Python and XML

Python and XML

Christopher A. Jones and Fred L. Drake, Jr.

O'REILLY®

Beijing · Cambridge · Farnham · Köln · Paris · Sebastopol · Taipei · Tokyo

Python and XML
by Christopher A. Jones and Fred L. Drake, Jr.

Published by O'Reilly & Associates, Inc., 1005 Gravenstein Highway North, Sebastopol, CA 95472.

O'Reilly & Associates books may be purchased for educational, business, or sales promotional use. Online editions are also available for most titles (*safari.oreilly.com*). For more information contact our corporate/institutional sales department: 800-998-9938 or *corporate@oreilly.com*.

Editor:	Laura Lewin
Production Editor:	Mary Brady
Cover Designer:	Emma Colby
Interior Designer:	David Futato

Printing History:

January 2002:	First Edition.

ISBN: 0-596-00128-2
[M]

*We would like to dedicate this book to
Frank Willison, O'Reilly Editor-in-Chief
and Python Champion.*

—Christopher A. Jones and Fred L. Drake, Jr.

*Frank will be remembered in the Python
community for the several great Python books
that he made possible, memories of his
participation in many Python conferences, and
his Frankly Speaking columns. The Python world
(and the world at large) won't be the same
without Frank.*

—Guido van Rossum, Python creator

Table of Contents

Preface

This book comes to you as a result of the collaboration of two authors who became interested in the topic in very different ways. Hopefully our motivations will help you understand what we each bring to the book, and perhaps prove to be at least a little entertaining as well.

Chris Jones started using XML several years ago, and began using Python more recently. As a consultant for major companies in the Seattle area, he first used XML as the core data format for web site content in a home-grown publishing system in 1997. But he really became an XML devotee when developing an open source engine, which eventually became the key technology for Planet 7 Technologies. As a consultant, he continues to use XML on an almost daily basis for everything from configuration files to document formats.

Chris began dabbling in Python because he thought it was a clean, object-oriented alternative to Perl. A long-time Unix user (but one who frequently finds himself working with Windows in Seattle), he has grown accustomed to scripting languages that place the full Unix API in the hands of developers. Having used far too much Java and ASP in web development over the years, he found Python a refreshing way to keep object-orientation while still accessing Unix sockets and threads—all with the convenience of a scripting language.

The combination of Python and XML brings great power to the developer. While XML is a potent technology, it requires the programmer to use objects, interfaces, and strings. Python does so as well, and therefore provides an excellent playpen for XML development. The number of XML tools for Python is growing all the time, and Chris can produce an XML solution in far less time using Python than he can with Java or C++. Of course, the cross-platform nature of Python keeps our work consistently usable whether we're developing on Windows, Linux, or a Unix variant—the combination of which we both seem to find powerful.

Fred Drake came to Python and XML from a different avenue, arriving at Python before XML. He discovered Python while in graduate school experimenting with a number of programming languages. After recognizing Python as an excellent language for rapid development, he convinced his advisors that he should be able to write his masters project using Python. In the course of developing the project, he became increasingly interested in the Python community. He then made his first contributions to the Python standard library, and in so doing became noticed by a group of Python programmers working on distributed systems projects at the research organization of CNRI. The group was led by Guido van Rossum, the creator of Python. Fred joined the team and learned more about distributed systems and gluing systems together than he ever expected possible, and he loved it.

While still in graduate school, Fred argued that Python's documentation should be converted to a more structured language called SGML. After a few years at CNRI, he began to do just that, and was able to sink his teeth into the documentation more vigorously. The SGML migration path eventually changed to an XML migration path as XML acceptance grew. Though that goal has not yet been achieved (he is still working on it), Fred has substantially changed the way the documentation is maintained, and it now represents one of the most structured applications of the typesetting and document markup system developed by Donald Knuth and Leslie Lamport.

Over time, the team from CNRI became increasingly focused on the development of Python, and moved on to form PythonLabs. Fred remained active in XML initiatives around Python and pushed to add XML support to the standard library. Once this was achieved, he returned to the task of migrating the Python documentation to XML, and hopes to complete this project soon.

Audience

This book is for anyone interested in learning about using Python to build XML applications. The bulk of the material is suited for programmers interested in using XML as a data interchange format or as a transformable format for web content, but the first half of the book is also useful to those interested in building more document-oriented applications.

We do not assume that you know anything about XML, but we do assume that you have looked at Python enough that you are comfortable reading straightforward Python code; however, you do not need to be a Python guru. If you do not know at least a little Python, please consult one of the many excellent books that introduce the language, such as *Learning Python*, by Mark Lutz and David Ascher and Lutz (O'Reilly, 1999). For the sections where web applications are developed, it helps to be familiar with general concepts related to web operations, such as HTTP and HTML forms, but sufficient information is included to get you started with basic CGI scripting.

Organization

This book is divided into ten chapters and six appendixes, as follows:

Chapter 1, *Python and XML*
> This chapter offers a broad overview of XML and why Python is particularly well-suited to XML processing.

Chapter 2, *XML Fundamentals*
> This chapter provides a good introduction to XML for newcomers and a refresher for programmers who have some familiarity with the standard.

Chapter 3, *The Simple API for XML*
> This chapter gives a detailed introduction to using Python with the SAX interface, for generating parse events from an XML data stream.

Chapter 4, *The Document Object Model*
> This chapter provides an introduction to working with DOM, which is the dominant object-oriented, tree-based API to an XML document.

Chapter 5, *Querying XML with XPath*
> This chapter discusses using a traversal language to extract portions of documents that meet your application's requirements.

Chapter 6, *Transforming XML with XSLT*
> This chapter details using XSLT to perform transformations on XML documents.

Chapter 7, *XML Validation and Dialects*
> This chapter discusses validating XML generated from other sources.

Chapter 8, *Python Internet APIs*
> This chapter provides an overview of Python's high-level support for Internet protocols, including tools for building both clients and servers for HTTP.

Chapter 9, *Python, Web Services, and SOAP*
> This chapter offers discussion of and examples showing how to build and use web services with Python.

Chapter 10, *Python and Distributed Systems Design*
> This chapter is an extended example that shows a variety of approaches to applying Python in constructing an XML-based distributed system.

Appendix A, *Installing Python and XML Tools*
> This appendix provides instructions on installing Python and the major XML packages used throughout this book.

Appendix B, *XML Definitions*
> This appendix gives a list of definitions from the XML specification and a Python script to extract them from the specification itself.

Appendix C, *Python SAX API*
> This appendix offers detailed API information for using the dominant event-based XML interface in Python.

Appendix D, *Python DOM API*

This appendix provides detailed interface documentation for using the standard tree-oriented API for XML from Python.

Appendix E, *Working with MSXML3.0*

This appendix gives information on Microsoft's XML libraries available for Python.

Appendix F, *Additional Python XML Tools*

This appendix is a summary of the many additional tools that are available for using XML with Python, and a list of starting points for additional information on the Web.

Conventions Used in This Book

The following typographical conventions are used throughout this book:

Bold

Used for the occasional reference to labels in graphical user interfaces, as well as user input.

Italic

Used for commands, URLs, filenames, file extensions, directory or folder names, emphasis, and new terms where they are defined.

`Constant width`

Used for constructs from programming languages, HTML, and XML, both within running text and in listings.

`Constant width italic`

Used for general placeholders that indicate that an item should be replaced by some actual value in your own program. Most importantly, this font is used for formal parameters when discussing the signatures of API methods.

How to Contact Us

We have tested and verified all the information in this book to the best of our abilities, but you may find that features have changed or that we have let errors slip through the production of the book. Please let us know of any errors that you find, as well as suggestions for future editions, by writing to:

O'Reilly & Associates, Inc.
1005 Gravenstein Highway North
Sebastopol, CA 95472
1-800-998-9938 (in the United States or Canada)
1-707-829-0515 (international/local)
1-707-829-0104 (fax)

You can also send us messages electronically. To be put on the mailing list or to request a catalog, send email to:

info@oreilly.com

To ask technical questions or comment on the book, send email to:

bookquestions@oreilly.com

We have a web site for the book, where we'll list examples, errata, and any plans for future editions. You can access this page at:

http://www.oreilly.com/catalog/pythonxml/

For more information about this book and others, see the O'Reilly web site:

http://www.oreilly.com/

Acknowledgments

While it is impossible to individually acknowledge everyone that had a hand in getting this book from an idea to the printed work you now hold in your hand, we would like to recognize and thank a few of these special people.

We are both very grateful for the support of our families, without which this would not have even gotten started. Chris would like to thank his family (Barb, Miles, and Katherine); without their support he would never get any writing completed, ever. Fred owes a great deal of gratitude to his wife (Cathy), who spent many a lonely evening wondering if he'd remember to come to bed. His children (William, Christopher, and Erin) made sure he didn't forget why he spends so much time on all this. Those late-night trips to the coffee shop with Erin will never be forgotten!

We'd especially like to thank Guido van Rossum and Fred's compatriots at PythonLabs (Tim Peters, Jeremy Hylton, and Barry Warsaw) for making sure Python could grow to be such a wonderful tool for building applications, and for leading the incredible community efforts which have gone into both Python itself and the excellent selection of additional packages of Python code.

Python's development has been beleaguered by regular employment changes, but we all owe a debt of gratitude to the employers of the contributors and the PythonLabs team. Now at Zope Corporation (formerly Digital Creations), PythonLabs has finally found a home that offers both a rich environment for Python and comfortable place to settle down. Previous employers of Python's lead developers, including the Corporation for National Research Initiatives (CNRI) and Stichting Mathematisch Centrum, deserve credit for allowing Python to germinate and blossom.

Our reviewers' efforts were invaluable and made this book what it is today. (They were helpful, and showed great faith in our ability to pull this off, even when we weren't so sure.) Martin von Löwis, Paul Prescod, Simon St.Laurent, Greg Wilson, and Frank Willison all contributed generously of their time and helped to ensure that our mistakes were noticed. The feedback they provided, both from a development and from a technical support perspective, was invaluable. Any mistakes in the finished book are our own. Fred Drake, who began working on this project as a technical reviewer, must still answer for any mistakes he's introduced!

Many people at O'Reilly played an important part in the development of this book, and without the help of their editorial staff, this book would seem rambling and incoherent (well, more so at least!). Laura Lewin deserves special recognition. Without her editorial skill and faith in our ability to present the important aspects of our subject, you wouldn't be reading this; her penchant for reminding us of the big picture when we became mired in the particulars of topics kept us on track and focused. Frank Willison deserves a great deal of credit not only for bringing Laura to O'Reilly, but in shepherding O'Reilly's efforts to bring together their line of books on Python; we'll all miss him. Finally, we'd like to thank the production staff at O'Reilly for their hard work in getting the book to print.

CHAPTER 1
Python and XML

Python and XML are two very different animals, each with a rich history. Python is a full-scale programming language that has grown from scripting world roots in a very organic way, through the vision and guidance of Python's inventor, Guido van Rossum. Guido continues to take into account the needs of Python developers as Python matures. XML, on the other hand, though strongly impacted by the ideas of a small cadre of visionaries, has grown from standards-committee roots. It has seen both quiet adoption and wrenching battles over its future. Why bother putting the two technologies together?

Before the Python/XML combination, there seemed no easy or effective way to work with XML in a distributed environment. Developers were forced to rely on a variety of tools used in awkward combination with one other. We used shell scripting and Perl to process text and interact with the operating system, and then used Java XML API's for processing XML and network programming. The shell provided an excellent means of file manipulation and interaction with the Unix system, and Perl was a good choice for simple text manipulation, providing access to the Unix APIs. Unfortunately, neither sported a sophisticated object model. Java, on the other hand, featured an object-oriented environment, a robust platform API for network programming, threads, and graphical user interface (GUI) application development. But with Java, we found an immediate lack of text manipulation power; scripting languages typically provided strong text processing. Python presented a perfect solution, as it combines the strengths of all of these various options.

Like most scripting languages, Python features excellent text and file manipulation capabilities. Yet, unlike most scripting languages, Python sports a powerful object-oriented environment with a robust platform API for network programming, threads, and graphical user interface development. It can be extended with components written in C and C++ with ease, allowing it to be connected to most existing libraries. To top it off, Python has been shown to be more portable than other popular interpreted languages, running comfortably on platforms ranging from massive parallel Connection Machines to personal digital assistants and other embedded systems. As a result, Python is an excellent choice for XML programming and distributed application development.

It could be said that Python brings sanity and robustness to the scripting world, much in the same way that Java once did to the C++ world. As always, there are trade-offs. In moving from C++ to Java, you find a simpler language with stronger object-oriented underpinnings. Changing to a simpler language further removed from the low-level details of memory management and the hardware, you gain robustness and an improved ability to locate coding errors. You also encounter a rich API equipped with easy thread management, network programming, and support for Internet technologies and protocols. As may be expected, this flexibility comes at a cost: you also encounter some *reduced performance* when comparing it with languages such as C and C++.

Likewise, when choosing a scripting language such as Python over C, C++, or even Java, you do make some concessions. You trade performance for robustness and for the ability to develop more rapidly. In the area of enterprise and Internet systems development, choosing reliable software, flexible design, and rapid growth and deployment are factors that outweigh the performance gains you might get by using a language such as C++. If you do need some of the performance back, you can still implement speed-sensitive components of your application in C or C++, but you can avoid doing so until you have profiling data to help you pinpoint what is really a problem and what only might be a problem. (How to perform the analysis and write extensions in C/C++ is a topic for other books.)

Regardless of your feelings on scripting languages, Java, or C++, this book focuses on XML and the Python language. For those who are new to XML, we will start with an overview of why it is interesting, and then we'll move on to using it from Python and seeing how we make our XML applications easier to create.

Key Advantages of XML

XML has a few key advantages that make it the data language of choice on the Internet. These advantages were designed into XML from the beginning, and, in fact, are what make it so appealing to Internet developers.

Application Neutrality

First, XML is both human- and machine-readable. This is not a subtle point. Have you ever tried to read a Microsoft Word document with a text editor? You can't if it was saved as a *.doc* file, because the information in a *.doc* document is in a *binary* (computer readable only) format, even though most Word documents primarily consist of text. A Word document cannot be shared with any other application besides Word—unless that application has been taught the intricacies of Word's binary format. In this case, the application must also be taught to expect changes in Word's format each time there is a new release from Microsoft.

This sounds annoying for the developer, but how bad is it, really? After all, Word is incredibly popular, so it must not be too hard to figure out. Let's look at the top of the Word file that contains this chapter:

```
Ï_à¡ _á                          >  _  ÿ      _              _  B_        _  D_   _
ÿÿÿ     ?_  @_   A_  ÿÿÿÿÿÿÿÿÿÿÿÿÿÿÿÿÿÿÿÿÿÿÿÿÿÿÿÿÿÿÿÿÿÿÿÿÿÿÿÿ
  ÿÿÿÿÿÿÿÿÿÿÿÿÿÿÿÿÿÿÿÿÿÿÿÿÿÿÿÿÿÿÿÿÿÿÿÿÿÿÿÿÿÿÿÿÿÿÿÿÿÿÿÿÿÿÿÿÿÿ
  ÿÿÿÿÿÿÿÿÿÿÿÿÿÿÿÿÿÿÿÿÿÿÿÿÿÿÿÿÿÿÿÿÿÿÿÿÿÿÿÿÿÿÿÿÿÿÿÿÿÿÿÿÿÿÿÿÿÿ
  ÿÿÿÿÿÿÿÿÿÿÿÿÿÿÿÿÿÿÿÿÿÿÿÿÿÿÿÿÿÿÿÿÿÿÿÿÿÿÿÿÿÿÿÿÿÿÿÿÿÿÿÿÿÿÿÿÿÿ
  ÿÿÿÿÿÿÿÿÿÿÿÿÿÿÿÿÿÿÿÿÿÿÿÿÿÿÿÿÿÿÿÿÿÿÿÿÿÿÿÿÿÿÿÿÿÿÿÿÿÿÿÿÿÿÿÿÿÿ
  ÿÿÿÿÿÿÿÿÿÿÿÿÿÿÿÿÿÿÿÿÿÿÿÿÿÿÿÿÿÿÿÿ 7 ÿÿÿÿÿÿÿÿÿÿÿÿÿÿÿÿÿÿÿÿÿÿÿÿ
  ÿÿÿÿÿÿÿÿÿÿÿÿÿÿÿÿÿÿÿÿÿÿÿÿì¥Á 7      _   _¿         _     _  >__
bjbjU_U_                       _  0,_ 7|  7|  W__        _   C
       ÿÿ_        ÿÿ_          ÿÿ_              1   Ê_
 Ê_   Ê_    Ê_      Ê_     Ê_     Ê_  ¶               _
```

This certainly looks familiar to anyone who has ever opened a Word file with a text editor. We don't see our recognizable text (the content we intended) so we must assume it is buried deep in the file. Determining what the true content is and where it is can be difficult, but it shouldn't be. It *is* our data, after all. Let's try another supported format: "Rich Text Format," or RTF. Unlike the *.doc* file, this format is text-based, and should therefore be a bit easier to decipher. We search down in the file to find the start of our text:

```
\par }\pard \s34\qr
\li0\ri0\sb80\sa480\sl240\slmult0\widctlpar\aspalpha\aspnum\faauto\out
linelevel0\widctlpar\aspalpha\aspnum\faauto\outlinelevel0\pnrauth1\pnr
date-967302179\pnrnot1\adjustright\rin0\lin0\itap0 {\b0\fs48 Combining
Python and XML}{
\b0\deleted\fs48\revauthdel1\revdttmdel-2041034726 Fundamentals}{\b0\f
s48\revised\revauth1\revdttm-2041034726 ?}{\b0\fs48
\par }\pard\plain \qj
```

This is better. The chapter title is visible, so we can try to decipher the structure from that point forward. The markup appears to be complex, and there's a hint of an old version of the chapter title. To extract the text we actually want, we need to understand the Word model for revision tracking, which still presents many challenges.

XML, on the other hand, is application-neutral. In other words, an XML document is usually processed by an XML parser or processor, but if one is not available, an XML document can be easily read and parsed. Data kept in XML is not trapped within the constraints of one particular software application. The ability to read rich data files can become very valuable when, for example, 20 years from now, you dig up a CD-ROM of old business forms that you suddenly find you need again. Will QuickBooks still allow you to extract this same data in 2021? With XML, you can read the data with any text editor.

Let's look at this chapter in XML. Using markup from a common document type for software manuals and documentation (DocBook), it appears somewhat verbose, and doesn't include change-tracking information, but we can identify the text quite easily now:

```
<chapter>
  <title>Python and XML</title>
  <para>Python and XML are two very different animals, each with a
    rich history.  Python is a full-scale programming language that has grown
    from scripting world roots, and has done so in a very organic way
```

Note that additional characters appear in the document (other than the document content); these are called *markup* (or *tags*). We saw this in the RTF version of the document as well, but there were many more bits of text that were difficult to decipher, and we can reasonably surmise that the strange data in the MS Word document would correspond to this in some way. Were this a book on RTF, you would quickly surmise two things: RTF is much more like a printer control language than the example of XML we just looked at, and writing a program that understands RTF would be quite difficult. In this book, we're going to show you that XML can be used to define languages that fit your application, and that creating programs that can decipher XML is not a difficult task, especially with the help of Python.

Hierarchical Structure

XML is hierarchical, and allows you to choose your own tag names. This is quite different from HTML. In XML, you are free to create elements of any type, and stack other elements within those elements. For example, consider an address entry:

```
<?xml version="1.0"?>
<address>
  <name>Bubba McBubba</name>
  <street>123 Happy Go Lucky Ln.</street>
  <city>Seattle</city><state>WA</state><zip>98056</zip>
</address>
```

In the above well-formed XML code, I came up with a few record names and then lumped them together with data. XML processing software, such as a *parser* (which you use to interpret the syntactic constructs in an XML document), would be able to represent this data in many ways, because its structure has been communicated. For example, if we were to look at what an application programmer might write in source code, we could turn this record into an object initialized this way:

```
addr = Address()
addr.name = "Bubba McBubba"
addr.street = "123 Happy Go Lucky Ln."
addr.city = "Seattle"
addr.state = "WA"
addr.zip = "98056"
```

This approach makes XML well-suited as a format for many serialized objects. (There are some constructs for which XML is not so well suited, including many formats for large numerical datasets used in scientific computing.) XML's hierarchical structure makes it easy to apply the concept of object interfaces to documents—it's quite simple to build application-specific objects directly from the information stream, given mappings from element names to object types. We later see that we can model more than simple hierarchical structures with XML.

Platform Neutrality

Remember that XML is cross-platform. While this is mainly a feature of its text-based format, it's still very much true. The use of certain text encodings ensures that there are no misconceptions among platforms as to the arrangement of an XML document. Therefore, it's easy to pass an XML purchase order from a Unix machine to a wireless personal digital assistant. XML is designed for use in conjunction with existing Internet infrastructure using HTTP, SSL, and other messaging protocols as they evolve. These qualities make XML lend itself to distributed applications; it has been successfully used as a foundation for message queuing systems, instant messaging applications, and remote procedure call frameworks. We examine these applications further in Chapter 9 and Chapter 10. It also means that the document example given earlier is more than simply application-neutral, and can be readily moved from one type of machine to another without loss of information. A chapter of a technical book can be written by a programmer on his or her favorite flavor of Unix, and then sent to a publisher using book composition software on a Macintosh. The many difficult format conversions can be avoided.

International Language Support

As the Internet becomes increasingly pervasive in our daily lives, we become more aware of the world around us—it is a culture-rich and diversified place. As technologists, however, we are still learning the significance of making our software work in ways that supports more than one language at a time; making our text-processing routines "8-bit safe" is not only no longer sufficient, it's no longer even close.

Standards bodies all over the world have come up with ways that computers can interchange text written in their national languages, and sometimes they've come up with several, each having varying degrees of acceptance. Unfortunately, most applications do not include information about which language or interchange standard their data is written in, so it is difficult to share information across the cultural and linguistic boundaries the different standards represent. Sometimes it is difficult to share information within such boundaries if multiple standards are prominent.

The difficulties are compounded by very substantial cultural differences that present themselves about how text is handled. There are many different writing systems in addition to the western European left-to-right, top-to-bottom style in which this book is written; right-to-left is not uncommon, and top-to-bottom "lines" of text arranged right-to-left on the page is used in China. Hebrew uses a right-to-left writing system, but numbers are written using Arabic numerals from left to right. Other systems support textual annotations written in parallel with the text. Consider what happens when a document includes text from different writing systems!

Standards bodies are aware of this problem, and have been working on solutions for years. The editors of the XML specification have wisely avoided proposing new solutions to most of these issues, and are instead choosing to build on the work of experts on the topic and existing standards.

The International Organization for Standardization (ISO) and the Unicode Consortium (*http://www.unicode.org/*) have arrived at a single standard that, while not perfect, is perhaps the most capable standard attempting to unify the world's text representations, with the intent that all languages and alphabets (including ideographic and hieroglyphic character sets) are representable. The standard is known as ISO/IEC 10646, or more commonly, Unicode. Not all national standards bodies have agreed that Unicode is the standard for all future text interchange applications, especially in Asia, but there is widespread belief that Unicode is the best thing available to serve everyone. The standard deals with issues including multidirectional text, capitalization rules, and encoding algorithms that can be used to ensure various properties of data streams. The standard does not deal specifically with language issues that are not tied intimately to character issues. Software sensitive to natural language may still need to do a lot beyond using Unicode to ensure proper collation of names in a particular language (or multiple languages!). Some languages will require substantial additional support for proper text rendering (Arabic, for instance, which requires different letterforms for characters based on their position within a word and based on neighboring letterforms).

The World Wide Web Consortium (W3C) made a simple and masterful stroke to make it easier to use both the older interchange standards and Unicode. It required that all XML documents be Unicode, and specified that they must describe their own encoding in such a way that all XML processors were able to determine what encoding the document was written in. A few specific encodings must be recognized by all processors, so that it is always possible to generate XML that can be read anywhere and represent all of the world's characters. There is also a feature that allows the content of XML documents to be labeled with the actual language it is written in, but that's not used as much as it could be at this time.

Since XML documents are Unicode documents, the languages of the world are supported. The use of Unicode and encodings in XML are discussed in some detail in Chapter 2. Unicode strings have been a part of Python since Version 2.0, and the Python standard library includes support for a large number of encodings.

The XML Specifications

In the trade press, we often see references about how XML "now supports" some particular industry-specific application. The article that follows is often confused, offering some small morsel of information about an industry consortium that has released a new specification for an XML-based language to support interoperability of data within the consortium's industry. As technical people, we usually note that it doesn't apply to the industries we're involved in, or else it does, but the specification is too early a draft to be useful. In fact, our managers will probably agree with us most of the time, or they'll be privy to some relevant information that causes them to disagree. If we step up the corporate ladder a couple more rungs, however, we often find an increase in the level of confusion over XML. Sometimes, this is accompanied by either a call to "adopt XML" (too often with a list of particular specifications that are not intended to be used together), or a reaction that XML is too immature to use at all.

So we need to think about just what we can work with that will meet the following criteria:

- It must make technical sense for our application.
- It should be sufficiently well-defined that implementation is possible.
- It must be able to be explained and justified to (at least) our direct managers.
- It won't freak out the upper management.

Ok, we're technical people, so we may have to ignore that last item; it certainly won't be covered in this book. In fact, most of this really can't be covered in technical material. There are many specifications in various stages of maturity, and most are specific to one industry or another. However, we can point out what the foundation specifications are, because those you will need regardless of your industry or other requirements.

XML 1.0 Recommendation

The XML specification itself is a document created and maintained by the W3C. As of this writing, the current version is *Extensible Markup Language (XML) 1.0* (Second Edition), and is available from the W3C web site at *http://www.w3.org/TR/REC-xml*. (The second edition differs from the first only in that some editorial corrections and clarifications have been made; the specification is stable.)

XML itself is not a markup language, but a *meta-language* that can be used to define specific markup languages. In this, it inherits much from SGML. The specification covers five aspects of markup languages:

- Range of structural forms which can be marked
- Specific syntax of markup components
- A schema language used to define specific languages

- Definition of validity constraints
- Minimum requirements for processing tools

Unlike SGML, XML allows itself to be used without defining an explicit markup language in any formal way. Whether or not this is useful for your applications, it has greatly accelerated the acceptance of XML-based technologies in some developer communities. This can happen because of the lower cost of entrance to the XML space. It is possible to adopt XML without learning some of the more esoteric corners of the specification, and development prototypes can start using XML technologies without a lot of advance planning.

Chapter 2 presents the most widely used parts of the specification and goes into more depth on what are the most important items to most readers of this book. If any of the details are of particular interest to you, please spend some time reading relevant parts of the specification. While it is at times a bit convoluted, it is not generally a difficult specification to read.

Namespaces in XML

While the XML 1.0 recommendation defines specific syntactic aspects of XML and one way of creating document types, it does not discuss how to combine components from multiple document types. The *Namespaces in XML* recommendation, available at *http://www.w3.org/TR/REC-xml-names* (referred to as Namespaces from now on), deals with the syntactic and structural mechanics of combining structured components from different specifications, but is largely silent on the meaning of resulting combinations. For this, it defers to specifications that had not been written when Namespaces was published.

This recommendation places some additional constraints on the syntactic construction of conformant documents. It allows a document to specify the source of each element or attribute by placing it in a *namespace*. Each namespace provides definitions for elements and attributes. How the elements and attributes are defined is not covered in this specification, so the concept of validation of an arbitrary document that uses namespaces is not entirely clear. It is possible to create a document type using XML 1.0 that has some support for namespaces, but such a schema loses much of the flexibility offered by the Namespaces specification. For example, the document type would have to specify the particular prefixes to which each namespace is bound, while the Namespaces specification allows prefixes to be determined by the document rather than the schema. Alternate schema languages that have better support for Namespaces have been defined; these are discussed briefly in Chapter 2.

XML as a Foundation

Like its predecessor SGML, XML provides a way to define languages that fit the requirements of your application. By specifying the exact syntax of the grammatical elements (such as the characters used to mark the start of an element), it has reduced the effort required to build conforming software—the components needed to extract an application's data from XML are far smaller and simpler to use than the corresponding components are for SGML.

The additional specifications, which the trade press so enjoy discussing every time a news release comes out, are generally built by defining new languages using the base XML and Namespaces recommendations. These are often documented by schema definitions (the forms that these take are described in Chapter 2) as well as committee-driven documents that attempt to explain how the language should be used. Since every industry has at least one consortium that deals in part with data interchange between different components of the industry (think of doctors, pharmacies, and hospitals in the health care field), many standards take this form. Many of the standards for XML are derived from earlier efforts using older SGML industry-specific languages, and many are new.

Locating information about the languages that have been defined for your industry may be easy or it may be difficult. There are many resources you can use to locate relevant specifications:

http://xml.schema.net/
> This web site contains information on a range of standards based on XML, including general business-oriented specifications, industry-specific standards, interoperable languages for academic research, and general Internet-related specifications.

http://www.biztalk.com/
> Information about the Microsoft-sponsored "BizTalk" range of business interoperability specifications can be found at this web site.

http://www.ebxml.org/
> The "e-business XML" initiative, or ebXML, grows out of the EDI community, and generally competes with BizTalk.

http://www.w3.org/
> For general Internet-related specifications, the World Wide Web Consortium is perhaps the best place to look; the working groups there have a broad constituency and the results of their efforts have a high level of uptake wherever they apply.

http://www.google.com/
> If all else fails, try searching here for "XML" and various keywords related to your industry (especially the names of major industry consortia).

The Power of Python and XML

Now that we've introduced you to the world of XML, we'll look at what Python brings to the table. We'll review the Python features that apply to XML, and then we'll give some specific examples of Python with XML. As a very high-level language, Python includes many powerful data structures as part of the core language and libraries. The more recent versions of Python, from 2.0 onward, include excellent support for Unicode and an impressive range of encodings, as well as an excellent (and fast!) XML parser that provides character data from XML as Unicode strings. Python's standard library also contains implementations of the industry-standard DOM and SAX interfaces for working with XML data, and additional support for alternate parsers and interfaces is available.

Of course, this much could be said of other modern high-level languages as well. Java certainly includes an impressive library of highly usable data structures, and Perl offers equivalent data structures also. What makes Python preferable to those languages and their libraries? There are several features, of which we briefly discuss the most important:

- Python source code is easy to read and maintain.
- The interactive interpreter makes it simple to try out code fragments.
- Python is incredibly portable, but does not restrict access to platform-specific capabilities.
- The object-oriented features are powerful without being obscure.

There are many languages capable of doing what can be done with Python, but it is rare to find all of the "peripheral" qualities of Python in any single language. These qualities do not so much make Python more capable, but they make it much easier to apply, reducing programming hours. This allows more time to be spent finding better ways to solve real problems or just allows the programmer to move on to the next problem. Here we discuss these features in more detail.

Easy to read and maintain

As a programming language, Python exhibits a remarkable clarity of expression. Though some programmers accustomed to other languages view Python's use of significant whitespace with surprise, everyone seems to think it makes Python source code significantly more readable than languages that require more special characters to be introduced to mark structure in the source. Python's structures are not simpler than those of other languages, but the different syntax makes source code "feel" much cleaner in Python.

The use of whitespace also helps avoid having minor stylistic differences, such as the placement of structural braces, so there's a greater degree of visual consistency across code by different programmers. While this may seem like a minor thing to many programmers, the effect is that maintaining code written by another programmer becomes much easier simply because its easier to concentrate on the actual structure and algorithms of the code. For the individual programmer, this is a nice side benefit, but for a business, this results in lower expenses for code maintenance.

Exploratory programming in an interactive interpreter

Many modern high-level programming languages offer interpreters, but few have proved as successful at doing so as Python. Others, such as Java, do not generally offer interpreters at all. If we consider Perl, a language that is arguably very capable when used from a command line, we see that it is not equipped with a rich interpreter. If we start the Perl interpreter without naming a script, it simply waits for us to type a complete script at the console, and then interprets the script when we're done. It does allow us to enter a few commands on the command line directly, but there's no ability to run one statement at a time and inspect the results as we go in order to determine if each bit of code is doing exactly what we expect. With Python, the interactive interpreter provides a rich environment for executing individual statements and testing the results.

Portability without restrictions

The Python interpreter is one of the most portable language interpreters available. It is known to run on platforms ranging from PDAs and other embedded systems to some of the most powerful multiprocessor platforms ever built. It can run on more operating systems than perhaps any other interpreter. Moreover, carefully written application code can share much of this portability. Python provides a great array of abstractions that do just enough to hide platform differences while allowing the programmer to use the services of specific platforms when necessary.

When an application requires access to facilities or libraries that Python does not provide, Python also makes it easy to add extensions that take advantage of these additional facilities. Additional modules can be created (usually in C or C++, but other languages can be used as well) that allow Python code to call on external facilities efficiently.

Powerful but accessible object-orientation

At one time, it was common to hear about how object-oriented programming (OOP) would solve most of the technical problems programmers had to deal with in their code. Of course, programmers knew better, pushed back, and turned the concepts into useful tools that could be applied when appropriate (though *how* and *when* it should be applied may always be the subject of debate). Unfortunately, many languages that have strong support for OOP are either very tedious to work with (such as C++ or, to a lesser extent, Java), or they have not been as widely accepted for general use (such as Eiffel).

Python is different. The language supports object orientation without much of the syntactic overhead found in many widely used object-oriented languages, making it very easy to define new object types. Unlike many other languages, Python is highly polymorphic; interfaces are defined in much less stringent ways than in languages such as C++ and Java. This makes it easy to create useful objects without having to write code that exists only to conform to an interface, but that will not actually be used in a particular application. When combined with the excellent advantage taken by Python's standard library of a variety of common interfaces, the value of creating reusable objects is easily recognized, all while the ease of implementing useful interfaces is maintained.

Python Tools for XML

Three major packages provide Python tools for working with XML. These are, from the most commonly used to the largest:

1. The Python standard library
2. PyXML, produced by the Python XML Special Interest Group
3. 4Suite, provided by Fourthought, Inc.

The Python standard library provides a minimal but useful set of interfaces to work with XML, including an interface to the popular Expat XML parser, an implementation of the lightweight Simple API for XML (SAX), and a basic implementation of the core Document Object Model (DOM). The DOM implementation supports Level 1 and much of Level 2 of the DOM specification from the W3C, but does not implement most of the optional features. The material in the standard library was drawn from material originally in the PyXML package, and additional material was contributed by leading Python XML developers.

PyXML is a more feature-laden package; it extends the standard library with additional XML parsers, has a much more substantial DOM implementation (including more optional features), has adapters to allow more parsers to support the SAX interface, XPath expression parsing and evaluation, XSLT transformations, and a variety of other helper modules. The package is maintained as a community effort by many of the most active Python/XML programmers.

4Suite is not a superset of the other packages, but is intended to be used in addition to PyXML. It offers additional DOM implementations tailored for different applications, support for the XLink and XPointer specifications, and tools for working with Resource Description Framework (RDF) data.

These are the packages used throughout the book; see Appendix A for more information on obtaining and installing them. Still more are available; see Appendix F for brief descriptions of several of these and references to more information online.

The SAX and DOM APIs

The two most basic and broadly used APIs to XML data are the SAX and DOM interfaces. These interfaces differ substantially; learning to determine which of these is appropriate for your application is an important step to learn.

SAX defines a relatively low-level interface that is easy for XML parsers to support, but requires the application programmer to manage more details of using the information in the XML documents and performing operations on it. It offers the advantage of low overhead: no large data structures are constructed unless the application itself actually needs them. This allows many forms of processing to proceed much more quickly than could occur if more overhead were required, and much larger documents can be processed efficiently. It achieves this by being an *event-oriented* interface; using SAX is more like processing user-input events in a graphical user interface than manipulating a pre-constructed data structure. So how do you get "events" from an XML parser, and what kind of events might there be?

SAX defines a number of handler interfaces that your application can implement to receive events. The methods of these objects are called when the appropriate events are encountered in the XML document being parsed; each method can be thought of as the actual event, which fits well with object-oriented approaches to parsing. Events are categorized as content, document type, lexical, and error events; each category of events is handled using a distinct interface. The application can specify exactly which categories of events it is interested in receiving by providing the parser with the appropriate handlers and omitting those it does not need. Python's XML support provides base classes that allow you to implement only the methods you're interested in, just inheriting do-nothing methods for events you don't need.

The most commonly used events are the content-related events, of which the most important are startElement, characters, and endElement. We look at SAX in depth in Chapter 3, but now let's take a quick look at how we might use SAX to extract some useful information from a document. We'll use a simple document; it's easy to see how this would extend to something more complex. The document is shown here:

```
<catalog>
  <book isbn="1-56592-724-9">
    <title>The Cathedral &amp; the Bazaar</title>
    <author>Eric S. Raymond</author>
  </book>
  <book isbn="1-56592-051-1">
    <title>Making TeX Work</title>
    <author>Norman Walsh</author>
  </book>
  <!-- imagine more entries here... -->
</catalog>
```

If we want to create a dictionary that maps the ISBN numbers given in the isbn attribute of the book elements to the titles of the books (the content of the title elements), we would create a content handler (as shown in Example 1-1) that looks at the three events listed previously.

Example 1-1. bookhandler.py

```
import xml.sax.handler

class BookHandler(xml.sax.handler.ContentHandler):
  def __init__(self):
    self.inTitle = 0
    self.mapping = {}
```

Example 1-1. bookhandler.py (continued)

```
def startElement(self, name, attributes):
  if name == "book":
    self.buffer = ""
    self.isbn = attributes["isbn"]
  elif name == "title":
    self.inTitle = 1

def characters(self, data):
  if self.inTitle:
    self.buffer += data

def endElement(self, name):
  if name == "title":
    self.inTitle = 0
    self.mapping[self.isbn] = self.buffer
```

Extracting the information we're looking for is now trivial. If the code above is in *bookhandler.py* and our sample document is in *books.xml*, we could do this in an interactive session:

```
>>> import xml.sax
>>> import bookhandler
>>> import pprint
>>>
>>> parser = xml.sax.make_parser()
>>> handler = bookhandler.BookHandler()
>>> parser.setContentHandler(handler)
>>> parser.parse("books.xml")
>>> pprint.pprint(handler.mapping)
{u'1-56592-051-1': u'Making TeX Work',
 u'1-56592-724-9': u'The Cathedral & the Bazaar'}
```

For reference material on the handler object methods, refer to Appendix C.

The DOM is quite the opposite of SAX. SAX offers a very small window of view that passes over the input document, relying on the application to infer the whole; the DOM gives the whole document to the application, which must then extract the finer details for itself. Instead of reporting individual events to the application as the parser handles the corresponding syntax in the document, the application creates an object that represents the entire document as a hierarchical structure. Although there is no requirement that the document be completely parsed and stored in memory when the object is provided to the application, most implementations work that way for simplicity. Some implementations avoid this; it is certainly possible to create a DOM implementation that parses the document lazily or uses some kind of persistent storage to keep the parsed document instead of an in-memory structure.

The DOM provides objects called *nodes* that represent parts of a document to the application. There are several types of nodes, each used for a different kind of construct. It is important to understand that the nodes of the DOM do not directly correspond to SAX events, although many are similar. The easiest way to see the difference is to look at how elements and their content are represented in both APIs. In SAX, an element is represented by start and end events, and its content is represented by all the events that come between the start and the end. The DOM provides a single object that represents the element, and it provides methods that allow the application to get the child nodes that represent the content of the element. Different node types are provided for elements, text, and just about everything else that can exist in an XML document.

We go into more detail and see some extended examples using the DOM in Chapter 4, and a detailed reference to the DOM API is given in Appendix D. For a quick taste of the DOM, let's write a snippet of code that does the same thing we do with SAX in Example 1-1, but using the basic DOM implementation from the Python standard library, as shown in Example 1-2.

Example 1-2. dombook.py

```
import pprint

import xml.dom.minidom
from xml.dom.minidom import Node

doc = xml.dom.minidom.parse("books.xml")

mapping = {}

for node in doc.getElementsByTagName("book"):
  isbn = node.getAttribute("isbn")
  L = node.getElementsByTagName("title")
  for node2 in L:
    title = ""
    for node3 in node2.childNodes:
      if node3.nodeType == Node.TEXT_NODE:
        title += node3.data
    mapping[isbn] = title

# mapping now has the same value as in the SAX example:
pprint.pprint(mapping)
```

It should be clear that we're dealing with something very different here! While there's about the same amount of code in the DOM example, it can be very difficult to develop reusable components, while experience with SAX often points the way to reusable components with only a small bit of refactoring. It is possible to reuse DOM code, but the mindset required is very different. What the DOM provides to compensate is that a document can be manipulated at arbitrary locations with full knowledge of the complete document, and the document contents can be extracted in different ways by different parts of an application without having to parse the document more than once. For some applications, this proves to be a highly motivating reason to use the DOM instead of SAX.

More Ways to Extract Information

SAX and the DOM give us some powerful tools for working with XML, but they clearly require a lot of code and attention to detail to use effectively in a large application. In both cases, working with complex data requires a great deal of work just to extract the interesting bits from the XML documents that contain the data. Now, what sorts of tools would we normally turn to when dealing with complex data sets? Two that come to mind are higher-level abstractions (such as APIs that do more work, and specialized task-oriented languages), and preprocessing techniques (transforming data from one form to another more suitable to the task at hand). Fortunately, both of these are available to us when working with XML from Python.

When an XML user wants to specify a portion of a document based on possibly complex criteria, she uses a language which lets her write the specification concisely; that language is called the *XML Path Language*, or *XPath*. Support for XPath is available in the 4Suite package, and has recently been added to the PyXML package as well. Using XPath, a query can be written that selects nodes from a DOM tree based on the element names, attribute values, textual content, and relationships between the nodes. We cover XPath in some detail, including how to use it with a DOM tree in Python, in Chapter 5.

Other times, what we'd really like is a new document that either contains less information or arranges it very differently. For this, we need a way to specify a transformation of a document that generates another document. This is provided by XML Stylesheet Language Transformations (XSLT). Originally developed as part of a new specification for stylesheets, XSLT is an XML-based language that is used to define transformations from XML to other formats. XSLT is most commonly used with XML or HTML as the output format. Chapter 6 describes this language and shows how to use it in Python.

What Can We Do with It?

Now that we've looked at how we can use XML with Python, we need to look at how we can apply our knowledge of XML and Python to real applications. In the Internet age, this means widely distributed systems operating across the Internet.

There's a lot to working with the Internet beyond XML and the CGI programming done in many of the examples in the book. In case you're not already familiar with this topic, we include an introduction to the facilities in the Python standard library that help create clients and servers for the Internet in Chapter 8. We review how to retrieve data from remote servers, and how to submit form-based requests programmatically and read the result. We then learn to build custom web servers that respond to HTTP requests, allowing us to build servers that do exactly what we need them to.

With these skills under our hat, we proceed to look at the emerging world of "web services." Chapter 9 describes what we mean by web services and introduces the specifications coming out in that area. We look at two packages that allow us to use SOAP to call on web services and demonstrate how to create one in Python.

In Chapter 10, we pull together much of what we've learned with an extended example that demonstrates how it all works together. Using XML as a communications medium, we are able to build an application that uses a variety of technologies and operates in diverse environments.

CHAPTER 2

XML Fundamentals

XML is not new! XML, the Extensible Markup Language, began development in 1996 and became an official World Wide Web Consortium (W3C) standard in 1998. XML is derived from the Standard Generalized Markup Language (SGML), which has been around for a great while. SGML has long been used as a means of document management, and is the parent of HTML. XML, on the other hand, is an outgrowth of these earlier markup languages intended for information sharing on the Internet. While HTML is effective for communicating how a page should look inside a web browser, XML speaks more to how information should be structured or used between or among applications (including web browsers) running on the Internet.

XML Structure in a Nutshell

The basic structure of an XML document is simple. Most can be reduced to a few simple components. Consider the following:

```
<?xml version="1.0"?>
<PurchaseOrder>
  <account refnum="2390094"/>
  <item sku="33-993933" qty="4">
    <name>Potato Smasher</name>
    <description>Smash Potatoes like never before.</description>
  </item>
</PurchaseOrder>
```

In this example, the first line, starting with the <? characters, is the *XML declaration*. It states which version of XML is being used and can also include information about the character encoding of the document. The text starting with <PurchaseOrder> and ending with </PurchaseOrder> is an XML *element*. An element must have an opening and closing *tag*, or the opening tag must end with the characters /> if it is to be empty. The account element shown here is an example of an *empty* element that ends with a `/>`. The `item` element opens, contains two other elements, and then closes. The `sku="33-993933"` expression is an *attribute* named `sku` with its value `33-993933` in quotes. An element can have as many attributes as needed. Both the `name` and `description` elements are followed by character data or text. Finally, the elements are closed and the document terminates.

In the remainder of this chapter, we walk through the relevant parts of the XML specification, highlighting the most important items for you to be aware of as you embark on coding with Python and XML.

Document Types and Schemas

When we talk about *document types*, we are speaking of something very similar to the notion of types in a programming language. Programming language types are used to describe structures that can be composed in particular ways, and document types do the same thing. The primitive components and the types of composition that are allowed differ, but they are conceptually aligned. A document type is commonly referred to as a *schema*. The difference between a document type and a database schema can be shallow in many applications, though the similarity is not always relevant. We often use *schema* to refer to a document type when it is not important how it was defined, because the phrase "document type" has historical associations with a particular schema language.

Schemas are valuable for several reasons, but two dominate: they require critical thinking about the applications and data to design, and they can be used to help specify how documents should constructed and interpreted when exchanged across organizational boundaries. The latter can be especially critical in applications such as supply-chain integration, where the automated exchange of dynamically generated documents can incur contractual obligations—it becomes very important that everyone agree what the documents mean, because misinterpretation can be very costly!

Document types are built on top of *data types* as well as on top of structuring rules, in which data types are very analogous to the primitive types provided by most programming languages. Different schema languages use different sets of data types, some being extensible and others allowing the use of arbitrary typing systems rather than providing their own. Some schema languages allow data types to be specified for any document content, and others limit the ability to apply data types to specific constructs.

All schema languages let the allowed ordering and nesting of elements be defined, and let attributes be associated with element types. Everything else is open to variation, so it helps to be aware of the general differences and select a schema language based on the requirements of the application, the availability of tools, and interoperability requirements.

Document Type Definitions

The XML 1.0 recommendation specifies one way to define a document type known as a *Document Type Definition*, or DTD. The language used to specify a DTD is really just part of XML itself, but is also informally known as the DTD language. This is a subset of XML that has a slightly different set of syntactic rules and does not allow arbitrary content to mix with the markup.

The DTD language for XML is derived from the DTD language for SGML, but drops many of the less commonly used constructs in favor of simplicity. The newfound simplicity pertains both for the language itself and for processing tools. The specific features that were omitted are only of interest if you already know the SGML version of the language, and so are not discussed in this book. Please refer to the XML recommendation and books focused on document type development to learn more about the differences.

We discuss the specific construction and interpretation of DTDs later in this chapter, but it is interesting to note that while the DTD language allows fairly flexible composition of elements, it defines very few data types that can be used to specify the types of attribute content, and provides almost no way to extend the set of data types. In spite of the limitations of DTDs, they are still an important type of schema due to their early specification as part of the XML 1.0 recommendation, their similarity to SGML DTDs, the widespread availability of tools, and the relative ease of learning how to create and use them.

Alternate Schema Languages

The XML sublanguage used to specify document types is largely inherited from the SGML roots of XML, and is perhaps the least appreciated aspect of the specification. The use of this language does represent a trade-off, no matter how useful it may be to particular projects. While there is no doubt that it is better than having only well-formed XML defined by the XML specification, there is a broadly perceived need for something better. As with all standards, however, one size does not fit all, so a number of alternate languages have been developed for specifying document types. Together, these are known as *schema languages*.

The application of each language varies, as does the level of complexity and availability of tool support. In this section, we examine some of the more popular languages and describe the intended uses for each of these, as well as what form of support is available for Python programmers. Two common aspects of the schema languages described here involve the fact that they all use XML to provide their own syntax, and they all are namespace-aware: the schema they can specify can contain elements and attributes from multiple namespaces. Both are significantly different from the DTD language, and both can easily be argued to be significant improvements.

XML Schema

The World Wide Web Consortium has been active in efforts to develop and standardize a schema language that was intended to work for everyone, and XML Schema is the result. As with all committee-driven designs, there is widespread dissatisfaction with XML Schema, not because it is not powerful enough, but because it is considered by many practitioners to be too complex. It defines ways to describe the allowed structures for a document type, as well as describe data types that can be used to describe both element and attribute content much more precisely and flexibly than what the DTD language supports.

XML Schema does offer the advantage that it provides ways to define both document types and data types, and includes a selection of basic data types to build on. These types range from numbers to strings that must match some regular expression, to more complex types such as dates or times. XML Schema data types are very rich compared to the data types supported by the DTD language. Schemas may be defined that constrain values of attributes or element content to be of these types, making it possible to describe larger document types much more precisely than the DTD language allows. This makes it possible to build tools that can validate a document against a schema, allowing application code to deal with far less specialized error-checking code. XML Schema data types are used briefly in Chapter 9, but are not discussed in detail.

There is an XML Schema validator for Python; see Appendix F for more information.

TREX

Tree Regular Expressions for XML (TREX) is a schema language designed by the notable James Clark, who has been active in developing usable XML standards for as long as XML has been around, and is known for his significant contributions to the SGML community before XML. TREX does not define fine-grain data types the way XML Schema does. It is intended to be used in conjunction with data types defined using external specifications, which can include XML Schema–defined data types.

The PyXML package includes a TREX validator in the xml.schema.trex module; this was added in PyXML Version 0.7.0.

RELAX-NG

RELAX-NG is a language derived from two well-received schema languages, TREX and RELAX; the specification is still under active development at the time of this writing. This specification is the combined effort of James Clark and Makoto Murata, the authors of TREX and RELAX, and is sponsored by the Organization for the Advancement of Structured Information Standards (OASIS). RELAX-NG takes the same approach to data types as TREX. Complete information on RELAX-NG is available at *http://www.oasis-open.org/committees/relax-ng/*. An alternate, non-XML syntax has also been proposed.

Schematron

The Schematron Assertion Language defined by Rick Jelliffe is a bit different from the other schema languages. Instead of defining what elements are allowed, their content models, and their attributes, Schematron makes assertions about the relationships among elements and attributes. Extensive documentation is available online at *http://schematron.sourceforge.net/*, and a Python validator is available from Fourthought, Inc. (*http://www.fourthought.com/*).

Types of Conformance

As with any specification, the primary reason for the XML specification's existence is to hold documents against it and make sure they conform to the specification. If so, then the rules within the specification can be used in reading, transforming, or applying the document. However, we must remember that XML defines two things: syntax for document instances, and a way to define new language using XML. It also tells us that we can use the former without the latter, so it must define what it means to conform to the specification in both cases.

If a document uses the XML syntax but does not depend on a specific markup language defined using the means provided by the XML recommendation, it needs to be *well-formed* in order to conform with XML. This is a form of conformance introduced by XML rather than inherited from SGML. On the other hand, a document that declares that it uses a specific markup language defined by a DTD is said to be *valid* if it is both well-formed and the elements and character data are arranged in a way that complies with the rules given by the specified Document Type Definition.

The XML specification defines a collection of text to be an XML document if it is well-formed according to the rules of the specification. The term well-formed is widely used in XML, and it refers to a document that is syntactically acceptable. For example:

```
<?xml version="1.0"?>
<book>
   <title>Python and XML</title>
</book>
```

The preceding document is well-formed. That is, beyond the *XML declaration* (described in more detail in "The Document Prolog," later in this chapter) pointing out that the document uses Version 1.0 of XML, both the book and title *elements* are opened and closed so that elements nest within each other in a strictly hierarchical way. You can't open a book and close a magazine.

Being well-formed is required but not sufficient to describe the concept of validity, which deals with the conformance of a document to a Document Type Definition. It's one thing to have the structure arranged such that it is syntactically acceptable, but quite another to ensure that the information contained within the document is

---

organized in the appropriate fashion and contains all of the necessary elements to be of use in an application or transaction.

The XML specification describes all XML processors as belonging to two classes: *validating* and *nonvalidating*. Regardless of validation, both types of processors must report violations of the specification's well-formedness constraints; otherwise, an XML document may be impossible to parse. A validating processor must be able to report violations of the DTD to the application. This requires that a validating processor read the entire DTD, and resolve and parse any external entities (described in the next section) referenced within the DTD itself and in the document instance. In contrast, nonvalidating processors need check only the document and internal DTD subset for well-formedness. Checking that a document is well-formed does not require accessing any external entities.

Since the arrival of alternate schema languages, a third form of conformance has been described informally. A document is said to be *schema valid* with respect to a particular schema, regardless of the language in which the schema is expressed, if the document is well-formed and the structure of the document conforms to the specific schema using the rules defined for that specific schema language. This is a generalization of the concept of validity given by the XML recommendation; all valid documents are also schema valid for the schema defined by their DTD (though they may be invalid for other schema).

Physical Structures

XML text is stored in *entities*. Entities are identified in various ways, but most commonly by filename or URI. There is no constraint on this, however, and many systems do use alternate means for entity storage—for example, many live happily in large databases. Many XML documents involve more than one entity; perhaps the most common arrangement is that the document is in one entity and its type definition is in another. As documents get larger, increasing numbers of entities are often involved with each document. This may be more common with document-centric applications than with data-communication applications of XML.

Entities are typically given names in one or more global namespaces. XML requires that entities be given *system identifiers*, which are always URIs. The term has roots in the SGML community, where system identifiers were used to refer to storage locations using whatever syntax the tools in use happened to understand. An additional global namespace is shared with the SGML world; the identifiers in that space are called *formal public identifiers* (FPIs). Use of this namespace is very limited in the XML world, as it is not always easily mapped to URLs that can be used to retrieve arbitrary resources, although there are ways to do it. They do see some use, and extensible support for FPIs is available in the PyXML toolkit.

Entities are used for several things in XML:

Document entities
> Regardless of the application, all documents start somewhere. With XML, they are also guaranteed to end in the same entity. The entity containing the start of the document is called the *document entity*. The document entity is interesting because it is the only entity that may be completely anonymous. An application can provide the content of the entity directly to the XML parser, allowing it to operate without extracting the text from a disk file or another local or remote data source.

External entities
> Other physical storage units that contribute to a document are *external entities*. These entities may contain all or part of the type specification for the document, or they may contain document content. While external entities are defined by their system and formal public identifiers, most are given local names for easy reference.

External DTD subset
> If a document contains a document type declaration that specifies an external document type subset, that subset is given in an entity. This entity is special in that it is not given a local name, but otherwise is simply an external entity.

Linked resources
> Some documents refer to other documents without making them a part of themselves. Whether or not these external resources are really entities is not always clear if they are not referenced via a name defined in an entity declaration. One typical example of this is the resources identified by URI in the href attribute of HTML's a element—it is not referenced by a named entity, and it is not always known just what the linked resource will contain when the reference is created. The fact that the external resource is identified as the target of a link is important to the linking document.

Constructing XML Documents

Documents are the heart of XML. Any amount of usable XML is presented as a document, often stored in a file. One of the very first things you must understand in order to use XML is how to create a well-formed document. In this section, we examine the syntactic components of a document, starting with the individual characters and looking at how they are viewed when building larger syntactic constructs. Then we look at the constructs defined for all documents by the XML recommendation.

Characters in XML Documents

The XML Specification defines a *character* as "an atomic unit of text as specified by ISO/IEC 10646." (Remember, ISO/IEC 10646 is more commonly referred to as

Unicode.) Of course, this explanation is exactly what you should say at a party if someone asks. One of the goals of both standardization and XML is to make documents easily understandable by platforms around the globe. As such, simple things like ASCII characters can become quite complex.

Regardless, the specification states that legal characters are "tab, carriage return, line feed," as well as belonging to the aforementioned Unicode specification. If you were to write an XML parser, the topic of characters and standardization would be of incredible importance to you. For the rest of us, it's usually enough to choose an XML parser that gets it right.

You can declare the character encoding used in an XML document using the optional XML declaration:

```
<?xml version="1.0" encoding="UTF-8"?>
```

For an external entity that is not a document itself, a variation of the XML declaration, called an *encoding declaration*, is used:

```
<?xml encoding="UTF-8"?>
```

More information on the XML declaration is provided in "The Document Prolog" later in this chapter. For now, let's look at some of the most widely used character sets and encodings. (A character set that can be mapped into Unicode can be considered an encoding of Unicode, even if it does not directly support everything defined in Unicode.)

The ASCII character set

The American Standard Code for Information Interchange (ASCII) is a 7-bit text format (meaning that it takes a sequence of seven 1's and 0's to form a character). ASCII is understood by virtually ever computer in use. Unicode extends ASCII, so the first 128 characters of Unicode coincide with the first 128 characters of ASCII.

The ISO-8859-1 character set

The character set *ISO-8859-1* is also known as *Latin-1*. The ISO-8859-1 set is very widely used as it contains support for most (but not all) Western European languages. The first 256 characters of Unicode are identical to ISO-8859-1 for compatibility reasons. The first 128 characters of ISO-8859-1 are identical to ASCII. The second 128 are a combination of control characters, special characters, and accented letters. ISO-8859-1 was inspired by DEC Multinational Character Set, but there are a few differences. There are also various *ISO-8859-X* sets with support for additional languages and characters.

UTF-8 Encoding

Universal Transformation Format, 8-bit (UTF-8), is documented in *IETF RFC 2279* by F. Yergeau. UTF-8 is the most popular complete encoding of Unicode.

UTF-8 extends ASCII to some degree. The first 128 positions of UTF-8 are transparently encoded to their ASCII counterparts. Since Unicode can supposedly support over 2 billion characters (way beyond 128), getting it to fit in a stream of discrete 8-bit bytes requires some encoding. UTF-8 solves this problem by representing each Unicode character with a unique sequence of bytes. In a UTF-8 stream, ASCII characters occupy only one byte in the stream, whereas all other characters are represented by two or more bytes the stream. Your XML declaration using UTF-8 appears as follows:

```
<?xml version="1.0" encoding="UTF-8"?>
```

The most detailed information for dealing with UTF-8 encoding comes from the RFC.

Text, Character Data, and Markup

The specification states "text consists of intermingled character data and markup." The main point here is that every character within an XML document is either *character data* (the actual information content we're most interested in, such as an address or item quantity), or it is *markup* (containing all of the special characters needed to create start tags, end tags, entities, comments, CDATA delimiters, DTDs, processing instructions, and declarations). All the characters together constitute *text*.

Character data in the content of elements is "any string of characters that does not contain the start-delimiter of any markup." Clearly, it is important to know the difference between the two, since it is markup that allows our programs to interpret the character data correctly.

All markup begins with one of two characters: the less-than sign (<) and the ampersand (&). All markup that begins with the less-than sign ends with the greater-than sign (>), and markup that begins with an ampersand ends with a semi-colon (;). These are the only special characters you need to be aware of most of the time. In some situations, the single-quote (') and double-quote (") characters need special attention. This does not mean that your documents and data cannot include these characters, only that they require some special encoding in the XML text. Any Unicode character can be part of the character data.

One result is you're unable to use literal special characters such as ampersands (&), or angle brackets (<, >) within your text. For example, the following would confound an XML processor:

```
<question>Is 5 < 7 ≤ 9?</question>
```

The text of the question element contains characters not allowed by the specification. The < is expected to start a new markup component, so the following space is interpreted as a syntax error. The less-than sign is used to start a variety of markup constructs, the most common of which are the element start and end tags. The ampersand is used to mark entity references.

In order to use these special characters within your XML document, you'll need to encode them using entity or character references. To turn the example into proper XML, we need to use this:

```
<question>Is 5 &lt; 7 &#x2263; 9?</question>
```

Entity references are discussed later in this chapter, although many of you who have worked with HTML will find them familiar as they include ' ('), " ("), < (<), and > (>). XML allows you to define your own entities as well, and they can contain more than a single character, but those four are defined by the XML specification and do not need to be defined specially for your documents. *Character references* are slightly different in that they specify individual Unicode characters without attempting to use mnemonic identifiers for them. A character reference you might have seen used in HTML would be something like ® (®, the registered trademark symbol). In XML, the numeric portion of the reference may be given using hexadecimal digits as well if the letter x is inserted between the sharp sign and the first digit. The reference ® also refers to the registered trademark symbol. Character references cannot be defined by authors, and they always refer to Unicode characters by the ordinal value assigned to them in the Unicode specification.

Names

The XML specification defines several small lexical details, but perhaps one of the most important is the *name*. Names are tokens composed of some combination of legal characters including letters, digits, underscores, hyphens, or colons; the first character of a name cannot be a digit. Name tokens are used for naming anything that needs a name in XML, including element types, attributes, and entities. Some names cannot be used in day-to-day XML markup. First, names beginning with the string xml (in any mixture of upper- and lowercase) are "reserved for standardization in [the XML specification] or future versions of this specification." Secondly, when naming your elements, you must avoid use of the colon (:), as it is the basis for *XML namespaces* (a method of prefixing element names with tokens to give them domain context). While the XML 1.0 specification allows colons in element and attribute names, the more recent Namespaces specification assigns a particular syntactic significance that constrains their use. In other words, if you're defining a whole class of elements related specifically to books, such as bookTitle or bookAuthor, its better to use capitalization, hyphenation, or underscores to separate the words (such as book_title, book-title, or bookTitle) as opposed to using the colon, such as book:Title. Using an expression like book:Title leads XML processors to believe that you are referring to a Title element within the namespace URI attached to the local name book. Of course, it may be that Namespaces are appropriate for your application, in which case you should take the time to read the Namespaces specification very carefully and define any that are needed.

Whitespace in Character Data

When working with XML-based markup languages, it can be difficult to know how to treat whitespace. For many applications, whitespace can be handled as just more normal character data, while this is not sufficient for others. The problem most often manifests itself when presentation to the user is being controlled by the application. While the XML specification does not attempt to solve the problem, it does provide a way to include a hint for processing tools and applications that the whitespace in a particular element should be preserved as given, rather than treated as malleable space.

The easiest way to visualize the problem is to consider the way program source code is most commonly presented in HTML. Most HTML authors wrap source code in a pre element:

```
<pre>
def hello( ):
    print "Hello, world!"
</pre>
```

This is certainly the easiest way to present source code in HTML. Now consider what happens if, instead of using a pre element, we use a paragraph, or p, element:

```
<p>
def hello( ):
    print "Hello, world!"
</p>
```

This creates a very different effect in most web browsers, typically causing the entire program text to be shown on a single line with only a single space separating each word, even though the example includes multiple lines and multiple adjacent spaces.

The solution looks simple, at least for HTML. Simply use a pre element when we want to preserve whitespace. This obvious solution unfortunately has an equally obvious problem—it only works for HTML, not for arbitrary XML-based markup languages. A solution is needed that also works for a non-HTML document like this:

```
<Poem>
  Ode to a node,
  Nested beneath its tree,
  Snug as a bug in its XML rug
  Dreaming of the W3C.
</Poem>
```

How is an XML tool to know that the line breaks and other presentation for a poem are significant?

The XML specification defines an attribute called xml:space that you can attach to an element to communicate to the application that whitespace should be preserved. It is the responsibility of the client application to act on this information and indeed preserve whitespace when handling or formatting the data. A typical compliant XML parser passes the whitespace from the document through to the application regardless of whether the xml:space attribute has been seen (in either the document or the schema). An application can use the attribute to determine just what manipulations it can perform on the document content.

The value of the xml:space attribute can be either default or preserve. If the value is default, the application is allowed to treat the whitespace in whatever way it normally would; the XML specification imposes no limitations on how the whitespace is affected in this case. If, however, the value is preserve, the application is expected to avoid interfering with the whitespace in the element to which the attribute applies, as well as all child elements, until it encounters a child that specifies a value for xml:space. At that point, the child's value for xml:space takes precedence for itself and it's descendents.

The xml:space attribute can be used in a couple of different ways. The first is to simply include it in the document instance, which is sufficient for well-formed XML. The first line of our poem becomes:

```
<Poem xml:space="preserve">
```

While this seems reasonable for small quantities of XML text, it proves unworkable for large volumes of documents that are edited by humans. Think about what HTML would be like if we had to always include a special attribute to get the effect of the pre element! For this reason, the xml:space attribute is most often used by including it in the document schema. In a DTD, we would write something like this:

```
<!ATTLIST Poem xml:space (default|preserve) 'preserve'>
```

Attribute list declarations will be discussed in more detail in "Attribute Declarations" later in this chapter.

From a practical point of view, most applications that parse XML look at the names of the elements to determine what to do with the character data contained therein. For example, while parsing the text of a book formatted in XML, you may come across a code element that tells you to preserve the whitespace within that section. If you look carefully, however, often the document type specifies that xml:space has a default value of preserve for those elements.

End-of-Line Handling

The specification is straightforward where end-of-line handling is concerned. An XML parser must pass characters to applications with normalized line endings. That is, any combination of the hexadecimal characters 0x0D and 0x0A, or a standalone 0x0D character not followed by 0x0A, is converted to a single 0x0A character. For the less hexadecimal among us, it means that typical formatting codes such as \r\n and \r are converted to \n. And for those of you who have never used those weird backslash characters, it means that text coming from platforms that commonly use carriage-returns plus linefeed characters to terminate lines (such as Windows) is converted to use only linefeed characters.

Language Identification

An attribute named `xml:lang` is provided by the specification and can be placed inside documents to indicate the language used in the content. Again, this attribute must be declared in valid documents, much like `xml:space`. The values that can be used within this attribute are defined in *IETF RFC 1766*, or in a later version. Most language character codes have two letters, such as en for English, but dialects may be specified using an underscore character and an additional two-letter code; United States English can be specified as en_US, while the Queen's English can be specified as en_GB.

The Document Prolog

An XML document contains a *prolog*, which includes everything that precedes the single element that is the document content. The prolog consists of an optional declaration called the *XML declaration*, followed by an optional *Document Type Declaration*, followed by any number (including zero!) of comments and processing instructions. So the prolog may completely empty, but often contains the XML declaration as a matter of good form. The Document Type Declaration is required if the document is intended to conform to a DTD.

The XML declaration looks much like a processing instruction, but is slightly different because of a special purpose it serves. Since XML requires that all documents are Unicode—but does not constrain the encoding of the Unicode characters to bytes in the data stream that contains the document—there must be a way to determine that encoding. Some encodings can be recognized by the leading bytes of the data stream. A set of specific rules for determining the encoding from the leading bytes of the data stream is given as part of the XML recommendation. For many encodings however, that is not possible. The XML specification states that in those cases where the encoding is not known *a priori* (as when the encoding is returned in the headers of an HTTP response), the document must be encoded in UTF-8 or include an XML declaration that specifies the encoding. The declaration always includes the version of the XML specification with which the document conforms (only XML 1.0 has been defined at this time). A typical XML declaration would look like:

```
<?xml version="1.0" encoding="iso-8859-1"?>
```

This declares that the document is encoded in the character set ISO 8859-1, more commonly known as Latin-1. It's entirely legal to omit the encoding from the declaration as well, so the minimal declaration looks like this:

```
<?xml version="1.0"?>
```

I'm sure this already appears on coffee mugs.

After the XML declaration, a Document Type Declaration may appear. Note that this is different from the Document Type Definition, although the first two words and obvious abbreviations are the same. To avoid confusion, the acronym "DTD" is never used to refer to this; it is usually called the "DOCTYPE declaration." If given, this declaration specifies the name of the document element, and may specify both internal and external components of the DTD. Let's look at the simplest form of this declaration:

```
<!DOCTYPE book>
```

This tells us that the document element is of the type named book, but nothing else; this is not very useful by itself. There are actually two additional components to this declaration, each of which is optional, but one or both must be provided for the declaration to be particularly useful. Let's look at an example that contains both of these components:

```
<!DOCTYPE book SYSTEM "http://xml.example.com/dtds/book.dtd" [
  <!ENTITY myCompany "Super Mega Ultra Corporation">
]>
```

Here, we include a specification for an external subset of the DTD (the SYSTEM and the quoted string), and an internal subset enclosed in brackets.

If the Document Type Declaration is given, the name of the document type must match the name of the root element. If you declare your document type as <!DOCTYPE Tool [...]>, then your root element must be Tool. Furthermore, all the specific relationships in the DTD concerning nesting, character data, and attributes must be enforced against the document if it is to pass the test for validity.

If you decide to use both the internal and external subsets, the internal subset overrules the external. That is, the rules contained within the DTD inside your XML document prevails over rules for the same construct in an external DTD subset.

Start, End, and Empty Element Tags

An element's name communicates its type. The attributes contained within a start tag are not recognized in any particular order. The specification sees no difference between <name first="Chris" last="Jones"> and <name last = "Jones" first = "Chris">.

There are several constraints to keep in mind when working with tags. First, there is a constraint on attributes: they must be unique. No attribute name can appear twice in the same start tag. Next, if the document is to be considered valid, the attributes must have been declared, and the values must be of the types specified. Additionally, attribute values cannot be, nor can they contain, external entity references. Finally, an attribute of a start tag, or its entity replacement text, must not contain the character <. As for end tags, the specification requires only that they exactly match the start tag's name. Attributes are not allowed in end tags.

Elements can contain just about any type of character data, as long as it is not confused with surrounding XML markup itself. This has been addressed earlier in this chapter in the "Character Data and Markup" section.

Empty elements are elements without content. They may contain attributes as shown in this example:

```
<names>
  <name first="Chris" last="Jones"/>
  <name/>
</names>
```

This XML represents two well-formed name elements. Both are empty, but the first expresses two attributes as well.

Quotes around attribute values

The specification defines *literals* as "any quoted string not containing the quotation mark used as a delimiter for that string." Functionally, literals are used to indicate the content for an internal entity and the values of attributes. Typically, attribute and value combinations look like this:

```
<account refnum="23908403"/>
```

In this example, refnum is an attribute of the account element and has a value of 23908403. Either single or double quotation marks may be used, with the restriction that whichever is used to quote the value may not be directly used in the value, though it may be included using entity references or numeric character references.

As an example of an attribute value that contains both types of quotation marks, let's use this phrase:

The cat said "The dog yelled 'Help!,' then I pounced."

Encoded as an attribute, we end up with this:

```
<talltale text=
  'The cat said "The dog yelled &apos;Help!,&apos; then I pounced."'
  />
```

Comments

Comments in XML are similar to comments in HTML. The specification states that *comments* can reside anywhere outside of other markup. A simple XML comment looks like this:

```
<!-- This is a comment. -->
```

Since comments are not allowed inside other markup, you can't embed a comment inside an XML start tag:

```
<book name="Python and XML" <!--comment here-->>
```

This type of expression is not allowed by the XML specification. Interestingly enough, comments can appear inside a DTD. In addition, comments are not considered part of the document's character data. A couple of other caveats are that the double-hyphen (--) cannot be used inside the text of a comment as the characters -->

are used to indicate that the comment is being closed. Since one of the goals of XML is to avoid the syntactic difficulties of preceding markup languages, XML simply does not allow a double-hyphen within the body of comments. Entities and other markup are not handled within the text of a comment, so you can use the characters special to the rest of XML in your comments without worry that they'll cause syntax errors in your data. The correct version of the earlier comment element is as follows:

```
<book name="Python and XML">
This book is about the Python programming language
and XML markup language.
<!--comment here-->
</book>
```

By placing the comment inside the element instead of in the start tag, we've made it follow the rules.

Processing Instructions

Processing Instructions (PI) allow an XML document to pass instructions to a handling application. The XML processor does not consider Processing Instructions to be part of the document's character data. The point of PIs is to hand information to an application. For example, if you are communicating an urgent piece of news and want the receiving application to present some sort of alert to the user, you might place the following instruction within the XML, so that varying applications can act accordingly (i.e., a Palm VII could beep, an X Window application could raise an alert box, and so on):

```
<?newsAlert title="Martians Invade"?>
```

In this example, newsAlert is commonly referred to as the *target*; the rest of the text does not have a special name. The distinction between the two portions of the processing instruction is entirely a matter on convention; the specification mandates only the leading <?, trailing ?>, and the lack of the character pair ?> within the PI. (Note that most of the APIs used to work with PIs refer to the two parts as the *target* and the *data*.) There is no specific syntax associated with the content of processing instructions, though it is recommended practice to begin each with a *target* (usually the name of the tool expected to handle it). It is becoming common for applications to expect the content following the target to look much like a series of attributes with values, which are commonly referred to as *pseudo-attributes*. Clients of this XML document are able to handle or ignore the PI in whatever way is appropriate to them. Processing Instructions are useful because they provide an XML-oriented way of passing events between applications or adding annotations to the data that are specific to particular applications. Historically, PIs were used in the SGML community to encode instructions to formatting applications, with semantics such as "add a page break here."

CDATA Sections

A *CDATA section* is used to escape special characters in character data in your document. For example:

```
<![CDATA[The <ool <utter Knife & Sharpening Set]]>
```

This is actually an encoding of the character data:

```
The <ool <utter Knife & Sharpening Set
```

Without using a CDATA section, this must be encoded using general entities or character references:

```
The &lt;ool &lt;utter Knife &amp; Sharpening Set
```

The CDATA section is a good way to escape longer stretches of text that contain many characters that would otherwise be treated as markup if included directly in the text. Note that a CDATA section starts with the markup '<![CDATA['; no whitespace is allowed around the word CDATA. Once inside a CDATA section, no XML syntax is recognized until the characters ']]>' are encountered. Entity and character references aren't resolved or recognized, so the text ­ does not resolve to the trademark registration symbol, though it would in normal character data or in a CDATA attribute value.

Document Type Definitions

As discussed earlier, Document Type Definitions, or DTDs, are the form of document types specified by the XML 1.0 recommendation. Though there are alternatives, DTDs remain one of the most common ways of specifying a document type. In this section, we discuss the syntax of the various declarations that can occur in the Document Type Declaration; these can all appear in both the internal and external subsets.

Entity Declarations

Entities are sources of data that are used to compose a larger construct. Most, called *general entities*, are used to construct documents, but some, known as *parameter entities*, are used to construct the document type itself. Both are defined using an *entity declaration* in the Document Type Definition. Each kind of entity is defined in a separate namespace; there can be a general entity named myEntity and a parameter entity of the same name, and the names do not clash.

Entities can be declared more than once—the first definition for a name takes precedence. This allows the internal subset to override a definition provided in the external subset; when used with parameter entities, this mechanism can be used to extend DTDs. Document type extension generally works best when the DTD being extended has been carefully designed with this in mind. The DocBook DTD for technical documentation is an excellent example of this.

General entities can take a variety of forms: they may be *parsed* entities, consisting of XML text, or *unparsed*, such as an image stored as a Portable Network Graphics (PNG) file. The text of a parsed entity may be included in the entity declaration, or it may reside in an external source. The body of an unparsed entity is always stored externally. Most entities used with XML are parsed entities; unparsed constructs, such as images, are typically referenced using an absolute or relative URL rather than by a named entity.

Parsed general entities are used to define substitution text for a (typically) shorter name. Recall that in XML, text includes not only character data, but markup as well, so the substitution can actually insert additional structure into the document as long as all structures are complete within the substitution. At production time, a parser resolves the entity into its substitution text, and evaluates the document based on how it looks after the entities have been resolved. A simple internal entity is as easy to create as a symbol and its replacement text:

```
<!ENTITY sandwich "Crabby Patty">
```

In your document, any reference to &sandwich; yields the replacement text of "Crabby Patty" into the document. For example:

```
I am hungry for a &sandwich;.
```

This sentence renders as:

I am hungry for a **Crabby Patty.**

External entities are defined using an entity declaration that gives a URL to an external resource containing the replacement text:

```
<!ENTITY legal SYSTEM "http://www.example.com/legal.xml">
```

Any reference to &legal; within a document yields:

```
<legal>Copyright 2001, Example Corporation</legal>.
```

Like internal entities, external entities replace symbols with the appropriate text. Sometimes this must be done when the text uses characters that would otherwise be considered markup (such as the use of special characters like <, >, and & in your XML). Other times, entities are used to keep boilerplate information that is normally maintained somewhere else available to the document.

Parameter entities are different in both usage and applicability. They can only be used to create the Document Type Definition, and not to directly compose the document. The syntax of an XML document does not allow parameter entities to be referred to from within the document content, but only allows their use with the internal and external DTD subsets. There are no unparsed parameter entities, though a nonvalidating parser may ignore them. Validating parsers are required to parse all referenced parameter entities.

The declaration for a parameter entity looks much like the declaration for a general entity, with just a couple of additional characters added:

```
<!ENTITY % node-decls SYSTEM "node-decls.dtd">
```

What this declaration has that the general entity declaration doesn't is a percent sign (%) between the keyword ENTITY and the name of the entity, with whitespace on both sides to set it off (the whitespace is required). This parameter entity would be used like this:

```
%node-decls;
```

Note that the reference to the parameter entity uses the percent sign instead of the ampersand to mark the beginning of the name; this is necessary since the two sets of names may overlap.

The effect of entity replacement is much like the use of general entities. The replacement text effectively replaces the entity reference, and interpretation of the document type continues using the modified text.

The usefulness of parameter entities is highest when working with modularized document types, which can provide carefully designed extension mechanisms using parameter entities. A large DTD, such as the industry-standard DocBook DTD for software documentation, can be customized by creating a new document type that simply defines several parameter entities and then incorporates the standard DocBook definition. Since the entity declarations in the customization layer override the definitions provided by DocBook, this mechanism can be used to either extend or restrict the specific document type in ways that are suitable for a specific project.

Element Type Declarations

Element type declarations are used to constrain an element's content. They indicate what element types can be used as children of the element, and show how the children may be arranged. Element type declarations may look like this:

```
<!ELEMENT br      EMPTY>
<!ELEMENT generic ANY>
<!ELEMENT name    (address+)>
<!ELEMENT para    (#PCDATA | list | picture)*>
```

We can break up the declaration in particular systactic components, each with a specific purpose:

```
<!ELEMENT name content-model>
```

The text <!ELEMENT tells the parser that this is an element type declaration. *name* gives a name to the element type; this allows it to be referenced from elsewhere in the Document Type Definition. The *content-model* is used to specify what can appear as content of the element, whether it can contain character data, other elements, or both. No element type may be declared more than once.

It is interesting to note that there is not a place for attributes to be declared. While attributes are associated with element types, they are defined using attribute declarations, described later in this chapter, in the section "Attribute Declarations."

Content models

A *content model* describes what elements are allowed as children of the declared element type, in what order and combination they are allowed, and whether arbitrary character data is allowed.

The content models of all elements can be broken into two categories:

Element Content

This describes content made up only of elements. That is, you define an address element that requires no character data, but instead requires child elements. The specification defines content particles that "consist of names, choice lists of content particles, or sequence lists of content particles."

Mixed Content

This content may contain character data. This is the most common arrangement in text documents:

```
<news title="XML from Outer Space">
    This article describes XML transmissions from outer space.

    <h1>Not a Meteor</h1>
    <para>Contrary to earlier reports, the XML that has landed from
        outer space is not a meteor.</para>
</news>
```

In this example, elements and character data are mixed beneath the news element. Elements that have a mixed content model are not required to allow other elements as content. In fact, an element type with only character data in the content model may be completely empty; there is no way to specify that there must be characters in the character data.

Let's take another look at our example element declarations:

```
<!ELEMENT br     EMPTY>
```

These element type declarations are simple. The content model of the first, EMPTY, can be used to describe an empty br element as found in XHTML. It can contain no child elements and no character data. It can still contain noncontent constructs, such as comments or processing instructions. An element type declared as EMPTY is considered a degenerate special case of element content.

```
<!ELEMENT generic ANY>
```

Next, we have an element named generic that can contain any kind of element defined in the document type (this does *not* allow undefined element types!). In addition to other elements, character data is allowed as well, so a content model of ANY is mixed content.

```
<!ELEMENT name     (address+)>
```

The third example is simple, but very different from the others. Instead of a simple name such as ANY or EMPTY, the model is described by something that closely resembles a regular expression. In this particular example, we have a name element that requires one or more address elements to be included. This form of content model is perhaps the most commonly used and allows for fine control. Content models can take on varying levels of complexity, but the goal is always the same: to define the content that is allowed or expected within the element.

The content model is specified with parentheses, as well as with commas indicating a sequence. Vertical bar characters (|) indicate a choice. For example:

```
<!ELEMENT name (first, last)>
```

This element type requires a `first` child element followed by a `last` child element, and nothing else. If you want to offer a choice between `first` or `last`, but not allow both, use a vertical bar:

```
<!ELEMENT name (first | last)>
```

These expressions can be nested within each other as well:

```
<!ELEMENT order (sku, quantity, (account | name), price)>
```

The above `order` element requires a child `sku` element, followed by a `quantity` element, then followed by either an `account` or a `name` element, and finally followed by a `price` element.

Additionally, the operators +, *, and ? can be tacked onto the end of content expressions to indicate the number of times an element or sequence must occur, or whether it is repeatable or even required. Without a modifier, the element must appear exactly once in that location. They are explained in the following list:

+   Content must appear one or more times.

*   Content may appear zero or more times.

?   Content may appear zero times or one time.

For example, to require an `order` element to have only one `account`, followed by at least one or more `sku`s, contain one or more `price` elements, and optionally provide a shipping address (`ship`) once only, you could use an Element type such as the following:

```
<!ELEMENT order (account, sku+, price+, ship?)>
```

To mix a combination of character data or elements, you can use the or operator to specify your mixed content, as shown here:

```
<!ELEMENT paragraph (#PCDATA | list | picture)*>
```

This `paragraph` element type allows for repeatable sequences of character data (denoted by the asterisk), `list` elements, or `picture` elements within `paragraph` elements. #PCDATA can only be combined with elements using the or operator in a group that has a * modifier, and it can only occur in the outermost parenthesized group of a content model.

Attribute Declarations

As discussed earlier, *attributes* are used to provide name/value combinations as properties of elements. Attributes can appear only in start tags and empty element tags.

An attribute-list declaration would be a part of a DTD, used to validate the XML document. An example follows:

```
<!ATTLIST news
    title  CDATA #REQUIRED
    author CDATA #IMPLIED>
```

This is an attribute-list declaration that indicates that any news element is required to have a title attribute consisting of character data, and may optionally have an author attribute, also consisting of character data.

Attribute data types

The specification states that *attribute types* are of three kinds: *string, tokenized,* and *enumerated*. In the earlier attribute list example, you saw that a news element required a title attribute with the string type CDATA.

There are several tokenized attribute types:

ID

    A unique identifier for this element. The identifier must be a name unique in the current document instance.

IDREF

    Must match an ID somewhere in the XML document.

IDREFS

    A list of one or more names, separated by spaces. Each must match an ID in the document.

ENTITY

    Matches the name of an unparsed entity declared in the document.

ENTITIES

    A space-separated list containing one or more entity names.

NMTOKEN

    The most seldom used, this matches an NMTOKEN production as defined in the XML recommendation; refer to the recommendation for more information.

NMTOKENS

    A list of one or more space-separated NMTOKEN values; this is the least used attribute type.

The remaining attribute types, the enumerated types, are defined in the attribute list itself. An enumerated type is a type that takes a name from a defined list of names, in which the list is given in an attribute declaration. Each distinct set of names forms a separate type, but these types do not have names of their own. An example should help clarify this:

```
<!ATTLIST ship
        type (sloop | frigate | dinghy) #IMPLIED>
```

This declaration defines an attribute type that may have a value of dinghy, frigate, or sloop, but no other value. The element `<ship type="yacht"/>` would trigger a validation failure.

Attribute values and constraints

An attribute declaration allows the document type to specify a default value for an attribute if the attribute is missing. It can also indicate whether the attribute may be omitted from the document. Let's look at a more interesting example of an attribute declaration:

```
<!ATTLIST chapter
    synopsis  CDATA                      #IMPLIED
    author    CDATA                      #REQUIRED
    email     CDATA                      "info@example.com"
    version   CDATA #FIXED               "1.0"
    type      (normal|reference|appendix) "normal">
```

The synopsis attribute is required to be a string (CDATA) if it is given at all, but it is not required, and does not have a default value because it is marked as #IMPLIED. (Most of the attributes in HTML are declared this way.) The #REQUIRED constraint means just what it says; the author attribute must be specified in the document. Because it is a string, it may be empty. If a string value is specified instead of #IMPLIED or #REQUIRED, as with the email attribute in our example attribute list, it becomes the default value that is used if no value is given in the document.

The #FIXED constraint can only be used in conjunction with a default value, which we see for the version attribute. When this constraint is used, the document is allowed to include the attribute, but the value must match that given by the default exactly, though it may be encoded using a different mixture of characters, entity references, and character references. If the value differs, an error is reported by the parser.

The type attribute is an example of an enumerated type, similar to what we looked at earlier. Default values and constraints are specified for enumerated types in the same way as for other types, with the additional constraint that if a value is specified, it must be one of the names included in the enumeration.

ID attributes offer some unique behavior. Let's create an attribute for the news element we defined previously:

```
<!ATTLIST news
        newsID ID #REQUIRED>
```

With this attribute list, news elements are required to have a newsID attribute. The allowed values are governed by the rules of the ID tokenized type. Specifically, the ID value is a name (as defined in this chapter in the section "Names") and must not appear more than once in an XML document as the value of any attribute of type ID.

In other words, ID values must uniquely represent an element within the document. Consider a legal example:

```
<news newsID="id39">Text</news>
<news newsID="id40">Text</news>
```

Since the values of ID attributes are required to be unique within a document, the following is illegal:

```
<news newsID="id39">Text</news>
<news newsID="id39">Text</news>
```

Additionally, no element may have more than one ID attribute specified. An element type may define more than one attribute of the ID type, but at most, one ID value may be specified for any element. As a result, some of the programming APIs can use the values of ID attributes to retrieve specific elements from a document.

What is most interesting about ID attributes, however, is not the attributes themselves, but the IDREF attribute type. While a particular value may only appear once in a document as an ID type, it may appear any number of times as the value of an IDREF or IDREFS attribute. In particular, attributes of those types may *only* take values that also appear as the value of an ID attribute somewhere in the same document. (An IDREFS attribute can take a value that is a space-separated list of ID values, each of which must exist in the document.) These values can be used to forge internal links between elements that a validating parser must check. This can be very convenient when a basic tree structure is not sufficient to model your data; the ID, IDREF, and IDREFS attributes can be used to extend the data model to include connected, directed graphs with typed arcs.

Canonical XML

The term *canonicalization* originally was "borrowed" loosely from its more ancient context to indicate that one structure of an instance document is the same as the master, or commonly accepted, structure of the document. Canonicalization is sometimes referred to as C14N for brevity; this is similar to the more common use of I18N for internationalization.

Canonical XML is an emerging W3C recommendation that allows you to see if one physical representation of a document is equivalent to another physical representation of the same document in order to determine if they are "canonically" equivalent. In this section, we explore some of the technical features of Canonical XML to gain a better understanding of its application to suit your needs.

The Canonical XML Data Model

To begin the process of converting a document to canonical form, you, or rather your Canonical XML processor, must start with some form of XML that it can understand. Therefore, your first parameter to a canonical translator should be an XPath node set, or a serialized XML document. The second parameter is a Boolean value, which indicates whether comments should be analyzed.

In the case of a node set, it must have normalized line feeds, normalized attribute values, substituted CDATA sections with their character content, and resolved character and parsed entity references. In other words, each node must be fully cooked. No stranded entities and no superfluous whitespace are allowed. All whitespace within the root element must be preserved with the exception of line-delimiter normalization. The whole approach leads you to think that the document is being worked over—flattened, stretched, and pulled like pizza dough just prior to being cooked.

Document Order

Although Canonical XML depends on XPath, it imposes a few rules on the XPath node sets that are sent into any Canonical XML processor.

1. An element's namespace and attribute nodes must follow the element but precede any children.
2. Namespace nodes must exist prior to attribute nodes.
3. Namespace nodes for an element are sorted lexicographically by local name.
4. Attribute nodes for an element are sorted lexicographically with the namespace URI as a primary key and the local name as a secondary key.

Canonical XML Structure

Canonical XML does away with the XML declaration and DTD, and also normalizes whitespace outside of the root element. Abbreviated empty elements (in the style of `<element-name/>`) are converted to start- and end-tag pairs (`<element-name></element-name>`). Namespace and attributes may be lexicographically reorganized to comply with canonical expectations as described in the previous section, "Document Order." In addition to these modifications, a canonical representation replaces CDATA sections with their actual characters, and applies character reference replacement when appropriate. Attribute values and text also have their special characters replaced with references.

Canonical XML is quite new, and we have yet to see significant amounts of Python software developed for Canonical XML processing. The vision of Canonical XML is blurry, but it is a method for checking two instances (regardless of DTD or Schema) and working them over like cleaned fish to see if they share the same skeletons. Version 0.7 of PyXML will include support for rendering XML in canonical form.

Going Beyond the XML Specification

The standards developed at the W3C ensure interoperability between distributed systems and the applications developers around the world. As we progress in this book from XML tools and strategies in your local applications to distributed application development, several new XML terms and issues come into the forefront.

XML Namespaces

As discussed in "Namespaces in XML" in Chapter 1, namespaces provide a means to combine elements from different knowledge domains or schemas. The Namespaces specification accomplishes this by allowing element and attribute names to be qualified with a URI; every URI corresponds to a unique namespace. Namespaces are used for several purposes in practice, but the most important is to allow a document to contain elements defined by different schema (possibly originating from different organizations) without having naming conflicts.

Namespaces are used by associating a named `xmlns` attribute with a URI. Namespaces are communicated in an XML document using the reserved colon character in an element name, prefixed with the `xmlns` symbol. For example:

```
<sumc:purchaseOrder refnum="389473984-38844"
    xmlns:sumc="http://www.superultramegacorp.com">
  <sumc:product name="Magical Widget" sku="398-4993833">
    <sumc:qty value="24">One Case Order</sumc:qty>
    <sumc:amount value="34.56">34.56</sumc:amount>
    <sumc:shipping value="overnight">Next-day</sumc:shipping>
  </sumc:product>
</sumc:purchaseOrder>
```

In this document, the namespace of *SuperUltraMegaCorp* is defined. The prefix `sumc` has been associated with it in the `xmlns:sumc` attribute. Elements prefixed with `sumc:` are within this namespace. This `purchaseOrder` now has a context that can set it apart from a similarly structured purchase order intended for a different business domain.

Extracting Information Using XPath

XPath is discussed at length in Chapter 5. For now it is worth a mention, lest you start to develop your own method for querying XML without understanding what standards are offered. XPath offers a standardized method of querying XML for specific information, whether it's a single element or node, or a collection of elements. The standardization is of value not when you're writing the backend part of your application, but rather when you need to expose search capabilities either programmatically or via the web.

Using XLink to Link XML Documents

The XLink language allows for the insertion of elements into XML documents to create and describe links between different resources. XLink uses XML syntax to create structures representing links similar to hyperlinks used in HTML, as well as more complex linking structures. Link specifications are encoded in the attributes of the source document, or in supplemental documents that can describe links among other documents. The most common applications embed link information at the link source. The target of a link is described using a URI and an XPath expression; the URI specifies the target resource, and the XPath expression specifies a specific location in the linked resource. XLink is still a young specification and is not discussed further in this book.

Communicating with XML Protocols

The XML Protocol working group is a W3C group tasked with investigating the development of XML-based messaging and communications standards. These standards are attempting to define a method of packaging information and sending it across the Internet. Some are focused on transactions, some are focused on guaranteed delivery, and others are focused on routing and enveloping mechanisms. The Protocol Activity page (*http://www.w3.org/2000/03/29-XML-protocol-matrix*) is an excellent online resource for comparing these different protocols when developing distributed systems. The Web Distributed Authoring and Versioning specifications from the IETF, collectively known as WebDAV, use XML to support interoperable tools for web site management and authoring. Chapter 9 covers such items as remote procedure calls and web services (including SOAP) in greater detail. Additional specifications deal with other aspects of distributed computing, especially topics such as authentication and secure communications.

Replacing HTML with XHTML

The Extensible Hypertext Markup Language, or XHTML (*http://www.w3.org/TR/xhtml1/*), is a welcome gift to those of us who have had to struggle with parsing HTML. Though there is a W3C specification for HTML, most implementations conform only partially. This is due in part to the growth of HTML from some early implementations rather than a formal specification, and also to the browser implementers' attempts to do "the right thing" even with badly broken markup. The attempts to force HTML to fit into an SGML mold after the fact probably hindered compliance further, if only because the rules for parsing it became more complex and implementers' don't like to start over. When a browser parses HTML, it concerns itself with display attributes, not organization of the information in the document. While XHTML doesn't change the focus on appearance, it is an XML-based markup language, allowing you to parse it with an XML parser. This can drastically reduce the handling time of XHTML. It also allows you to leverage XHTML into other XML applications, as well as use XML Namespaces in conjunction with XHTML that has migrated into other domains and systems.

The first version of the XHTML specification, XHTML 1.0, defines a monolithic document type that corresponds closely with the HTML 4 specification. Future versions of XHTML, starting with XHTML 1.1, are moving toward a modular approach; different aspects of the language will be defined in separate components, and different applications will have the flexibility to determine which components they support. Part of the intent is to allow browsers with simpler displays, such as mobile phones, to avoid having to implement portions of XHTML that do not make sense for the application (such as tables for very small textual displays). An additional benefit is that application developers can define new modules that allow documents to be created that can be used for both presentation to people and improved computer-to-computer communications.

Transforming XML with XSLT

The XML Stylesheet Language, or XSL, consists of two component specifications: XSL Transformations (XSLT) and XSL Formatting Objects (XSL-FO). The transformation language is used to translate XML documents from their original form to some other form, which may be XML, HTML, or anything else (including plain text). XSLT is covered in more detail in Chapter 6. The XSL-FO specification describes specific presentational styling and is used to describe a formatted document that could be printed to a typesetting device or displayed on a screen. It is not as widely implemented as XSLT and is not covered further in this book.

## CHAPTER 3

The Simple API for XML

The Simple API for XML, otherwise known as SAX, is a popular interface for working with XML data. Let's start by looking at the background and history of SAX, after which we'll describe the major components of the interface. Once the overview is complete, we can look at several examples to help you see how to use it in your own applications.

The Birth of SAX

Before SAX, almost every XML parser offered its own interface, so applications were built to use specific parsers. The interfaces were low-level and generally similar in structure; the differences were mostly in the details. When new parsers were made available, applications had to be modified extensively to work with the different interface in order to take advantage of the new parser, even though the fundamental structure was essentially unchanged.

As is so often the case, the solution lay in introducing another layer of indirection. A group of XML developers using Java, led by David Megginson on the XML-DEV mailing list, defined a set of Java interfaces that allowed an application to work with any parser. The only requirement was that there be a *driver* for the new API for each parser. The driver was a class that used the parser-specific interface to make calls back to the application using the new, general interface. The application would create *handler* objects that implemented methods the driver would use to call back to the application. When Megginson released the specification, he also released a set of drivers for many of the more popular Java XML parsers. The initial specification supported the XML 1.0 recommendation, but not any of the more complex layers that have been built on top of it; the initiatives to create those were largely in their infancy at the time. The group of developers called the new API the "Simple API for XML," or SAX, because it was actually simpler than most of the parser-specific interfaces it was designed to abstract away.

The new API was widely received as a major step forward for application writers—it was easy to use, allowed the use of arbitrary parsers with an application, and was carefully defined before any other common APIs were available. Java programmers became extremely happy as the stress levels dropped in their professional lives. Developers in other languages adapted the specification in ways that allowed SAX to remain an identifiable API even as it was made to work with the native conventions used in those languages. Python programmers in the XML-SIG, led by Lars Marius Garshol, created an adaptation of the API and implemented drivers for several parsers. This implementation was accepted as part of the PyXML package.

The W3C then released the Namespaces recommendation. This recommendation changed the very concept of what constituted a name. While there was great debate over the value of the new recommendation, most people recognized that it did solve real problems and that it was here to stay. No one wanted a return of having to chase incompatible APIs, so the SAX developers quickly dug in and worked on a version of SAX that could support Namespaces. The revised API is known as SAX2. It is interesting to note that some of the first implementations of namespaces were filters written as SAX handlers; the SAX events were used to drive the SAX2 handlers with a little bit of processing in the middle to add the Namespaces support. Information on the Java version of SAX2 and links to additional SAX resources can be found at the SAX home page at *http://sax.sourceinfo.new/*.

Python developers rapidly adopted the SAX2 interface, taking the opportunity to clean up some warts of the early mapping of SAX from the Java-based specification. The SAX2 API rapidly became part of PyXML and was adopted for use in the Python standard library. When Python programmers speak of the SAX API, they are generally referring to the second version.

Understanding SAX

The first job of using SAX is to design and implement a handler that works with your specific XML documents. When dealing with a large project or working with a vast catalogue of valid documents, it may make sense to implement a few comprehensive handlers to deal with multiple document types. However, for smaller projects, it may be more desirable to implement handlers for each specific document type that you encounter. As you start to build more complex applications, you will see that the things you're attempting to do with the XML as well as the XML documents themselves can drive the way you develop your document handlers. Often, the SAX methods that you implement extract data from the event stream, which you can then hand off to another application (such as a database). Or you might want to apply intelligent business logic to it. It's likely that the task will drive your development strategy.

In all practical use, SAX is a callback-based API in which you implement handler objects to process XML. You pass a reference to your SAX handler objects to a SAX-capable parser (or driver; we'll use "parser" to refer to either). When parsing begins, the parser calls the methods on your handler objects and allows you to process the XML, so that you can do something useful with it in your applications and distributed systems.

SAX is an excellent stream-based API. It allows for faster processing of documents, as well as handling of documents that are simply too large to load into memory. Additionally, the event-based API allows you to react to parsing events and errors in "real-time," as they occur, while parsing the document, rather than waiting for the entire document to load. This can be especially valuable when used in a graphical application that needs to remain responsive to the user. Another huge win for many applications is the lower memory consumption when compared to DOM-based code; by allowing the application control over any objects created during parsing, the application can minimize the needed storage overhead and discard objects as soon as they are no longer required.

SAX is the interface to use when you need to construct some application-specific data structures from one or more documents, but you don't need to maintain the XML structure within your application. Since SAX reports low-level events to the handlers installed by the application, the programmer needs to be careful about keeping track of the application state during parsing—it lends itself toward modeling the application as a state machine. Fortunately, the programmer is not required to pay a high memory or a performance penalty, which is often associated with loading potentially large documents. This would be difficult to avoid when using the DOM interface, which usually keeps the entire document tree in memory until the tree is discarded. (We look at the DOM in detail in the next chapter.)

Using SAX in an Application

When an application is built using SAX, it can be helpful to think of the application as a set of components. The XML parser itself, including the SAX driver, is a black-box component that only needs a small amount of control information from the application. The handler objects are the only way for the XML parser to communicate with the application, but the logic they contain should be more concerned with interpreting the events reported by the parser than in implementing the application—these often form a separate layer that provides the application with the data model it needs. The application itself uses the derived data structures and higher-level events from the handler objects to perform the real work of the application. The relationship of these components is shown in Figure 3-1.

For smaller applications, it is common for the application and the handlers to be the same objects, often with the application code in the callback methods. While this does not work well for larger applications, it is a reasonable approach for simple applications. While learning about SAX, it offers excellent pedagogical side effects as

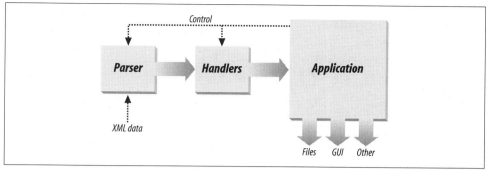

Figure 3-1. Components of a SAX application

well, so our examples embed the application code directly in the handler implementations. It is not difficult to see how to create abstractions between the SAX handler objects and a larger application.

SAX refers to the parser object as a *reader*. It reads input from some source and generates calls to the handler methods for particular events in the input. (There isn't any requirement that the source be an XML document, though it usually is.) The application registers handler objects using methods on the reader, and may set some additional properties of the parser. In our overview of the API, we start by examining the handler objects that can be provided to the parser and then take a quick look at the reader interface.

SAX Handler Objects

SAX is composed of four primary interfaces that are called by parsers for the different events that are encountered during the parsing phase. Python has tailored these methods slightly (mostly by using Python's more powerful native data types) from its native Java to faithfully implement SAX in the Python environment. By implementing the different interfaces of the callback API, you can receive all the events generated by the parser as it encounters the different parts of the XML document. Let's take a quick look at the different handler objects that can be implemented. (Complete reference information on the methods invoked by the parser for each object is given in Appendix C.)

ContentHandler

The ContentHandler interface is the most commonly used of all SAX interfaces, and is the primary way in which your applications receive parsing events. Parsing events are geared towards the primary markup and character data present in documents. Tell your SAX-capable parser about your implementation of this interface via the setContentHandler method.

The callback API is the part of SAX that users of XML are most interested in. This is the API that you implement to receive the stream of events generated by the parser. As each element comes through, it triggers the parser to call a startElement method on the handler you implemented. The startElement handler, designed for the XML in use, must know what to do with any element it encounters in the document:

```
def startElement(self, name, attrs):
    if name == "webArticle":
        subcat = attrs["subcategory"]
        if subcat.find("tech") > -1:
            self.inArticle = 1
            self.isMatch = 1

    elif self.inArticle:
        if name == "header":
            self.title = attrs["title"]
            self.inBody = 1
        if name == "body":
            self.inBody = 1
```

ErrorHandler

The ErrorHandler interface allows applications to respond to errors encountered by the parser at runtime. This object must be registered with the reader object (using setErrorHandler) to be effective. All parse errors are classified into three categories based on their severity; the handler object implements a different method for each level of severity. The least severe errors are passed to the warning method, while real violations of the specifications are passed to the error method if the parser can continue to look for additional errors in the input. They are passed to fatalError if this is not possible.

Each of these methods receives a single parameter, which is always an instance of the SAXException interface. This interface offers a number of methods to allow information about the error to be retrieved, including where the error occurred and in which input source. If the handler decides to terminate processing, the SAXException object can simply be raised as an exception.

If you do not supply an error handler, the default behavior is to print an error message to sys.stdout for warnings, and to raise the exception for both normal and fatal errors.

If you have installed the PyXML package, a couple of convenient implementations are provided in the xml.sax.saxutils module. The ErrorPrinter class is an error handler that prints a report of the error on standard output, regardless of the severity. The ErrorRaiser simply raises the exception, so errors always terminate processing.

DTDHandler

When an application needs to know about notations and unparsed entities, it can use the SAX parser's setDTDHandler method to specify a DTDHandler object to receive this information. Objects with this interface need only implement two interfaces—one to receive notation definitions, and one to receive entity definitions. Only definitions of unparsed entities (entities with specified notations) are passed to this interface.

While this doesn't sound like it covers much of the information specified in a DTD, it does cover what an application is normally expected to need if using unparsed entities. Remember, the "S" in SAX stands for "Simple"—most applications do not actually need the details of the content models and other entity definitions. If you do need more information from the DTD, many mechanisms are available:

- The optional SAX DeclHandler handler, which may not be supported by all parsers
- The native interface of the Expat parser; see the documentation for the standard library module xml.parsers.expat
- The xml.parsers.xmlproc.dtdparser module from PyXML

EntityResolver

This handler, if implemented, must also be registered with the parser prior to parsing, using the parser's setEntityResolver method. When the parser encounters external entities, it calls the resolveEntity method in your implementation. Application developers can use this method to point the parser at an alternative location to resolve entities, such as a cache. If it returns None or a system identifier, the parser tries to load the entity using the basic facilities for HTTP and FTP provided by the Python standard library.

Other handler objects

There are actually two more handler objects defined for use with SAX, but these are considered optional and do no have methods on the parser to set them as conveniently. Most applications will not need these, but being aware of them helps when they are needed.

DeclHandler

> An object with methods that are called when the parser encounters definitions of the structural model of the document. The methods are called for element and attribute declarations, and for declarations of both internal and external entities.

LexicalHandler

> The methods of this object are called for events that applications are not supposed to care about, but that can be useful when performing a transform that should not affect the document any more than necessary. The events reported to this handler include comments, entity boundaries, the start and end of the DTD, and CDATA section boundaries.

There are no setDeclHandler or setLexicalHandler methods on a SAX parser. These handlers are installed using the *property* interface of the parser, which we discuss shortly.

SAX Reader Objects

To use the handler objects, we must register them with a SAX *reader*, or parser. All parsers are required to support the four most commonly needed handlers, and convenient methods are defined to set and retrieve the values of each of these. The routines `setContentHandler`, `setDTDHandler`, `setEntityResolver`, and `setErrorHandler` all have matching routines to retrieve the current handler; these methods have names that start with get instead of set. There is an additional method, `setLocale`, which can be used to specify the locale for errors and warnings.

In addition to these configuration methods, SAX provides the concepts of *features* and *properties*. A feature is some bit of functionality that may be turned on or off, and a property is a named value associated with the parser's state. Depending on the specific feature or property and the parser implementation, each may be either read-only or modifiable, or perhaps modifiable only when a parse is not in progress. The `DeclHandler` and `LexicalHandler` discussed previously are configured by setting properties on the parser. Most applications will not need to use properties or features.

Reading an Article

In this example, we look at how we can extract and use information from an XML document using SAX. The particular documents our script works with are simple news articles, but we'll see how to work with elements, attributes, and textual content.

Some of the trade-offs of using SAX depend on what you're trying to accomplish, and how the XML is structured. SAX treats XML as a continuous stream, firing events to your handler as they happen. Example 3-1 shows *article.xml*.

Example 3-1. article.xml

```
<?xml version="1.0"?>
<webArticle category="news" subcategory="technical">
    <header title="NASA Builds Warp Drive"
            length="3k"
            author="Joe Reporter"
            distribution="all"/>
    <body>Seattle, WA - Today an anonymous individual
            announced that NASA has completed building a
            Warp Drive and has parked a ship that uses
            the drive in his back yard.  This individual
            claims that although he hasn't been contacted by
            NASA concerning the parked space vessel, he assumes
            that he will be launching it later this week to
            mount an exhibition to the Andromeda Galaxy.
    </body>
</webArticle>
```

Example 3-1 contains markup that is structured in a few different ways, and can be interesting to parse via SAX. A document such as *article.xml* requires that we

---

understand how the document is structured prior to writing a handler to parse it. Therefore, the handler is tightly coupled to the document's structure.

Writing a Simple Handler

You can write the ArticleHandler class to a new file, *handlers.py*; we'll keep adding new handlers to this file throughout the chapter. Keep it simple at first, just to see how SAX works:

```
# - ArticleHandler (add to handlers.py file)
class ArticleHandler(ContentHandler):
    """
    A handler to deal with articles in XML
    """
    def startElement(self, name, attrs):
      print "Start element:", name
```

Now we need to create a script to instantiate the parser, assign the handler, and do the actual work.

Creating the Main Program

No matter how complex your handler objects become, there is rarely much code involved in setting up the parser. Let's look at Example 3-2, in which we use only the ArticleHandler class just created, and parse what we find on the standard input stream. The file *art.py*, shown in Example 3-2, demonstrates how to do this.

Example 3-2. art.py

```
#!/usr/bin/env python
# art.py

import sys

from xml.sax  import make_parser
from handlers import ArticleHandler

ch = ArticleHandler()
saxparser = make_parser()

saxparser.setContentHandler(ch)
saxparser.parse(sys.stdin)
```

Once created, you can run the code from the command line using file redirection to populate standard input (both Unix and Windows):

```
$> python art.py < article.xml
```

The output using the simple article handler appears as:

```
Start element: webArticle
Start element: header
```

```
Start element: title
Start element: body
```

The output reflects the simple rule in your `ArticleHandler` class, which just prints out the name of each tag it encounters. To really use the XML, you have to add more functionality to the handler class in the *handlers.py* file.

Adding Intelligence

XML allows information to be parsed for different purposes. If you create a news article in XML, one application can grab it and display it as HTML, while another can index it to a search database. It's easy to imagine that a service might like to offer intelligent agents to scour Internet sources for news items, special offers, and other items of interest for you based on preferences that you set up. XML makes this process manageable, as opposed to the alternative of reliably parsing HTML for structured information, which is nearly impossible. HTML only communicates the appearance of a document and not its organizational structure. In HTML, two documents may look exactly alike in the browser, but use wildly different tags under the hood. Parsing the HTML for its information won't work, unless of course the page designer had that goal in mind when setting out to create the page.

Your news agent is configured to go after technology stories, especially ones that relate to space travel. When it discovers such an article, it displays a message, the headline, and the first few words of the body text. You can add functionality to your handler class to support this.

Since SAX is stream-based, it's sometimes necessary to set flags so that you can track when you've entered certain elements in and when you haven't. If you find that you're setting too many different flags, you might consider using a DOM approach as opposed to SAX. SAX is perfect when doing bulk operations on a lengthy XML stream. However, if you are trying to pull a complex data structure out of the document, you may be better off using the DOM.

To keep our example simple, set a few flags as the events are propagated, and go after the desired information. In the `startElement` method, check to see if you're indeed inside a news article and if your article is indeed technical. If it satisfies both of these requirements, change a Boolean data member so that other methods start paying attention to the data they receive. Also set a property on the handler itself so that the main application knows the handler has found a technical article, as that was its assignment:

```
def startElement(self, name, attrs):
  if name == "webArticle":
    subcat = attrs.get("subcategory", "")
    if subcat.find("tech") > -1:
      self.inArticle = 1
      self.isMatch = 1
```

```
elif self.inArticle:
    if name == "header":
        self.title = attrs.get("title", "")
    if name == "body":
        self.inBody = 1
```

The last conditional test is to see if the parser has entered the body element of a relevant article. If so, the characters method now knows to begin buffering data as the it is called:

```
def characters(self, characters):
    if self.inBody:
        if len(self.body) < 80:
            self.body += characters
        if len(self.body) > 80:
            self.body = self.body[:78] + "..."
            self.inBody = 0
```

Finally, look for the close of the body tag to indicate to the characters method that it no longer needs to pay attention to character data:

```
def endElement(self, name):
    if name == "body":
        self.inBody = 0
```

Beyond implementing these three methods, the class is also modified to initialize data members, and to provide an isMatch data member to indicate to the main application whether this handler has found something worth keeping. The complete class (replacing the earlier class of the same name) is shown in Example 3-3.

Example 3-3. Enhanced ArticleHandler

```
from XML.sax.handler import ContentHandler

class ArticleHandler(ContentHandler):
    """
    A handler to deal with articles in XML
    """
    inArticle = 0
    inBody    = 0
    isMatch   = 0
    title     = ""
    body      = ""

    def startElement(self, name, attrs):
        if name == "webArticle":
            subcat = attrs.get("subcategory", "")
            if subcat.find("tech") > -1:
                self.inArticle = 1
                self.isMatch = 1

        elif self.inArticle:
            if name == "header":
```

Example 3-3. Enhanced ArticleHandler (continued)

```
        self.title = attrs.get("title", "")
    if name == "body":
        self.inBody = 1

  def characters(self, characters):
    if self.inBody:
      if len(self.body) < 80:
        self.body += characters
      if len(self.body) > 80:
        self.body = self.body[:78] + "..."
        self.inBody = 0

  def endElement(self, name):
    if name == "body":
      self.inBody = 0
```

Using the Additional Information

Now that the handler has been modified to collect more information and determine if the article is interesting, we can add a little more code to *art.py* so that when an interesting article is found, it prints a report for the user and ignores everything else. To do this, we need only append this code to the end of *art.py*, which was originally shown in Example 3-2:

```
if ch.isMatch:
    print "News Item!"
    print "Title:", ch.title
    print "Body:", ch.body
```

With *article.xml* as input, you should see the following output:

```
$> python art.py < article.xml
News Item!
Title: NASA Builds Warp Drive
Body: Seattle, WA - Today an anonymous individual
                announced that NASA has completed building a...
```

Searching File Information

In this section, we create a file indexing script that can generate an XML document representing your entire filesystem or a specific portion of it. Indexing files with XML is a powerful way to keep track of information, or perform bulk operations on groups of particular files on a disk. You can create an XML-generating indexing routine easily in Python. The *index.py* program in Example 3-4 (which shows up a little later in the chapter) starts in any directory you specify and generates an element for each file or directory that exists beneath the starting point. Once we have the index of file information, we look at how to use SAX to search the information to filter the list of files for whatever criteria interests us at the time.

Creating the Index Generator

The main part of this routine works by just checking each file in a starting directory, and then recursing into any directories it finds beneath the starting directory. Recursion allows it to index an entire filesystem if you choose. On Unix, the program performs a lot of work, as it does content checking via a popen call to the file command for each file. (While this could be made more efficient by calling find less often and requiring it to operate on more than one file at a time, that isn't the topic of this book.) One of the key methods of this class is indexDirectoryFiles:

```python
def indexDirectoryFiles(self, dir):
    """Index a directory structure and creates an XML output file."""
    # prepare output XML file
    self.__fd = open(self.outputFile, "w")
    self.__fd.write('<?xml version="1.0" encoding="' +
                    XML_ENC + '"?>\n')
    self.__fd.write("<IndexedFiles>\n")

    # do actual indexing
    self.__indexDir(dir)

    # close out XML file
    self.__fd.write("</IndexedFiles>\n")
    self.__fd.close()
```

An XML file is created with the name given in outputFile and an XML declaration and root element are added. The indexDirectoryFiles method calls its internal __indexDir method—this is the real worker method. It is a recursive method that descends the file hierarchy, indexing files along the way.

```python
def __indexDir(self, dir):
    """Recursive function to do the actual indexing."""
    # Create an indexFile for each regular file,
    # and call the function again for each directory
    files = listdir(dir)
    for file in files:
        fullname = os.path.join(dir, file)
        st_values = stat(fullname)

        # check if its a directory
        if S_ISDIR(st_values[0]):
            print file

            # create directory element
            self.__fd.write("<Directory ")
            self.__fd.write(' name="' + escape(fullname) + '">\n')
            self.__indexDir(fullname)
            self.__fd.write("</Directory>\n")

        else:
            # create regular file entry
```

```
        print dir + file
        lf = IndexFile(fullname, st_values)
        self.__fd.write(lf.getXML())
```

The actual work is just determining those files that are directories and those that are regular files. XML is created accordingly during this process, and written to the output file. When all of the __indexDir calls eventually return, the XML file is closed.

Now the program is essentially finished. A helper function named escape is imported from the xml.sax.saxutils module to perform entity substitution against some common characters within XML character data to ensure they do not appear to be markup in the resulting XML.

Creating the IndexFile class

The IndexFile class is used for an XML representation of file information. This information is derived primarily from the os.stat system call. The class copies information from the stat call into its member variables in its __init__ method, as shown here:

```
def __init__(self, filename, st_vals):
    """Extract properties from supplied stat object."""
    self.filename = filename
    self.uid = st_vals[4]
    self.gid = st_vals[5]
    self.size = st_vals[6]
    self.accessed = ctime(st_vals[7])
    self.modified = ctime(st_vals[8])
    self.created = ctime(st_vals[9])

    # try for filename extension
    self.extension = os.path.splitext(filename)[1]
```

In this method, important file information is extracted from the tuple st_vals. This contains the filesystem information returned by the stat call. The __init__ method also tries for a filename extension if possible by checking for the "." character. If you are running Unix, the script tries to use the os.popen function to call the file command, which returns a human-readable description of the content of both text and binary files. It can take much longer to generate, but once in, the XML is valuable and does not need to be regenerated every time we want it:

```
    # check contents using file command on linux
    if os.name == "posix":
        # Open a process to check file contents
        fd = popen("file \"" + filename + "\"")
        self.contents = fd.readline().rstrip()
        fd.close()
    else:
        # No content information
        self.contents = self.extension
```

If you're not using Unix, the file command is unavailable, and so the contents information is given the file extension. For example, in a Word file, the XML is `<contents>.doc</contents>`. On Unix, however, the call to popen returns a file object. The output text of the command is read in using the readline method of the file object. The results are then stripped and used as a description of the files contents. The class features a single method, getXML, which returns the file information as a single XML element in string format:

```python
def getXML(self):
    """Returns XML version of all data members."""
    return ("<file name=\"" + escape(self.filename) + "\">" +
            "\n\t<userID>" + str(self.uid) + "</userID>" +
            "\n\t<groupID>" + str(self.gid) + "</groupID>" +
            "\n\t<size>" + str(self.size) + "</size>" +
            "\n\t<lastAccessed>" + self.accessed +
            "</lastAccessed>" +
            "\n\t<lastModified>" + self.modified +
            "</lastModified>" +
            "\n\t<created>" + self.created + "</created>" +
            "\n\t<extension>" + self.extension +
            "</extension>" +
            "\n\t<contents>" + escape(self.contents) +
            "</contents>" +
            "\n</file>")
```

In the preceding code, the XML is thrown together as a series of strings. Another way is to use a DOMImplementation object to create individual elements and insert them into the document's structure (illustrated in Chapter 10).

Both of these classes are used to develop a lengthy XML document representing files and metadata for any given section of your filesystem. The complete listing of *index.py* is shown in Example 3-4

Example 3-4. index.py

```python
#!/usr/bin/env python
"""

index.py
usage: python index.py <starting-dir> <output-file>
"""

import os
import sys

from os    import stat
from os    import listdir
from os    import popen
from stat import S_ISDIR
from time import ctime

from xml.sax.saxutils import escape

XML_ENC = "ISO-8859-1"
```

Example 3-4. index.py (continued)

```
"""""""""""""""""""""""""""""""""""""""""""""""""""""""""""""
  Class: Index(startingDir, outputFile)
"""""""""""""""""""""""""""""""""""""""""""""""""""""""""""""
class Index:
    """
    This class indexes files and builds
    a resultant XML document.
    """
def __init__(self, startingDir, outputFile):
    """ init: sets output file """
    self.outputFile = outputFile
    self.startingDir = startingDir

    def indexDirectoryFiles(self, dir):
        """Index a directory structure and creates an XML output file."""
        # prepare output XML file
        self.__fd = open(self.outputFile, "w")
        self.__fd.write('<?xml version="1.0" encoding="' +
                        XML_ENC + '"?>\n')
        self.__fd.write("<IndexedFiles>\n")

        # do actual indexing
        self.__indexDir(dir)

        # close out XML file
        self.__fd.write("</IndexedFiles>\n")
        self.__fd.close()

    def __indexDir(self, dir):
        """Recursive function to do the actual indexing."""
        # Create an indexFile for each regular file,
        # and call the function again for each directory
        files = listdir(dir)
        for file in files:
            fullname = os.path.join(dir, file)
            st_values = stat(fullname)

            # check if its a directory
            if S_ISDIR(st_values[0]):
                print file

                # create directory element
                self.__fd.write("<Directory ")
                self.__fd.write(' name="' + escape(fullname) + '">\n')
                self.__indexDir(fullname)
                self.__fd.write("</Directory>\n")

            else:
                # create regular file entry
                print dir + file
                lf = IndexFile(fullname, st_values)
                self.__fd.write(lf.getXML())
```

Example 3-4. index.py (continued)

```
"""""""""""""""""""""""""""""""""""""""""""""""""""""""""""""""
 Class: IndexFile(filename, stat-tuple)
"""""""""""""""""""""""""""""""""""""""""""""""""""""""""""""""
class IndexFile:
    """

    Simple file representation object with XML
    """

    def __init__(self, filename, st_vals):
        """Extract properties from supplied stat object."""
        self.filename = filename
        self.uid = st_vals[4]
        self.gid = st_vals[5]
        self.size = st_vals[6]
        self.accessed = ctime(st_vals[7])
        self.modified = ctime(st_vals[8])
        self.created = ctime(st_vals[9])

        # try for filename extension
        self.extension = os.path.splitext(filename)[1]

        # check contents using file command on linux
        if os.name == "posix":
            # Open a process to check file
            # contents
            fd = popen("file \"" + filename + "\"")
            self.contents = fd.readline().rstrip( )
            fd.close( )
        else:
            # No content information
            self.contents = self.extension

    def getXML(self):
        """Returns XML version of all data members."""
        return ("<file name=\"" + escape(self.filename) + "\">" +
                "\n<userID>" + str(self.uid) + "</userID>" +
                "\n<groupID>" + str(self.gid) + "</groupID>" +
                "\n<size>" + str(self.size) + "</size>" +
                "\n<lastAccessed>" + self.accessed +
                "</lastAccessed>" +
                "\n<lastModified>" + self.modified +
                "</lastModified>" +
                "\n\t<created>" + self.created + "</created>" +
                "\n\t<extension>" + self.extension +
                "</extension>" +
                "\n\t<contents>" + escape(self.contents) +
                "</contents>" +
                "\n</file>")

"""""""""""""""""""""""""""""""""""""""""""""""""""""""""""""""
Main
"""""""""""""""""""""""""""""""""""""""""""""""""""""""""""""""
if __name__ == "__main__":
    index = Index(sys.argv[1], sys.argv[2])
```

Example 3-4. index.py (continued)

```
print "Starting Dir:", index.startingDir
print "Output file:", index.outputFile

index.indexDirectoryFiles(index.startingDir)
```

Running index.py

Running *index.py* from the command line requires supplying both a starting directory and an XML filename to use as output:

```
$> python index.py /usr/bin/ usrbin.xml
```

The script prints directory names similar to the *find* command, but after completion, the file *usrbin.xml* contains something similar to the following:

```
<?xml version="1.0" encoding=" ISO-8859-1"?>
<IndexedFiles>
<Directory  name="/usr/bin/X11">
<file name="/usr/bin/X11/Magick-config">
        <userID>0</userID>
        <groupID>0</groupID>
        <size>1786</size>
        <lastAccessed>Fri Jan 19 22:29:34 2001</lastAccessed>
        <lastModified>Mon Aug 30 20:49:06 1999</lastModified>
        <created>Mon Sep 11 17:22:01 2000</created>
        <extension>None</extension>
        <contents>/usr/bin/X11/Magick-config: Bourne shell script text</contents>
</file><file name="/usr/bin/X11/animate">
        <userID>0</userID>
        <groupID>0</groupID>
        <size>16720</size>
        <lastAccessed>Fri Jan 19 22:29:34 2001</lastAccessed>
        <lastModified>Mon Aug 30 20:49:09 1999</lastModified>
        <created>Mon Sep 11 17:22:01 2000</created>
        <extension>None</extension>
        <contents>/usr/bin/X11/animate: ELF 32-bit LSB executable,
         Intel 80386,version 1, dynamically linked (uses
         shared libs), stripped</contents>
</file>
```

The XML file's size depends on the particular directory it originated in. By default, the program follows symbolic links (on Unix, symbolic links allow one directory or filename to refer to another), introducing the possibility of forming infinite recursion, so beware! Indexing your home directory or indexing a directory of open source software that you've downloaded is probably the most effective thing to do in this case.

Searching the Index

Now that your file data has been abstracted to XML, you can write a SAX event handler to search for items within the file list. SAX is a good choice here, because this document could easily be several megabytes in size, and interpreting it as it is being read is the least resource-intensive approach.

The *saxfinder.py* script takes a single argument (the search text) and parses the supplied XML file checking via its SAX handler interfaces, in order to see if any of the files are of interest to you.

The script expects to work on XML as created earlier with *index.py*.

If the contents element of your XML file contains the character data that you supplied on the command line, the file is considered a match and the script prints a message accordingly. If you are running Windows, your contents tags only have the file extension, so your searches are limited to file extensions, unless you alter the code to watch something besides just the contents element.

Use three methods of the SAX interface to implement your metadata finder. First, startElement is implemented to both capture the name of the current file element as well as mark when you've entered the character data portion following a contents tag:

```
def startElement(self, name, attrs):
  if name == "file":
    self.filename = attrs.get('name', "")

  elif name == "contents":
    self.getCont = 1
```

If you're entering a content element, a flag (self.getCont) is set so that the characters method knows when to gobble up character data and store it in another member variable:

```
def characters(self, ch):
  if self.getCont:
    self.contents += ch
```

When an endElement event rolls around, the script examines the contents that have been captured (if any) to see if they match the original command-line parameter. If so, the ·filename is printed; if not, SAX happily moves on to the next file element within the XML document:

```
def endElement(self, name):
  if name == "contents":
    self.getCont = 0
    if self.contents.find(self.contentType) > -1:
      print self.filename, "has", self.contentType, "content."
    self.contents = ""
```

In addition, the self.getCont flag is disabled after leaving a contents element, to instruct the characters method not to capture data.

SAX helps you here by allowing you to process an XML index file that represents an entire filesystem and easily takes up 20 megabytes on your disk. Parsing such a gigantic document with the DOM can be difficult and unbearably slow.

Example 3-5 shows the complete listing of *saxfinder.py*.

Example 3-5. saxfinder.py

```
"""
saxfinder.py - generates HTML from pyxml.xml
"""
import sys

from xml.sax import make_parser
from xml.sax import ContentHandler

class FileHandler(ContentHandler):
  def __init__(self, contentType):
    self.getCont  = 0
    self.contents = ""
    self.filename = ""
    self.contentType = contentType

  def startElement(self, name, attrs):
    if name == "file":
      self.filename = attrs.get('name', "")

    elif name == "contents":
      self.getCont = 1

  def characters(self, ch):
    if self.getCont:
      self.contents += ch

  def endElement(self, name):
    if name == "contents":
      self.getCont = 0
      if self.contents.find(self.contentType) > -1:
        print self.filename, "has", self.contentType, "content."
      self.contents = ""

# Main

fh = FileHandler(sys.argv[1])
parser = make_parser( )
parser.setContentHandler(fh)
parser.parse(sys.stdin)
```

You can run *saxfinder.py* from the command line on both Unix and Windows. You need to supply a search string as the first parameter, and be sure and redirect or pipe an XML document (created with *index.py*) into standard input:

```
$> python saxfinder.py "C program" < nard.xml
```

The result should be something like this:

```
/home/shm00/nard/xd/server.cpp has C program content.
/home/shm00/nard/xd/shmoo.cpp has C program content.
/home/shm00/nard/gl-misc/array.cpp has C program content.
```

```
/home/shm00/nard/gl-misc/vertex.cpp has C program content.
/home/shm00/nard/gl-misc/mecogl.cpp has C program content.
/home/shm00/nard/gl-misc/drewgl/smugl.cpp has C program content.
/home/shm00/nard/gl-misc/drewgl/pal.cpp has C program content.
/home/shm00/nard/gl-misc/drewgl/pal.h has C program content.
/home/shm00/nard/gl-misc/drewgl/gl.cpp has C program content.
```

Building an Image Index

If you've ever visited an image library on the Internet, you've probably enjoyed (even taken for granted) the way a collection of small thumbnail images acts as links for full-sized counterparts. Many artists, when presenting a portfolio online, adopt this effective approach to displaying their work. With the rise of digital cameras and scanners, more and more people are finding themselves pulling directories full of images onto the Web in a format that makes for easy browsing. In the next section, we build a Python script that takes a full directory of images and thumbnail images and creates a master HTML page with the thumbnails acting as links to the full-size image. The *saxthumbs.py* program expects you to have a pre-existing directory of images and thumbnails, and operates on the output of the *index.py* script we created earlier.

In order for the *saxthumbs.py* SAX handler to correctly process a thumbnail directory, the images need to follow a naming convention (easily changeable by editing the code). Currently, the *saxthumbs.py* handler expects to find `file` elements within the XML document that have a corresponding *<imagename>.jpg* file that is the entire image, and a *t-<imagename>.jpg* file that is a thumbnail-size image.

When using *index.py* to create a list of your image files, point it to a directory that has image files named accordingly:

```
$> ls -l *newimage*
-rw-rw-r--   1 shm00    shm00        98197 Jan 18 11:08 newimage.jpg
-rw-rw-r--   1 shm00    shm00         5272 Jan 18 11:42 t-newimage.jpg
```

In this manner, every file that ends in *.jpg* and has a corresponding *t-<imagename>.jpg* file (note the size differences) is assimilated into the thumbnail index.

Creating Thumbnail Images

There is an easy way to set up your image files on Unix systems, using the convert command. This command is part of the ImageMagick package, and is installed by default by most modern Linux distributions. For other Unix systems, the package is available at *http://www.imagemagick.org/*.

```
$> convert image.jpg -geometry 192x128 t-image.jpg
```

This will take *image.jpg*, no matter how large it is, and make a 192x128 size thumbnail in JPEG format. Of course, if the image is a Windows bitmap image (with the *.bmp* extension), you can do a two-step operation to get JPEG files:

```
$> convert image.bmp image.jpg
$> convert image.jpg -geometry 192x128 t-image.jpg
```

Now that you understand how convert works, you can use a simple shell loop to produce small thumbnail images for every *.jpg* in your image directory:

```
$> for each in *jpg
> do
> convert $each -geometry 192x128 t-$each
> echo $each
> done
```

You should end up with the following:

```
-rwxrwxr-x  1 shm00    shm00         97003 Jan 16 22:40 mvc-001s.jpg
-rwxrwxr-x  1 shm00    shm00         93373 Jan 16 22:40 mvc-002s.jpg
-rwxrwxr-x  1 shm00    shm00         86619 Jan 16 22:40 mvc-003s.jpg
-rwxrwxr-x  1 shm00    shm00         94894 Jan 16 22:40 mvc-004s.jpg
-rwxrwxr-x  1 shm00    shm00         76210 Jan 16 22:40 mvc-005s.jpg
-rwxrwxr-x  1 shm00    shm00         73704 Jan 16 22:40 mvc-006s.jpg
-rwxrwxr-x  1 shm00    shm00         80292 Jan 16 22:40 mvc-007s.jpg
-rw-rw-r--  1 shm00    shm00          4434 Jan 21 11:46 t-mvc-001s.jpg
-rw-rw-r--  1 shm00    shm00          4181 Jan 21 11:46 t-mvc-002s.jpg
-rw-rw-r--  1 shm00    shm00          3604 Jan 21 11:46 t-mvc-003s.jpg
-rw-rw-r--  1 shm00    shm00          4634 Jan 21 11:46 t-mvc-004s.jpg
-rw-rw-r--  1 shm00    shm00          3339 Jan 21 11:46 t-mvc-005s.jpg
-rw-rw-r--  1 shm00    shm00          2777 Jan 21 11:46 t-mvc-006s.jpg
-rw-rw-r--  1 shm00    shm00          2996 Jan 21 11:46 t-mvc-007s.jpg
```

This listing represents the convert program applied against *mvc-00*.jpg* files taken with a digital camera. The *saxthumbs.py* script produces markup to display both the thumbnails and each individual image.

If you run *index.py* against this directory, you create an XML file that we are able to use a little later in the chapter when we go over the *saxthumbs.py* process:

```
$> ./index.py /home/shm00/images/ img.xml
```

The new file, *img.xml*, contains file elements that detail your image files in a format appropriate for the script to manipulate.

Creating thumbnails on Windows

If you don't have access to Unix (or a scriptable image processor for your operating system), you can create your own image directory on Windows. Just be sure to resize originals and prefix the thumbnails with *t-*, and make sure that all of the images to be displayed on the Web are in JPEG format (ending with *.jpg*). For example, if you open the *My Pictures* directory in Photoshop, you can take each image, resize it to 192x128, and save it as a *t-* version of its original self.

To come back around to our example, once you prepare the directory, you can point *index.py* at it and generate an XML index file for the images.

Implementing the SAXThumbs Handler

The SAXThumbs handler creates an anchor for each thumbnail in the HTML output file, and creates a standalone HTML document to display the full size image. Then, SAXThumbs leaves you with an HTML page showing all of your thumbnails, as well as an HTML page for each full size image.

The SAXThumbs handler is implemented as a class inheriting from ContentHandler. The name of the output file, which should contain a preview of all of the thumbnails, is supplied as a command-line parameter and passed to the constructor:

```python
def __init__(self, thumbsFilename):
    self.filename = thumbsFilename

def startDocument(self):
    self.fd = open(self.filename, "w")
    self.fd.write("<html><body>\n")

def endDocument(self):
    self.fd.write("</body></html>\n")
    self.fd.close()
```

When the end of the XML document is reached, it's assumed that there are no more image files to process, and the thumbnails document is closed.

The rest of the work is done in the startElement method. First, the image name is copied without its path information:

```python
def startElement(self, name, attrs):
    if name == "file":
        filename = attrs.get("name", "")

        # pull out just the filename
        dir, localname = os.path.split(filename)
        localname, ext = os.path.splitext(localname)
```

Then, the file is examined to determine whether it's a thumbnail or a full image. Thumbnails have HTML anchors around them, which are then added to the thumbnails output file:

```python
if localname.startswith("t-") and ext == ".jpg":
    # create anchor tag in thumbs.html
    fullImgLink = localname[2:] + ".html"
    self.fd.write('<br><a href="%s"><img src="%s%s"></a>\n'
                  % (fullImgLink, localname, ext))
```

If the image is not a thumbnail, but a full image, then a separate HTML file is created that displays the image:

```python
fullImageFile = os.path.join(dir, localname) + ".html"
print "Will create:", fullImageFile

fullImageHTML = ('<html><body><img src="%s%s"></body></html>\n'
```

```
                                      % (localname, ext))

          lfd = open(fullImageFile, "w")
          lfd.write(fullImageHTML)
          lfd.close( )
```

The full-image HTML file is created in the same directory that holds the image. The thumbnails file is created in the same directory from which you're running *thumbmaker.py*. Example 3-6 shows *saxthumbs.py*.

Example 3-6. saxthumbs.py

```python
from xml.sax import ContentHandler

class SAXThumbs(ContentHandler):
    """
    This is the SAX handler that generates a full-
    image display (an .html page) for each image file
    contained in the XML file.

    It also adds an anchor on the thumbs page showing
    the thumbnail, and linking to the big image page
    that was created first.
    """
    def __init__(self, thumbsFilename):
        self.filename = thumbsFilename

    def startDocument(self):
        self.fd = open(self.filename, "w")
        self.fd.write("<html><body>\n")

    def endDocument(self):
        self.fd.write("</body></html>\n")
        self.fd.close( )

    def startElement(self, name, attrs):
        if name == "file":
            filename = attrs.get("name", "")
            # slice out just the filename
            dir, localname = os.path.split(filename)
            localname, ext = os.path.splitext(localname)

            if localname.startswith("t-") and ext == ".jpg":
                # create anchor tag in thumbs.html
                fullImgLink = localname[2:] + ".html"
                self.fd.write('<br><a href="%s"><img src="%s%s"></a>\n'
                              % (fullImgLink, localname, ext))

                fullImageFile = os.path.join(dir, localname) + ".html"
                print "Will create:", fullImageFile

                fullImageHTML = ('<html><body><img src="%s%s"></body><html>\n'
                                 % (localname, ext))
```

Example 3-6. saxthumbs.py (continued)

```
        lfd = open(fullImageFile, "w")
        lfd.write(fullImageHTML)
        lfd.close( )
```

The *thumbmaker.py* file is a script that loads the XML from standard input, and registers the SAXThumbs class as the chosen handler to use with the SAX parser. Example 3-7 shows *thumbmaker.py* in its entirety.

Example 3-7. thumbmaker.py

```
#!/usr/bin/env python
# thumbmaker.py

import sys

from xml.sax    import make_parser
from saxthumbs import SAXThumbs

# Main

ch = SAXThumbs(sys.argv[1])
parser = make_parser( )

parser.setContentHandler(ch)
parser.parse(sys.stdin)
```

It is interesting to note the similarity to the first script that we wrote in Example 3-2.

To run *thumbmaker.py*, you first need to make sure you have created the right type of directory containing image files and that you've run *index.py* across the directory to generate an XML file containing the list of files. Once you have these items, you can pick a name for the index file (such as *mythumbs.html*) and pass it to the script:

```
$> python thumbmaker.py mythumbs.html < img.xml
```

In this case, *mythumbs.html* is the output file, and the XML source is received from the file *img.xml*.

Viewing Your Thumbnails

After executing *thumbmaker.py*, you are left with a thumbnails file that is sitting in your current working directory. You should move this file to the directory that is holding your images:

```
$> mv mythumbs.html /home/shm00/tw/zero/images/
```

Converting XML to HTML

The PyXML package contains XML parsers, including PyExpat, as well as support for SAX and DOM, and much more. While learning the ropes of the PyXML package, it would be nice to have a comprehensive list of all the classes and methods. Since this is a programming book, it seems appropriate to write a Python program to extract the information we need—and in XML, no less!

Let's generate an XML file that details each of the files in the PyXML package, the classes therein, and the methods of the class. This process allows us to generate quick, usable XML. Rather than a replacement for all the snazzy code-to-documentation generators out there, Example 3-8 shows a simple, quick way to generate XML that we can experiment with and use throughout the examples in this chapter. After all, when manipulating XML, it helps to have a few hundred thousand bytes of it sitting around to play with. (This program also demonstrates the simplicity of examining all the files in a directory tree in using the os.path.walk function.)

Example 3-8. genxml.py

```
"""
genxml.py

Descends PyXML tree, indexing source files and creating
XML tags for use in navigating the source.
"""

import os
import sys

from xml.sax.saxutils import escape


def process(filename, fp):
  print "* Processing:", filename,

  # parse the file
  pyFile = open(filename)
  fp.write("<file name=\"" + filename + "\">\n")
  inClass = 0
  line = pyFile.readline()
  while line:
    line = line.strip()
    if line.startswith("class") and line[-1] == ":":
      if inClass:
        fp.write(" </class>\n")
      inClass = 1
      fp.write(" <class name='" + line[:-1]  + "'>\n")

    elif line.find("def") > 0 and line[:-1] == ":" and inClass:
      fp.write("  <method name='" + escape(line[:-1]) + "'/>\n")

    line = pyFile.readline()

  pyFile.close()
  if inClass:
    fp.write(" </class>\n")
```

Example 3-8. genxml.py (continued)

```
    inClass = 0

  fp.write("</file>\n")

def finder(fp, dirname, names):
  """Add files in the directory dirname to a list."""
  for name in names:
    if name.endswith(".py"):
      path = os.path.join(dirname, name)
      if os.path.isfile(path):
        process(path, fp)

def main( ):
  print "[genxml.py started]"

  xmlFd = open("pyxml.xml", "w")
  xmlFd.write("<?xml version=\"1.0\"?>\n")
  xmlFd.write("<pyxml>\n")

  os.path.walk(sys.argv[1], finder, xmlFd)

  xmlFd.write("</pyxml>")
  xmlFd.close( )

  print "[genxml.py finished]"

if __name__ == "__main__":
  main( )
```

The main function in Example 3-8 uses the os.path.walk function to search your PyXML directory for Python files. For each Python source file that exists beneath the starting directory (the argument to the script), the process function is called to extract class information. That function writes the extracted information into the open XML file.

At this point, the script proceeds to parse each Python source file, highlighting each of the classes and methods contained within them by parsing each line for relevant keywords such as class and def:

```
    def process(filename, fp):
      print "* Processing:", filename,

      # parse the file
      pyFile = open(filename)
      fp.write("<file name='" + filename + "'>\n")
      inClass = 0
      line = pyFile.readline()
      while line:
        line = line.strip()
```

When the program finds a class declaration, it creates the appropriate class tag and attributes within the XML document:

```
if line.startswith("class") and line[-1] == ":":
        if inClass:
          fp.write(" </class>\n")
        inClass = 1
        fp.write(" <class name='" + line[:-1]  + "'>\n")
```

When the program encounters a method definition, it replaces special characters with entities so they don't cause problems in the XML. The method definition string is trimmed, and then surrounded with the appropriate markup:

```
elif line.find("def") > 0 and line[:-1] == ":" and inClass:
        fp.write("  <method name='" + escape(line[:-1]) + "'/>\n")

    line = pyFile.readline()
```

After a file is complete, the program closes out the last class it was in, if any, and closes out the file tag as well:

```
pyFile.close()
    if inClass:
      fp.write(" </class>\n")
      inClass = 0

    fp.write("</file>\n")
```

Python simplifies the work of parsing the text. Each line is manipulated quite a bit, quotation marks are escaped with entities (using the escape function from the xml. sax.saxutils module), and XML tags are placed around class definitions and method names.

To run this program from the shell:

```
$> python genxml.py /home/chris/PyXML/xml
```

The parameter to the script is the path to your PyXML source directory (including the *xml* subdirectory).

The Generated Document

The XML that is generated is placed in a file called *pyxml.xml*. Each file element looks something like this:

```
<file name="../xml/dom/ext/reader/Sax2Lib.py">
 <class name="class LexicalHandler">
  <method name="def xmlDecl(self, version, encoding, standalone)"/>
  <method name="def startDTD(self, doctype, publicID, systemID)"/>
  <method name="def endDTD(self)"/>
  <method name="def startEntity(self, name)"/>
  <method name="def endEntity(self, name)"/>
```

```
  <method name="def comment(self, text)"/>
  <method name="def startCDATA(self)"/>
  <method name="def endCDATA(self)"/>
 </class>
 <class name="class EntityRefList">
  <method name="def getLength(self)"/>
  <method name="def getEntityName(self, index)"/>
  <method name="def getEntityRefStart(self, index)"/>
  <method name="def getEntityRefEnd(self, index)"/>
  <method name="def __len__(self)"/>
 </class>
 <class name="class NamespaceHandler">
  <method name="def startNamespaceDeclScope(prefix, uri)"/>
  <method name="def endNamespaceDeclScope(prefix)"/>
 </class>
 <class name="class SAXNotSupportedException(Exception)">
 </class>
</file>
```

Note that the name attribute of the file tag varies depending upon what your parameter is to the script (your PyXML source path). Functions not defined as methods in a class are not included by the simple parsing loop (hey, this isn't a compiler!), but you should be aware that the XML support provided by both the standard library and the PyXML package includes many useful functions—read the reference documentation for more information on those. The escape function we use in this script is a perfect example of this. If you're new to Python, you'll find that little helper functions are characteristic of Python libraries; most of the small utilities needed to make the larger facilities easier to use have already been included, allowing you to concentrate on your application.

If you spend some time reviewing this XML file, you will start to become familiar with the scope of the PyXML toolkit. A script is provided a little later in this chapter that converts this XML to HTML using the SAX API and Python string manipulation features. Figure 3-2 shows the XML within a browser.

The Conversion Handler

You can finish off this program by implementing the PyXMLConversionHandler class. This class generates HTML from the XML file we created earlier. The process allows you to load the HTML file into your browser and see all of the files, classes, and methods within PyXML in formatted text. Create this class, as shown in Example 3-9, in the file *handlers.py*.

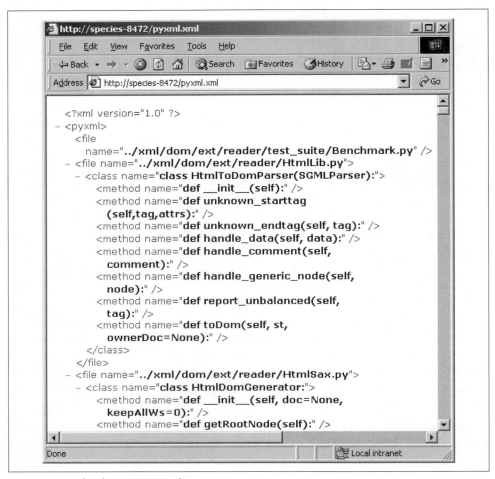

Figure 3-2. genhtml.py output in a browser

Example 3-9. handlers.py

```python
from xml.sax import ContentHandler

class PyXMLConversionHandler(ContentHandler):
    """A simple handler implementing 3 methods of
    the SAX interface."""

    def __init__(self, fp):
        """Save the file object that we generate HTML into."""
        self.fp = fp

    def startDocument(self):
        """Write out the start of the HTML document."""
        self.fp.write("<html><body><b>\n")
```

Example 3-9. handlers.py (continued)

```python
    def startElement(self, name, attrs):
        if name == "file":
            # generate start of HTML
            s = attrs.get('name', "")
            self.fp.write("<p>File: %s<br>\n" % s)
            print "* Processing:", s

        elif name == "class":
            self.fp.write(" " * 3 + "Class: "
                        + attrs.get('name', "") + "<br>\n")

        elif name == "method":
            self.fp.write(" " * 6 + "Method: "
                        + attrs.get('name', "") + "<br>\n")

    def endDocument(self):
        """End the HTML document we're generating."""
        self.fp.write("</b></body></html>")
```

While the conversion itself is very straightforward, one interesting thing to note is that this class writes its output to a file object passed to the constructor instead of building a string of XML text in memory. This avoids storing a potentially large buffer in memory and building it incrementally with many memory copies. If the string is required to be in memory when the process is complete, the creator can provide a `StringIO` instance as the file to write to; the `StringIO` implementation is more efficient at building a large string than many string concatenations. This is a Python idiom that has proven its utility over a wide range of projects.

Driving the Conversion Handler

The main script really isn't any different from the others we've looked at so far. We create the parser and instantiate our handler class, register the handler, and set the parser in motion. This process is shown in Example 3-10.

Example 3-10. genhtml.py

```python
#!/usr/bin/env python
#
# generates HTML from pyxml.xml

import sys

from xml.sax  import make_parser
from handlers import PyXMLConversionHandler

dh = PyXMLConversionHandler(sys.stdout)
parser = make_parser( )
```

Example 3-10. genhtml.py (continued)

```
parser.setContentHandler(dh)
parser.parse(sys.stdin)
```

The output from this script is written to the standard output stream.

Advanced Parser Factory Usage

PyXML features several parsers, and multiple ways to instantiate them, depending on whether you're using SAX, trying to create a DOM tree, or doing something completely different. Designed for portable code, a ParserFactory class is provided that supplies a SAX-ready parser guaranteed available in your runtime environment. Additionally, you can explicitly create a parser (or SAX driver) by dipping into any specific package, such as PyExpat. We illustrate an example of both, but normally you should rely on the parser factory to instantiate a parser.

The make_parser function (imported from xml.sax) returns a SAX driver for the first available parser in the list that you supply, or returns an available parser if no list is specified or if the list contains parsers that are not found or cannot be loaded. The make_parser function has its roots as part of the xml.sax.saxexts.ParserFactory class, but it is better to import the method from xml.sax (more on this in a bit). For example:

```
from xml.sax import make_parser
parser = make_parser( )
```

At the time of this writing, if you have PyXML installed, a call to make_parser without an argument is sure to return either a PyExpat or xmlproc driver. If you dig into the source of the xml.sax module, you will see this list supplied to the ParserFactory class. If you instantiate a parser factory directly out of xml.sax.saxexts, you need to be sure to supply a list containing the name of at least one valid parser, or it won't be able to create a parser:

```
>>> from xml.sax.saxexts import ParserFactory
>>> p = ParserFactory( )
>>> parser = p.make_parser( )
Traceback (most recent call last):
  File "<stdin>", line 1, in ?
  File "/usr/local/lib/python2.0/site-packages/_xmlplus/sax/saxexts.py",
      line 77, in make_parser
    raise SAXReaderNotAvailable("No parsers found", None)
xml.sax._exceptions.SAXReaderNotAvailable: No parsers found
```

If you supply a list of parsers or drivers, you get what you're after:

```
>>> from xml.sax.saxexts import ParserFactory
>>> p = ParserFactory(["xml.sax.drivers.drv_pyexpat"])
>>> parser = p.make_parser( )
```

In most cases, it's a good idea to use the make_parser function from xml.sax, but it's also valuable to know what is going on under the hood. Several factory classes are available, with variations for HTML, SGML, non-validating XML, and validating XML parsers.

Native Parser Interfaces

Now that we've looked at how SAX can be used and have seen just how regular the code is to set up the parser and the `ContentHandler`, you may be wondering how much of that ease comes from using SAX and how much is a matter of convenience functions in the Python libraries. While we won't delve deeply into the native interfaces of the individual parsers, this is a good question, and can lead to some interesting observations.

The key advantage to using SAX is that the callback methods have the same names and significance regardless of the actual parser you use. There are at least two nice results of this: changing parsers does not affect your application, and your code is more maintainable because someone new to the code is more likely to know the SAX interface than any particular parser-specific interface.

So just how do the native interfaces to the individual parsers differ from SAX, and why would we choose to use them instead? Let's take a quick look at the PyExpat parser to get a taste of the differences.

Using PyExpat Directly

Of course, to use PyExpat, you need to have it installed. It is included as part of the Python installer for Windows, and is built automatically on Unix if you have the Expat library installed. If you did not install PyExpat as part of Python, it is installed as part of the PyXML package.

PyExpat resides in the `xml.parsers.expat` module. If we want to modify our last example to use PyExpat directly, we don't have a lot of work to do, but there are a few changes. Since the PyExpat handler methods closely match the SAX handlers, at least for the basic use we demonstrate here, we can use the same handler class we've already written. The imports won't need to change much:

```
#!/usr/bin/env python

import sys

from xml.parsers import expat
from handlers     import PyXMLConversionHandler
```

Once the parser is imported, it can be created and used:

```
parser = expat.ParserCreate()
```

Were we to do this at the interactive prompt, we could poke at the parser object to see what attributes it has:

```
>>> from xml.parsers import expat
>>> parser = expat.ParserCreate()
```

```
>>> dir(parser)
['CharacterDataHandler', 'CommentHandler', 'DefaultHandler', 'DefaultHandlerExpa
nd', 'EndCdataSectionHandler', 'EndElementHandler', 'EndNamespaceDeclHandler', '
ErrorByteIndex', 'ErrorCode', 'ErrorColumnNumber', 'ErrorLineNumber', 'ExternalE
ntityParserCreate', 'ExternalEntityRefHandler', 'GetBase', 'NotStandaloneHandler
', 'NotationDeclHandler', 'Parse', 'ParseFile', 'ProcessingInstructionHandler',
'SetBase', 'StartCdataSectionHandler', 'StartElementHandler', 'StartNamespaceDec
lHandler', 'UnparsedEntityDeclHandler', 'ordered_attributes', 'returns_unicode',
'specified_attributes']
```

That certainly doesn't look like a SAX parser!

There is no setContentHandler method, nor is there anything that takes its place. To register our content handler, we need to set various attributes to the methods of a content handler instance:

```
dh = PyXMLConversionHandler(sys.stdout)

parser.StartElementHandler = dh.startElement
parser.EndElementHandler = dh.endElement
parser.CharacterDataHandler = dh.characters
```

This isn't hard, but it is certainly more tedious than the SAX setContentHandler method, and the code actually needs to be changed, as we need to use more methods on the handler object.

Once we've initialized the handler methods we're interested in using, we can start the parse. Again, this is a little different from the SAX version:

```
parser.Parse(sys.stdin.read(), 1)
```

We know what sys.stdin.read() does, but the 1 used for the second parameter looks suspiciously like a magic number in our source code. It is actually a Boolean value indicating that the string being passed to the Parse method is the final chunk of the input; Parse can be called multiple times with smaller portions of the input and the flag set to 0, and then called with an indicator of 1 for the final chunk of data. This can be useful when reading data asynchronously from a network connection.

When parsing XML from a file object, the following method is also available:

```
parser.ParseFile(sys.stdin)
```

The complete script that uses the handler with PyExpat is shown in Example 3-11.

Example 3-11. genhtml2.py with PyExpat

```
"""
genhtml2.py - generates HTML from pyxml.xml
"""

import sys

from xml.parsers import expat
from handlers    import PyXMLConversionHandler
```

Example 3-11. genhtml2.py with PyExpat (continued)

```
dh = PyXMLConversionHandler(sys.stdout)
parser = expat.ParserCreate( )

parser.StartElementHandler = dh.startElement
parser.EndElementHandler = dh.endElement
parser.CharacterDataHandler = dh.characters
parser.ParseFile(sys.stdin)
```

The output is to the standard output stream. If opened in your browser, it shows you all of the classes of the PyXML package and their methods, exactly as the pure SAX version of this example did.

CHAPTER 4

The Document Object Model

The Document Object Model (DOM) is an interface that exposes document structure programmatically to developers. Perhaps the most common application of the DOM is "Dynamic HTML" (DHTML), where an HTML document can be modified programmatically within the browser using an embedded scripting language. Typically, the scripting language is some flavor of ECMAScript (such as JavaScript or JScript), since most browsers support it, but others can be used as well. (For browsers on Windows, this can even be Python!) This allows you to change the background color of a table cell, or dynamically change font faces after the page is in the browser. The DOM defines the interface for vendors to offer compatible APIs.

The DOM is also extremely useful when exposed by a library such as the Python Standard Library or PyXML. It can allow you to use Python to manipulate an XML document already in memory. With the DOM interfaces, you can either change or extract portions of the document.

The DOM Specifications

The Document Object Model is defined in a series of recommendations from the W3C. The specifications clearly cover XML (or we would not be describing them in this book), but they cover other things as well. The initial version of the DOM actually came from the HTML world; browser vendors invented it in various flavors as part of the APIs available to client-side scripts embedded in web pages. Since the vendors each implemented different interfaces, there was a call from content creators to have a standardized interface so their pages would work in at least roughly equivalent ways on the different browsers. Since the W3C is the best available shared ground on which the vendors could build a common specification, the DOM specifications are developed there.

All standards organizations face issues regarding the longevity of their specifications, and the W3C is no exception, no matter that it is quite young compared to more traditional standards groups such as ANSI and ISO. Given the relative youth of the

W3C, it has had to deal with these issues almost from the start due to the rapid pace of development and the way standards are applied on the Internet. It does follow a traditional model however, rather than following the less formal (though highly effective) model of the Internet Engineering Task Force (IETF).

Most of the W3C recommendations provide a version number of the *major.minor* style favored by software developers, perhaps due to the origins of the organization. This is probably most prominent when we look at the HTML specifications; many versions have been released, and each is distinct from the others. Documents that contain anything beyond the simplest content cannot hope to comply with more than one version of the recommendation. This seems difficult to avoid for a markup language, but the effect is often that the standards are not as valuable as they could be if it were possible to maintain a higher degree of version independence.

The W3C is doing something different with the DOM. The specifications for the DOM do not have versions in the same sense that the HTML specification does. The new versioning model is also being used with the Cascading Style Sheets (CSS) recommendations, although those specifications are outside the scope of this book.

The DOM specification has been developed as a family of individual specifications, and the family can be described along two different axes: breadth and depth. When we think about the breadth of the recommendations, we can describe a broad family as including many features. For depth, we can describe a deep family as reaching further into the details as well as covering basic functionality. A broad family does many things, while a deep family tree covers many details. The W3C describes functional areas as *features*, while it describes depth of detail as *levels*.

Levels of the Specification

The *levels* of a specification are interesting to discuss first because they can be most confusing for many people. It is common to hear levels described as being just a strange name for the traditional notion of versions, but they are quite different. (Unfortunately, the DOM specifications themselves are not always clear about this.) As each feature of the DOM is enhanced, new levels are defined. This similarity to traditional versions certainly makes it easy to confuse the two concepts, but there is an important difference: an implementation of the second level must include an implementation of the first; advancing beyond the first level does not break compatibility for code that only expects to work with the older variant of the specification.

Each level of the DOM specifications cuts across the entire breadth of the DOM family, as it existed when it was defined (with one exception). Successive levels have introduced new features as well. Implementations are not required to implement all the features of the DOM, but generally need to implement the features they include at the same level.

At the time of this writing, two levels of the DOM have been defined by W3C recommendations, with a third level being developed by working groups within the W3C.

The primordial interfaces defined by browser implementations before the DOM standardization began are often described as "Level 0." The Level 1 specification from the W3C consists of a single recommendation that defines only two features, Core and HTML. This level provides general support for HTML and the XML 1.0 recommendation, but nothing else. For Level 2, the W3C broke the specification into six different documents. The Core feature was split into the Core and XML features, and support for Namespaces was added. New features added in Level 2 include an events model (mostly, but not entirely, for use in browsers), Cascading Style Sheets, document traversal, range specifications, and a vague concept of document views. Oddly, the HTML feature for Level 2 has not been completed and there has been no visible progress for quite some time.

The third level of the DOM, still only available as a set of working drafts, contains just four documents at this time. The Core, XML, and Events features are further refined, but most of the interesting work is taking place in new features. The current plans include new features for schemas (supporting at least the DTD and XML Schema languages), loading and saving XML documents, and an object model for XPath expressions. (We look at XPath in the next chapter, but it's too early to consider that the XPath feature of the DOM is ready.)

Feature Specifications

The *features* defined by the DOM vary from level to level, with new features being added and old features being split into separate features. The former is not a problem because code that works with an implementation of earlier levels simply will not need the newer features. In practice, the second has not been demonstrated to introduce any difficulty either, if only because Level 2 implementations always implement both the Core and XML features. For any implementation, the only required feature is the Core.

Since most Python implementations of the DOM provide at least some features from Level 2, and Level 3 exists only in draft form, let's take a look at what each feature defined for Level 2 provides to the application developer.

Core
    This includes basic structures required to expose well-formed XML documents without exposing any DTD information. In particular, entities, notations, entity references, and processing instructions are not provided. These are the interfaces with which we are concerned with in this chapter.

XML
    This feature set adds additional interfaces used to represent entity and notation declarations provided by the document type declaration (though not the document type itself), and some lexical information helpful in generating a modified document, including CDATA sections, entity references, and processing instructions.

Events

This feature is interesting in that it is broken down into several specific subfeatures. All implementations that support any type of events must support the basic Events feature, but only need to support the specific subfeatures which make sense for the implementation. The subfeatures include support for various classes of user-interface events and document-modification events.

Range

The range feature provides interfaces that make it possible to describe a portion of a document that cannot be represented as a sequence of nodes; this can be especially useful when describing a selection from the document as might be highlighted by the user.

Traversal

This provides support for traversal over the nodes of a document (or part of a document) in either the order in which they are found in the document, or as a tree-based traversal where the application guides a cursor to visit child nodes, parent nodes, or siblings during the traversal. Nodes can be filtered so the application need not deal with nodes it is not interested in.

Views

A vague specification that deals with providing multiple types of views on a document. This is not clearly useful.

StyleSheets

An abstract interface used to represent stylesheets. This is not specifically bound to Cascading Style Sheets, but may be used to represent other kinds of stylesheets as well. Since each stylesheet language is substantially different, this does not provide much styling information.

CSS

The CSS feature includes extensions of the Style Sheets interfaces that provide substantially more style information. These interfaces provide a great deal of information about CSS Level 2 stylesheets. This is intended to be used in browsers and editors, which are expected to update their presentation based on changes to the stylesheets using these interfaces.

Additional DOM features are being prepared outside the DOM working group for specific XML-based languages. Information about these and the specifications from the DOM working group is available online at *http://www.w3.org/DOM/DOMTR*.

Understanding the DOM

The DOM structure is essentially a hierarchy of *node* objects. Beginning with the root of the document (not the same as the document element), all constructs in the document are represented by nodes of various types, whether an element, text, attributes of elements, or other less common node types. Each node contains a list of references to child nodes, which can in turn be of the same types as those contained by the parent node. Therefore, a complete document looks just like a tree, all the way from the "trunk" (or root element of the tree) out to the leaf nodes representing text, childless elements, comments, processing instructions, and possibly other constructs. Figure 4-1 shows a very simple DOM hierarchy including a root element, two child elements, and their respective child text elements. Usually the character data of an element consists of multiple text nodes depending on the parser in use. Contiguous strings of textual data become sequences of text nodes.

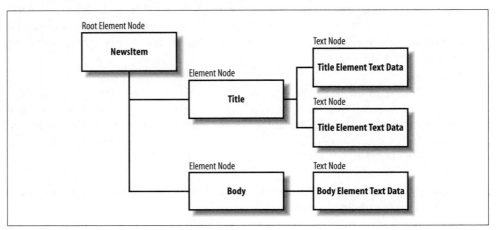

Figure 4-1. A simple DOM hierarchy

When a document is represented by the DOM, an object hierarchy represents the entire document. As with other nodes, it can contain children; the outermost element of the document is simply a child of the document node. The document can have other children; comments and processing instructions can precede or succeed the document element and appear in the proper order as children of the document. The document type declaration is also represented as a child of the document.

The W3C was careful to specify the DOM in a language-independent way, and each programming language has its own way to present the interfaces to the application programmer; each of these mappings of the DOM into the idioms of the target language is called a *binding* of the DOM. The W3C includes bindings for Java and ECMAScript as part of the DOM specifications. For Python, the official source of the DOM binding is the Python XML-SIG. The binding developed by the SIG members has been documented in the *Python Library Reference*, which is part of the standard documentation package for Python. Reference material for the DOM has been included in Appendix D of this book, but the standard documentation should be considered the authoritative document for this binding.

The DOM specifications provide the interfaces as CORBA IDL modules and Java interfaces, but does not specify (or even recommend) that the language-specific IDL mappings adopted by the Object Management Group (OMG) be used. In fact, the

Java interfaces provided by the W3C do not match the IDL-to-Java mapping. For Python, the XML-SIG decided that a somewhat more Python-friendly mapping would be used, with some concessions made to the IDL-to-Python mapping. Since no one seems to be using the IDL-derived form of the binding, we cover only the Python-centric version of the DOM binding in this book.

Python DOM Offerings

Python has several different ways for working with the DOM. The one you choose should best fit your needs. minidom is smaller and faster than a fully compliant DOM, but suits the needs of most users. pulldom provides a way to build only the portion of the DOM needed for a particular application, allowing the DOM to be more easily used when working with large documents or tight memory constraints. 4DOM is a full-fledged DOM Level 2 implementation. While these are the dominant implementations of the DOM for Python, and the only implementations described here, realize that there are additional implementations available that may be more tailored to your requirements.

Streamlining with Minidom

minidom, part of the xml.dom package included with both the Python standard library and PyXML, is a lightweight DOM implementation. Its goal is to provide a simple implementation and smaller memory footprint than a full DOM implementation. The methods for creating the DOM are simple as well. minidom also supports functions for working with string-length XML chunks and methods for extracting them.

Overall, minidom may be best for loading simple (not necessarily small) configuration files for your applications, dealing with form submissions from web pages, handling user authorization, and using it anywhere a "little" bit of XML is needed. You can reduce memory and time overhead by using minidom. These are two elements of significant importance in web application development.

Using Pulldom

pulldom, which also may be imported from the xml.dom package, may be just the thing to save your life when faced with the task of taking a portion of a large XML document and creating a DOM instance of the subset for manipulation. pulldom essentially allows for the construction of selected portions of a DOM based on SAX events. The module uses minidom for the actual nodes it returns.

pulldom seeks to be a middle ground between the DOM and SAX. pulldom wants to overcome the state-management (the place-marking mentioned earlier) of SAX, but also preserve its stream-based processing for speed and efficiency. pulldom also seeks to simplify the self-similar, intricately complex nature of a complete DOM tree, its many nodes and lists, and its memory-gobbling nature.

4DOM: A Full Implementation

Both `minidom` and `pulldom` have their specific fits, but for the remainder of this book, we work with 4DOM. This is a DOM implementation that implements most of the Level 2 features that actually make sense outside a browser.

After your experience with SAX earlier in this chapter, interacting with the DOM may seem incredibly easy by comparison. However, dealing with a seemingly endless intricacy of stacked node classes may send you running back to SAX to do your string comparisons. However you fare, the next sections seek to introduce you to working with the DOM in Python, and to provide a reference to its interfaces.

Regardless of the implementation you use, there are two basic types of operations you can perform with the DOM. The most common operations involve retrieving information from the document, which we discuss first. Once we cover that, we move on to explain how to use the DOM to modify and create documents.

Retrieving Information

Retrieving information from a document is easy using the DOM. Most of the work lies in traversing the document tree and selecting the nodes that are actually interesting for the application. Once that is done, it is usually trivial to call a method of the node (or nodes), or to retrieve the value of an attribute of the node. In order to extract information using the DOM, however, we first need to get a DOM document object.

Getting a Document Object

Perhaps the most glaring hole in the DOM specifications is that there is no facility in the API for retrieving a document object from an existing XML document. In a browser, the document is completely loaded before the DOM client code in the embedded or linked scripts can get to the document, so the document object is placed in a well-known location in the script's execution environment. For applications that do not live in a web browser, this approach simply does not work, so we need another solution.

Our solution depends on the particular DOM implementation we use. We can always create a document object from a file, a string, or a URL.

Loading a document using 4DOM

Creating a DOM instance to work with is easy in Python. Using 4DOM, we need call only one function to load a document from an open file:

```
from xml.dom.ext.reader.Sax2 import FromXmlStream
doc = FromXmlStream(sys.stdin)
```

Loading a document using minidom

There are two convenient functions in the `xml.dom.minidom` module that can be used to load a document. The `parse` function takes a parameter that can be a string containing a filename or URL, or it can be a file object open for reading:

```
import xml.dom.minidom
doc = xml.dom.minidom.parse(sys.stdin)
```

Another function, `parseString`, can be used to load a document from a buffer containing XML text that has already been loaded into memory:

```
doc = xml.dom.minidom.parseString("<doc>My tiny document.</doc>")
```

Determining a Node's Type

You can use the constants built in to the DOM to see what type of node you are dealing with. It may be an element, an attribute, a CDATA section, or a host of other things. (All the node type constants are listed in Appendix D.)

To test a node's type, compare its `nodeType` attribute to the particular constant you're looking for. For example, a `CDATASection` instance has a `nodeType` equal to `CDATA_SECTION_NODE`. An `Element` (with potential children) has a `nodeType` equal to `ELEMENT_NODE`. When traversing a DOM tree, you can test a node at any point to determine whether it is what you're looking for:

```
for node in nodes.childNodes:
    if node.nodeType == node.ELEMENT_NODE:
        print "Found it!"
```

The `Node` interface has other identifying properties, such as its *value* and *name*. The `nodeName` value represents the tag name for elements, while in a text node the `nodeName` is simply #text. The `nodeValue` attribute may be null for elements, and should be the actual character data of a text element or other leaf-type element.

Getting a Node's Children

When dealing with a DOM tree, you primarily use nodes and *node lists*. A node list is a collection of nodes. Any level of an XML document can be represented as a node list. Each node in the list can in turn contain other node lists, representing the potential for infinite complexity of an XML document.

The `Node` interface features two methods for quickly getting to a specific child node, as well as a method to get a node list containing a node's children. `firstChild` refers to the first child node of any given node. The interface shows `None` if the node has no children. This is handy when you know exactly the structure of the document you're dealing with. If you are working with a strict content model enforced by a schema or DTD, you may be able to count on the fact that the document is organized in a certain way (provided you included a validation step). But for the most part, it's best to leverage the spirit of XML and actually traverse the document for the data you're looking for, rather than assume there is logic to the location of the data. Regardless, firstChild can be very powerful, and is often used to retrieve the first element beneath a document element.

The lastChild attribute is similar to firstChild, but returns the last child node of any given node. Again, this can be handy if you know the exact structure of the document you're working with, or if you're trying to just get the last child regardless of the significance of that child.

The childNodes attribute contains a node list containing all the children of the given node. This attribute is used frequently when working with the DOM. When iterating over children of an element, the childNodes attributes can be used for simple iteration in the same way that you would iterate over a list:

```
for child in node.childNodes:
    print "Child:", child.nodeName
```

The value of the childNodes attribute is a NodeList object. For the purpose of retrieving information from the DOM, it behaves like a Python list, but does not support "slicing." NodeList objects should not be used to modify the content of the DOM as the specific behaviors may differ among DOM implementations.

The NodeList interface features some additional interfaces beyond those provided by lists. These are not commonly used with Python, but are available since the DOM specifies their presence and behavior. The length attribute indicates the number of nodes in the list. Note that the length returns the total number, but that indexing begins at zero. For example, a NodeList with a length of 3 has nodes at indices 0, 1, and 2 (which mirrors the way an array is normally indexed in Python). Most Python programmers prefer to use the len built-in function, which works properly with NodeList objects.

The item method returns the item at the specific index passed in as a parameter. For example, item(1) returns the second node in the NodeList, or None if there are fewer than two nodes. This is distinct from the Python indexing operation, for which a NodeList raises IndexError for an index that is out of bounds.

Getting a Node's Siblings

Since XML documents are hierarchical and the DOM exposes them as a tree, it is reasonable to want to get the siblings of a node as well as its children. This is done using the previousSibling and nextSibling attributes. If a node is the first child of its parent, its previousSibling is None; likewise, if it is the last child, its nextSibling is None. If a node is the only child of its parent, both of these attributes are None, as expected.

When combined with the firstChild or lastChild attributes, the sibling attributes can be used to iterate over an element's children. The required code is slightly more verbose, but is also better suited for use when the document tree is being modified in certain ways, especially when nodes are being added to or removed from the element whose children are being iterated over.

For example, consider how Directory elements could be removed from another Directory element to leave us with a Directory containing only files. If we iterate over the top element using its childNodes attribute and remove child Directory elements as we see them, some nodes are not properly examined. (This happens because Python's for loops use the index into the list, but we're also shifting remaining children to the left when we remove one, so it is skipped as the loop advances.) There are many ways to avoid skipping elements, but perhaps the simplest is to use nextSibling to iterate:

```
child = node.firstChild
while child is not None:
  next = child.nextSibling
  if (child.nodeType == node.ELEMENT_NODE
      and child.tagName == "Directory"):
    node.removeChild(child)
  child = next
```

Extracting Elements by Name

The DOM can provide some advantages over SAX, depending on what you're trying to do. For starters, when using the DOM, you don't have to write a separate handler for each type of event, or set flags to group events together as was done earlier with SAX in Example 3-3. Imagine that you have a long record of purchase orders stacked up in XML. Someone has approached you about pulling part numbers, and only part numbers, out of the document for reporting purposes. With SAX, you can write a handler to look for elements with the name used to identify part numbers (sku in the example), and then set a flag to gobble up character events until the parser leaves the part number element. With the DOM, you have a different approach using the getElementsByTagName method of the Document interface.

To show how easy this can make some operations, let's look at a simple example. Create a new XML file as shown in Example 4-1, *po.xml*. This document is the sample purchase order for the next script:

Example 4-1. po.xml

```
<?xml version="1.0"?>
<purchaseOrder>
  <item>
    <name>Mushroom Lamp</name>
    <sku>229-987488</sku>
    <price>$34.99</price>
    <qty>1</qty>
  </item>
  <item>
    <name>Bass Drum</name>
```

Example 4-1. po.xml (continued)

```
    <sku>228-988347</sku>
    <price>$199.99</price>
    <qty>1</qty>
  </item>
  <item>
    <name>Toy Steam Engine</name>
    <sku>221-388833</sku>
    <price>$19.99</price>
    <qty>1</qty>
  </item>
</purchaseOrder>
```

Using the DOM, you can easily create a list of nodes that references all nodes of a single element type within the document. For example, you could pull all of the sku elements from the document into a new list of nodes. This list can be used like any other NodeList object, with the difference that the nodes in the list may not share a single parent, as is the case with the childNodes value. Since the DOM works with the structural tree of the XML document, it is able to provide a simple method call to pull a subset of the document out into a separate node list. In Example 4-2, the getElementsByTagName method is used to create a single NodeList of all the sku elements within the document. Our example shows that sku elements have text nodes as children, but we know that a string of text in the document may be presented in the DOM as multiple text nodes. To make the tree easier to work with, you can use the normalize method of the Node interface to convert all adjacent text nodes into a single text node, making it easy to use the firstChild attribute of the Element class to retrieve the complete text value of the sku elements reliably.

Example 4-2. po.py

```python
#!/usr/bin/env python

from xml.dom.ext.reader.Sax2 import FromXmlStream
import sys

doc = FromXmlStream(sys.stdin)

for sku in doc.getElementsByTagName("sku"):
  sku.normalize()
  print "Sku: " + sku.firstChild.data
```

Example 4-2 requires considerably less code than what is required if you are implementing a SAX handler for the same task. The extraction can operate independently of other tasks that work with the document. When you run the program, again using *po.xml*, you receive something similar to the following on standard output:

```
    Sku: 229-987488
    Sku: 228-988347
    Sku: 221-388833
```

You can see something similar being done using SAX in Example 3-3.

Examining NodeList Members

Let's look at a program that puts many of these concepts together, and uses the *article.xml* file from the previous chapter (Example 3-1). Example 4-3 shows a recursive function used to extract text from a document's elements.

Example 4-3. textme.py

```
#!/usr/bin/env python

from xml.dom.ext.reader.Sax2 import FromXmlStream
import sys

def findTextNodes(nodeList):
  for subnode in nodeList:
    if subnode.nodeType == subnode.ELEMENT_NODE:
      print "element node: " + subnode.tagName

      # call function again to get children
      findTextNodes(subnode.childNodes)

    elif subnode.nodeType == subnode.TEXT_NODE:
      print "text node: ",
      print subnode.data

doc = FromXmlStream(sys.stdin)
findTextNodes(doc.childNodes)
```

You can run this script passing *article.xml* as standard input:

```
$> python textme.py < article.xml
```

It should produce output similar to the following:

```
element node: webArticle
text node:

element node: header
text node:

element node: body
text node:  Seattle, WA - Today an anonymous individual
             announced that NASA has completed building a
             Warp Drive and has parked a ship that uses
             the drive in his back yard.  This individual
             claims that although he hasn't been contacted by
             NASA concerning the parked space vessel, he assumes
             that he will be launching it later this week to
             mount an exhibition to the Andromeda Galaxy.

    text node:
```

You can see in the output how whitespace is treated as its own text node, and how contiguous strings of character data are kept together as text nodes as well. The exact output you see may vary from that presented here. Depending on the specific parser you use (consider different versions or different platforms as different parsers since the buffering interactions with the operating system can be relevant), the specific boundaries of text nodes may differ, and you may see contiguous blocks of character data presented as more than one text node.

Looking at Attributes

Now that we've seen how to examine the hierarchical content of an XML document using the DOM, we need to take a look at how we can use the DOM to retrieve XML's only nonhierarchical component: attributes. As with all other information in the DOM, attributes are described as nodes. Attribute nodes have a very special relationship with the tree structure of an XML document; we find that the interfaces that allow us to work with them are different as well.

When we looked at the child nodes of elements earlier (as in Example 4-3), we only saw nodes for child elements and textual data. From this, we can reasonably surmise that attributes are not children of the element on which they are included. They are available, however, using some methods specific to Element nodes. There is an attribute of the Node interface that is used only for attributes of elements.

The easiest way to get the value of an attribute is to use the getAttribute method of the element node. This method takes the name of the attribute as a string and returns a string giving the value of the attribute, or an empty string if the attribute is not present. To retrieve the node object for the attribute, use the getAttributeNode method instead; if the attribute does not exist, it returns None. If you need to test for the presence of an attribute without retrieving the node or attribute value, the hasAttribute method will prove useful.

Another way to look at attributes is using a structure called a NamedNodeMap. This object is similar in function to a dictionary, and the Python version of this structure shares much of the interface of a dictionary. The Node interface includes an attribute named attributes that is only used for element nodes; it is always set to None for other node types. While the NamedNodeMap supports the item method and length attribute much as the NodeList interface does, the normal way of using it in Python is as a mapping object, which supports most of the interfaces provided by dictionary objects. The keys are the attribute names and the values are the attribute nodes.

Changing Documents

Now that we've looked at how we can extract information from our documents using the DOM, we probably want to be able to change them. There are really just a few things we need to know to make changes, so we describe the basic operations and then show a few examples. The basic operations involved in modifying a document center around creating new nodes, adding, moving, and removing nodes, and modifying the contents of nodes. Since we often want to add new elements and textual content, we start by looking at creating new nodes.

Creating New Nodes

Most of the time, new nodes need to be created explicitly. Since the DOM is defined as a set of interfaces rather than as concrete classes, the only way to create new nodes is to make call methods on the objects we already have in hand. Fortunately, the Document interface includes a large selection of factory methods we can use to create new nodes of most types. (Methods for creating entity and notation nodes are noticeably absent, but most applications should not find themselves constrained by that.)

The most used of these factory methods are very simple, and are used to create new element and text nodes. For elements, use the createElement method, with the tag name of the element to create as the only parameter. Text nodes can be created using the createTextNode method, passing the text of the new node as the parameter. For the details on the other node factory methods, see the reference material in Appendix D.

Adding and Moving Nodes

There are some very handy methods available for moving nodes to different locations on the tree. These methods appear on the basic Node interface, so all DOM nodes provide these. There are constraints on the use of these nodes: you cannot use them to construct documents which do not make sense structurally, and well-formedness of the document is ensured at all times. For example, an exception is raised if you attempt to add a child to a text node, or if you try to add a second child element to the document object.

appendChild(*newChild*)
> Takes a *newChild* node argument and appends it to the end of the list of children of the node.

insertBefore(*newChild, refChild*)
> Takes the node *newChild* and inserts it immediately before the *refChild* node you supply.

replaceChild(*newChild, oldChild*)
> Replaces the *oldChild* with the *newChild*, and *oldChild* is returned to the caller.

removeChild(*oldChild*)
> Removes the node *oldChild* from the list of children of the node this is called on.

The brief descriptions do not replace the reference documentation for these methods; see Appendix D for more complete information.

Removing Nodes

Let's look at how to examine a tree, and how to remove specific nodes on the tree. Example 4-4 uses a few nested loops to dive three levels deep into an XML document created using the *index.py* script from Example 3-4. The design has its limitations, as it assumes you are only dealing with elements no more than three levels deep, but demonstrates the DOM methods we're interested in.

Example 4-4. domit.py

```python
#!/usr/bin/env python
import sys

from xml.dom.ext.reader.Sax2 import FromXmlStream
from xml.dom.ext            import PrettyPrint

# get DOM object
doc = FromXmlStream(sys.stdin)

# remove unwanted nodes by traversing Node tree

for node1 in doc.childNodes:
  for node2 in node1.childNodes:
    node3 = node2.firstChild
    while node3 is not None:
      next = node3.nextSibling
      name = node3.nodeName
      if name in ("contents", "extension", "userID", "groupID"):
        # remove unwanted nodes here via the parent
        node2.removeChild(node3)
      node3 = next

PrettyPrint(doc)
```

After getting a document from standard input, a few nested for loops are executed to descend three levels deep into the tree and look for specific tag names. When running the script against the XML document we created with *index.py*, your file elements should look like this:

```xml
<file name='c:\windows\desktop\G-Force\G-Force.doc'>


        <size>12570</size>
        <lastAccessed>Tue May 09 00:00:00 2000</lastAccessed>
        <lastModified>Tue May 09 11:56:14 2000</lastModified>
        <created>Wed Jan 17 23:31:23 2001</created>


  </file>
```

The whitespace around the removed elements remains in place as you can see by the gaps between elements; we did not look for adjacent text nodes, so they remain unaffected. This text was the result of a call to the PrettyPrint function at the end of the script. Of course, the element looks the same regardless of hierarchical position within the document. When writing DOM processing code, you should try to keep it

---

independent from the structure of the document. Instead of using `firstChild` to get what you're after, consider enumerating the children and examining each one. This may cost some processing time, but it does give the document's structure more flexibility. As long as the target element appears beneath the parent node, the child will be found. When you use `firstChild`, you might be setting yourself up for trouble if someone gives you a document with a slightly different structure, such as a peer element coming before another in the document. You can write this type of operation using a recursive function, so that you can handle similar structures, regardless of position in the document. If you really don't care where within the subtree an element is found, you can use the `getElementsByTagName` method described earlier.

Another common requirement is to locate a node that you know must be a child of a particular node, but not require a specific ordering of the child nodes. A simple loop in a utility function handles this nicely:

```python
from xml.dom import Node

def findChildrenByTagName(parent, tagname):
    """Return a list of 'tagname' children of 'parent'."""
    L = []
    for child in parent.childNodes:
        if (child.nodeType == Node.ELEMENT_NODE
            and child.tagName == tagname):
            L.append(child)
    return L
```

An even simpler helper function that can come in handy is a function that finds the first child element with a particular tag name, or the first to have one of several tag names. These are all minor variations of the function just presented.

Changing a Document's Structure

In addition to doing replacements and additions, you can also restructure a document entirely using the DOM.

In Example 4-5, we take the nested loops from the last section, and replace them with a traveling recursive function. The script can also work with XML output from the *index.py* script we worked with earlier in this chapter. In this version however, the `file` element's `size` child is used as a replacement for itself. This process leaves the document filled with `directory` and `size` elements only.

Example 4-5 shows *domit2.py* using a recursive function.

Example 4-5. domit2.py

```python
#!/usr/bin/env python

from xml.dom.ext.reader.Sax2 import FromXmlStream
```

Example 4-5. domit2.py (continued)

```
from xml.dom.ext          import PrettyPrint

import sys

def makeSize(nodeList):
  for subnode in nodeList:
    if subnode.nodeType == subnode.ELEMENT_NODE:
      if subnode.nodeName == "size":
        subnode.parentNode.parentNode.replaceChild(
          subnode, subnode.parentNode)
      else:
        makeSize(subnode.childNodes)

# get DOM object
doc = FromXmlStream(sys.stdin)

# call func
makeSize(doc.childNodes)

# display altered document
PrettyPrint(doc)
```

You can run the script from the command line:

```
$> python domit2.py < wd.xml
```

The file *wd.xml* is an XML file created with the *index.py script*—you can use any file you like, as long as has the same structure as the files created by *index.py*. The output should be something like this:

```
<Directory name='c:\windows\desktop\gl2'>
<size>230444</size>
    <size>3035</size>
    <size>8904</size>
    <size>722</size>
    <Directory name='c:\windows\desktop\gl2/Debug'>
<size>156672</size>
        <size>86016</size>
        <size>3779068</size>
        <size>25685</size>
        <size>17907</size>
        <size>250508</size>
        <size>208951</size>
        <size>402432</size>
    </Directory>
<size>3509</size>
    <size>33792</size>
    <size>722</size>
    <size>48640</size>
    <size>533</size>
  </Directory>
```

Building a Web Application

Now you can use your new knowledge of the DOM to create a simple web application. Let's build one that allows for the posting and viewing of articles. The articles are submitted and viewed via a web browser, but stored by the web server as XML, which allows the articles to be leveraged into different information systems that process XML. HTML articles, on the other hand, are unusable outside of a web browser.

Preparing the Web Server

In order to run the examples in this chapter, you must have a web server available that lets you execute CGI scripts. These examples were designed on Apache, so the CGI scripts contain a *sh-bang* line that specified the path to the Python executable (the #!/usr/bin/python expression at the top of the file) so that Apache can run them just like any other CGI script. (Understanding the term "*sh*-bang" requires a little bit of knowledge of Unix history. The traditional command-line environment for Unix was originally implemented using the *sh* program. The exclamation point was named the "bang" character because it was always used after words such as "bang" and "pow" in comic books and cartoons. Since the lines at the top of scripts that started with #! were interpreted by the *sh* program, they came to be known as *sh*-bang lines.)

Ensuring the script's execution

You must enable the execution of your Python scripts on your web server. On Apache, this means enabling CGI within the web directory, ensuring that the actual CGI scripts contain the pointer to the Python interpreter so they run correctly, and setting the "execute" permission on the script. This last item can be accomplished using the *chmod* program:

```
$> chmod +x start.cgi
```

On other web servers and on Windows, you need to assign a handler to your CGI scripts so that they are executed by the Python interpreter. This may require that you name your scripts with a *.py* extension, as opposed to a *.cgi* extension, if *.cgi* is already assigned to another handler.

Enabling write permission

Beyond just being able to execute scripts within a web directory, the web user must also have write access to the directory for the examples to work. The examples are meant to illustrate the manipulation of XML and the ability to repurpose accessible XML into different applications.

To avoid dependency on a database in this chapter, and to provide easy access to the XML, these examples use the filesystem directly for storage. Articles are stored to disk as *.xml* files.

For Apache, you must give the user nobody write access to the specific web directory. If you are serving pages out of */home/httpd/myXMLApplication*, you need to set up something like the following:

```
$> mkdir /home/httpd/myXMLApplication
$> chown nobody /home/httpd/myXMLApplication
$> chmod 755 /home/httpd/myXMLApplication
```

This gives the user nobody (the user ID that Apache runs under) write access to the directory. There are many other ways to securely set this up; this is simply one option. In general, for production web applications, it's a good idea *not* to give write access to web users.

The Web Application Structure

The web application is driven mainly by one script, *start.cgi*. The script does most of the processing, serves the content templates, and invokes the objects capable of storing and retrieving your XML articles. The primary components consist of the article object, the storage object, the article manager, the SAX-based article handler, and the *start.cgi* script that manages the whole process. Figure 4-2 shows a diagram of the major components.

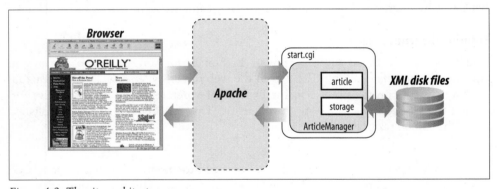

Figure 4-2. The site architecture

In the next few sections, we examine the code and operation of the CGI components in detail.

The Article class

The Article class represents an article as XML information. It's a thin class with methods only for creating an article from existing XML, or for retrieving the XML that makes up the article as a string. In addition, it has modifiable attributes that allow you to manipulate the content of the article:

```
def __init__(self):
    """Set initial data attributes."""
    self.reset()
```

```
def reset(self):
    self.title       = ""
    self.size        = 0
    self.time        = "" # pretty-printing time string
    self.author      = ""
    self.contributor = ""
    self.contents    = ""
```

The attributes can be modified during the life of an article to keep you from having to create XML in your program. For example:

```
>>> from article import Article
>>> art = Article()
>>> art.title = "FirstPost"
>>> art.contents = "This is the first article."
>>> print art.getXML()
<?xml version="1.0"?>
<article title="FirstPost">
  <contents>
This is the first article.
  </contents>
</article>
```

The getXML method call has the logic to recreate the XML when necessary. You can create articles with a well-formed string of XML, or by loading a string of XML from a disk file. The getXML method exists as a means for you to pull the XML back out of the object. Note the use of the escape function, which we imported from the xml. sax.saxutils module; this ensures that characters that are syntactically significant to XML are properly encoded in the result.

```
def getXML(self):
    """Returns XML after re-assembling from data
    members that may have changed."""

    attr = ''
    if self.title:
      attr = ' title="%s"' % escape(self.title)
    s = '<?xml version="1.0"?>\n<article%s>\n' % attr
    if self.author:
      s = '%s  <author name="%s" />\n' % (s, escape(self.author))
    if self.contributor:
      s = '%s  <contributor name="%s" />\n' % (s, escape(self.contributor))
    if self.contents:
      s = ('%s  <contents>\n%s\n  </contents>\n'
           % (s, escape(self.contents)))
    return s + "</article>\n"
```

The fromXML method of the article class populates the current XML article object with the values from the supplied string. This method uses the convenience function parseString, from xml.dom.minidom, to load the XML data into a document object, and then uses the content retrieval methods of the DOM to collect the required information:

```
def fromXML(self, data):
    """Initialize using an XML document passed as a string."""
    self.reset()
    dom              = xml.dom.minidom.parseString(data)
    self.title       = get_attribute(dom, "article", "title")
    self.size        = int(get_attribute(dom, "size", "bytes") or 0)
    self.time        = get_attribute(dom, "time", "stime")
    self.author      = get_attribute(dom, "author", "name")
    self.contributor = get_attribute(dom, "contributor", "name")
    nodelist         = dom.getElementsByTagName("contents")
    if nodelist:
        assert len(nodelist) == 1
        contents = nodelist[0]
        contents.normalize()
        if contents.childNodes:
            self.contents = contents.firstChild.data.strip()
```

This method uses a convenience function defined elsewhere in the module. The function get_attribute looks into the document for an attribute and returns the value it finds; if the attribute it is looking for does not exist (or the element it expects to find it on does not exist), it returns an empty string instead. If it finds more than one element that matches the requested element type, it complains loudly using the assert statement. (For a real application, you would not use assert in this way, but this is sufficient for our examples since we're mainly interested in the XML aspect.)

When working with the web site logic, most manipulation on article objects occurs by either using the Storage class to load an article from disk, or by parsing a form submission to create an article for a user and then using the Storage class to save the XML file to disk. Example 4-6 shows the complete listing of the Article class.

Example 4-6. Article class from article.py

```
import xml.dom.minidom
from xml.sax.saxutils import escape

class Article:
    """Represents a block of text and metadata created from XML."""

    def __init__(self):
        """Set initial data properties."""
        self.reset()

    def reset(self):
        """Re-initialize data properties."""
        self.title       = ""
        self.size        = 0
        self.time        = ""       # pretty-printing time string
        self.author      = ""
        self.contributor = ""
```

Example 4-6. Article class from article.py (continued)

```python
    self.contents    = ""

  def getXML(self):
    """Returns XML after re-assembling from data
    members that may have changed."""

    attr = ''
    if self.title:
      attr = ' title="%s"' % escape(self.title)
    s = '<?xml version="1.0"?>\n<article%s>\n' % attr
    if self.author:
    s = ('<?xml version="1.0"?>\n'
         '<article%s>\n' % attr)
    if self.author:
      s = '%s  <author name="%s" />\n' % (s, escape(self.author))
    if self.contributor:
      s = '%s  <contributor name="%s" />\n' % (s, escape(self.contributor))
    if self.contents:
      s = ('%s  <contents>\n%s\n  </contents>\n'
           % (s, escape(self.contents)))
    return s + "</article>\n"

  def fromXML(self, data):
    """Initialize using an XML document passed as a string."""
    self.reset()
    dom = xml.dom.minidom.parseString(data)
    self.title       = get_attribute(dom, "article", "title")
    self.size        = int(get_attribute(dom, "size", "bytes") or 0)
    self.time        = get_attribute(dom, "time", "stime")
    self.author      = get_attribute(dom, "author", "name")
    self.contributor = get_attribute(dom, "contributor", "name")
    nodelist         = dom.getElementsByTagName("contents")
    if nodelist:
      assert len(nodelist) == 1
      contents = nodelist[0]
      contents.normalize()
      if contents.childNodes:
        self.contents = contents.firstChild.data.strip()

# Helper function:

def get_attribute(dom, tagname, attrname):
  """Return the value of a solitary element & attribute,
  if available."""
  nodelist = dom.getElementsByTagName(tagname)
  if nodelist:
    assert len(nodelist) == 1
    node = nodelist[0]
    return node.getAttribute(attrname).strip()
  else:
    return ""
```

The Storage class

The Storage class is used to place an article on disk as an XML file, and to create article objects from XML files that are already on disk:

```
>>> from article import Article
>>> from storage import Storage
>>> a = Article()
>>> a.title = "FirstPost"
>>> a.contents = "This is the FirstPost."
>>> a.author = "Fred L. Drake, Jr."
>>> s = Storage()
>>> s.save(a)
>>>
>>> b = s.load("FirstPost.xml")
>>> print b.getXML()
<?xml version="1.0"?>
<article title="FirstPost">
  <author name="Fred L. Drake, Jr." />
  <contents>
This is the FirstPost.
  </contents>
</article>
```

Here, you create an article from scratch as a, store it to disk using the Storage object, and then reincarnate the article as b using Storage's load method. Note that the load method takes the actual filename that is a concatenation of the article.title and the *.xml* extension.

The Storage.save method takes an article instance as the only parameter and saves the article to disk as an XML file using the form *article.title*.xml:

```
sFilename = article.title + ".xml"
fd = open(sFilename, "w")

# write file to disk with data from getXML() call
fd.write(article.getXML())
fd.close()
```

The getXML method is used to retrieve an XML string containing an XML version of the article; the string is then saved to the disk file. The Storage.load method takes an XML file from disk, reads in the data from the file, and then creates an article using the fromXML method of the Article class:

```
fd = open(sName, "r")
sxml = fd.read()
fd.close()

# create an article instance
a = Article()
a.fromXML(sxml)

# return article object to caller
return a
```

The return result is an `Article` instance. Example 4-7 shows *storage.py* in its entirety.

Example 4-7. storage.py

```
# storage.py
from article import Article

class Storage:
    """Stores and retrieves article objects as XML files
    -- should be easy to migrate to a database."""

    def save(self, article):
        """Save as <article.title>.xml."""
        sFilename = article.title + ".xml"
        fd = open(sFilename, "w")

        # write file to disk with data from getXML() call
        fd.write(article.getXML())
        fd.close()

    def load(self, sName):
        """Name must be filename.xml--Returns an article object."""
        fd = open(sName, "r")
        sxml = fd.read()

        # create an article instance
        a = Article()

        # use fromXML to create an article object
        # from the file's XML
        a.fromXML(sxml)
        fd.close()

        # return article object to caller
        return a
```

Implementing Site Logic

The `Article` and `Storage` classes are not web-oriented. They could be used in any type of application, as the articles are represented in XML, and the `Storage` class just handles their I/O to disk. Conceptually at least, you could use these classes anywhere to create an XML-based information store.

On the other hand, you could write a single CGI script that has all of the logic to store articles to disk and read them, as well as parse the XML, but then your articles and their utility would be trapped within the CGI script. By breaking core functionality off into discrete components, you're free to use the `Article` and `Storage` classes from any type of application you envision.

In order to manage web interaction with the article classes, we will create one additional class (`ArticleManager`) and one additional script (*start.cgi*). The `ArticleManager` class builds a web interface for article manipulation. It has the ability to display articles as HTML, to accept posted articles from a web form, and to handle user interaction with the site. The *start.cgi* script handles I/O from the web server and drives the ArticleManager.

The ArticleManager class

The ArticleManager class contains four methods for dealing with articles. The manager acts as a liaison between the article objects and the actual CGI script that interfaces with the web server (and, indirectly the user's browser).

The viewAll method picks all of the XML articles off the disk and creates a section of HTML hyperlinks linking to the articles. This method is called by the CGI script to create a page showing all of the article titles as links:

```
def viewAll(self):
    """Displays all XML files in the current
    working directory."""
    print "<p>View All<br><br>"

    # grab list of files in current directory
    fl = os.listdir(".")
    for xmlFile in fl:
      # weed out XML files
      tname, ext = os.path.splitext(xmlFile)
      if ext == ".xml":
        # create HTML link surrounding article name
        print '<br><a href="start.cgi?cmd=v1a&af=%s">%s</a><br>'
              % (quote(xmlFile), tname)
```

The method is not terribly elegant. It simply reads the contents of the current directory, picks out the XML files, and strips the *.xml* extension off the name before displaying it as a link. The link connects back again to the same page (*start.cgi*), but this time with query string parameters that instruct *start.cgi* to invoke the viewOne method to view the content of a single article. The quote function imported from urllib is used to escape special characters in the filename that may cause problems for the browser. URL construction and quoting is discussed in more detail in Chapter 8.

The viewOne method uses the storage object to reanimate an article stored on disk. Once the article instance is created, its data members are mined (one by one), and wrapped with HTML for display in the browser:

```
def viewOne(self, articleFile):
    """ takes an article file name as a parameter and
        creates and displays an article object for it.
    """
    # create storage and article objects
    store = Storage()
    art = store.load(articleFile)
```

```
# Write HTML to browser (standard output)
print "<p>Title: " + art.title + "<br>"
print "Author: " + art.author + "<br>"
print "Date: " + art.time + "<br>"
print "<table width=500><tr><td>" + art.contents
print "</td></tr></table></p>"
```

It's important to note here that the parameter handed to viewOne is a real filename, not just the title of the XML document.

The postArticle method is probably the simplest method discussed yet, as its job is simply to create HTML. The HTML represents a submittal form whereby users can write new articles and present them to the server for ultimate storage in XML. Since the HTML form does not change, this method can simply print the value of a constant that contains the form as a string.

The postArticleData method is slightly more complicated. Its job is to extract key/value pairs from a submitted HTTP form, and create an XML article based on the obtained values. Once the XML is created, it must be stored to disk. It does this by creating an article object and setting the members to values retrieved from the form, then using the Storage class to save the article.

```
def postArticleData(self, form):
    """Accepts actual posted form data, creates and
    stores an article object."""
    # populate an article with information from the form
    art = Article()
    art.title       = form["title"].value
    art.author      = form["author"].value
    art.contributor = form["contrib"].value
    art.contents    = form["contents"].value

    # store the article
    store = Storage()
    store.save(art)
```

Example 4-8 shows *ArticleManager.py* in its entirety.

Example 4-8. ArticleManager.py

```
# ArticleManager.py
import os
from urllib  import quote
from article import Article
from storage import Storage

class ArticleManager:
  """Manages articles for the web page.

  Responsible for creating, loading, saving, and displaying
  articles."""

  def viewAll(self):
```

Example 4-8. ArticleManager.py (continued)

```
    """"Displays all XML files in the current working directory."""
    print "<p>View All<br><br>"

    # grab list of files in current directory
    fl = os.listdir(".")
    for xmlFile in fl:
      # weed out XML files
      tname, ext = os.path.splitext(xmlFile)
      if ext == ".xml":
        # create HTML link surrounding article name
        print '<br><a href="start.cgi?cmd=v1a&af=%s">%s</a><br>' \
              % (quote(xmlFile), tname)

  def viewOne(self, articleFile):
    """"Takes an article file name as a parameter and
    creates and displays an article object for it.
    """
    # create storage and article objects
    store = Storage()
    art = store.load(articleFile)

    # Write HTML to browser (standard output)
    print "<p>Title: " + art.title + "<br>"
    print "Author: " + art.author + "<br>"
    print "Date: " + art.time + "<br>"
    print "<table width=500><tr><td>" + art.contents
    print "</td></tr></table></p>"

  def postArticle(self):
    """"Displays the article posting form."""
    print POSTING_FORM

  def postArticleData(self,form):
    """"Accepts actual posted form data, creates and
    stores an article object."""
    # populate an article with information from the form
    art = Article()
    art.title       = form["title"].value
    art.author      = form["author"].value
    art.contributor = form["contrib"].value
    art.contents    = form["contents"].value

    # store the article
    store = Storage()
    store.save(art)

POSTING_FORM = '''\
<form method="POST" action="start.cgi?cmd=pd">
<p>
Title:      <br><input type="text" length="40" name="title"><br>
Contributor:<br><input type="text" length="40" name="contrib"><br>
Author:     <br><input type="text" length="40" name="author"><br>
```

Example 4-8. ArticleManager.py (continued)

```
Contents:    <br><textarea rows="15" cols="80" name="contents"></textarea><br>
<input type="submit">
</form>
'''
```

Controlling the Application

The CGI script is the main program for the web application. It is also the only "page" that will ever be in the browser. When the user types *start.cgi* in the address bar, Apache runs the script on the server.

The script begins by importing the cgi and os modules:

```
import cgi
import os
```

The script then prints the content header, as well as the opening HTML. This HTML is the same regardless of the type of operation *start.cgi* is performing; therefore, it is defined as the constant HEADER (not shown) and printed for every request:

```
# content-type header
print "Content-type: text/html"
print
print HEADER
```

After the common portion of the result page is printed, the query string is checked for the cmd parameter, which specifies what actions *start.cgi* should perform. The hyperlinks produced and sent to the browser by *start.cgi* are all fitted with this same parameter indicating a specific instruction such as view or post. The query string is checked using the cgi module. It is inspected to see if it contains the cmd parameter. If so, processing continues; if not, the user is presented with an error message.

```
query = cgi.FieldStorage()
if query.has_key("cmd"):
  cmd = query["cmd"][0].value

  # instantiate an ArticleManager
  am = ArticleManager()
```

The ArticleManager is instantiated as am, and command processing continues by checking cmd for its four possible values. For viewing article titles, the command sequence va is used:

```
# Command: viewAll - list all articles
if cmd == "va":
  am.viewAll()
```

For viewing a specific article, the command sequence v1a is used:

```
# Command: viewOne - view one article
if cmd == "v1a":
  aname = query["af"].value
  am.viewOne(aname)
```

For posting articles, a form is displayed. The CGI script looks for the pa sequence:

```
# Command: postArticle - view the post-article page
  if cmd == "pa":
    am.postArticle( )
```

When the user submits the article form, the data is posted to the web server. The CGI script looks for the command sequence pd to indicate that the article data is posted. It then passes the CGI form to the ArticleManager's postArticleData method:

```
# Command: postData - take an actual article post
if cmd == "pd":
  print "<p>Thank you for your post!</p>"
  am.postArticleData(query)
```

If cmd is not present in the query string, or if cmd has a value that is not one of the four, an error message is presented as the else clause to the first if statement:

```
else:
  # Invalid selection
  print "<p>Your selection was not recognized</p>"
```

The HTML is then closed by a final print statement:

```
# close the HTML
print "</body></html>"
```

The complete listing of *start.cgi* is shown in Example 4-9.

Example 4-9. start.cgi

```
#!/usr/local/bin/python
#
# start.cgi - a Python CGI script

import cgi
import os

from ArticleManager import ArticleManager

HEADER = """\
<html>
<body>
<p>
<table cellspacing="0" cellpadding="1">
  <tr><td>
      <h1>XML Articles</h1>
    </td></tr>
  <tr><td>
      <h3><a href="start.cgi?cmd=va">View All</a>  | 
        <a href="start.cgi?cmd=pa">Post Article</a></h3>
    </td></tr>
</table>
"""
```

Example 4-9. start.cgi (continued)

```
#
# MAIN
#

# content-type header
print "Content-type: text/html"
print
print HEADER

# retrieve query string
query = cgi.FieldStorage( )
if query.has_key("cmd"):
  cmd = query["cmd"].value

  # instantiate an ArticleManager
  am = ArticleManager( )

  # do something for each command

  # Command: viewAll - list all articles
  if cmd == "va":
    am.viewAll( )

  # Command: viewOne - view one article
  if cmd == "v1a":
    aname = query["af"].value
    am.viewOne(aname)

  # Command: postArticle - view the post-article page
  if cmd == "pa":
    am.postArticle( )

  # Command: postData - take an actual article post
  if cmd == "pd":
    print "<p>Thank you for your post!</p>"
    am.postArticleData(query)

else:
  # Invalid selection
  print "<p>Your selection was not recognized.</p>"

# close the HTML
print "</body></html>"
```

Take note of the initial #!/usr/local/bin/python expression. As this is a CGI script, the operating system needs a hint on how to run it. If it is compiled C code, it could be executed by the web server; however, if it is a script, it likely needs to be handed off to the services of a script interpreter. Such is the case with Python. Note that we did not use the *sh*-bang line #!/usr/bin/env python; that could open a security hole when used with CGI scripts. See the documentation of Python's cgi module for more information about CGI security issues and how to address them properly when using Python.

Going Beyond SAX and DOM

In this chapter, we discussed the DOM and how it differs from SAX. In the next chapter, we explore another method of extracting interesting portions of an XML document using a basic traversal language called XPath. Once you've learned a little about XPath, we move on in Chapter 6 to a transformation technology called XSLT.

## CHAPTER 5

Querying XML with XPath

The XML Path Language (XPath) is a language that allows you to easily perform searches against XML documents using a path-like string. XPath searches return individual nodes or collections of nodes based on expressions. XPath does not use XML syntax. In fact, it is not a procedural programming language in the normal sense; there is no concept of control flow. XPath expressions are usually single strings. XPath does, however, support some functional manipulation (usually found in programming languages) but one doesn't write XPath scripts or programs. Instead, one writes XPath expressions that are evaluated against XML documents and result in node lists being returned. In this chapter, we discuss the origin of XPath, as well as its syntax, capabilities, and how it is used from within Python.

XPath at a Glance

XPath 1.0 is a W3C recommendation available for your perusal from the W3C web site (*http://www.w3.org/TR/xpath*). XPath allows for the retrieval of portions of an XML document via XPath expressions. The specification defines a concrete syntax for expressions and offers a well-defined meaning for the expressions when interpreted. When an XPath expression is processed with a DOM, the nodes that match the expression are returned to the caller. XPath expressions target a specific node, or groups of nodes, within an XML document. The result is one of four types:

- A collection of nodes
- A Boolean value
- A floating-point number
- A string

In XPath, the term *context* refers to the location in the document where the XPath expression is being applied. You may start from the document element (the root element) or from any descendent element. XPath may inform you of the current context node (representing the current location in the document). A pair of integers may represent context position and context size. There may also be variable bindings in the context, available functions, and a namespace relevant to the current position.

Where Is XPath Used?

XPath is not stored within a particular type of document. Instead, XPath expressions are used primarily in XSLT (a transformation language used with XML), but can be used elsewhere as well. (XSLT is covered in more detail in Chapter 6.) In the case of APIs such as 4XPath, expressions can be used against a DOM to return results programmatically in your Python programs. Microsoft's MSXML3.0 (covered in Appendix E) processes XPath expressions as well.

Location Paths

The most commonly used type of XPath expression is the *location path*. A location path can be thought of as similar to a path for a file on a disk, but on steroids. Where a path for a filesystem contains only names of directories and a file, an XPath location path can specify much more. At each step along the path, it can perform selection based on complex tests of the nodes in a document, and the result may be several nodes. The tests, or predicates, for each step of the path can match based on element name, attribute presence or value, or textual content.

The full syntax of location paths is complex, but the specification is considerate enough to define abbreviated forms for the most commonly used tests; these are called *abbreviated location paths*. All of the location paths we describe in this chapter use the abbreviated syntax; for more information on the full syntax and selection capabilities of XPath, please refer to the specification.

Location paths are used within XSLT elements, but may also be used programmatically with an XPath API to return node sets from an XML document at runtime. The latter technique will come into greater focus as you read this chapter; the former is covered in Chapter 6.

An Example Document

Let's start with an example document that represents data records. The records are all fairly similar, but of course the field values are different in each one. This is typical of the type of documents you might mine with XPath. In Example 5-1, we apply XPath expressions against an XML document representing starships from some popular science-fiction television series.

Example 5-1. ships.xml

```
<?xml version="1.0" encoding="UTF-8"?>
<shiptypes
 name="United Federation of Planets">
  <ship name="USS Enterprise">
    <class>Sovereign</class>
    <captain>Jean-Luc Picard</captain>
```

Example 5-1. ships.xml (continued)

```
    <registry-code>NCC-1701-E</registry-code>
  </ship>
  <ship name="USS Voyager">
    <class>Intrepid</class>
    <captain>Kathryn Janeway</captain>
    <registry-code>NCC-74656</registry-code>
  </ship>
  <ship name="USS Enterprise">
    <class>Galaxy</class>
    <captain>Jean-Luc Picard</captain>
    <registry-code>NCC-1701-D</registry-code>
  </ship>
  <ship name="USS Enterprise">
    <class>Constitution</class>
    <captain>James T. Kirk</captain>
    <registry-code>NCC-1701</registry-code>
  </ship>
  <ship name="USS Sao Paulo">
    <class>Defiant</class>
    <captain>Benjamin L. Sisko</captain>
    <registry-code>NCC-75633</registry-code>
  </ship>
</shiptypes>
```

A Path Hosting Script

The *ships.xml* file provides a good stretch of XML data to write paths against. Now you can write a small program to apply path expressions to the document, and report on the nodes that are returned. In Example 5-2, we create a small script, *xp.py*, which invokes the xml.xpath.Evaluate function provided with 4Suite and more recent versions of PyXML.

Example 5-2. xp.py

```
"""
xp.py (requires xml doc on stdin)
"""
import sys

from xml.dom.ext.reader import PyExpat
from xml.xpath            import Evaluate

path0 = "ship/captain"  # all captain elements

reader = PyExpat.Reader()
dom = reader.fromStream(sys.stdin)

captain_elements = Evaluate(path0, dom.documentElement)
for element in captain_elements:
  print "Element: ", element
```

To run this program, you need to supply the previously created *ships.xml* from Example 5-1 as input:

```
$ python xp.py < ships.xml
```

In Example 5-2, the path `ship/captain` is used to extract all captain elements from the *ships.xml* document. The result is a node list containing the following:

```
<captain>Jean-Luc Picard</captain>
<captain>Kathryn Janeway</captain>
<captain>Jean-Luc Picard</captain>
<captain>James T. Kirk</captain>
<captain>Benjamin L. Sisko</captain>
```

Of course, this is not a complete or standalone document, but rather a node list. These nodes are processed by the remaining code in the program:

```
captain_elements = Evaluate(path0, dom.documentElement)
for element in captain_elements:
    print "Element: ", element
```

The path `ship/captain` is a relative location path, as it does not specify an exact location from the root of the document to the element, as does `/shiptypes/ship/captain`. The `ship/captain` expression returns `captain` elements that are children of a `ship` element, relative to the document node passed to `Evaluate`.

Getting Character Data

You will often want to target text beneath an element. For example, you may want to search just for the captain's name, rather than the element node. You could append the XPath text function to your expression:

```
path1 = "ship/captain/text( )"
```

This addition to the path expression selects all text nodes beneath the `captain` element. If you replace the original production lines with the following code:

```
captainnodes = Evaluate(path1, dom.documentElement)
for captainnode in captainnodes:
    print "Starfleet Captain: ", captainnode.nodeValue
```

you see the following result:

```
$ python xp.py < ships.xml
Starfleet Captain:  Jean-Luc Picard
Starfleet Captain:  Kathryn Janeway
Starfleet Captain:  Jean-Luc Picard
Starfleet Captain:  James T. Kirk
Starfleet Captain:  Benjamin L. Sisko
```

Specifying an Index

Often, when working with data, you become interested in the ordinal positions of elements within columns, rows, or arrays. XML is no different in this regard. XPath provides indexed elements with syntax similar to array indexes, but it is important to know that XPath indexes are one-based, while Python sequence indexes are zero-based. To target an element using an index, use brackets next to the element name:

```
path2 = "ship[2]/captain/text( )"
```

In this case, ship[2] indicates that the second ship element for each parent of any ship element should have the text nodes beneath its captain element selected. To see the output, change the processing code:

```
capnode = Evaluate(path2, dom.documentElement)
print "Captain of ship[2] is: ", capnode[0].nodeValue
```

Using path2, the output is:

```
$ python xp.py < ships.xml
Captain of ship[2] is:  Kathryn Janeway
```

It is important not to allow the visual similarity between ship[2] and Python sequence indexing to confuse you; they are very different. The notation is actually shorthand for ship[position( )=2], which indicates that the second ship child element of some other element will match. Consider the following XML fragment:

```
<fleet name="Atlantic">
  <ship id="id1"/>
  <lifeboat id="id2"/>
</fleet>
<fleet name="Pacific">
  <lifeboat id="id3"/>
  <ship id="id4"/>
  <ship id="id5"/>
</fleet>
```

The XPath expression ship[2] matches only the ship element with an id attribute of id5. This is not a trick, but it is an excellent reason to keep a copy of the XPath specification close by.

Testing Descendent Nodes

You may also want to query the text content beneath an element name. Say you have a structure of book chapters, each containing headings and paragraphs. You may want to search for text that appears underneath a certain heading. XPath provides a convenient way for you to check the character data of a text node that is the child of an element. If you are searching for a <ship> element with a <class> element beneath it that contains the word Intrepid, you could use the following path:

```
path3 = 'ship[class="Intrepid"]'
```

This expression selects ship elements that have a child class element with child character data of Intrepid. You can further explore the returned node list with a processing code:

```
shipnodes = Evaluate(path3, dom.documentElement)
for shipnode in shipnodes:
```

```
shipname = shipnode.getAttribute("name")
captain = Evaluate("captain/text()", shipnode)
print "------------ Intrepid Class Ship ------------"
print "Name: ", shipname
print "Captain: ", captain[0].nodeValue
```

In this code, we select all ship nodes that have a child `class` element indicating that they are `Intrepid` class ships. We can then reprocess this node to further select ship names and captains to generate the following output:

```
$ python xp.py < ships.xml
------------ Intrepid Class Ship ------------
Name:  USS Voyager
Captain:  Kathryn Janeway
```

Instead of just checking that a descendent element contains necessary information as in path3, you can continue building the path expression to grab something specific beneath the matching element:

```
path4 = 'ship[class="Constitution"]/@name'
```

In this path, you drill down further. First, a `ship` element is selected only if its child `class` element contains the character data `Constitution`. This path is further extended when we select the `name` attribute of the ship element that contains the specific child character data (the `@` symbol is used to indicate that we're interested in an attribute rather than a child element). Again, we change the processing code a little to use the new node list:

```
ship = Evaluate(path4, dom.documentElement)
print "Name of Constitution Class Ship: ", ship[0].nodeValue
```

The output follows:

```
$ python xp.py < ships.xml
Name of Constitution Class Ship:  USS Enterprise
```

Testing Attributes

Of course, evaluating XML attributes and their contents involves a slightly different process than evaluating element names and text node character data. In XPath, the `@` character is used to indicate an attribute. Brackets are also used to surround the node when it is being tested against character data. In order to test the character contents of an attribute, use a path such as the following:

```
path5 = 'ship[@name="USS Enterprise"]'
```

This expression selects all ship elements that have a name attribute containing the word *Enterprise*. In your *ships.xml* file, there are three starships named Enterprise, each with slightly different registry codes. You can mine the node list for more information:

```
ships = Evaluate(path5, dom.documentElement)
for shipnode in ships:
  registry = Evaluate("registry-code/text()", shipnode)
```

```
captain = Evaluate("captain/text( )", shipnode)
print "Found Enterprise with registry: ", registry[0].nodeValue
print "Captain: ", captain[0].nodeValue
```

These subsequent expressions are relative paths that select `captain` and `registry-code` text from the current element with each hop through the node list. This time using the preceding code, the output appears as:

```
$ python xp.py < ships.xml
Found Enterprise with registry:  NCC-1701-E
Captain:  Jean-Luc Picard
Found Enterprise with registry:  NCC-1701-D
Captain:  Jean-Luc Picard
Found Enterprise with registry:  NCC-1701
Captain:  James T. Kirk
```

Selecting Elements

As with any ordered data set, you are usually interested in pulling one specific type of information out from the entire document. You may only be interested in the names of employees in a human resources database. Or you may have heavily nested data that you want to make sure you pull out with each occurrence of a given data type, regardless of its position in the document. With XPath, you can use the path expression // to indicate that all matching elements beneath the root should be selected:

```
path6 = "/shiptypes//captain"
```

This expression selects all captain elements beneath the route, regardless of where they appear. Since you are working with elements, obtaining character data requires some of the work shown earlier, or a traversal of the node structure:

```
captains = Evaluate(path6, dom.documentElement)
for captain in captains:
    print "Captain: ", captain.firstChild.nodeValue
```

Running path6 generates the following output:

```
$ python xp.py < ships.xml
Captain:  Jean-Luc Picard
Captain:  Kathryn Janeway
Captain:  Jean-Luc Picard
Captain:  James T. Kirk
Captain:  Benjamin L. Sisko
```

Additional Operators

If you are familiar with filesystem paths on Windows or Unix, you may have seen the . and .. operators. The . operator indicates the current directory (or current element in XPath) while .. refers to the parent directory (or parent element in XPath). Using *ships.xml*, shown in Example 5-1, we can search for a specific ship's name and then reference the parent element to see which organization the ship belongs to.

```
path7 = "ship[@name='USS Voyager']/../@name"
```

This expression searches for a ship element that has a name attribute of "USS Voyager." The path then continues to select the name attribute of this ship element's parent. In *ships.xml*, this is the name attribute of the shiptypes element. To generate output, change your processing code in *xp.py*:

```
org = Evaluate(path7, dom.documentElement)
print "USS Voyager is owned by", org[0].nodeValue
```

This time *xp.py* generates output attributing the Voyager to the Federation of Planets:

```
$ python xp.py < ships.xml
USS Voyager is owned by United Federation of Planets
```

XPath Arithmetic Operators

In addition to selecting elements by location paths, XPath also provides capability for data manipulation. The numerical parts of an XML document can be added, divided, subtracted, and multiplied. Likewise, strings can be compared for equality.

XPath provides arithmetic operators for use within XPath expressions. This capability comes in very handy in XSL transformations that involve totaling an item list or applying discounts to product prices for display in HTML. The operators available in XPath are +, -, *, div, and mod (addition, subtraction, multiplication, division, and modulus, respectively.) There are also functions such as sum that allow you to total sets of numbers and perform other tasks. We cover functions in the next section.

Imagine that you have an XML file containing a list of products, and you want to display these products in another application (such as your web site) but need to apply a 20% discount to all retail prices. You can use the XPath arithmetic operators to solve this problem. Let's turn to the source XML document (*products.xml*) shown in Example 5-3.

Example 5-3. products.xml

```
<?xml version="1.0" encoding="UTF-8"?>
<products>
        <item name="bowl" price="19.95"/>
        <item name="spatula" price="4.95"/>
        <item name="power mixer" price="149.95"/>
        <item name="chef hat" price="39.95"/>
</products>
```

To apply a blanket 20% discount to all products, you can use XPath from within an XSLT document. The XSLT shown in Example 5-4 (*products.xsl*) does the trick.

Example 5-4. products.xsl

```
<?xml version="1.0" encoding="iso-8859-1"?>
<xsl:stylesheet version="1.0"
 xmlns:xsl="http://www.w3.org/1999/XSL/Transform">
```

Example 5-4. products.xsl (continued)

```
<xsl:template match="/">
  <html>
    <body>
      <xsl:apply-templates/>
    </body>
  </html>
</xsl:template>

<xsl:template match="item">
  <p><b>Item:</b> <xsl:value-of select="@name"/>
  Orig. Price: <xsl:value-of select="@price"/>, Our Price:
  <xsl:value-of select="@price * 0.8"/>
  </p>
</xsl:template>

</xsl:stylesheet>
```

The XPath numerical expressions are in the `xsl:value-of` elements. The discount is achieved by multiplying the value of the price attribute by `0.8`. You can run the transformation using the *4xslt* tool illustrated in the previous chapter:

```
$ 4xslt.bat products.xml products.xsl
<html>
  <body>
    <p>
      <b>Item: </b>bowl
  Orig. Price: 19.95, Our Price: 15.96</p>
    <p>
      <b>Item: </b>spatula
  Orig. Price: 4.95, Our Price: 3.96</p>
    <p>
      <b>Item: </b>power mixer
  Orig. Price: 149.95, Our Price: 119.96</p>
    <p>
      <b>Item: </b>chef hat
  Orig. Price: 39.95, Our Price: 31.96</p>
    </body>
  </html>
```

The `div` and `mod` operators work as the others do. For example, `@price div 2` divides all prices designated by 2.

XPath Functions

XPath provides numerous functions for working with numbers and strings, and allows you to complete transformations and mine XML data without having to constantly bridge other APIs or technologies to do simple string and arithmetic operations. Adding, simple division, multiplication, and string searching are available as built-in functions of XPath.

Working with Numbers

Several XPath functions are available to you. In Example 5-4, multiplication is used to apply a 20% discount to products. If you need to total a list of products, you can use the sum function, working with the same products data again:

```
<?xml version="1.0" encoding="UTF-8"?>
<products>
        <item name="bowl" price="19.95"/>
        <item name="spatula" price="4.95"/>
        <item name="power mixer" price="149.95"/>
        <item name="chef hat" price="39.95"/>
</products>
```

This time, in Example 5-5, you can use a single XPath expression to generate a total. The expression sum(//@price) returns the sum of the values of all price elements in the products document. Now go back and modify the stylesheet you created to discount the products, but this time add in an xsl:value-of element to generate a total.

Example 5-5. products.xsl

```
<?xml version="1.0" encoding="iso-8859-1"?>
<xsl:stylesheet version="1.0"
                xmlns:xsl="http://www.w3.org/1999/XSL/Transform">
<xsl:template match="/">
  <html>
    <body>
      <table>
        <xsl:apply-templates/>
      </table>
      <p>Your Total:
        <xsl:value-of select="sum(//@price)"/>
      </p>
    </body>
  </html>
</xsl:template>

<xsl:template match="item">
  <tr><td><b>Item: </b><xsl:value-of select="@name"/></td>
      <td><b>Price: </b><xsl:value-of select="@price"/></td>
  </tr>
</xsl:template>

</xsl:stylesheet>
```

Figure 5-1 shows the result of the transformation (the HTML) in a browser.

In addition to sum, several other functions exist for working with numbers. The floor function returns the largest integer that is not greater than the argument. In other words, floor(3.4) returns 3. The ceiling function, floor's counterpart, returns the smallest integer that is greater than the argument, e.g., ceiling(3.4) returns 4. The round function does exactly what you think it should: round your decimal-ridden

---

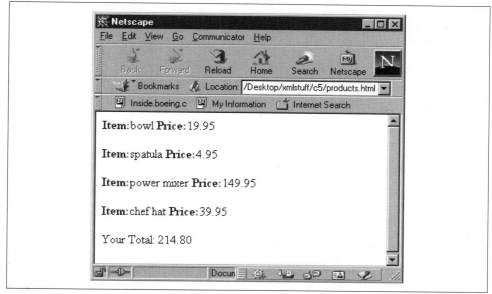

Figure 5-1. Using the sum( ) XPath function

number to its closest integer. For example, round(3.4) returns 3, while round(3.8) returns 4.

Working with Strings

In addition to functions for numbers, XPath supports functions for manipulating text. Most of these are valuable when doing conditional testing. Earlier you checked character data of child attributes with syntax such as:

```
ship[class="Intrepid"]
```

This expression returns any ship element with a class element beneath it containing the character data *Intrepid*. This is a fine approach for exact comparisons, but sometimes you'll want finer control.

For example, the starts-with function takes two arguments. The first argument is what you're looking for: the letters the string may start with. The second argument is the node to evaluate. The function returns true or false. For example, to get a true or false return (in XSL) on whether a ship element has a registry code that starts with NCC, you can try the following expression:

```
<xsl:value-of select="starts-with('NCC', ./registry-code/text())"/>
```

This expression returns true for every ship in the *ships.xml* file. This type of Boolean return may be of most benefit in XSLT, where you can use its if-then-else language features for conditional processing. A variation on this theme is the contains function, which returns true if the second argument contains the first argument.

If you know you have the string you want and are looking to slice and dice it, the substring and string-length functions can help you out. The substring function takes up to three arguments. The first argument is the string to manipulate; the second argument is the starting index within the string; the third argument is the ending index. If the third argument is omitted, it's assumed to be the end of the string. The string-length function is straightforward, and returns the total length of the string as a number.

The translate function takes a string parameter, as well as a list of characters to replace and a list of corresponding replacement characters. Each character in the second argument is replaced by the corresponding character in the same position in the third argument. For example, the expression translate("Wee Willy Winky", "eily", "oaps") returns the string Woo Wapps Wanks. The concat function returns the concatenation of its two arguments.

Working with Nodes

Some functions in XPath are designed to work with elements and element traversal itself. These functions supply information related to XPath's current position, and other positional type of information such as first matching element and last matching element. Node functions are fairly straightforward.

The position function returns a number equal to the context position from the expression evaluation context. For example, to create a numbered list for the ships of *ships.xml*, you could use the position function as shown in the following stylesheet:

```
<?xml version="1.0" encoding="iso-8859-1"?>
<xsl:stylesheet version="1.0"
 xmlns:xsl="http://www.w3.org/1999/XSL/Transform">
  <xsl:template match="shiptypes">
    <html>
      <body>
        <xsl:apply-templates select="ship"/>
      </body>
    </html>
  </xsl:template>
  <xsl:template match="ship">
    <p>
      <xsl:value-of select="position()"/>.
      <xsl:value-of select="@name"/>
    </p>
  </xsl:template>
</xsl:stylesheet>
```

This code generates the following HTML output:

```
<html>
  <body>
    <p>1.
      USS Enterprise</p>
```

```
    <p>2.
      USS Voyager</p>
    <p>3.
      USS Enterprise</p>
    <p>4.
      USS Enterprise</p>
    <p>5.
      USS Sao Paulo</p>
  </body>
</html>
```

The count function returns the number of nodes in the node set matching the argument. In other words, count(//@name) returns the total number of name attributes within a document. The last function returns a number equal to the context size (the number of nodes) in the current expression.

The id function returns a node by specific id. If you create an element <name id="a345">Chris Jones</name> and then use id('a345') in your expression, this node is returned. The localname and name functions return both the local name and the qualified name of the node in the current node set that appears first in document order.

Compiling XPath Expressions

In this chapter, we use the Evaluate function from the 4XPath API to apply XPath expressions against node sets. For programmatic use of XPath within Python, the 4XPath API is readily available and offers considerable power.

Most of the XPath API is geared towards supporting XPath expressions, as XPath is a standard. But for the programmer embedding XPath processing functionality into their applications, there is some optimization found in 4XPath.

The Compile and Context functions aid the developer to create compiled XPath expressions for repeated use against multiple documents. For example, if you are accepting large numbers of XML documents from customers or suppliers, you may want to apply an XPath expression to each one (as it arrives) to figure out what to do with it, or where to route it within your organization. Having your XPath expression readily compiled and applied against each unique document adds speed to your application, as you've done away with the need to parse the XPath expression.

The Compile function returns an expression object that supports an evaluate method similar to the Evaluate function used thus far in this chapter. However, the method expects a Context object, not a node. The task of compiling an expression, and then using the compiled version, is fairly simple:

```
expression = Compile("ship/@name")
context = Context(dom.documentElement)
nodes = expression.evaluate(context)
```

The first step is to generate an expression; the second step is to generate context for the document or node set you're working with. You can run the expression by calling the evaluate method of the compiled expression object, as demonstrated in Example 5-6 (which makes use of the *ships.xml* file).

Example 5-6. xp.py

```
#!/usr/local/bin/python

import sys

from xml.dom.ext.reader import PyExpat
from xml.xpath          import Compile
from xml.xpath.Context  import Context

reader = PyExpat.Reader()
dom = reader.fromStream(sys.stdin)

expression = Compile("ship/@name")
context = Context(dom.documentElement)
nodes = expression.evaluate(context)

print "Nodes: ", nodes
```

When executed from the command line with *ships.xml* as input, the program generates the following output:

```
$ python compx.py < ships.xml
Nodes:  [<Attribute Node at a1cd9c: Name="name", Value="USS Enterprise">,
<Attribute Node at a2305c: Name="name", Value="USS Voyager">,
<Attribute Node at a2b7fc: Name="name", Value="USS Enterprise">,
<Attribute Node at a33fdc: Name="name", Value="USS Enterprise">,
<Attribute Node at a3a30c: Name="name", Value="USS Sao Paulo">]
```

Your Python and XML toolkit is almost complete; we look at one more core technology in the next chapter. After that, we delve into topics that deal with actually integrating XML with your existing systems and building new systems using Python and XML.

## CHAPTER 6

Transforming XML with XSLT

We've covered using SAX to capture XML parsing events and output corresponding HTML for display in a web browser. XML's power lies in its ability to represent data for data's sake. XML is not concerned with displays such as web pages, handheld devices, PostScript files, etc. Instead, XML is concerned only with the structure of your information. For this reason, we frequently parse XML and convert it to another format for viewing, such as HTML.

In this chapter, we discuss Extensible Stylesheet Language Transformations (XSLT). One of the simplest things that XSLT does is transform your XML documents into HTML documents for consumption by browsers. We go over how to construct an XSLT stylesheet that performs the same transformation for you that SAX did earlier, but with considerably less effort. Keep in mind, however, that XSLT is more powerful than mere HTML production as it transforms one XML document written for a specific DTD or dialect into another dialect. These XML to XML transformations can be very powerful when exchanging business documents between Internet domains that use different dialects. Dialects and validation are covered in Chapter 7.

The XSLT Specification

The XSLT specification is available from the World Wide Web Consortium web site at *http://www.w3.org/TR/xslt.html*. Reading the specification is a perfect cure for insomnia, so to keep you awake, I summarize key parts of XSLT here as they relate to Python.

In any working XSLT setup, three distinct files exist and at least one piece of software is utilized. The first is the source XML file, which is your original document. The next is the XSL stylesheet, which represents the rules of the transformation and is itself an XML-compliant document. The third and final document is the result of the transformation. This is most likely either HTML or XML. The essential software used to create the transformation is the XSLT processor. This software loads the original XML document, applies the transformation rules, and spits out the result of the transformation. Figure 6-1 shows an example of this arrangement.

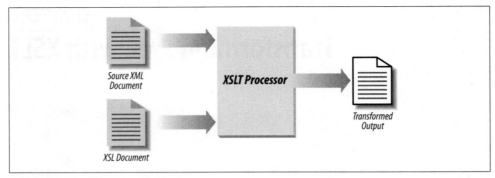

Figure 6-1. The XSLT transformation process

The XSLT language is an XML-based language. It is defined as a set of elements and attributes with carefully defined semantics. XSLT is very straightforward, as you'll discover.

XSLT Processors

There are a variety of XSLT processors available on the market, both free and commercial. The power of XSLT is in the transformations that the language allows, but the actual work is completed by the processor. Depending on your environment, you may choose a processor based on speed or on accessibility from a particular platform such as Python. Alternatively, you may choose a processor that you can drive programmatically.

The XSLT processor's job is to take an XSL stylesheet and perform its transformation rules against an existing XML document to produce a new transformed document. The W3C states that XSLT is for transforming XML to XML, which is true, but it can be used to generate HTML or other formats as well. It is frequently used to transform XML to HTML or XHTML for viewing in a web browser.

XSLT is a language unto itself, and has nothing in particular to do with Python. As such, you can convert documents for use in your Python programs with any XSLT processor. However, if you are hoping to embed XSLT functionality within your Python programs, you need a processor accessible from Python either natively (such as 4XSLT) or by a bridge mechanism (such as using MSXML3.0 from Python, as covered in Appendix E).

For Python, the 4XSLT package is an open source XSLT processor that can be driven from the command line as well as embedded in your Python programs—it is primarily implemented in Python, but includes some modules written in C for improved performance. 4XSLT is available from Fourthought, Inc. as part of the 4Suite package (see *http://www.4suite.org/*).

Other XSLT processors exist for other languages and platforms, but can still batch process transformations for use in your Python applications. Microsoft's Internet

Explorer has an XSLT processor embedded within it, and can transform an XML document into HTML in the client's browser (though versions prior to 6.0 are horribly noncompliant). SAXON is a collection of XML tools, including a Java-based XSLT processor capable of running in any Java virtual machine. Sablotron is a fast C++ XSLT processor. The W3C's XSLT site (*http://www.w3.org/Style/XSL/*) contains numerous links to XSLT processing software.

For the remainder of this chapter, we use the 4XSLT processor as it's completely Python-based, and its functionality is accessible at runtime from your Python applications.

Defining Stylesheets

If you are familiar with the Cascading Style Sheets (CSS) specification often used on the Web, you are probably aware that CSS stylesheets can be stored in a separate file, or embedded as a special element within an HTML document. Also, specific styling information can be attached to individual attributes within the document. In this section, we examine the corresponding approaches to using XSLT.

Each of the three ways of using CSS have an analogous technique using XSLT, but the XSLT stylesheets are substantially more powerful. While this discussion refers to some specific XSLT elements and shows several in the examples, it does not expect that you know anything about them. These elements are described in more detail later in this chapter; this section simply introduces you to the ways stylesheets can be written and how that relates to the documents being processed.

Simplified Stylesheets

Simplified stylesheets are more like using the STYLE attribute in HTML documents than anything else, but the similarity is minimal. This approach is somewhat less powerful than using embedded or standalone stylesheets; the `xsl:stylesheet` element is not allowed since the entire stylesheet is interpreted as the body of an `xsl:template` element. Many features of XSLT require using additional "top-level" elements (peers of the `xsl:template` element), so they are not allowed in this context. This kind of stylesheet is more difficult to use when the basic structure of the source document needs to be preserved, but is perfectly able to make queries about the structure and content of the source document. Simplified stylesheets are most often applied when the output documents are very regular and only need to extract very specific portions of the input document.

Since simplified stylesheets are also about the easiest to start with when learning XSLT, let's take a look at one. In the previous chapter, we use a list of spaceships from a group of well-known television shows to provide input data (see Example 5-1); we use that input here as well. Instead of using the DOM and XPath to retrieve a list of nodes, we use XSLT to create a list of spaceships sorted by their registry numbers, nicely presented as an HTML table. Example 6-1 shows the stylesheet. Notice the root element of the stylesheet document declares the namespace for XSLT and specifies the XSLT version that is being used; these are required for the use of simplified stylesheets.

Example 6-1. ships-template.html

```
<html xmlns:xsl="http://www.w3.org/1999/XSL/Transform"
      xsl:version="1.0">
  <head>
    <title>Ships of the
           <xsl:value-of select="/shiptypes/@name" /></title>
  </head>
  <body>
    <table border="1">
      <tr><th>Ship</th>
          <th>Class</th>
          <th>Registration</th>
          <th>Captain</th>
        </tr>
      <xsl:for-each select="/shiptypes/ship">
        <xsl:sort select="registry-code" />
        <tr><td><xsl:value-of select="@name" /></td>
            <td><xsl:value-of select="class" /></td>
            <td><xsl:value-of select="registry-code" /></td>
            <td><xsl:value-of select="captain" /></td>
          </tr>
      </xsl:for-each>
    </table>
  </body>
</html>
```

The result of processing the *ships.xml* file from Example 5-1 with the stylesheet *ships-template.html* in Example 6-1 is given in *ships.html*, shown in Example 6-2. The transformation was performed using 4XSLT.

Example 6-2. ships.html

```
<html>
  <head>
    <meta http-equiv='Content-Type' content='text/html; charset=iso-8859-1'>
    <title>Ships of the
           United Federation of Planets</title>
  </head>
  <body>
    <table border="1">
      <tr>
        <th>Ship</th>
        <th>Class</th>
        <th>Registration</th>
        <th>Captain</th>
      </tr>
      <tr>
```

Example 6-2. ships.html (continued)

```
      <td>USS Enterprise</td>
      <td>Constitution</td>
      <td>NCC-1701</td>
      <td>James T. Kirk</td>
    </tr>
    <tr>
      <td>USS Enterprise</td>
      <td>Galaxy</td>
      <td>NCC-1701-D</td>
      <td>Jean-Luc Picard</td>
    </tr>
    <tr>
      <td>USS Enterprise</td>
      <td>Sovereign</td>
      <td>NCC-1701-E</td>
      <td>Jean-Luc Picard</td>
    </tr>
    <tr>
      <td>USS Voyager</td>
      <td>Intrepid</td>
      <td>NCC-74656</td>
      <td>Kathryn Janeway</td>
    </tr>
    <tr>
      <td>USS Sao Paulo</td>
      <td>Defiant</td>
      <td>NCC-75633</td>
      <td>Benjamin L. Sisko</td>
    </tr>
  </table>
 </body>
</html>
```

Note that the transformation added a meta element near the top of the generated HTML, and that the indentation and whitespace inside the replacement for the xsl: for-each element has been adjusted somewhat. Figure 6-2 shows what the resulting HTML document looks like in a web browser.

Standalone Stylesheets

Stylesheets stored in separate files are perhaps the most commonly used form of stylesheets for both CSS and XSLT. The root element of the stylesheet must be an xsl:stylesheet or xsl:transform element. This is what we use for most of the examples in this book. Standalone stylesheets offer more power and flexibility than simplified stylesheets, and lend themselves to better modularization, allowing use of a powerful import mechanism as well as strong pattern matching abilities.

Let's look at the previous example expressed as a standalone stylesheet. We could use a trivial wrapper around the template document to create a stylesheet that is technically correct, but let's go ahead and change it to reflect a more typical way of

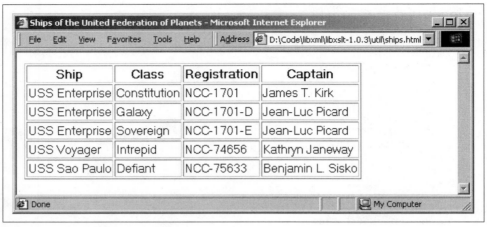

Figure 6-2. ships.html in a browser

structuring a stylesheet. This particular version no longer sorts the table of ships, but maintains their order from the original document. This is a common way of structuring a stylesheet for a document-oriented application. Our new stylesheet is shown in Example 6-3. Notice that the XSLT namespace is declared here as well, along with the version attribute, but we need not include the namespace prefix when the attribute is attached to an xsl:stylesheet element.

Example 6-3. ships.xsl

```
<xsl:stylesheet xmlns:xsl="http://www.w3.org/1999/XSL/Transform"
                version="1.0">

<xsl:template match="/">
<html>
  <head>
    <title>Ships of the
           <xsl:apply-templates mode="head" /></title>
  </head>
  <body>
    <xsl:apply-templates />
  </body>
</html>
</xsl:template>

<xsl:template match="shiptypes" mode="head">
<xsl:value-of select="@name" />
</xsl:template>

<xsl:template match="shiptypes">
<table border="1">
  <tr><th>Ship</th>
      <th>Class</th>
      <th>Registration</th>
```

Example 6-3. ships.xsl (continued)

```
      <th>Captain</th>
    </tr>
  <xsl:apply-templates />
</table>
</xsl:template>

<xsl:template match="ship">
  <tr><td><xsl:value-of select="@name" /></td>
      <td><xsl:value-of select="class" /></td>
      <td><xsl:value-of select="registry-code" /></td>
      <td><xsl:value-of select="captain" /></td>
    </tr>
</xsl:template>

</xsl:stylesheet>
```

This version is structured as a set of templates that match particular constructs in the input document; the matched constructs are specified by the match attribute of the xsl:template elements. The XSLT constructs used in this stylesheet are explained in detail later in this chapter. Example 6-4 shows the result of transforming *ships.xml* (see Example 5-1) using *ships.xsl* (see Example 6-3).

Example 6-4. ships2.html

```
<html>
  <head>
    <meta http-equiv='Content-Type' content='text/html; charset=iso-8859-1'>
    <title>Ships of the
           United Federation of Planets</title>
  </head>
  <body>
    <table border="1">
      <tr>
        <th>Ship</th>
        <th>Class</th>
        <th>Registration</th>
        <th>Captain</th>
      </tr>
      <tr>
        <td>USS Enterprise</td>
        <td>Sovereign</td>
        <td>NCC-1701-E</td>
        <td>Jean-Luc Picard</td>
      </tr>
      <tr>
        <td>USS Voyager</td>
        <td>Intrepid</td>
        <td>NCC-74656</td>
        <td>Kathryn Janeway</td>
      </tr>
      <tr>
```

Example 6-4. ships2.html (continued)

```
      <td>USS Enterprise</td>
      <td>Galaxy</td>
      <td>NCC-1701-D</td>
      <td>Jean-Luc Picard</td>
    </tr>
    <tr>
      <td>USS Enterprise</td>
      <td>Constitution</td>
      <td>NCC-1701</td>
      <td>James T. Kirk</td>
    </tr>
    <tr>
      <td>USS Sao Paulo</td>
      <td>Defiant</td>
      <td>NCC-75633</td>
      <td>Benjamin L. Sisko</td>
    </tr>
  </table>
  </body>
</html>
```

The only difference between this output and Example 6-2 is that the table is not sorted in this version.

Embedded Stylesheets

XSLT stylesheets can be embedded within other documents in much the same way that CSS stylesheets can be embedded in an HTML document. When embedding an XSLT stylesheet, it is typically embedded in the document to which it applies. The embedded element must be the xsl:stylesheet (or xsl:transform) element. This usage pattern is not commonly used since it doesn't allow the stylesheet to be re-used as easily with other documents, and few XSLT processors support embedded stylesheets. Given the lack of broad tool support for embedded stylesheets, we won't bother showing any examples.

Using XSLT from the Command Line

Before we learn how to embed XSLT transformations in Python programs, we need to concentrate on learning more about XSLT itself. As we're learning, it will generally be easier to run our transformations from the command line than from a Python script. Many of the processors provide a command-line tool for performing transformations. We use the 4XSLT package provided as part of 4Suite; if you choose to use a different tool, please consult its documentation to determine how to use it.

4XSLT includes a script that performs transformations from the command line. On Windows, the *4xslt.bat* script is installed in the *Scripts* directory of your Python installation by the 4Suite installer. To make the script more easily usable, either add the *Scripts* directory to your PATH environment variable or copy the *4xslt.bat* file to a directory that is already included in the PATH.

The basic operation of *4xslt* simply requires two parameters: the XML document to transform, and the stylesheet to apply. This example was used to apply the stylesheet from Example 6-3 to produce the output shown in Example 6-4:

```
C:\my-dir> 4xslt ships.xml ships.xsl > ships2.html
```

Output redirection is used to save the result of the transformation to a file.

4XSLT and the *4xslt* script support the use of both simplified and standalone stylesheets. Embedded stylesheets are not supported.

XSLT Elements

Much of XSLT's functionality is exercised in the form of elements that perform functions and tasks. In fact, the whole language is XML-based and describing its features is already the subject of several books. This section presents some of the XSLT elements and fundamentals so you can begin using it in your daily work.

The Stylesheet Element

The xsl:stylesheet element is always the root element of standalone stylesheets, and is also used for embedded stylesheets. The stylesheet element contains some optional and mandatory attributes that provide more details about the stylesheet to the XSLT processor. The specification defines a second root element in the XSLT namespace, called xsl:transform. This element is identical to xsl:stylesheet in every way but name, and can be used in place of xsl:stylesheet with no change in meaning.

The id attribute is optional. However, an identifier would certainly come in handy if this stylesheet were part of a larger XML document (as would be the case for an embedded stylesheet). The XML specification states that any attribute of type ID (not necessarily named id, but of the *data type* ID declared in the DTD) must be unique within any XML document. Use of an ID attribute on a stylesheet is powerful if you are dynamically generating several stylesheets collected together in a larger composite document.

The version attribute is required as it indicates which version of XSLT is being used. All xsl:stylesheet elements must have the version attribute. The root element of simplified stylesheets must also have a version attribute explicitly associated with the XSLT namespace, as shown in Example 6-1.

It is strongly recommended that you give a namespace prefix to the stylesheet elements to distinguish it from other elements that are part of the transformation or part of a larger document that contains the stylesheet. The URI of the namespace must be the W3C URI *http://www.w3.org/1999/XSL/Transform*.

A typical stylesheet element may start like this:

```
<xsl:stylesheet
  xmlns:xsl="http://www.w3.org/1999/XSL/Transform"
                  version="1.0">
```

In this example, the namespace and the version have been presented, but no `id` attribute is present.

Since XSLT can generate output, which is XML, HTML, or any other format, it is important to specify which form the output should take. This is done using the `xsl:output` element, which requires a single attribute:

```
<xsl:output method="xml"/>
```

The value of the `method` attribute can be `xml`, `html`, or `text`. The meaning of each of these values is roughly what you would expect. If the output should be XHTML, use the `xml` value. For all formats that are not XML or HTML, the `text` method allows control over each byte of the output, but the intended use is to generate text-based formats. If you need to generate formats such as RTF or any of the TeX-based languages, `text` is the right value to use. Many applications that require other formats can be satisfied by generating an XSL-FO document and then processing it using a processor that has a lot of information about details of the target format.

If the stylesheet does not contain an `xsl:output` element, or if the `method` attribute is not specified, the output is XML.

Creating a Template Element

The `xsl:template` element is regularly used to accomplish a great deal of work in the transformation process. This element is an XSLT instruction, and usually specifies a pattern for its invocation or defines a name so that it can be called by other parts of the XSL document. The body of the `xsl:template` element contains the output markup for when the template is either called or matched by the XSLT processor.

The attributes of the template element define optionally its `name` and matching rule (`match`). In addition to these attributes, `mode` and `priority` are available as well. The `mode` is used to indicate a namespace prefix to be considered by the XSLT processor when the `xsl:apply-templates` instruction (described in the next section) is used with a specific mode. The `priority` attribute is used to define a priority when the template is part of a collection of template elements that match the same pattern. In other words, when the XSLT processor has multiple templates to choose from, it defers to `priority` if specified.

The most important attribute here is `match`. The `match` attribute contains an XPath expression used to determine when the processor has hit the target element in the source XML document. For example, in the earlier address record, rather than parsing the document with SAX waiting for your event, use the following `match` attribute and XPath syntax to hit the first address line:

```
<xsl:template match="/addr-record/address1">
```

This expression starts with the root element `addr-record` and then further selects its child `address1`. To display the contents of this field, you could use the same expression in your `select` attribute (covered a little later in this chapter).

Earlier we created a template element to match an entire XML document and produce a complete HTML document. You can also use the template elements to match any element within the XML source document:

```
<xsl:template match="/addr-record/address1">
<html>
<head>
        <title>Transformed Address Record</title>
</head>
<body>
        <p>We have matched /addr-record/address1</p>
        <p><xsl:value-of select="/addr-record/address1"/></p>
</body>
</html>
</xsl:template>
```

In this example, you are matching an element `address1` that is a child of the root `addr-record` element and then processing several rules and content. When the template is instantiated by the XSLT processor, it outputs the child elements of the template (in this case HTML) and processes any other XSLT elements contained therein. The result is the HTML written to standard output by the XSLT processor. If you run this modified version of the stylesheet against the XML document, you get the HTML expected in the previous code listing, but you also get the rest of the XML document's character data trailing the HTML. This is because no instructions were given for the rest of the character data, so it is simply dumped out. The `xsl:apply-templates` element allows you to nest rules within each other to produce deeply nested documents that are transformed as expected.

Applying Templates

When you have a document that contains nested structures, the `apply-templates` element is used to recursively apply transformation rules throughout the document. An easy example that demonstrates the concept of nested structures is formatted text, wherein paragraphs may contain sentences with bold typeface of multiple colors, code examples, or other formatting structures that may appear nested within themselves.

Another deeply nested structure is a filesystem. A directory can contain any number of files and subdirectories. Each subdirectory follows the same content rule as any other and may contain any number of files and subdirectories. The resultant tree can become quite complex.

When dealing with XML documents containing nested structures, it may be desirable to establish a set of rules (templates) for specific tags, but allow those tags and rules to be nested inside each other. You can use the `apply-templates` elements to accomplish this. Consider the following XML:

```
<deep-nest>
        <title>Sample Text</title>
        <big>T</big>his is an example of
        <red>Fancy Text</red> that comes in
        <blue>m<big>u</big></blue><green>l<big>
        t</big></green><blue>i<big>p</big>
        </blue><green>l<big>e</big></green>
        colors.  Many of <bold>these</bold>
        elements are <big><green>N</green>
        <blue>E</blue><green>S</green><blue>T</blue>
        <green>E</green><blue>D</blue></big> within
        each other.
</deep-nest>
```

This XML fragment contains elements with other elements within them. There is no set order as to which tags can be embedded within others, as there is not a specified DTD. To account for this nesting in your template elements, use the `xsl:apply-templates` instruction. For example, the `big` element can occur within a color element, a bold element, or a `title` element. Therefore, its `template` element is:

```
<xsl:template match="big">
        <font size="5"><xsl:apply-templates/></font>
</xsl:template>
```

Wherever there is a `big` element, it is replaced with the `font` tag. Furthermore, any content within the big tag is processed against any other template patterns since the `xsl:apply-templates` instruction is specified. Now let's take a look at the whole stylesheet used to process the XML:

```
<?xml version="1.0" encoding="iso-8859-1"?>
<xsl:stylesheet version="1.0"
 xmlns:xsl="http://www.w3.org/1999/XSL/Transform">
<xsl:output method="html"/>
<xsl:template match="deep-nest">
        <html><body><xsl:apply-templates/></body></html>
</xsl:template>

<xsl:template match="title">
        <h1><xsl:apply-templates/></h1>
</xsl:template>

<xsl:template match="big">
        <font size="5"><xsl:apply-templates/></font>
</xsl:template>

<xsl:template match="red">
        <font size="3" color="#FF0000"><u>
        <xsl:apply-templates/></u></font>
</xsl:template>
```

```
<xsl:template match="blue">
        <font color="#0000FF"><xsl:apply-templates/></font>
</xsl:template>

<xsl:template match="green">
        <font color="#00FF00"><b><xsl:apply-templates/></b></font>
</xsl:template>

<xsl:template match="bold">
        <b><i><xsl:apply-templates/></i></b>
</xsl:template>

</xsl:stylesheet>
```

The key to this stylesheet is well-formedness. Every XML element in the source document is accounted for in the stylesheet, and each defers to further processing by placing xsl:apply-templates square in the middle. If you run the XML and stylesheet through your XSLT processor, you get the following HTML:

```
<html>
  <body>
    <h1>Sample Text</h1>
    <font size='5'>T</font>his is an example of
        <font color='#FF0000' size='3'>
      <u>Fancy Text</u>
    </font> that comes in
        <font color='#0000FF'>m<font size='5'>u</font>
    </font>
    <font color='#00FF00'>
      <b>l<font size='5'>
        t</font></b>
    </font>
    <font color='#0000FF'>i<font size='5'>p</font>
    </font>
    <font color='#00FF00'>
      <b>l<font size='5'>e</font></b>
    </font>
        colors. Many of <b><i>these</i></b>
        elements are <font size='5'>
      <font color='#00FF00'>
        <b>N</b>
      </font>
      <font color='#0000FF'>E</font>
      <font color='#00FF00'>
        <b>S</b>
      </font>
      <font color='#0000FF'>T</font>
      <font color='#00FF00'>
        <b>E</b>
      </font>
      <font color='#0000FF'>D</font>
    </font> within
        each other.
  </body>
</html>
```

Getting the Value of a Node

The xsl:value-of element generates output from an expression. It has two possible attributes: select and disable-output-escaping. The select attribute is mandatory as it's used to generate the replacement content. The select attribute takes an XPath expression. Given the XML <a><c id="c">content</c></a>, the following expression produces the word "content."

```
<xsl:value-of select="/a/b/c"/>
```

To retrieve an attribute of an element, use the @ symbol in your select attribute:

```
<xsl:value-of select="/a/b/c/@id"/>
```

The disable-output-escaping attribute causes the XSLT processor to suppress encoding of characters that could be confused with markup. This can be useful when generating text output. For example, consider the document:

```
<doc>A &amp; B</doc>
```

and this template:

```
<xsl:template match="doc">
  <xsl:value-of select="text()" disable-output-escaping="yes"/>
</xsl:template>
```

If disable-output-escaping were allowed to have its default value of no, the result of the template would be presented as A & B—but when the attribute is set to yes, the presentation is A & B. This is not needed if the output method is set to text using the xsl:output element.

We have already used the xsl:value-of element in the previous examples in this chapter, as it is core to XSLT.

Iterating over Elements

The xsl:for-each element allows you to iterate through certain element types inside a template match. It has a mandatory select attribute that defines the node set to be iterated. The select attribute can contain anything that results in a collection of elements or nodes, and can be as simple as an element name or another type of path expression.

The xsl:for-each element is helpful when you are working with mixed content and want only to transform a subset of elements within a document. For example, the following purchases XML document describes multiple types of purchases:

```
<?xml version="1.0"?>
<purchases>
        <product name="floppy disk" price="3.50"/>
        <service name="web updates" price="6.95"/>
        <product name="ink-jet cartridge" price="19.95"/>
        <service name="consulting" price="150h"/>
</purchases>
```

If you are interested only in the product purchases and not services, you could use the for-each element to select only the product elements:

```
<?xml version="1.0" encoding="iso-8859-1"?>
<xsl:stylesheet version="1.0"
 xmlns:xsl="http://www.w3.org/1999/XSL/Transform">
<xsl:output method="html"/>
<xsl:template match="/">
        <html><body><xsl:apply-templates/>
        </body></html>
</xsl:template>
<xsl:template match="purchases">
        <xsl:for-each select="product">
            <p>Product: <xsl:value-of select="./@name"/>
                Price: <xsl:value-of select="./@price"/></p>
        </xsl:for-each>
</xsl:template>
</xsl:stylesheet>
```

This stylesheet generates HTML detailing information about products, but not about services.

XSLT is a substantial programming language and extends well beyond the scope of this book. In addition to the elements covered here that allow you to select, search, and iterate source XML, XSLT features all sorts of standard language features such as control structures, conditionals, variables, and functions. There are several resources available from which you can learn more about XSLT; if you are considering using XSLT for your projects, a good tutorial introduction is well worth the time.

A More Complex Example

In Chapter 3, we created an XML document that represents the Python classes in the PyXML package (*index.py*). The *pyxml.xml* file from Chapter 3 is a lengthy XML document, and makes a good test subject.

In this section, we convert the *pyxml.xml* file back to HTML, but this time using XSLT instead of a SAX driver. After using XSLT to perform this, the SAX and string approach from Chapter 2 will not seem nearly as powerful. However, this type of conversion work is exactly what XSLT is designed to accomplish. The basic structure of the *pyxml.xml* document consists of a file element, followed by one or more class elements, followed by one or more method definition elements:

```
<file name="../xml/dom/ext/reader/HtmlLib.py">
        <class name="class HtmlToDomParser(SGMLParser):">
                <method name="def __init__(self):"/>
                <method name="def unknown_starttag(self,tag,attrs):"/>
                <method name="def unknown_endtag(self, tag):"/>
                <method name="def handle_data(self, data):"/>
                <method name="def handle_comment(self, comment):"/>
                <method name="def handle_generic_node(self, node):"/>
```

```
                <method name="def report_unbalanced(self, tag):"/>
                <method name="def toDom(self, st, ownerDoc=None):"/>
        </class>
    </file>
```

The above XML represents only a few lines of the 2600 line file. The stylesheet used to convert this XML to HTML uses a combination of apply-templates and value-of elements to traverse the structure and generate appropriate output.

The stylesheet starts by creating the HTML opening and closing elements, and calling apply-templates to fill in the content:

```
<xsl:template match="pyxml">
  <html>
    <body bgcolor="#FFFFFF" text="#3333FF">
      <xsl:apply-templates/>
    </body>
  </html>
</xsl:template>
```

Three separate templates, one for each of the element types generated by *index.py*, are defined in the next section and catch the content and generate the appropriate HTML output.

File Template

To catch file elements in *pyxml.xml*, create a template that uses the element's name as a match. Once found, HTML is formatted to produce the name of the file in red text in a new table row:

```
<xsl:template match="file">
    <p>
    <table cellpadding="0" cellspacing="0" border="1"
           bordercolor="#000000" width="540">
      <tr>
        <td align="center">Source File:
          <b class="filename"><xsl:value-of select="./@name"/></b>
        </td>
      </tr>
      <xsl:apply-templates/>
    </table></p>
</xsl:template>
```

Inside the template, a value-of element is used with a path expression that targets the name attribute. After the table row is complete, apply-templates is used to fill in the content beneath this element, which may consist of multiple class and method elements.

Class Template

The class template creates a new table row with the classname, then simply prints out the classname:

```
<xsl:template match="class">
    <tr>
      <td>Class:
        <b class="classname"><xsl:value-of select="./@name"/></b>
      </td>
    </tr>
    <xsl:apply-templates/>
</xsl:template>
```

As shown earlier, the `apply-templates` instruction is used to further fill in the content beneath this element.

Method Template

The method template follows suit and creates its own unique HTML to display method names, this time in black text:

```
<xsl:template match="method">
    <tr>
      <td align="left">
        <span class="methodname"
          ><xsl:value-of select="./@name"/></span>
      </td>
    </tr>
</xsl:template>
```

Here `apply-templates` is not used because there are no child elements of a `method` element in the *pyxml.xml* document.

Example 6-5 shows the complete listing of *pyxml.xsl*.

Example 6-5. pyxml.xsl

```
<?xml version="1.0" encoding="UTF-8" ?>
<xsl:stylesheet
 xmlns:xsl="http://www.w3.org/1999/XSL/Transform"
 version="1.0">

<xsl:output method="html"/>

<xsl:template match="pyxml">
<html>
  <body bgcolor="#FFFFFF" text="#3333FF">
    <xsl:apply-templates/>
  </body>
</html>
</xsl:template>

<xsl:template match="file">
    <p><table cellpadding="0" cellspacing="0" border="1"
       bordercolor="#000000" width="540">
    <tr>
      <td align="center">Source File:
        <b><font color="#FF0000">
```

Example 6-5. pyxml.xsl (continued)

```
            <xsl:value-of select="./@name"/>
          </font></b>
        </td>
      </tr>
      <xsl:apply-templates/>
    </table></p>
</xsl:template>

<xsl:template match="class">
  <tr>
    <td>Class: <b><xsl:value-of
                    select="./@name"/></b>
    </td>
  </tr>
  <xsl:apply-templates/>
</xsl:template>

<xsl:template match="method">
  <tr>
    <td align="left">
      <font color="#000000">
        <xsl:value-of select="./@name"/>
      </font>
    </td>
  </tr>
</xsl:template>

</xsl:stylesheet>
```

When you run the transformation in Example 6-5, you produce a *pyxml.html* document that shows all of the classes in the PyXML package.

```
C:\my-dir> 4xslt pyxml.xml pyxml.xsl > pyxml.html
```

Embedding XSLT Transformations in Python

XML is frequently used to store the "core" version of a document while transformations are used to integrate the data into other systems. For example, you may receive a purchase order as XML over the Web and dispatch it in several different directions (and in different formats) to your other data systems. You may parse the XML inserting the data into Oracle tables, transform it to HTML, add it to an internal web site, transform the purchase order into another flavor of XML, and pass it on to your suppliers.

Regardless of where you're sending your XML, the ability to perform XSLT transformations at runtime is critical. The 4XSLT package works nicely from inside your Python programs. In this section, we create a Python CGI executable for use within Linux and Apache, or in any web server that is configured to run external CGI programs.

The process involves two stylesheets, one XML document, and one CGI executable. The first stylesheet converts the XML document into HTML for your browser. The second stylesheet converts the XML document into HTML for your browser, but adds additional HTML allowing you to edit the text of the XML document and update it on the server. The Python CGI script exists to run the XML through the appropriate stylesheet based on your actions. The script also takes care of updating the source XML on disk. In order for the script to run correctly, it must be placed in a directory where the web user (user *nobody* on Apache and Unix) has permission to write a new XML file.

Creating the Source XML

For starters, we need to create an XML document. Further updates to the XML can be accomplished through the web browser once you've created the CGI script. For now, you can get by with the following code saved to disk as *story.xml*:

```
<?xml version="1.0"?>
<story>
  <title>Web Sites Use XML</title>
  <body>
  It is no surprise, web sites are using XML these days.
  </body>
</story>
```

Be sure to save the document as *story.xml* so that the CGI script can find it when applying stylesheets.

Creating a Simple Stylesheet

The first stylesheet used by the CGI script displays the XML as simple HTML in the browser. It uses the XSLT apply-templates method, and contains a form button labeled **Edit Me** that reloads the CGI script. When the CGI executes in edit mode, it uses the second stylesheet to present the edit form. The simple stylesheet is shown below in Example 6-6. Be sure and save it to disk as *story.xsl*.

Example 6-6. story.xsl

```
<?xml version="1.0" encoding="iso-8859-1"?>
<xsl:stylesheet version="1.0"
 xmlns:xsl="http://www.w3.org/1999/XSL/Transform">

<xsl:template match="story">
  <html>
    <head><title>The Story Page</title></head>
    <body><xsl:apply-templates/>
    </body>
  </html>
</xsl:template>
```

Example 6-6. story.xsl (continued)

```
<xsl:template match="title">
  <h1><xsl:apply-templates/></h1>
</xsl:template>

<xsl:template match="body">
  <p><xsl:apply-templates/></p>
  <p>
    <form action="xslt.cgi" method="get">
      <input type="hidden" name="mode" value="edit"/>
      <input type="submit" value="Edit Me"/>
    </form>
  </p>
</xsl:template>

</xsl:stylesheet>
```

Figure 6-3 shows the transformed XML within a web browser.

Figure 6-3. Transformation using a simple stylesheet

Creating a Stylesheet with Edit Functions

The second stylesheet is similar to the first, except this time the contents of the XML are placed within form fields that are editable within your browser. When the form is submitted, the CGI script updates the XML file on disk, and then reprocesses it through the simple stylesheet sending the result back to the browser.

The editing stylesheet is shown in Example 6-7. Be sure to save this to disk as *edstory.xsl*.

Example 6-7. edstory.xsl

```xml
<?xml version="1.0" encoding="iso-8859-1"?>
<xsl:stylesheet version="1.0"
 xmlns:xsl="http://www.w3.org/1999/XSL/Transform">

<xsl:template match="story">
  <html>
    <head><title>The Story Page</title></head>
    <body>
      <form action="xslt.cgi" method="get">
        <xsl:apply-templates/>
      </form>
    </body>
  </html>
</xsl:template>

<xsl:template match="title">
  <h1><xsl:value-of select="."/></h1>
  <p>New Title:
    <input type="text" name="title" length="20"/>
  </p>
</xsl:template>

<xsl:template match="body">
  <p>New Body:
    <textarea rows="10" cols="50" name="body">
     <xsl:value-of select="."/>
    </textarea>
    <input type="hidden" name="mode" value="change"/>
    <p><input type="submit"/></p>
  </p>
</xsl:template>

</xsl:stylesheet>
```

Figure 6-4 shows the edit form displayed in a web browser. Selecting the submit button updates the XML file on disk and reapplies the simple transformation.

Creating the CGI Script

The *xslt.cgi* script pulls the stylesheets together and coordinates the processing and updating of the XML on disk. While this application lets you edit and display XML in your browser, it only consists of a single CGI script and two XSL sheets. The source data that may constantly change is also stored on disk as XML.

XSLT transformations can be done programmatically using the xml.xslt.processor. Processor class (provided 4XSLT is installed, as shown earlier). When the CGI script launches, it imports and instantiates the XSLT processor:

```python
#!/usr/local/bin/python
# xlst.cgi
```

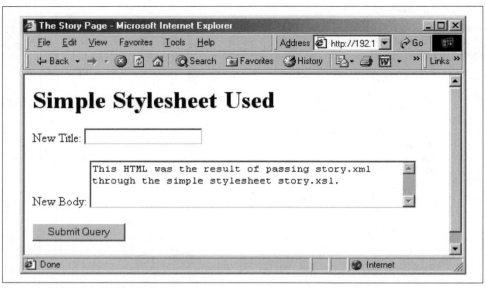

Figure 6-4. Editing the XML inside a web browser

```
import cgi
import os
import sys

from xml.xslt.Processor import Processor

# parse query string & instantiate xlst proc
query = cgi.FieldStorage()

xsltproc = Processor()
```

Using the XSLT processor in the CGI is simple. Two methods are exposed to establish a stylesheet and perform a transformation returning the result as a string:

```
xsltproc.appendStylesheetUri("story.xsl")
html = xsltproc.runUri("story.xml")
```

The appendStylesheetUri method is used to establish which stylesheet is used during a transformation. The runUri method performs the transformation against a source XML document and returns the result as a string.

The CGI script does not get around to transformations until it figures out what you're trying to do. Your choices are communicated to the script using a query string passed to the server as part of the request.

Selecting a Mode

After the CGI has fetched the QUERY_STRING, it's used to determine which mode (edit, change, or display) you are selecting. In the case of no mode whatsoever, the script sends back a complaint and exits:

```
mode = query.getvalue("mode", "")
if not mode:
  print "<html><body>"
  print "<p>No mode given</p>"
  print "</html></body>"
  sys.exit(0)
```

In the case of a show command, the simple stylesheet and source XML are loaded by the XSLT processor and the resultant HTML is sent to the browser:

```
if mode[0] == "show":
  # run XML through simple stylesheet
  xsltproc.appendStylesheetUri("story.xsl")
  html = xsltproc.runUri("story.xml")
  print html
```

In the case of an edit command, the XML is processed through the editing stylesheet, which adds the necessary form markup. This is nearly identical to a show command, but this time the name of the stylesheet is different.

```
elif mode[0] == "edit":
  # run XML through form-based stylesheet
  xsltproc.appendStylesheetUri("edstory.xsl")
  html = xsltproc.runUri("story.xml")
  print html
```

If you were to press the submit button after editing the XML, the result would be sent to the server along with a change command. The script would then update the XML file on disk, reapply the transformation, and send the results back to your browser.

```
elif mode[0] == "change":
  # change XML source file, rerun stylesheet and show
  newXML  = '<?xml version="1.0"?>\n'
  newXML += "\t<story>\n\t<title>"
  newXML += query.getvalue("title")[0] + "</title>\n"
  newXML += "\t<body>\n"
  newXML += query.getvalue("body")[0] + "\n\t</body>\n</story>\n"
  fd = open("story.xml", "w")
  fd.write(newXML)
  fd.close()

  # run updated XML through simple stylehseet
  xsltproc.appendStylesheetUri("story.xsl")
  html = xsltproc.runUri("story.xml")
  print html
```

If the script doesn't have write access when running as the web user, it fails.

Example 6-8 shows the complete listing of *xslt.cgi*.

Example 6-8. xslt.cgi

```
#!/usr/local/bin/python
# xlst.cgi
```

Example 6-8. xslt.cgi (continued)

```python
import cgi
import os
import sys

from xml.xslt.Processor import Processor

# parse query string & instantiate xslt proc
query = cgi.FieldStorage( )

xsltproc = Processor( )

print "Content-type: text/html\r\n"

mode = query.getvalue("mode", "")
if not mode:
    print "<html><body>"
    print "<p>No mode given</p>"
    print "</html></body>"
    sys.exit( )

if mode[0] == "show":
    # run XML through simple stylesheet
    xsltproc.appendStylesheetUri("story.xsl")
    html = xsltproc.runUri("story.xml")
    print html

elif mode[0] == "change":
    # change XML source file, rerun stylesheet and show
    newXML  = '<?xml version="1.0"?>\n'
    newXML += "\t<story>\n\t<title>"
    newXML += query.getvalue("title")[0] + "</title>\n"
    newXML += "\t<body>\n"
    newXML += query.getvalue("body")[0] + "\n\t</body>\n</story>\n"
    fd = open("story.xml", "w")
    fd.write(newXML)
    fd.close( )

    # run updated XML through simple stylehseet
    xsltproc.appendStylesheetUri("story.xsl")
    html = xsltproc.runUri("story.xml")
    print html

elif mode[0] == "edit":
    # run XML through form-based stylesheet
    xsltproc.appendStylesheetUri("edstory.xsl")
    html = xsltproc.runUri("story.xml")
    print html
```

Choosing a Technique

XSLT is extremely powerful when you need to transform XML from one flavor to another, or to convert XML to HTML for display in a web browser. If you have converted your web site contents to XML on disk, you may want to use a fast XSLT processor to batch convert all of your XML to HTML as the files change. Converting your XML to HTML as a batch process allows your server to continue handling requests for static HTML, which can provide a substantial performance improvement, especially if the stylesheets are large or complex. The performance aspect improvements are accentuated by allowing the use of simpler web servers and easier server configurations, which also makes it easier to take advantage of a variety of caching and load balancing architectures.

Sometimes you may need to convert XML to HTML on a per-request basis, or at runtime in your applications. When this is the case, you can embed XSLT functionality in your application as shown earlier in the CGI example.

## CHAPTER 7

XML Validation and Dialects

When XML is used as the basis for a transaction between two parties, the ability to know whether a document is properly formed is important when working across organizational boundaries where contractual obligations are used to define the responsibilities of each party. In this chapter, we work with structured XML formats, convert non-XML information to structured XML, and validate XML documents against their DTDs. We examine aspects of working with official XML dialects, the impact the process of validation can have on your system design, and explore *ebXML* (Electronic Business XML) at a high level.

Let's first look at the base technologies: Document Type Definitions (DTDs; discussed in Chapter 2), *validating parsers*, and *web forms*. These technologies make exchanging XML documents reliable and flexible. Afterwards, we'll dive into some in-depth examples that touch on different aspects of working with validation.

Working with DTDs

Schemas and validation play a major role in reliable application communication. Developing a firm understanding of how to express document relationships within a schema is crucial to using them effectively. In this chapter, we concentrate on DTDs, but the concepts presented here apply to all schema languages. See the discussion of alternate schema languages in Chapter 2 for pointers to Python modules that support schema languages other than the DTD language defined as part of XML 1.0.

The DTD is represented in the internal DTD subset, the external DTD subset, or the combination of the two. As the name suggests, the internal subset rides along with the XML document instance, whereas the external subset is stored as a link telling the parser where to find the DTD.

The `xmlproc` package is a validating parser for Python. As of this writing, it is the only validating parser available for Python that is also *implemented* in Python. If you have the PyXML package installed, as we assume throughout this book, you already have `xmlproc` available and may already use it in your programs. The `xmlproc` package can be imported from the `xml.parsers` package:

```
>>> from xml.parsers import xmlproc
```

Validating with the Internal DTD Subset

There is a good chance that if you have been working with XML for a while, you are able to easily pick up the basic syntax of DTDs just by seeing a few examples. The `xmlproc` package features a command-line routine called *xvcmd.py*. This simple utility tests documents for validity against their DTDs. You can use *xvcmd.py* to try out a few simple DTDs, both external and internal. Be sure that you have *xvcmd.py* in your path (typically located beneath your PyXML installation directory in *xmldoc/ demo/xmlproc/xvcmd.py*).

Here is a small XML document called *product.xml* (Example 7-1), which shows an internal DTD subset. For illustration purposes, the document doesn't faithfully implement the DTD. You may not notice this just by glancing at the code; therefore it's good that we have *xvcmd.py* handy to actually test for validation.

Example 7-1. product.xml with a bad product element

```
<?xml version="1.0"?>
<!DOCTYPE product [
        <!ELEMENT name (#PCDATA)>
        <!ELEMENT price (#PCDATA)>
        <!ELEMENT product (name, price)>
]>
<product>
        <name>Bean Crusher</name>
</product>
```

Try out *xvcmd.py* (the validator) from your command line:

```
C:\>python c:\python20\xmldoc\demo\xmlproc\xvcmd.py product.xml
xmlproc version 0.70

Parsing 'product.xml'
E:product.xml:9:11: Element 'product' ended, but not finished

Parse complete, 1 error(s) and 0 warning(s)
```

As suspected, an error occurs. The problem is that in the DTD, we explicitly stated the content model for a product element. We stated that it must contain exactly one name element and one price element:

```
<!ELEMENT product (name, price)>
```

Furthermore, the DTD instructs that each of those elements (`price` and `name`) must contain only character data as shown in the following element declarations:

```
<!ELEMENT name (#PCDATA)>
<!ELEMENT price (#PCDATA)>
```

We can correct the problem in your XML, as we show in Example 7-1. The product element needs a price element inside of it, and this price element can only have character data. Let's change the document *products.xml* in Example 7-1 to the following, by adding a price element:

```
<?xml version="1.0"?>
<!DOCTYPE product [
        <!ELEMENT name (#PCDATA)>
        <!ELEMENT price (#PCDATA)>
        <!ELEMENT product (name, price)>
]>
<product>
        <name>Bean Crusher</name>
        <price>3.95</price>
</product>
```

Now, return to the command line to try out the *xvcmd.py* validator once again:

```
C:\>python c:\python20\xmldoc\demo\xmlproc\xvcmd.py product2.xml
xmlproc version 0.70

Parsing 'product.xml'

Parse complete, 0 error(s) and 0 warning(s)
```

This time Example 7-1 works just fine, because the XML instance document is now in compliance with the DTD. The DTD places strict control over the content model of basic XML constructs (elements, attributes, and character data) allowed with any given XML document.

Validating with an External DTD Subset

We've looked at an internal DTD subset. Now let's explore an external DTD subset. Typically, when dealing with a DTD that is applied to many document instances, the DTD is stored externally. By keeping the DTD external, you can maintain one DTD that can be applied to many documents. If you store your DTD within the document, each document instance needs its own copy. With a large collection of instance documents, reliably maintaining an internal DTD is problematic. An external DTD is sometimes a better idea in these cases. Import the DTD into the document, as shown in Example 7-2.

Example 7-2. order.xml with an external DTD

```
<?xml version="1.0"?>
<!DOCTYPE order SYSTEM "order.dtd">
<order>
        <customer_name>eDonkey Enterprises</customer_name>
        <sku>343-3940938</sku>
        <qty>4</qty>
        <unit_price>39.95</unit_price>
        <product_name>eDonkey Feed Bags</product_name>
</order>
```

Note that there is no internal DTD subset. The file *order.dtd* contains the Document Type. The *order.dtd* file is shown in Example 7-3:

Example 7-3. order.dtd

```
<!ELEMENT customer_name (#PCDATA)>
<!ELEMENT sku (#PCDATA)>
<!ELEMENT qty (#PCDATA)>
<!ELEMENT unit_price (#PCDATA)>
<!ELEMENT product_name (#PCDATA)>
<!ELEMENT order (customer_name,
                 sku,
                 qty,
                 unit_price,
                 product_name)>
```

While the exact syntax of element type declarations is covered in the next section, here it's relevant to explain the general composition of the DTD. In Example 7-3, five XML elements are created, each with a character data content model. A sixth element is created named order, but it takes precisely one of each of the other elements within it as its content model. Any valid document using this DTD must adhere to this structure. You can test the new document and DTD by running the *xvcmd.py* command, as shown here:

```
C:\>python c:\python20\xmldoc\demo\xmlproc\xvcmd.py order.xml
xmlproc version 0.70

Parsing 'order.xml'

Parse complete, 0 error(s) and 0 warning(s)
```

The document *order.xml* is valid. If you arbitrarily change the document, it breaks. Let's modify your *order.xml* document to look like the one following by deleting the qty and product_name elements. This ensures that the document breaks under the eyes of validation:

```
<?xml version="1.0"?>
<!DOCTYPE order SYSTEM "order.dtd">
<order>
        <customer_name>eDonkey Enterprises</customer_name>
        <sku>343-3940938</sku>
        <unit_price>39.95</unit_price>
</order>
```

In this case, the parser complains about the new document structure:

```
$ python c:\python20\xmldoc\demo\xmlproc\xvcmd.py order.xml
xmlproc version 0.70

Parsing 'badorder.xml'
E:badorder.xml:6:14: Element 'unit_price' not allowed here
E:badorder.xml:7:9: Element 'order' ended, but not finished

Parse complete, 2 error(s) and 0 warning(s)
```

Generally, it's a good idea to place the DTD externally. This is a far more flexible way of doing things as it allows multiple document instances to be compared to one single DTD. For example, a DTD is much better when your documents are published on the Internet. You can easily have XML instance documents scattered all over the world, but if their document type declarations point to a URL for a valid DTD, they can still be validated. Using a URL to indicate the DTD allows you to keep a single copy of a DTD online.

Validation at Runtime

At runtime, one means of validating XML documents from Python is using `xmlproc` in conjunction with its callback interfaces and parser API. By implementing both the `ErrorHandler` and `DTDConsumer` interfaces, you can capture events about validity errors within the document (via `ErrorHandler`) and events about the DTD's structure (via `DTDConsumer`).

To catch errors in the validity of the document, you can implement the `ErrorHandler` interface and provide it to the `XMLValidator`, all part of `xmlproc`. Create the file *xpHandlers.py* and add the `BadOrderErrorHandler` class to it, as shown in Example 7-4.

Example 7-4. A BadOrderErrorHandler class implements ErrorHandler in xpHandlers.py

```
from xml.parsers.xmlproc.xmlapp import DTDConsumer
from xml.parsers.xmlproc.xmlapp import ErrorHandler

"""
BadOrderErrorHandler -- implement xmlproc's ErrorHandler Interface
"""
class BadOrderErrorHandler(ErrorHandler):
  def warning(self,msg):
    print "Warning received!:", msg

  def error(self,msg):
    print "Error received!: ", msg

  def fatal(self,msg):
    print "Fatal Error received!: ", msg
```

To catch events related to the construction of the DTD itself, you can implement the `DTDConsumer` interface. In order to do this, add the class to *xpHandlers.py*, as shown in Example 7-5.

Example 7-5. A DTDHandler class implements DTDConsumer in xpHandlers.py

```
"""
DTDHandler -- implements xmlproc's DTDConsumer Interface
"""
class DTDHandler(DTDConsumer):
```

```
def __init__(self,parser):
  self.parser=parser

def dtd_start(self):
  print "Starting DTD..."

def dtd_end(self):
  print "Finished DTD..."

def new_general_entity(self,name,val):
  print "General Entity Received: ", name

def new_external_entity(self,ent_name,pub_id,sys_id,ndata):
  print "External Entity Received: ", ent_name

def new_element_type(self,elem_name,elem_cont):
  print "New Element Type Declaration: ", elem_name, \
        "Content Model: ", elem_cont

def new_attribute(self,elem,attr,a_type,a_decl,a_def):
  print "New Attribute Declaration: ", attr
```

Example 7-5 is self-explanatory. Each method represents an event related to the parsing of the DTD. Your methods can capture and utilize this information in any way you see fit.

Implementing the interfaces is where the real work happens. To actually do productive work and use the validator, you can create an instance, provide it your interface objects, and set it to work on a particular resource. The file *val.py*, shown in Example 7-6, contains the simple amount of code to parse a document.

Example 7-6. Command-line validator (val.py)

```
""" xml validation """
import sys
from xml.parsers.xmlproc import xmlval
from xpHandlers import BadOrderErrorHandler, DTDHandler

xv = xmlval.XMLValidator()
dt = DTDHandler(xv.parser)
bh = BadOrderErrorHandler(xv.app.locator)

xv.set_error_handler(bh)
xv.set_dtd_listener(dt)
xv.parse_resource(sys.argv[1])
```

You can use *val.py* to see if XML documents pass muster against their DTDs from the command line:

```
$ python val.py order.xml
New Element Type Declaration:  customer_name
```

```
Content Model:  ('', [('#PCDATA', '')], '')
New Element Type Declaration:  sku
Content Model:  ('', [('#PCDATA', '')], '')
New Element Type Declaration:  qty C
ontent Model:  ('', [('#PCDATA', '')], '')
New Element Type Declaration:  unit_price
Content Model:  ('', [('#PCDATA', '')], '')
New Element Type Declaration:  product_name
Content Model:  ('', [('#PCDATA', '')], '')
New Element Type Declaration:  order
Content Model:  (',', [('customer_name', ''), ('sku', ''), ('qty', ''),
                ('unit_price', ''), ('product_name', '')], '')
Finished DTD...
```

By supplying xmlproc's XMLValidator with handlers, you can capture the information related to a document's validity to suit your needs. In the next section, we put validation to the test by creating a translation and validation example that runs on a web server.

The BillSummary Example

To pull together some of the validation techniques presented in this chapter, we develop an example application that utilizes a DTD, flat-file conversion, and XML validation.

In the following set of programs, we develop an Internet system that parses a flat file submitted by a web browser, converts the flat text to XML, validates the XML, stores the XML to disk under a unique ID for publishing, and communicates success or failure back to the browser (or HTTP) client. Such an arrangement can act as an HTTP-based interface for converting flat files to XML (and making the resultant XML files available over HTTP) in a distributed system.

To accomplish this, use Python's CGI libraries to grab a flat file from an HTTP request. Use string and file APIs to parse the flat file submitted by the browser, and a DOM implementation to construct a document object based on the flat file's contents. A validating parser is used to ensure that the constructed DOM faithfully adheres to the established *Bill Summary* DTD.

All of the files for this example are available as part of the examples archive.

The files used in this example should be placed in a CGI-capable directory on your web server. In this section, we create the following files:

flatfile.html
> Allows you to send the flat file to CGI script using a browser. *BillSummary.txt*, the flat file, is preloaded as the form submission.

FlatfileParser.py
> A class that parses the flat file and returns a DOM document.

ValidityError.py
> A class that handles validation errors for `xmlproc`.

BillSummary.dtd
> A DTD for validating converted XML.

flat2xml.cgi
> A CGI that accepts the flat file, converts it to XML, validates it, publishes it to disk (and therefore HTTP) and communicates the results back to the browser.

The CGI script *flat2xml.cgi* is the real workhorse and pulls everything together. It's presented in its entirety at the end of the section.

The Flat File

The flat file we use in this application is a sample billing statement from a fictitious consulting corporation. As a typical small business might, this particular imaginary company has used spreadsheet software for invoices and exporting them as text. Our job is to allow something useful to eventually happen with these invoices. Your goal is to migrate the forms into XML for easier manipulation in the future. Converting them to XML and making them available via HTTP is a good start. The text shown in Example 7-7, *BillSummary.txt*, is used throughout this section extensively.

Example 7-7. BillSummary.txt

```
#
# Bill Summary
#
Bill Summary, Format 1.2
Section: Customer
customer-id: 34287-AUHE-39383947579
name: Zeropath Corporation
address1: 123 Zeropath Street
address2:
city: Redmond
state: WA
zip: 98052
phone: 425-555-1212
billing-contact: Larry Boberry
billing-contact-phone: 425-555-1212

Section: Bill Highlights
bill-id: 3453439789-6454-77
customer: 34287-AUHE-39383947579
customer-name: Zeropath Corporation
total-hours: 80
hours-rate: 150
total-svcmtrls: 950
total-bill-amount: 12950
```

Example 7-7. BillSummary.txt (continued)

```
Section: Item
item-id: 8289893
bill-id: 3453439789-6454-77
item-name: Continued Project Work (Backend)
total-hours: 40
total-svcmtrls: 450

Section: Item
item-id: 8289894
bill-id: 3453439789-6454-77
item-name: Continued Project Work (UI)
total-hours: 40
total-svcmtrls: 500
```

Once we have this file on disk, we can begin the process of creating a web form that sends this flat file over the wire via HTTP. We explore this particular application in the remaining sections of this chapter.

The Web Form

We first develop a web form to let you submit your flat files for XML conversion. If a company's invoices are uploaded onto a shared disk as flat files each day, a batch process can pick them all up, and submit them via HTTP to your conversion application.

Choosing HTTP as your interface leaves communication pathways open for a variety of clients (i.e., browsers across the Internet, applications speaking HTTP from behind a firewall, etc.). You can have people submit text-based invoices directly from their browsers, or they can send them programmatically using intelligent clients that know how to speak HTTP.

The web form is a simple HTML document, as shown in Example 7-8. The area to pay attention to is the `form` tag and its `method` and `action`. These elements define where the browser sends the flat text when you press the submit button. A `textarea` tag is used to contain the flat file, and the text from Example 7-7 is then present as the default text when you load the form.

Example 7-8. The web form flatfile.html will post your flat file

```
<html>
<body bgcolor="#FFFFFF" text="#000000">
<h1>Flat File Selection</h1>
<p>Click the button below to post the flat file to
   the server.  You may also edit the flat file to
   cause errors on the server and in the handling
   code.
</p>
<p>
```

Example 7-8. The web form flatfile.html will post your flat file (continued)

```
<form action="flat2xml.cgi" method="POST">
<textarea name="flatfile" rows=20 cols=80>
#
# Bill Summary
#
Bill Summary, Format 1.2
Section: Customer
customer-id: 34287-AUHE-39383947579
name: Zeropath Corporation
address1: 123 Zeropath Street
address2:
city: Redmond
state: WA
zip: 98052
phone: 425-555-1212
billing-contact: Larry Boberry
billing-contact-phone: 425-555-1212

Section: Bill Highlights
bill-id: 3453439789-6454-77
customer: 34287-AUHE-39383947579
customer-name: Zeropath Corporation
total-hours: 80
hours-rate: 150
total-svcmtrls: 950
total-bill-amount: 12950

Section: Item
item-id: 8289893
bill-id: 3453439789-6454-77
item-name: Continued Project Work (Backend)
total-hours: 40
total-svcmtrls: 450

Section: Item
item-id: 8289894
bill-id: 3453439789-6454-77
item-name: Continued Project Work (UI)
total-hours: 40
total-svcmtrls: 500

</textarea>
<br><input type=submit>
</form>
</p>
</body>
</html>
```

When loaded in a browser, the web page generated from the code in Example 7-8 appears as shown in Figure 7-1.

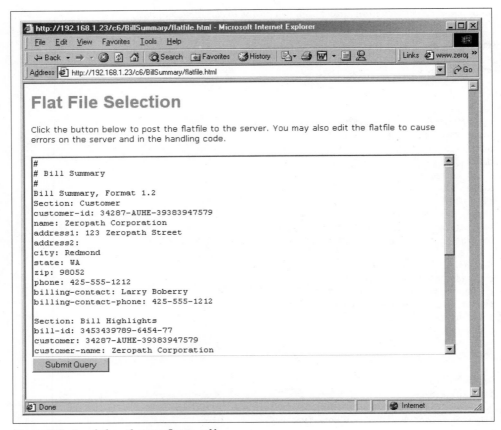

Figure 7-1. A web form hosts a flat text file

Starting the CGI

You should now have two components of the example: a sample flat file representing a billing summary, and an HTML web form that sends the flat file over HTTP to a Python script named *flatfile.cgi*, as identified by the form element's action attribute.

Before we dive into the complex CGI complete with validation, let's simply test your CGI waters and confirm that you're able to receive the flat file from your web browser. Example 7-9 offers a good milestone for establishing CGI execution and browser connectivity. Your CGI needs to capture the flat file out of the HTTP request and send it back to the user to demonstrate that everything is working well. XML and validation come afterward. The baseline CGI should look something like the early version of *flat2xml.cgi* shown in Example 7-9.

Example 7-9. flatfile.cgi, a first step version of the CGI

```
#!/usr/local/bin/python
# flat2xml.cgi
```

Example 7-9. flatfile.cgi, a first step version of the CGI (continued)

```python
import cgi
import os
import sys

#
# Start HTTP/HTML Output
#
print "Content-type: text/html"
print
print "<html><body>"

#
# Parse query string for flat file
#
try:
  query = cgi.FieldStorage()
  flatfile = query.getvalue("flatfile", "")[0]
except:
  print "Conversion request not found or incorrectly formatted."
  print "</body></html>"
  sys.exit(0)

#
# Display flat file
#
print "<h1>Flat File</h1>"
print "<p>Flat file received:</p> "
print "<p><pre>" + flatfile + "</pre></p>"
print "</body></html>"
```

Most of Example 7-9 is fairly basic Python. The contents of the flat file are sent by the browser in the form of a GET request as the variable flatfile inside the form. If it is unavailable, an error occurs. When Example 7-9 is up and running, you should see a screen similar to the one shown in Figure 7-2.

In the following sections, we build on this base functionality and add conversion of the flat file to XML. Validation of the XML follows to ensure that everything is going as planned.

Conversion and Validation

To convert the flat file to XML, we first need to parse the file. While parsing a unique flat file format may seem tedious, there is no getting around this aspect of XML integration. In fact, the tediousness of having to parse every "one-off" flat file structure is perhaps the leading impetus behind XML. XML enforces a format that is easily parsed by all applications. The good news is that the flat files should take essentially the same structure in any given system, and you can write a single chunk of parsing routines for each type of flat file you encounter.

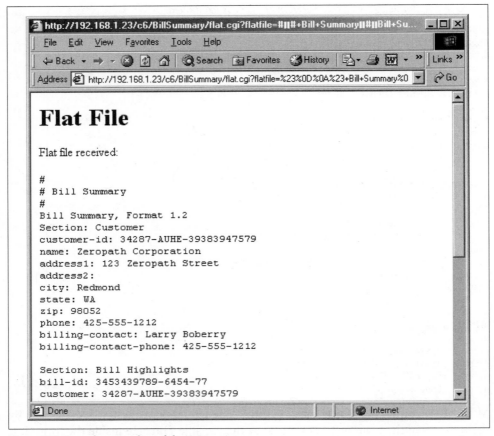

Figure 7-2. Base functionality of the CGI script

Converting text to XML

The flat file used in this example is organized into sections, with additional data filling in each section. We cannot be completely sure how many sections there will ultimately be in the document, as that number depends on the number of "consulting hours" that are placed on the customer's bill. The FlatfileParser you create needs to be flexible; it can't assume a rigid ordering of sections within the document, or their uniqueness or grouping with other sections. To accomplish its goal of taking flat text and organizing it into an XML document, the FlatfileParser uses the DOM implementation to create a DOM structure to hold the various pieces of text that the FlatfileParser extracts:

```
#
# FlatfileParser.py
#
from xml.dom      import implementation
```

```
class FlatfileParser:
  def parseFile(self, fileAsString):
```

The class `FlatfileParser` has one method, named `parseFile`. This method takes a single string representing the contents of a file. Python also features the `StringIO` class, which allows a string to support read and write operations, such as a file. `StringIO` is a good choice for this class, but to keep things simple, we work with a complete string in this example.

The next couple of steps are critical. Here, we create a new DOM document as `BillSummary`, and retrieve its root element. We append children to the element as our `FlatfileParser` works the flat text:

```
# Create DocType Declaration
doctype = implementation.createDocumentType('BillSummary', '',
                                            'BillSummary.dtd')

# Create empty DOM Document and get root element
doc = implementation.createDocument('', 'BillSummary', doctype)
elemDoc = doc.documentElement
```

The implementation class is imported from `xml.dom.implementation`, and its `createDocumentType` method is used to construct a `BillSummary` type referencing a file called *BillSummary.dtd* (shown in Example 7-12). A document object is created with the `createDocument` method adding the freshly created doctype as a parameter. Finally the document's root element is retrieved via the `doc.documentElement` method.

Now that the basis for the document is created, the code can loop over the lines in the file, examining the contents. New sections result in new section elements, and the data within these elements results in new children for the section elements. Here is a cross-section of the structure of the flat file:

```
Section: Bill Highlights
bill-id: 3453439789-6454-77
customer: 34287-AUHE-39383947579
customer-name: Zeropath Corporation
total-hours: 80
hours-rate: 150
total-svcmtrls: 950
total-bill-amount: 12950
```

In your `FlatfileParser`, encountering a "Section" string creates a new element. This element is then added to the document and set as the "current" element. All other lines of the document, such as `bill-id` and `total-hours`, are added to the "current" element as children until a new "Section" is discovered. The first half of the code checks to see if you're dealing with a Section element. If it finds that this is true, the second half of the code dumps the current line to XML as an element and CDATA pair:

```
# Read in each line of flat file for processing
for line in fileAsString.splitlines():
  # Test to see if we're in a section or not
```

```
    if bInElement:
      # Check to see if we're leaving a section
      if ':' in line:
        # Append section element, reset section switch
        elemDoc.appendChild(elemCurrent)
        bInElement = 0
      else:
        # Parse a section line on ':'
        k,v = line.split(':', 1)

        # Create element name and child text from key/value pair
        elem = doc.createElement(k.strip())
        elem.appendChild(doc.createTextNode(v.strip()))

        # append element to current section element
        elemCurrent.appendChild(elem)
```

The code first checks to see if you have encountered a blank line or completed a Section. If it finds you have not, the current line is assumed to be a child of the current section and is split upon its colon (:). The doc.createElement method is then used to create the element and its tag name from the left half of the text string, while the character data of the element is appended as a child, and is taken from the right half of the text string. This process continues until there are no lines left in the file.

What the previous code snippet doesn't show is what happens when bInElement is false (zero in the case of Python). Based on the structure of the flat file, when bInElement is false it's time to start a new section. The code then searches for another "Section" string. When found, it is converted to an element and set as the "current" element, and bInElement is flipped back to true.

```
# Create a new element based on which section of
# the flat file we are in...
if line.startswith("Section: Customer"):
  elemCustomer = doc.createElement("Customer")
  bInElement = 1

  # Set current working element for the Customer section
  elemCurrent = elemCustomer

if line.startswith("Section: Bill Highlights"):
  elemBillHighlights = doc.createElement("BillHighlights")
  bInElement = 1

  # Set current working element for the BillHighlights section
  elemCurrent = elemBillHighlights

if line.startswith("Section: Item"):
  elemItem = doc.createElement("Item")
  bInElement = 1

  # Set current working element for the Item section
  elemCurrent = elemItem
```

For every line of code that you have in your file, the FlatfileParser assumes that you are within a section or dealing with a section's children. If miscellaneous data appears after a section and before a new one, it is ignored because the parsing loops you have created only consider things based on what section they are in. Finally, when the document has no more lines left within it, the new DOM document is returned:

```
return doc
```

Example 7-10 shows the complete listing of *FlatfileParser.py*. The CGI script shown later in this section uses the FlatfileParser class.

Example 7-10. FlatfileParser.py

```
#
# FlatfileParser.py
#
from xml.dom    import implementation

class FlatfileParser:
  def parseFile(self, fileAsString):

    # Create DocType Declaration
    doctype = implementation.createDocumentType('BillSummary', '',
                                      'BillSummary.dtd')

    # Create empty DOM Document and get root element
    doc = implementation.createDocument('', 'BillSummary', doctype)
    elemDoc = doc.documentElement

    # boolean text parsing switch to help
    # navigate flat file
    bInElement = 0

    # Read in each line of flat file for processing
    for line in fileAsString.splitlines():
      # Test to see if we're in a section or not
      if bInElement:
        # Check to see if we're leaving a section
        if ':' in line:
          # Append section element, reset section switch
          elemDoc.appendChild(elemCurrent)
          bInElement = 0
        else:
          # Parse a section line on ':'
          k,v = line.split(':')

          # Create element name and child text from key/value pair
          elem = doc.createElement(k.strip())
          elem.appendChild(doc.createTextNode(v.strip()))

          # append element to current section element
          elemCurrent.appendChild(elem)
```

Example 7-10. FlatfileParser.py (continued)

```
    # Create a new element based on which section of
    # the flat file we are in...
    section = line.strip( )
    if section == "Section: Customer":
      elemCustomer = doc.createElement("Customer")
      bInElement = 1

      # Set current working element for the Customer section
      elemCurrent = elemCustomer

    if section == "Section: Bill Highlights":
      elemBillHighlights = doc.createElement("BillHighlights")
      bInElement = 1

      # Set current working element for the BillHighlights section
      elemCurrent = elemBillHighlights

    if section == "Section: Item":
      elemItem = doc.createElement("Item")
      bInElement = 1

      # Set current working element for the Item section
      elemCurrent = elemItem

  return doc
```

Validating the XML

You may be wondering what XML is produced by running the FlatfileParser against the sample text shown in Example 7-7. If you apply FlatfileParser against *BillSummary.txt*, you should wind up with a DOM that looks like *BillSummary.xml*, shown in Example 7-11 (provided you display your DOM with PrettyPrint or the like).

Example 7-11. A well-formed, converted, valid, BillSummary.xml

```
<?xml version='1.0' encoding='UTF-8'?>
<!DOCTYPE BillSummary SYSTEM "BillSummary.dtd">
<BillSummary>
  <Customer>
    <customer-id>34287-AUHE-39383947579</customer-id>
    <name>Zeropath Corporation</name>
    <address1>123 Zeropath Street</address1>
    <address2>
    </address2>
    <city>Redmond</city>
    <state>WA</state>
    <zip>98052</zip>
    <phone>425-555-1212</phone>
    <billing-contact>Larry Boberry</billing-contact>
    <billing-contact-phone>425-555-1212</billing-contact-phone>
```

```
    </Customer>
    <BillHighlights>
       <bill-id>3453439789-6454-77</bill-id>
       <customer>34287-AUHE-39383947579</customer>
       <customer-name>Zeropath Corporation</customer-name>
       <total-hours>80</total-hours>
       <hours-rate>150</hours-rate>
       <total-svcmtrls>950</total-svcmtrls>
       <total-bill-amount>12950</total-bill-amount>
    </BillHighlights>
    <Item>
       <item-id>8289893</item-id>
       <bill-id>3453439789-6454-77</bill-id>
       <item-name>Continued Project Work (Backend)</item-name>
       <total-hours>40</total-hours>
       <total-svcmtrls>450</total-svcmtrls>
    </Item>
    <Item>
       <item-id>8289894</item-id>
       <bill-id>3453439789-6454-77</bill-id>
       <item-name>Continued Project Work (UI)</item-name>
       <total-hours>40</total-hours>
       <total-svcmtrls>500</total-svcmtrls>
    </Item>
</BillSummary>
```

One important aspect missing from our example thus far is the actual DTD. In order for flat files to convert to XML, and to subsequently have the XML deemed valid, there must be a DTD. The DTD for the BillSummary document is straightforward. It uses the concepts of content models and element ordering, discussed in Chapter 2.

You must have the DTD saved as *BillSummary.dtd* in order for validation to succeed. *BillSummary.dtd* is presented in Example 7-12.

Example 7-12. BillSummary.dtd

```
<!ELEMENT customer-id (#PCDATA)>
<!ELEMENT name (#PCDATA)>
<!ELEMENT address1 (#PCDATA)>
<!ELEMENT address2 (#PCDATA)>
<!ELEMENT city (#PCDATA)>
<!ELEMENT state (#PCDATA)>
<!ELEMENT zip (#PCDATA)>
<!ELEMENT phone (#PCDATA)>
<!ELEMENT billing-contact (#PCDATA)>
<!ELEMENT billing-contact-phone (#PCDATA)>
<!ELEMENT bill-id (#PCDATA)>
<!ELEMENT customer (#PCDATA)>
<!ELEMENT customer-name (#PCDATA)>
<!ELEMENT hours-rate (#PCDATA)>
<!ELEMENT total-bill-amount (#PCDATA)>
<!ELEMENT item-id (#PCDATA)>
```

Example 7-12. BillSummary.dtd (continued)

```
<!ELEMENT item-name (#PCDATA)>
<!ELEMENT total-hours (#PCDATA)>
<!ELEMENT total-svcmtrls (#PCDATA)>

<!ELEMENT Customer (customer-id, name, address1, address2,
                    city, state, zip, phone, billing-contact,
                    billing-contact-phone)>

<!ELEMENT BillHighlights (bill-id, customer, customer-name,
                          total-hours, hours-rate, total-svcmtrls,
                          total-bill-amount)>

<!ELEMENT Item (item-id, bill-id, item-name, total-hours,
                total-svcmtrls)>

<!ELEMENT BillSummary (Customer, BillHighlights, Item*)>
```

If you turn back to *val.py*, presented in Example 7-6, you can use it to check the validity of your freshly created *BillSummary.dtd* and your example *BillSummary.xml* (that is if you typed it in, or extracted it from the FlatfileParser). If you have the XML as a saved file, you can test it accordingly:

```
C:\pythonxml\c6>python val.py BillSummary.xml
```

Creating a validation handler

Now that you have a FlatfileParser, a generated XML version, and a DTD to hold it against, you need a validation handler for xmlproc. The XMLValidator class features a method called set_error_handler. You can use this method to supply XMLValidator with an error handler that does the things you need it to, such as write errors to your HTTP/HTML client.

To implement the ErrorHandler, derive an object from its interface and override the methods you wish to implement as part of your error scheme. Your error handler writes simple text messages wrapped in HTML. Example 7-13 shows the complete listing of *ValidityError.py*, which implements an ErrorHandler-compliant object.

Example 7-13. ValidityError.py

```
from xml.parsers.xmlproc.xmlapp import ErrorHandler

"""

ValidityErrorHandler -- implement xmlproc's ErrorHandler Interface
"""
class ValidityErrorHandler(ErrorHandler):

  def warning(self,msg):
    print "<p><b><font color=#FF0000>Warning received!:</b></font>"
    print "<br>" + msg + "</p>"
    self.errors = 0
```

Example 7-13. ValidityError.py (continued)

```
def error(self,msg):
  print "<p><b><font color=#aa0000>Error received!:</b></font>"
  print "<br>" + msg + "</p>"
  self.errors = 1

def fatal(self,msg):
  print "<p><b><font color=#aa0000>Fatal Error received!:</b></font>"
  print "<br>" + msg + "</p>"
  self.errors = 1
```

Each method of the error handler accepts a message. It writes the message to the web page with verbiage describing what type of error it is (warning, error, or fatal). Each method also flips a switch (`self.errors`) so that the CGI script can tell if errors have occurred.

Now that the handlers, DTD, and XML files are in place, we can return to the CGI for completion.

Completing the CGI

When we last left *flat2xml.cgi*, we instructed it to simply dump the flat file back out as text to confirm that your CGI setup is working correctly. Now we go back and add some real functionality to the setup. At the end of this section, the full listing of the CGI is presented in Example 7-14.

Defining success and error functions

The CGI script is the great coordinator in this sample application. The web server launches the CGI upon a page request, and the CGI in turn imports modules and classes and begins the process of completing the task. In the beginning, however, the CGI completes the imports and establishes success and failure methods:

```
#!/usr/local/bin/python
# flat2xml.cgi

import cgi
import os
import sys

from FlatfileParser     import FlatfileParser
from xml.dom.ext        import PrettyPrint
from xml.parsers.xmlproc import xmlval
from ValidityError      import ValidityErrorHandler

# customer failure message
def failure(msg):
  print "<h1>Failure</h1>"
  print "<p><b>Post received, Failure called:"
  print msg + "</b></p>"
```

```
# customer success message
def success(msg):
  print "<p><b>XML Document Received, is valid, and "
  print "has been written to disk. "
  print "Message: " + msg + "</b></p>"
```

The success function is called after the document has been successfully converted, validated, and stored to disk using the Customer ID number as part of the filename. The `failure` function is called whenever the CGI encounters a fatal error, although it is up to the caller to end the CGI when `failure` returns.

The next step is to prepare the HTTP/HTML output, and start communicating back to the browser. The CGI script works on a series of conditions that either result in a successful message sent to the browser, or a fatal error message stopping the script. To get the HTML started, use a few print statements:

```
#
# Start HTTP/HTML Output
#
print "Content-type: text/html"
print
print "<html><head>"
print "<link rel=stylesheet type=text/css href=bs.css>"
print "</head><body>"
```

The <head> element contains a link to a stylesheet that adds some text coloration to the example.

Converting the flat file to XML

The code to convert the flat file to XML is primarily inside the `FlatfileParser` created earlier. Use the Python CGI API to grab the flat file from the query string:

```
#
# Parse query string for flat file
#
try:
  querys = cgi.FieldStorage( )
  flatfile = query.getvalue("flatfile", "")[0]
except:
  failure("Conversion request not found or incorrectly formatted.")
  print "</body></html>"
  sys.exit(0)

# instatiate flat file parser & display file
ffp = FlatfileParser( )
print "<h1>Flat File</h1>"
print "<p>Flat file received:</p> "
print "<p><pre>" + flatfile + "</pre></p>"
```

After instantiating the `FlatfileParser`, use the `parseFile` method to convert the text to XML:

```
#
# Convert flatfile to XML
#
print "<h1>Conversion</h1>"
BillSummaryDOM = ffp.parseFile(flatfile)
CustomerIdElement = BillSummaryDOM.getElementsByTagName("customer-id")
if CustomerIdElement:
    # go after the Customer Id
    CustomerId = CustomerIdElement[0].firstChild.data
    print "<p>Converted to XML...</p>"
else:
    # No id found, boot document now
    failure("Unable to detect customer-id in DOM instance.")
    print "</body></html>"
    sys.exit(0)
```

Notice there is additional logic after the BillSummaryDOM, created to grab the customer ID element. Before you go through the trouble of validating the document, you need to save it to disk under a special identifier so that it's available to other systems from the web server, including the validator. To do this, extract the Customer ID character data from the customer-id element within the DOM. If it is present, the code moves along; if it's absent, a fatal error occurs and the script exits.

Validating the converted XML

Provided the document was well-formed enough to extract the ID, you can begin the process of validation. Validation gives the application a chance to ensure that the document conforms to standards and will not cause problems in the system. Assuming the ID is found, you can move into the validation step, which involves saving the document to disk, as shown here:

```
# Validate the DOM
#
print "<h1>Validation</h1>"
try:
    # Write document to disk based on Customer Id
    fd = open(CustomerId + ".xml", 'w')
    PrettyPrint(BillSummaryDOM, fd)
    fd.close()
except:
    # Problem writing document?
    failure("<p>Unable to write XML document to disk.</p>")
    print "</body></html>"
    sys.exit(1)
```

The PrettyPrint function is used to write the DOM into the file descriptor. The work is carried out within a try and except block to catch any file I/O problems before they propagate out of the script and cause an Internal Server Error for the browser to see. Next comes the actual instantiation of XMLValidator:

```
# instantiate parser
xv = xmlval.XMLValidator()
```

```
# instantiate the error handler
veh = ValidityErrorHandler(xv.app.locator)

# set up parser, call parse method
xv.set_error_handler(veh)
xv.parse_resource(CustomerId + ".xml")
```

If there are any errors during the validation steps, your custom error handler, ValidityErrorHandler, presents errors to the browser and continues to process.

Displaying the XML

Regardless of validity errors, the CGI script displays the XML to the browser in the HTML page with the help of the <pre> and <xmp> tags. If you are not familiar with these, the <pre> tag instructs the browser to display the text that follows the tag as preformatted text, preserving whitespace. This is a good tag to use when showing code snippets. But XML can be tricky, as the browser can mistake it for unsupported HTML tags. This is where the <xmp> tag comes in handy—originally intended for example HTML, it works to escape any text that is enclosed in '<' and '>' type characters, as shown here:

```
# Display XML Document
print "<h1>XML Document</h1><pre><xmp>"
PrettyPrint(BillSummaryDOM)
print "</xmp></pre>"
```

To make sure the DOM is displayed as raw XML in the HTTP stream, use the PrettyPrint function imported from xml.dom.ext. This method "prints" the XML into any file-like object you provide; however, if nothing is provided beyond the DOM, then the file-like object is assumed to be sys.stdout.

If there are no validation errors during your script's execution, a successful end occurs. However, if for some reason validation errors stack up, even when your flat file and XML make it past all of the other hurdles, the script still fails. Remember that the ValidityErrorHandler was configured with an error switch so that external objects could track its success rate. The CGI script uses this error switch to determine if there are any validation errors:

```
# confirm response to user
#
if veh.errors:
  failure("Validation Error(s).")
else:
  success("Success.")

# Finish Up
print "</body></html>"
```

If any validation errors are riding in ValidityErrorHandler, the script calls the failure method. Example 7-14 shows the complete version of *flat2xml.cgi*.

Example 7-14. flat2xml.cgi

```python
#!/usr/local/bin/python
# flat2xml.cgi

import cgi
import os
import sys

from FlatfileParser      import FlatfileParser
from xml.dom.ext         import PrettyPrint
from xml.parsers.xmlproc import xmlval
from ValidityError       import ValidityErrorHandler

# customer failure message
def failure(msg):
  print "<h1>Failure</h1>"
  print "<p><b>Post received, Failure called:"
  print msg + "</b></p>"

# customer success message
def success(msg):
  print "<p><b>XML Document Received, is valid, and "
  print "has been written to disk. "
  print "Message: " + msg + "</b></p>"

#
# Start HTTP/HTML Output
#
print "Content-type: text/html"
print
print "<html>"
print "<body>"

#
# Parse query string for flat file
#
try:
  query = cgi.FieldStorage()
  flatfile = query.getvalue("flatfile", "")[0]
except:
  failure("Conversion request not found or incorrectly formatted.")
  print "</body></html>"
  sys.exit(0)

# instatiate flat file parser & display file
ffp = FlatfileParser()
print "<h1>Flat File</h1>"
print "<p>Flat file received:</p> "
print "<p><pre>" + flatfile + "</pre></p>"

#
# Convert flatfile to XML
#
print "<h1>Conversion</h1>"
```

Example 7-14. flat2xml.cgi (continued)

```
BillSummaryDOM = ffp.parseFile(flatfile)
CustomerIdElement = BillSummaryDOM.getElementsByTagName("customer-id")
if CustomerIdElement:
  # go after the Customer Id
  CustomerId = CustomerIdElement[0].firstChild.data
  print "<p>Converted to XML...</p>"
else:
  # No id found, boot document now
  failure("Unable to detect customer-id in DOM instance.")
  print "</body></html>"
  sys.exit(0)

#
# Validate the dom
#
print "<h1>Validation</h1>"
try:
  # Write document to disk based on Customer Id
  fd = open(CustomerId + ".xml", 'w')
  PrettyPrint(BillSummaryDOM, fd)
  fd.close()
except:
  # Problem writing document?
  failure("<p>Unable to write XML document to disk.</p>")
  print "</body></html>"
  sys.exit(1)

# instantiate parser
xv = xmlval.XMLValidator()

# instantiate the error handler
veh = ValidityErrorHandler(xv.app.locator)

# set up parser, call parse method
xv.set_error_handler(veh)
xv.parse_resource(CustomerId + ".xml")

# Display XML Document
print "<h1>XML Document</h1><pre><xmp>"
PrettyPrint(BillSummaryDOM)
print "</xmp></pre>"

#
# confirm response to user
#
if veh.errors:
  failure("Validation Error(s).")
else:
  success("Success.")

# Finish Up
print "</body></html>"
```

Running the Application in a Browser

The CGI script can have a variety of different outcomes based on whether you edit the text before sending it. As is, the flat file is well-formed in the text box when you load *flatfile.html*. It produces HTML output as shown in Figure 7-3.

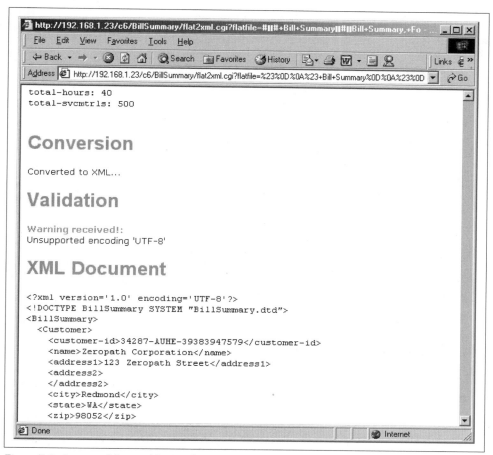

Figure 7-3. A successful run of flat2xml.cgi

However, if you were to edit the text before sending it, you would see wildly different results. For example, if you delete half of the Bill Highlights section and merge it into the first section, you generate a mess of validity errors as shown in Figure 7-4.

The errors you just introduced were caused by your arbitrary deletions of large swatches of content. The CGI captured the problems by using validation. The errors shown in Figure 7-4 clearly illustrate the validity errors in the document, and can be triggered to fire events in other parts of your system. In a real situation, you would

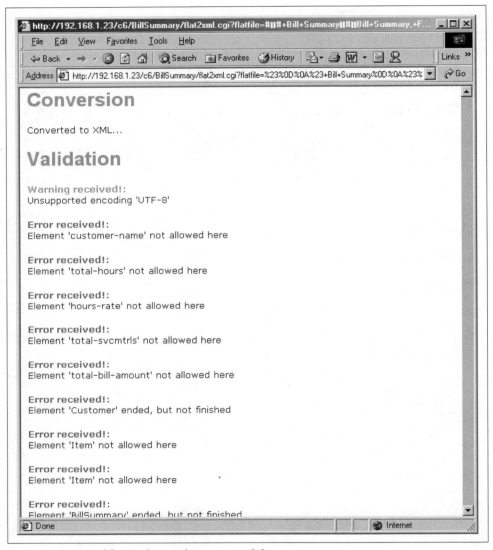

Figure 7-4. A run of flat2xml.cgi with excessive validation errors

have a certain business logic that would dictate what to do if a piece of data is missing. For example, in your business it might not be too bad if a document looks good but is missing a date field. However, if the document is missing an account number, it might be a fatal flaw requiring a different course of action. The level of logic you enforce may have something to do with the complexity of the document you're working with. This entire example is based around an XML document created from scratch. When creating documents from scratch you are able to tailor them to your exact situation (perhaps too much so). If you decide to work with a standardized dialect, there are even more stringent considerations and requirements for your documents, and your transactions may have to flow along the lines of someone else's business logic.

Dialects, Frameworks, and Workflow

Any cursory glance at a search engine tells you an XML dialect or framework exists for just about every type of business or system on the planet. In order to choose a fitting repository or dialect, you need to model your business or system processes. You may decide that your business largely counts on support for transactions and a reliable communications protocol. Choosing a dialect (or even inventing your own) requires development and enforcement of DTDs or Schema. Additionally, an understanding of the underlying XML technologies to support these activities is warranted. Often, when transferring a human-intensive business process to electronic form, you need to look at the workflow and then determine appropriate integration steps to mimic the process electronically. If there are any analytical or business logic steps involved, you need to incorporate those into the electronic version as well.

Designing a workflow may involve citing a primary objective (such as "complete sales transaction"), which can in turn involve many additional individual steps ("receive purchase order," "bill customer," "ship product," etc.) that can have their own conditional outcomes ("no inventory," "invalid account number," etc.). It's the goal of a system's architect to integrate the correct components to ensure the desired outcome, or to handle any of the other conditions that may arise.

In small applications (or small organizations), a developer completes much of the system logic. In more complex distributed systems, you frequently find third-party consultants and expensive commercial software involved, but it still comes down to the same technology building blocks. Understanding the objectives of your system may aid in choosing the correct XML dialect and framework. Some of the choices include ebXML, BizTalk, and commercial offerings such as Commerce One's and Ariba's proprietary e-business languages.

What Does ebXML Offer?

Electronic Business XML (*ebXML*) was formed to improve upon the EDI standard, and level the playing field between trading partners. The OASIS consortium, along with the United Nation's UN/CEFACT body, formed ebXML as a collaborative effort, and published information concerning ebXML at *http://www.ebxml.org/*.

So what does ebXML signify for programmers? In reality, it means a complex set of documents and even more complex set up of transactional document flows. Adopting ebXML means adopting not only a dialect of document instances, but a business process modeling flow to connect things together.

ebXML Document Structure

The dialect portion of ebXML deals with message formats. The specification puts forth guidelines that must be used when creating ebXML documents. Simple structure is used in ebXML. The specification requires that element and attribute names follow a standard capitalization arrangement, similar to Java names. Using a scheme described as upper and lower camel–case, ebXML element and attribute names have the following capitalization format:

```
<MyElementName myElementAttribute="..." myOtherElementAttr="...">
```

Additionally, underscores (_), periods (.), and dashes (-) are not allowed in element or attribute names, though they are legal in general XML.

Business Process and Modeling

In ebXML, business process and information modeling is not mandatory. But if it is used, it is required to be UMM (UN/CEFACT Modeling Methodology). This is a modeling language that uses UML (Universal Modeling Language), which is commonly used in object-oriented programming design.

The UMM approach separates operational and functional views and relies on two "view" constructs: the Business Operational View (BOV) and the Functional Service View (FSV). The operational view covers such things as the semantics involved in a transaction, as well as operational conventions, agreements, and arrangements. The functional view covers logistical and technological items such as user interfaces, data transfer interfaces, and capabilities for discovery and implementation runtime scenarios.

It is not a requirement that all adopters of ebXML utilize every aspect of the business modeling support. As a developer, you may choose to standardize upon a set of documents, but choose not to implement the routing and business logic these documents seem to suggest.

Phases of ebXML

Adopting new technology and business processes is a tough challenge. ebXML has defined phases of adoption that include considerations for the changes businesses usually undergo. Phases of ebXML are broken down into the *Implementation* phase, the *Discovery and Retrieval* phase, and an operational *Run Time* phase.

Items in the Implementation phase deal directly with creating an application of the ebXML infrastructure. In this scenario, a trading partner uses the Core and Business Libraries, coupled with any business process information of the other trading partners from the ebXML Registry.

Once you have implemented an ebXML business service interface, you can begin the Discovery and Retrieval phase. The discovery process is an attempt to understand the meaning of the information being requested and retrieving it as necessary.

The Run Time phase is where actual ebXML messages are being exchanged to support a transaction.

CHAPTER 8
Python Internet APIs

As the Internet continues to evolve, so do the toolboxes of the programmers who code for it. Just a few years ago, most Internet-related development usually involved tapping into a database or legacy system and presenting the information to the Web. This type of development is still very popular and necessary. However, the notion of exposing business processes and previously internal systems to the Internet as web services is picking up speed. The type of data exposed by business processes is meant for consumption by applications, not humans, and demands different solutions from programmers. There is also a rising interest in peer-to-peer services in which machines interrogate each other for available resources. This new evolution of the Internet and the interconnecting of distributed systems requires that programmers understand previously mysterious subsystems. Some of these new challenges involve making web sites talk to each other without the involvement of humans. This chapter shows you the programmatic APIs and Python modules you need to work with XML and the Internet.

Connecting Web Sites

Let's take a trip back to 1999. An imaginary beverage distributor sees value in allowing supermarkets to order beverage cases online. They hope this will replace the process of accepting a fax and manually keying in order details. The beverage company envisions a situation in which purchasing agents at the supermarkets could use their web browsers to quickly key in current needs and submit orders to the beverage company's system.

At this same time, the supermarkets are getting more and more interested in automating their inventory control. Instead of having people pour over stock statistics and sales numbers as they attempt to forecast demand, companies are installing sophisticated point-of-sale software at registers that perform these calculations for them. Once a week the system spits out printouts of the purchasers' needs based on buying patterns. The purchasing agent is then supposed to send out purchase orders as needed.

Continuing Improvement

Now let's go into the present. You are asked to take the information that is being automatically generated by the supermarket's inventory and sales forecasting system and plug it into the beverage company's order system without the involvement of a human. Ideally, this process should allow for supermarket computers to automatically send out purchase orders to suppliers when stock is low and demand dictates.

In order to perform this new task, you need to know how to interrogate the supermarket's inventory and forecasting system automatically, as well as how to submit the data you come up with as a purchase order to the beverage company. The ideal scenario, of course, is that both systems are web-enabled first. In this scenario, Python and its Internet APIs come to the rescue, allowing you to easily replace human-intensive browser operations with script and logic.

Python to the Rescue

We will now dive into Python's support for the Internet, as well as explore how to construct programs that mimic browsers or act like web servers, fetching URLs of all types, including FTP and HTTP.

Python's Internet support includes modules for working with URLs (Universal Resource Locators). Using the urllib module, you can build and deconstruct actual URLs, as well as retrieve them at runtime in your Python programs. Python also features an HTTP module that makes programmatic access to the HTTP protocol a breeze. For example, if there is specific stock price you are rabid about, and you know of a web site that retrieves live stock quotes, you can write a Python application to query that site for you periodically. Your program can extract the target stock quote and display it on your desktop instead of bringing up your browser every few hours to fetch the information from a specific site.

While this chapter presents a good view of the technologies needed to creatively develop Internet solutions, it's wise to start with the basics. The most fundamental building block of the Internet is the URL.

Working with URLs

The URL contains a great deal of Internet information in a single string. It tells you the name of the server, the name of the file on the server, any data that you are supplying to generate a dynamic response, and even the protocol to use to retrieve the information. In basic form, URLs look like this:

http://www.oreilly.com/oreilly/about.html

This URL has three elements. The first section tells you (or your software) the protocol in use for this resource. In this case, it is HTTP, shown by http:. The next section indicates the server name and its corresponding domain. In this case the server is named www, and the domain is oreilly.com, coming together as //www.oreilly.com. What follow are a pathname (/oreilly/) and a filename (about.html). Your browser uses this information as it comes to the brilliant conclusion to use HTTP in connecting with www in oreilly.com, and retrieves the /oreilly/about.html file.

Of course, URLs can become more complicated. If you type "Python" into a search box and click Submit, your browser may go after a URL similar to the following:

http://search.oreilly.com/cgi-bin/search?term=Python&category=All&pref=all

Now there are several more items to examine. First, the server has changed from www to search. Second, the path has changed from /oreilly/ to /cgi-bin/. The filename *about.html* has been replaced with a target named search. But most interesting is the question mark and the data that follows:

```
?term=Python&category=All&pref=all
```

This portion of the URL is known as the query string. If search is a CGI program (or something similar inside an application server) the query string is supplied to it in the form of an environment variable. The CGI program can pick the string apart to realize that a variable named term is set to Python, and that category and pref are equal to All and all respectively. As you can imagine, this information is relevant to the O'Reilly database and appropriate product information is returned to your browser.

However, suppose that instead of searching the O'Reilly site for "Python", you searched it for "Python!". What does the URL look like now? Well, the only difference is that the exclamation point is URL-encoded. That is, only a few special characters are allowed within a URL, all others are escaped to their respective hexadecimal code and delimited with a percent (%) sign. This time, the query string looks slightly different:

```
?term=Python%21&category=All&pref=all
```

The exclamation point is now replaced with %21, which is its URL-encoded cousin.

Encoding URLs

If you are constructing a URL programmatically for submission to a web site, you find yourself needing to supply parameters in the query string, as shown in the previous section.

Programmatic construction of URLs may be necessary when integrating your Python program with a dynamic web site expecting query parameters in the query string.

The Python urllib module features the method urlencode. This method accepts a dictionary of key/value pairs and returns a properly formatted query string that you could tag onto a URL. For example, if you have an arbitrarily sized dictionary, you could call urlencode with the dictionary as a parameter, as shown here:

```
>>> from urllib import urlencode
>>> myDict = {
... "Name" : "Chris Jones",
```

```
... "Address" : "Woodinville, WA",
... "Favorite Characters" : "#, @, $, and %"
... }
>>> strUrl = urlencode(myDict)
>>> print strUrl
Address=Woodinville%2c+WA&Name=Chris+Jones&Favorite+Characters=
    %23%2c+%40%2c+%24%2c+and+%25
```

What constitutes strURL here is not a complete URL. It's just the query data that comes at the end of the URL. The first half of the URL needs to include the protocol, as well as the server and domain pairing:

```
http://www.example.com/search.
cgi?Address=Woodinville%2c+WA&Name=Chris+Jones&Favorite+Characters=
    %23%2c+%40%2c+%24%2c+and+%25
```

The urlencode method takes care of escaping special characters as it translates #, @, $, and % into %23%2c+%40%2c+%24%2c+and+%25. Not only are the special characters translated, but the commas and spaces have also been converted to their hexadecimal values.

Quoting URLs

The quote method of urllib that takes a single string of data and performs the necessary encoding related to urlencode that takes a dictionary as a parameter. The primary difference is quote does not automatically generate key/value pairings based on a dictionary. The quote method exists to convert a single string into a URL-compliant syntax. For example, if a URL you are constructing consists of *http://www.example.com/addQuotation.cgi?myquote=*, but you need to add a URL-compliant value to it, you could use the quote method to encode it:

```
>>> from urllib import quote
>>> quote('Famous Quote: "I think, therefore I am."')
'Famous%20Quote%3a%20%22I%20think%2c%20therefore%20I%20am.%22'
```

Perhaps the most important thing to remember is that quote should be used to *encode a single string, not a key/value pair*. In any key=value combination, *only the value should be encoded with the quote command*. If you were to include the myquote= (or the key) portion of the query string when calling the quote method, the equal sign would also be encoded rendering the URL worthless.

Unquoting URLs

What goes up must come down. If you are encoding URLs programmatically, the odds are that you are going to need to decode one at some point or another. The unquote method of urllib takes an encoded string (such as that generated by quote) and returns the decoded version of it:

```
>>> from urllib import unquote
>>> unquote("Famous%20Quote%3a%20%22I%20think%2c%20therefore%20I%20am.%22")
'Famous Quote: "I think, therefore I am."'
```

If you are constructing and deconstructing URLs programmatically, it follows that actually connecting to these and retrieving their content is of value.

Opening URLs

The protocol portion of the URL can consist of anything that processing software can understand. Perhaps the most common URL protocols (also called schemes) are HTTP, FTP, and FILE. HTTP is used to connect to web servers, FTP is used to retrieve files, and FILE is used to retrieve a local file. All are easily accomplished using Python's urllib module.

The urllib.urlopen function takes care of opening URLs of all kinds and can give you back a file-like object to work with. To retrieve a local file, just use the filename. For example, to open an XML document in the local directory, you can use the following syntax:

```
>>> from urllib import urlopen
>>> fd = urlopen("order.xml")
>>> print fd.read()
<?xml version="1.0"?>
<!DOCTYPE order SYSTEM "order.dtd">
<order>
        <customer_name>eDonkey Enterprises</customer_name>
        <sku>343-3940938</sku>
        <unit_price>39.95</unit_price>
</order>

>>> fd.close()
```

The urlopen function returns a file-like object. This object can then be treated as a file to retrieve and display its contents. When the file object is closed, urlopen cleans up its business as well, terminating its connection to the remote server or local file.

Using FTP

The urlopen function works for remote files just as easily as it does for local files, provided you're connected to the Internet. For example, if you supply a URL for an FTP server's root directory, you may be able to pull back its contents, as shown here:

```
>>> fd = urlopen("ftp://ftp.oreilly.com")
>>> print fd.read()
total 64
drwxr-xr-x    3 61          512 Aug 29  2000 bin
drwxr-xr-x    2 3           512 Aug 30  2000 dev
drwxr-xr-x    4 61          512 Oct 16  2000 etc
lrwxrwxrwx    1 1            12 Aug 31  2000 examples -> pub/examples
drwxrwx-wx    2 100         512 May  7 22:22 incoming
drwxrws--x   48 61        17408 May  6 04:00 intl
drwxr-xr-x    2 1           512 Sep  1  2000 lost+found
drwxrws--x   55 61         4608 May  7 22:22 outgoing
drwxrwsr-x   21 61          512 Mar 30 21:47 pub
```

```
drwxr-xr-x   2 61             512 Aug 31  2000 published
drwxr-sr-x   4 100            512 Apr 17 17:17 software
dr-xr-xr-x   5 61             512 Aug 30  2000 usr

>>> fd.close( )
```

Retrieving URLs

urlretrieve is similar to urlopen. This function optionally accepts a filename if you wish to store the remote file locally, and the function returns a tuple of the filename and the actual data as a mime message, as shown here:

```
>>> from urllib import urlretrieve
>>> ob = urlretrieve("ftp://ftp.oreilly.com", "menu.txt")
>>> ob
('menu.txt', <mimetools.Message instance at 007F382C>)
```

The first argument is the actual URL to connect to, while the second argument is the name of a local file to hold the data.

One of the most exciting features of urlretrieve is its callback functionality. When retrieving a document, you can supply a callback method as an optional third parameter to receive progress reports as the resource is downloaded.

If you supply a callback method, urlretrieve expects your callback method to take three arguments. The first argument is the current block number on which the retrieval is operating. The second argument is the size of the blocks being used, and the third is the total size of the file. Example 8-1 shows a simple routine that reports on its progress.

Example 8-1. retrieve.py

```
"""
retrieve.py example
"""
from urllib import urlretrieve

def callback(blocknum, blocksize, totalsize):
  print "Downloaded " + str((blocknum * blocksize)),
  print " of ", totalsize

urlretrieve("http://www.example.com/pyxml.xml", "px.xml", callback)
print "Download Complete"
```

The running example shows you:

```
C:\WINDOWS\Desktop\oreilly\pythonxml\c8>python retrieve.py
Downloaded 0   of   116063
Downloaded 8192   of   116063
Downloaded 16384   of   116063
Downloaded 24576   of   116063
Downloaded 32768   of   116063
Downloaded 40960   of   116063
```

```
Downloaded 49152  of  116063
Downloaded 57344  of  116063
Downloaded 65536  of  116063
Downloaded 73728  of  116063
Downloaded 81920  of  116063
Downloaded 90112  of  116063
Downloaded 98304  of  116063
Downloaded 106496 of  116063
Downloaded 114688 of  116063
Downloaded 122880 of  116063
Downloaded 131072 of  116063
Download Complete
```

The callback functionality is excellent for keeping track of FTP progress. The callback functionality is also great anytime you need to keep tabs on a long download, or communicate progress information to a frustrated, busy end-user.

Connecting with HTTP

While `urllib` is suitable for working with Internet files, you may still have the need to perform more intricate communication with an HTTP server. For example, if you are writing a Python program to communicate between two web sites, you may need to adjust the headers to include any cookies the site may require. You may need to emulate a certain browser type (by placing its name in your `User-Agent` header) if the site requires the latest version of Internet Explorer. Working with `httplib` as opposed to `urllib` in cases such as these allows for finer control.

HTTP Conversations

HTTP conversations between browsers and servers involve headers and data. The interaction between a web browser and a web server reveals a great deal of information about both parties. The HTTP headers that precede content from the server and precede requests from the browser contain a lot of metadata about both client and server. For example, when you type a URL into your browser and press return, a complete HTTP request is sent to the remote server that can look something like this:

```
GET /c7/favquote.cgi HTTP/1.1
Host: www.python.org
Accept: image/gif, image/x-xbitmap, image/jpeg, image/pjpeg
Accept-Language: en-us
Accept-Encoding: gzip, deflate
User-Agent: Mozilla/4.0 (compatible; MSIE 5.5; Windows 98; Win 9x 4.90)
Connection: Keep-Alive
```

The headers tell the web server a great deal about the capabilities of the client browser. From the first line of the headers (`GET /c7/favquote.cgi HTTP/1.1`), we can tell that the request type is a `GET`, the target file is *c7/favquote.cgi*, and the HTTP version in use is `1.1`. Beyond this essential information is data telling the server what file types the browser can accept, what the browser is, and what type of HTTP connection to use. The Accept lines tell the server that your browser can handle *.gif* and *.jpeg* files, as well as any others. Notice there are three lines that start with Accept in the HTTP headers. They show the browser accepts en-us as its language, and both gzip and deflate as encoding:.

```
Accept: image/gif, image/x-xbitmap, image/jpeg, image/pjpeg
Accept-Language: en-us
Accept-Encoding: gzip, deflate
```

The User-Agent informs the server which browser or HTTP client you're using. Every browser (and every HTTP library) populates this field with one thing or another, letting web sites know how people are visiting. Some web sites are designed to specifically utilize the features of either Netscape Navigator or Internet Explorer and may redirect browsers to one set of pages or another based on what it sees in the User-Agent string:

```
User-Agent: Mozilla/4.0 (compatible; MSIE 5.5; Windows 98; Win 9x 4.90)
```

This User-Agent is Internet Explorer 5.5 running on Microsoft's desktop platform. The last header in the previous example tells the server what type of connection to use. In this case, it's Keep-Alive:

```
Connection: Keep-Alive
```

The Keep-Alive connection type tells the server to keep the socket between the client and the server open for additional resources. Typically, when downloading a web page, an initial request is made to retrieve the HTML page itself, and then a series of subsequent requests are made to retrieve images referenced with the <img> tag, as well as linked stylesheets and framesets. Initiating a new connection for each one of these resources would be very time-consuming, especially considering the graphics-laden web pages in use today. The Keep-Alive option lets the browser use the same channel it has already established to bring down all of the additional resources.

Request Types

In addition to the GET request, three other request types exist. Basically, a browser can do four things with a web server. It can GET a file. It can POST data to a file as well, such as sending a form to a CGI script. The two other lesser-known methods are HEAD and PUT. HEAD is used just to retrieve web server headers, and PUT is used to actually send a file to the server.

GET
>   Requests a file, and optionally contains a query string used by the file (if it's a CGI or other executable) to generate dynamic data.

POST
>   Sends URL-encoded data to the server in a large chunk. Frequently used to send form fields to the server. Anything POSTed can also be sent via GET, but the

difference is the query string becomes large and may look unsightly or be unmanageable in the browser when doing a GET. A POST is not carried on the query string, and so is not visible to an end user. Some servers may allow less data on a query string, and accept bigger chunks of data in a POST request.

HEAD

Similar to GET, but returns only the headers.

PUT

A seldom-used HTTP method to place files on the server. When using this method, the filename that normally goes after a GET or a POST request is used as the filename for the content being delivered to the server. In other words, instead of telling the server you want to GET a page called */index.html*, tell it you are going to PUT a file named */index.html* on the server. During a PUT operation, the contents of the file are sent after the headers, just like in a POST operation.

Getting a Document with Python

To manually use HTTP from Python, use httplib. The httplib module is standard and ships with Python 2.x. The HTTP class within httplib features several import methods for connecting to the server:

Req = HTTP(*address, [port]*)

Returns an instance of the HTTP class for use as a request object in this connection. The connection is also made to the given address and optional port. Most web servers run on port 80, and you would not need to supply this argument. However, some web sites are kept on different ports and this option then gives you the ability to select a specific port.

Req.putrequest(*method, file*)

Performs the initial HTTP request method with its accompanying filename and HTTP version indicator. This is the first line of the headers, as in:

```
GET /c7/favquote.cgi HTTP/1.1
```

Req.putheader(*header-type, value*)

Adds a new header to the request. This method would be used to add your custom User-Agent string, Accept-Types, or cookies.

Req.endheaders( )

Instructs the module to finish off the headers sent to the server. In HTTP, the headers are separated from data with a blank line. That is, when the server is sending back an HTML page, it gives the browser its headers, followed by a blank line, followed by the HTML document. Conversely, when the browser is making a form POST to a server, it does the same thing and separates its request headers from its post data with a blank line.

Req.send(*data*)

Sends data after your request. The send method must be called after endheaders to speak proper HTTP. You use this method when making a POST or PUT.

ErrorCode, ErrorMessage, Headers = *Req*.getreply( )

Gives you the server's headers and response code in one swoop. Both ErrorCode and ErrorMessage should be 200 and OK respectively if everything is going well. The Headers object is actually an instance of mimetools.Message.

fp. = *Req*.getfile( )

Returns a file-like object that you can use to access the actual HTML (or other) document.

Using the HTTP class from httplib is simple. Example 8-2 shows how to connect to a server and retrieve the *index.html* page.

Example 8-2. Making an HTTP Request

```
>>> from httplib import HTTP
>>> req = HTTP("www.example.com")
>>> req.putrequest("GET", "/index.html")
>>> req.putheader("Accept", "text/html")
>>> req.putheader("User-Agent", "MyPythonScript")
>>> req.endheaders( )
>>> ec, em, h = req.getreply( )
>>> print ec, em
200 OK
>>> fd = req.getfile( )
>>> textlines = fd.read( )
>>> fd.close( )
```

The steps taken in Example 8-2 are straightforward. The HTTP class is called with an argument indicating the server, *www.example.com*. Next, headers are added describing some minimal information for the server including the type of data expected and the name of your user agent as MyPythonScript. The error code and error message are retrieved with a call to getreply and the result is printed to the console:

```
>>> print ec, em
200 OK
```

Next, getfile is used to retrieve the file-like object containing the document contents. The getfile method returns a file descriptor that you can read with. After a call to read, the return result is assigned to the variable textlines that now contains the actual document. Calling close finishes off the request. You can print textlines to see what you have retrieved:

```
>>> print textlines
<html>
<head>
<link rel="stylesheet" type="text/css" href="/zpath.css">
</head>
<body BGCOLOR="#CDFF00">
<p>
<table WIDTH=100% height=100%>
    <tr>
```

```
    <td VALIGN="top" ALIGN="left">
        <a HREF="/cgi-bin/start.cgi?page=top">
            <img SRC="images/zplogo.gif" WIDTH=457
                HEIGHT=144 BORDER=0>
        </a>
    </td>
</tr>
</table>
</p>    \
</body>
</html>
```

Of special note in this request is the User-Agent string. Most web site administrators run access reports and generate neat sets of statistics detailing the browser types in use. By writing your own Python Internet programs, you can add to the statistics. In Example 8-2, we set the User-Agent string to MyPythonScript by calling:

```
req.putheader("User-Agent", "MyPythonScript")
```

This is captured in the server logs, and most likely show up in the *less-than-one-percent* category of the site administrator's browser statistics.

Building a Query String with httplib

Example 8-2 shows how to request a specific file. Say you'd like to also add a query string to your GET request. The second argument to HTTP.putrequest is the filename you're after. To add a query string to the HTTP request, you could couple the filename with your data, as shown here, properly URL-encoded:

```
req.putrequest("GET", "/handler.cgi?id=12345")
```

If you need to encode your data because it contains special characters, you could use the urllib's quote function described earlier in this chapter, in the section entitled "Quoting URLs."

```
req.putrequest("GET", "/handler.cgi?" + quote("numbers=1/2/3/4/5"))
```

Baking Cookies for the Server

Any hungry server administrator may be disappointed to learn that the cookies your browser sends to his web site are electronic. Cookies are frequently delivered to web servers by browsers to indicate a special identification for your browser. Your browser keeps the cookie and returns it whenever the same web site or document is requested. This lets the web server personalize site content for you, or connect you with some specific data that may be held in a database, such as your profile information or virtual shopping cart. If you are writing Python scripts to go between web sites, you may need to send cookies in your headers. You use the putheader method of the HTTP class to do so, as shown here:

```
req.putheader("Cookie", "key=value")
```

Conversely, when the server is sending cookies to your browser a set-cookie header is thrown in the mix with the other headers and digested by your browser.

Performing a POST Operation

If you are manually using HTTP from Python, odds are you're moving documents around. You may be hitting one URL to get information from a database, constructing a form, and submitting that data to another web site via the POST operation. Creating a POST with httplib is straightforward, but more intricate than the examples shown thus far in this chapter. This method is detailed in the following sections.

Creating a POST catcher

Any example illustrating a POST is of no value without something to post to. So, for the purpose of this example, you can create a simple CGI script that echoes back your posted data. To use, place this ten-line file in a CGI-capable directory of your web server as *favquote.cgi*, shown in Example 8-3.

Example 8-3. favquote.cgi

```
#!/usr/bin/python

import cgi
form = cgi.FieldStorage()
favquote = form["favquote"].value

print "Content-type: text/html"
print ""
print "<html><body>"
print "Your quote is: "
print favquote
print "</body></html>"
```

This simple CGI uses the cgi module to retrieve the data sent in the post. We make a post to this CGI in the next section.

Ensuring proper URL encoding

One of the more interesting points of making a POST is ensuring that your data is properly URL-encoded. This means ensuring the favquote key is not encoded in the data if your CGI script is looking for a variable named favquote. For example, a proper key=value pair should be:

```
favquote=This%20is%20my%20quote%3a%20%22I%20think%20therefore%20I%20am.%22
```

However, if in your enthusiasm you quote the entire string and not just the value portion, you wind up with:

```
favquote%3dThis%20is%20my%20favorite%20quote%3a%20...
```

Unfortunately, the server will not know what to do with the second flawed scenario, as there is no key to associate the value with, as favquote= has been transformed into favquote%3d.

Performing a POST with httplib

In Example 8-3, we created a GET request using the methods of httplib. Performing a POST requires a couple of extra method calls, and very precise order of events. The sequence of the HTTP calls is important, and making a post requires extra headers. The start of a POST request is similar to a GET, as shown here:

```
req = HTTP("192.168.1.23")
req.putrequest("POST", "/c7/favquote.cgi")
req.putheader("Accept", "text/html")
req.putheader("User-Agent", "MyPythonScript")
```

Note that this time, the first argument to putrequest is POST. Beyond the change from GET to POST, the call to putrequest looks the same. When posting data to the server, it's important that the server know exactly how many bytes of data the HTTP client is sending. While the HTTP headers rely on line breaks and a blank line as field delimiters, posted data may contain all sorts of special characters, binary data, or other nonprintable characters. Therefore, instead of relying on line breaks, the server requires that you specify how many bytes you're sending, and then reads that number of bytes from your request. Specify the content length using putheader (note that you must know the number of bytes):

```
myquote = 'This is my quote: "I think therefore I am."'
postdata = "favquote=" + quote(myquote)
req.putheader("Content-Length", str(len(postdata)))
```

In these calls, you assemble the post data by concatenating the key portion (favquote=) with the quoted value. Use the len function to size up your URL-encoded string named postdata. Finally, since putheader expects a string as a second argument and not a number, convert the length with the str function.

The HTTP.send method is used to submit the data after ending the headers:

```
req.endheaders()
req.send(postdata)
```

Now, you can get the reply and read the results as you did with your GET request earlier in Example 8-3. The result of the POST may be dynamically generated data such as search results, or it could be an HTML page detailing a problem associated with the POST.

Illustrating a complete POST operation

As you can see, performing a POST (rather than a GET) requires learning a few more steps. The file *post.py*, shown in Example 8-4, pulls these ideas together and illustrates a complete POST operation. If you copied Example 8-3, *favquote.cgi*, to a CGI-capable directory on your web server, you should be able to run *post.py* from the command line. Be sure and *put the appropriate IP address* or `localhost` in the call to the HTTP constructor!

Example 8-4. post.py

```
"""
post.py
"""
from httplib import HTTP
from urllib  import quote

# establish POST data
myquote = 'This is my quote: "I think therefore I am."'

# be sure not to quote the key= sequence...
postdata = "favquote=" + quote(myquote)

print "Will POST ", len(postdata), "bytes:"
print postdata

# begin HTTP request
req = HTTP("192.168.1.23") # change to your IP or localhost
req.putrequest("POST", "/c7/favquote.cgi")
req.putheader("Accept", "text/html")
req.putheader("User-Agent", "MyPythonScript")

# Set Content-length to length of postdata
req.putheader("Content-Length", str(len(postdata)))
req.endheaders()

# send post data after ending headers,
# CGI script will receive it on STDIN
req.send(postdata)

ec, em, h = req.getreply()
print "HTTP RESPONSE: ", ec, em

# get file-like object from HTTP response
# and print received HTML to screen
fd = req.getfile()
textlines = fd.read()
fd.close()
print "\nReceived following HTML:\n"
print textlines
```

The raw HTTP headers and post data that *post.py* produces are shown below:

```
POST /c7/favquote.cgi HTTP/1.1
Accept: image/gif, image/x-xbitmap, image/jpeg, image/pjpeg
Accept-Language: en-us
Content-Type: application/x-www-form-urlencoded
Accept-Encoding: gzip, deflate
User-Agent: Mozilla/4.0 (compatible; MSIE 5.5; Windows 98; Win 9x 4.90)
```

```
Host: 192.168.1.45
Content-Length: 70
Connection: Keep-Alive
```

```
favquote=This+is+my+favorite+quote%3A+%22I+think%2C+therefore+I+am.%22
```

As you can see, the content length is specified and the data follows exactly one blank line after the headers.

Thus far in this chapter, we've encountered `urllib` and `httplib`, and have retrieved generic URLs and created custom HTTP requests. Now we are going to take a look at Python's support for implementing the server side of the connection.

Using the Server Classes

Armed with an understanding of sockets, you are now ready to code your own network servers. But before you go out and try to implement an HTTP server, you should see what Python already offers in terms of modules.

Python features a base HTTP server, a simple HTTP server, and a CGI HTTP server. As for the simple server, the main task is returning files from the local directory to clients that ask for them over HTTP. The CGI server is similar, but is prepared to run CGI scripts and equip them with the environment variables they need, in order to be interactive with their browser clients. But the most interesting of all in this area is the `BaseHTTPServer`.

The `BaseHTTPServer` module contains a simple socket server (the `HTTPServer` class) that accepts HTTP requests. You can implement a few methods of the `BaseHTTPRequestHandler` to work with the request. The advantage to using these two classes is the power it gives you when working with clients. Instead of simply serving files or running external CGI programs, you have the ability to interpret URLs any way you wish, and return anything you like back to the client. If you've ever worked with application servers that offer their own inline scripting language (i.e. PHP, Cold Fusion, Active Server Pages, etc.) then you have seen base HTTP servers in practice. When an application server such as Cold Fusion is running with your web server, your web server hands over any HTTP request that has a *.cfm* extension to the Cold Fusion process. That is, the server does absolutely nothing with the request if it is marked for Cold Fusion. Cold Fusion is then free to examine the request and send back the appropriate data after executing any inline code placed in the file.

In this section, we implement a base HTTP server that can handle both GET and POST requests. Running on port 2112, all HTTP traffic sent to port 2112 is completely handled by the server—regardless of what filename is being requested. In fact there won't be any files served at all, but instead there will be a default response that all browsers receive, regardless of what information is in the URL.

BaseHTTPServer Module Classes

The `BaseHTTPServer` module features two classes: the `HTTPServer` and the `BaseHTTPRequestHandler`. You'll likely only encounter four methods between the two of these classes, as shown in this section.

The `HTTPServer` class constructor takes two arguments: an address tuple (hostname and port), and a reference to a request handler. The `HTTPServer` class, once instantiated, has two modes of operation. You can call `serve_forever` to handle an infinite number of clients, or you can call `handle_request` to handle a single client.

The `BaseHTTPRequestHandler` is a stub class, which you can override for custom functionality. You'll likely only override `do_GET` and `do_POST`. These methods are called whenever a fresh HTTP request has arrived and is asking for either a GET or POST operation. The request handler does have some properties that are of considerable importance:

`rh.headers`
> A dictionary of header/value pairs.

`rh.rfile`
> The "request" or "read" file descriptor of the socket. This allows you to read data beyond the headers into the server as you would during a POST operation.

`rh.wfile`
> The "write" file descriptor of the socket. This attribute allows you to send data to the HTTP requestor (back to the client or browser).

`rh.path`
> The request and path portion of the query string.

`rh.command`
> The type of HTTP request that is being asked for (GET, POST, HEAD, or PUT).

`rh.request_version`
> A string representing the current HTTP version in use.

`rh.client_address`
> A tuple representing the client address.

Server Core Concepts

The architecture of the base server class is quite simple. HTTP headers are given to you as a dictionary; beyond that, a few simple functions exist allowing you to write the different aspects of an HTTP request back down to the sender. At the core of the classes are the `rfile` and `wfile` members of the `BaseHTTPRequestHandler`. These two objects actually allow you to read and write directly from the client socket.

Instantiating a server class

To instantiate a server and start its operations, you can use the HTTPServer constructor. For example:

```
myServer = HTTPServer(('', 2112), myRequestHandler)
for lp in range(5):
  myServer.handle_request()
```

This code instructs the server to connect to localhost (via the blank line and port number tuple) and to supply a custom request handler. In addition to handle_request, the HTTPServer features a serve_forever method that never returns. The method you choose is really just a matter of preference. Example 8-5, presented later in this chapter, handles five requests and then exits. When choosing serve_forever, you are committing to running the server for a very long time. You will not be able to interrupt it from the command line. Basically, if you've chosen serve_forever, you need to wire in a way of stopping your server—either by sending a special command to it over the network, or by flipping a lock file or other filesystem switch on the server. Of course, you can always just hunt down the process and kill it (with a *kill -9* on Unix or a quick trip to the Task Manager on Windows).

Serving a GET

If you are indeed implementing a request handler, it's up to you to implement do_GET and do_POST. A GET operation is easiest, as most of the information you may need is in the headers.

```
class myRequestHandler(BaseHTTPRequestHandler):
  def do_GET(self):
```

For starters, you need to derive your request handler (myRequestHandler) from the BaseHTTPServer.BaseHTTPRequestHandler class. After this first step, you can use some of the methods of the HTTPServer to send a response back to the user.

```
self.send_response(200)
self.send_header("Content-type", "text/html")
self.end_headers()
```

After closing out the headers with a call to end_headers, you can use the write file to send data to the browser.

```
self.wfile.write("<html><body>")
self.wfile.write("<b>Hello</b>")
self.wfile.write("</html></body>")
```

The actual URI requested would be present in the request handler's path attribute (self.path in the previous example). You could use the path information to serve a particular file, or to invoke a specific method on an object. All other client information in the headers is held in the headers dictionary.

Serving a POST

Implementing a POST is a little more intricate, and requires some knowledge of what HTTP looks like during a POST operation. The most important difference is that after reading the browser (or client) headers, the server must figure out how many bytes to read off the client sockets that constitute a POST. To accomplish this, all POST operations from a browser supply a Content-length header, from which the size of the POST is retrieved.

The basic method calls used when dealing with a post are shown here:

```
def do_POST(self):

    self.send_response(200)
    self.send_header("Content-type", "text/html")
    self.end_headers( )

    self.wfile.write("<html><body>")
    self.printBrowserHeaders( )
    self.wfile.write("<b>Post Data:</b><br>")

    if self.headers.dict.has_key("content-length"):

        content_length = string.atoi(self.headers.dict["content-length"])

        raw_post_data = self.rfile.read(content_length)
        self.wfile.write(raw_post_data)
```

As you can see, the length of the posted data is kept in the header named content-length and is submitted along with the client headers. Of course the value of content-length must be converted from a string to an integer before being used in a read operation on the input file.

Building a Complete Server

An example is a great way to learn the steps necessary for implementing your own server. In Example 8-5, writing the HTTP response and parsing the input headers for return in HTML are relegated to function calls so that both the do_GET and do_POST methods can have access to them. The printBrowserHeaders function simply iterates through the browser headers and formats them in HTML, writing them back down the socket:

```
def printBrowserHeaders(self):
  # iterate through header dictionary and
  # display the name and value of each pair.
  self.wfile.write("<p>Headers: <br>")
  header_keys = self.headers.dict.keys( )
  for key in header_keys:
    self.wfile.write("<b>" + key + "</b>: ")
    self.wfile.write(self.headers.dict[key] + "<br>")
```

The `printCustomHTTPHeaders` method sends a response code to the browser and closes off the HTTP headers. If you want to add any additional headers, you should do so here.

```python
def printCustomHTTPResponse(self, respcode):
    # send back appropriate HTTP code
    self.send_response(respcode)

    # tell them we're sending HTML
    self.send_header("Content-type", "text/html")

    # describe the server software in use!
    self.send_header("Server", "myRequestHandler :-)")

    # close off headers
    self.end_headers()
```

Example 8-5, *HTTPServer.py*, shows the complete listing of the server, incorporating the techniques presented thus far.

Example 8-5. HTTPServer.py

```python
"""
HTTPServer.py - an simple implementation
of the BaseHTTPServer module
"""

from BaseHTTPServer import HTTPServer
from BaseHTTPServer import BaseHTTPRequestHandler
import string

"""
class myRequestHandler - Handles any and all request
    coming in, regardless of path, file, or request
    method (GET/POST)
"""
class myRequestHandler(BaseHTTPRequestHandler):
    """
    do_GET will be called if the browser does a GET
    request.
    """
    def do_GET(self):
        # give them back a 200 OK every time.
        self.printCustomHTTPResponse(200)

        # start HTML output
        self.wfile.write("<html><body>")
        self.wfile.write("<p>Hello, I am a web server, sort of.</p>")
        self.wfile.write("<p>GET string: " + self.path + "</p>")
```

Example 8-5. HTTPServer.py (continued)

```python
    # show browser headers
    self.printBrowserHeaders()

    # finish off HTML
    self.wfile.write("</html></body>")

"""
do_POST is called if the browser is POSTing data
from a form
"""
def do_POST(self):
    # send back a 200 OK
    self.printCustomHTTPResponse(200)

    # start HTML and show browser headers again
    self.wfile.write("<html><body>")
    self.printBrowserHeaders()
    self.wfile.write("<b>Post Data:</b><br>")

    # track down length of the post, so that you
    # can read in the correct number of bytes.  The
    # length of the post is in the browser header
    # named 'content-length'.
    if self.headers.dict.has_key("content-length"):
        # convert content-length from string to int
        content_length = string.atoi(self.headers.dict["content-length"])

        # read in the correct number of bytes from the client
        # connection and send it back to the browser
        raw_post_data = self.rfile.read(content_length)
        self.wfile.write(raw_post_data)

    # finish off HTML
    self.wfile.write("</html></body>")

"""
printBrowserHeaders - this method prints the HTTP
    headers sent by the client
"""
def printBrowserHeaders(self):
    # iterate through header dictionary and
    # display the name and value of each pair.
    self.wfile.write("<p>Headers: <br>")
    header_keys = self.headers.dict.keys()
    for key in header_keys:
        self.wfile.write("<b>" + key + "</b>: ")
        self.wfile.write(self.headers.dict[key] + "<br>")
```

Example 8-5. HTTPServer.py (continued)

```
    """
    printCustomHTTPResponse - this method takes a response
        code and sends the code and custom headers
        back to the browser
    """
    def printCustomHTTPResponse(self, respcode):
      # send back appropriate HTTP code
      self.send_response(respcode)

      # tell them we're sending HTML
      self.send_header("Content-type", "text/html")

      # describe the server software in use!
      self.send_header("Server", "myRequestHandler :-)")

      # close off headers
      self.end_headers()


# start the server on port 2112, requires browser URLs
# to be addressed as http://servername:2112/pathtofile
myServer = HTTPServer(('', 2112), myRequestHandler)

# loop to handle 5 requests
for lp in range(5):
  myServer.handle_request()
```

Running a GET request

To launch your new server, simply supply its name to Python:

```
C:\WINDOWS\Desktop\oreilly\pythonxml\c8>python HTTPServer.py
```

The prompt won't return, as the server keeps running until it has handled five requests. When running the server to test the GET functionality, just launch your browser and type in the name of your server, plus port 2112 (*http://hostname:2112*), to get a response. It doesn't matter which path you use, as it is ignored by the server. Figure 8-1 shows a browser making a GET request against the server with an address of *http://localhost:2112/this/path/and/pagename/are/made.up?its=true*. The only critical piece of the URL is the *host:port* combination *http://localhost:2112*.

Running a POST request

Performing a POST requires a web form. The simple HTML file *testServer.html* shown in Example 8-6 should work. It does not need to be placed on a web server, but rather loaded it in your browser, just as you would a file. When you press the submit button, the form tries to POST its data to your *HTTPServer.py* running at port 2112. Example 8-6 shows the markup for *testServer.html*.

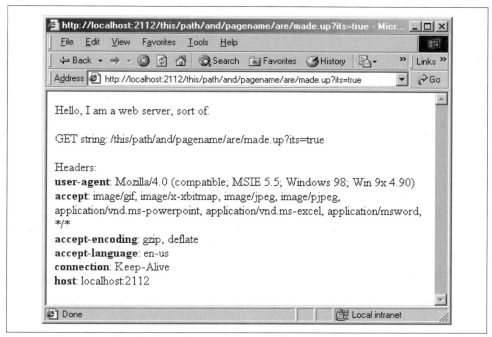

Figure 8-1. A browser connecting to the server with a GET request.

Example 8-6. testServer.html

```
<html>
<body>
<form action="http://localhost:2112/this/part/doesnt/matter" method="POST">
<textarea rows=10 cols=40 name="textdata">
This is some sample data for you to submit
if you like.
</textarea><br>
<input type=submit>
</form>
</body>
</html>
```

Figure 8-2 shows the web form from Example 8-6 sitting in your browser with the default text. The important thing to remember about the web form is that its action attribute points to port 2112, instead of just port 80.

When you submit the form, as with the GET request, the path and filename are ignored by the server, and instead *HTTPServer.py* simply uses the rfile to read data in from your request. The content-length header is sent by the browser to tell the server how many bytes to attempt to read from the socket. Figure 8-3 shows the response from the server. It's similar to the GET response, but your POST data is also presented, properly URL-encoded.

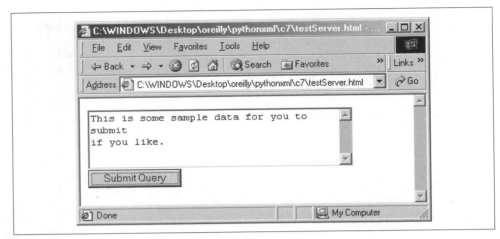

Figure 8-2. A web form to test the server

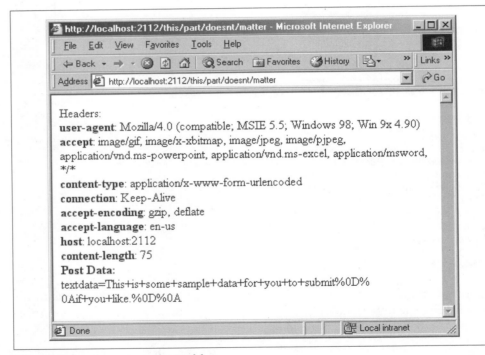

Figure 8-3. A response to a submitted form

In this chapter, we tie together many of the Internet's subsystems available to you
from Python. When writing applications that work with XML in distributed systems, it's important to understand how the different subsystems work together,
beyond just CGI. Having an understanding of how web servers operate, how URLs

are encoded and decoded, as well as understanding the nature of threads and sockets and their role in network programming, equips you to glue together distributed systems and XML with a more robust toolbox. XML is still very much a cutting-edge technology, and leveraging it effectively means having an advanced understanding of the distributed network environment in which its used including protocols, sockets, threads, and other APIs. In the next chapter we explore web services and SOAP. Given the nascent SOAP support in Python, the work done in this chapter will serve you well.

CHAPTER 9
Python, Web Services, and SOAP

The Internet has opened many eyes to the possibilities of easily accessible digital information. With systems connected together, there is no reason why an airline ticket agent can't have an email sent to your hotel when you're boarding your flight 45 minutes late. Likewise, an Internet-enabled PDA and GPS should have no trouble automatically updating driving directions for you when notified that your hotel has changed due to overbooking. In other words, web services enable distributed systems to communicate with each other, sharing relevant pieces of user information to trigger the right kinds of events, alerts, and notices. However, web services hold a great deal of promise for those other than end-users or business travelers. For corporations, web services provide a greater degree of interoperability with trading partners, allowing the automation of business transactions and tighter integration between production and supply-chain systems. As previously mentioned, for humans, web services hold the promise of tying together distributed information in such a way that the Web can become a unified, seamless whole, regardless of a user's location or device. Understanding the impact of such innovation can shed light on the current interest in and excitement over web services. Understanding the technology behind them can give you the tools to create more powerful, integrated, and dynamic web applications.

Web services are distributed systems on the Web. When you visit a rich Internet portal, chances are much of the content that you see there was derived from sites talking to one another before the actual content is delivered to you; this is commonly referred to as *content syndication*. The technology behind this distributed model is just beginning to emerge and take hold. Typically, the components needed for servers to talk to one another include a common wire protocol and a common transactional protocol. If the wire protocol encapsulates external data formats, those formats must also be agreed on. When these elements are in place, it becomes possible for one service (such as a credit bureau) to talk to another (such as a financial web site).

The Internet has given the world a common wire protocol. *Transmission Control Protocol/Internet Protocol* (TCP/IP) has established itself as the common network protocol used on the Internet. TCP/IP is taken for granted by applications that establish higher-level, file-like communications with each other all the time. While you may use a socket to connect to an HTTP server, the networking subsystems eventually speak TCP/IP on the wire to ensure your stream of bits gets to the server exactly as intended. On top of TCP/IP, there is a layer known as the Hypertext Transport Protocol (HTTP); on top of that, there is the layer Simple Object Access Protocol (SOAP). While SOAP can run over other communications protocols, HTTP makes the most sense due to its widespread adoption and agility with firewalls. SOAP is more of a transactional protocol giving response and request semantics to developers. SOAP also provides a common data format, as it successfully defines an encoding for data values in XML and can be shared easily shared between distributed systems.

The bulk of these technologies, coupled with supporting players such as Web Services Description Language (WSDL) and Universal Discovery, Description, and Integration (UDDI), constitutes web services for many industry analysts, though alternative technologies are used as well.

Python Web Services Support

For Python, web services are a nascent arena. In fact, as of this writing, several different SOAP implementations are in the works, yet none of them have reached maturity. The most mature SOAP implementations exist for both Java and Microsoft COM environments, and are supported by key industry heavyweights such as IBM and Microsoft. It's likely that these implementations will drive the adoption of web services, as well as help shape the standard. Fortunately, these implementations are available to your Python applications.

The Emerging SOAP Standard

Understanding SOAP helps you better use SOAP implementations, and more importantly allows you to adopt SOAP as a general XML messaging medium. SOAP is a work in progress but is slated to become a W3C recommendation. As of this writing, the latest SOAP specification is the W3C Note available from *http://www.w3c. org*. W3C members from various companies, including DevelopMentor, IBM, UserLand, Lotus Development, and Microsoft, develop SOAP.

SOAP is an XML-based protocol, and defines three basic concepts:

1. An envelope that describes a message and how to process it.
2. Encoding requirements that describe message data types.
3. Remote Procedure Call conventions that allow for distributed method invocations.

SOAP Messages

In its most basic form, SOAP is used over HTTP to send a message to a SOAP server. In turn, the server implements some specific functionality and returns a SOAP response message back to the caller. This type of interaction uses HTTP's inherent request/response design. The original SOAP message may be a method invocation and parameters; the response may be the return values.

A SOAP request may take the form of:

```
<SOAP-ENV:Envelope
    xmlns:SOAP-ENV="http://schemas.xmlsoap.org/soap/envelope/"
    SOAP-ENV:encodingStyle="http://schemas.xmlsoap.org/soap/encoding/">
    <SOAP-ENV:Body>
        <m:GetLocalTemperature xmlns:m="http://localhost/temperApp">
            <zipcode>90872</zipcode>
        </m:GetLocalTemperature>
    </SOAP-ENV:Body>
</SOAP-ENV:Envelope>
```

This message is sent over HTTP, and can be posted to a specific URI capable of interpreting and responding to the SOAP message. The return SOAP unit contains the response to the query GetLocalTemperature.

```
<SOAP-ENV:Envelope
    xmlns:SOAP-ENV="http://schemas.xmlsoap.org/soap/envelope/"
    SOAP-ENV:encodingStyle="http://schemas.xmlsoap.org/soap/encoding/"/>
    <SOAP-ENV:Body>
        <m:GetLocalTemperatureResponse
            xmlns:m="http://localhost/temperApp">
            <Farenheit>59</Farenheit>
        </m:GetLocalTemperatureResponse>
    </SOAP-ENV:Body>
</SOAP-ENV:Envelope>
```

In this return example, the result of the method invocation is returned to the caller in a SOAP packet.

Exchanging SOAP Messages

The current SOAP specification places no constraints on how a SOAP message is sent across the network. SOAP implementations are allowed to take advantage of any special features of their communications medium, be it HTTP, SMTP, or something yet to be imagined.

However, SOAP does define the concept of a *Message Path*. This critical concept allows a SOAP packet to be dealt with at intermediate steps along the way to its final destination. While it's simple to think of the message delivery process as one that simply hops a message to its end-point, in reality this powerful concept mimics that of *routing*. It's possible to add intelligence to a network to deal with SOAP packets, and distribute them where they need to go. This addition of intelligence to the network allows for a much greater level of scalability and traffic management by allowing multiple, distributed systems to route packets where they need to go, as opposed to forcing them through a central server.

SOAP requires intermediate processors to perform three steps in exact order:

1. The SOAP processor identifies any part of the SOAP message that's intended for itself; that is, the application must understand which parts of the SOAP message relate to its own operation, and which parts do not.

2. The application must make a decision as to whether it can support all of the required processing that the message expects of it. If the application cannot, it must discard the message.

3. The application must remove the portions of the message that it has processed if it isn't the end-point of the message, and is in fact just an intermediary or routing point. The removal must occur prior to the application forwarding the message to the next location.

For some middleware and routing applications, no parts of the SOAP message will be intended for them specifically. In these cases, the application may just look at the target URI or `SoapAction` value, and route the SOAP packet accordingly without modifying it.

Encoding SOAP Messages

The SOAP specification requires that all SOAP messages are encoded using XML. In addition, namespaces are used on elements and attributes, and any SOAP application must understand these concepts. The specification also dictates that messages with incorrect namespaces must be discarded—it defines two namespaces for use in SOAP. For envelopes, the correct namespace is *http://schemas.xmlsoap.org/soap/envelope/*. For serialization, the correct namespace is: *http://schemas.xmlsoap.org/soap/encoding/*.

These namespaces are associated with local names and inserted into element and attribute names per the W3C's *Namespaces in XML* document. Interestingly enough, given their native development in XML, SOAP messages are not allowed to contain either a Document Type Declaration or a Processing Instruction.

Constructing SOAP Envelopes

A composite SOAP message contains three broad parts. The first and outermost part is the *envelope*. Beneath the envelope is the *header*. The header is the place where routing information or other nonapplication metadata may be stored. It is permissible in the eyes of the specification to temporarily modify SOAP headers during a routing or transport period, leaving the message in its original state when it finally reaches the destination. The SOAP *body* is the place where the application-specific payload resides.

SOAP packet requirements

Let's consider the analogy of a physical package delivery. The envelope is obviously the shipping container, and the header data may be added and removed by transport stations regarding check-ins and checkouts. The body is the goods and materials nicely secured inside the box, not to be touched by anyone but the recipient.

From these constructs, the envelope and body are mandatory, whereas the header is optional. Furthermore, the specification requires that these additional constraints are minded when constructing packets:

1. For envelopes, SOAP requires that the element names be Envelope, with no exceptions. The Envelope element can optionally contain namespace declarations and additional, informative attributes. However, if any of these exist, they must be namespace-qualified. The specification requires that SOAP messages have an Envelope element marked with the *http://schemas.xmlsoap.org/soap/ envelope/* namespace. If not within this namespace context, the specification requires that the message is discarded.

2. For headers, SOAP requires element names to always be Header. The header is allowed to have immediate child elements. Any child element must be namespace-qualified.

3. For SOAP bodies, the element name must always be Body. The Body element must be an immediate descendant of the Envelope element, and if a Header element is present, it must immediately follow the header.

SOAP encoding style

SOAP allows for different serialization rules for SOAP messages. To that end, the encodingStyle attribute is used to indicate which serialization techniques are used in the message. The SOAP specification defines serialization rules within the document, and utilizes the URI *http://schemas.xmlsoap.org/soap/encoding/* to indicate that this encoding style is in use.

Using SOAP Headers

SOAP allows for the extension of messages through optional header data. The header data may never actually be seen by sending and receiving end-point applications, but may actually only be used and seen by intermediary and middleware applications along the message's path. However, there is no requirement that forbids the use of headers by applications.

According to the SOAP specification, headers must follow a few rules. First, a header entry must utilize a fully qualified element name within a namespace URI context. Second, the SOAP encodingStyle attribute may be used to denote the encoding style for header members. Third, the SOAP mustUnderstand attribute and actor attribute may also be used to indicate processing directions.

SOAP actor *Attribute*

The SOAP actor attribute names the recipient of a header element. The recipient is identified by URI.

SOAP mustUnderstand *Attribute*

The mustUnderstand attribute tells an application whether it is required to process the information contained within the element. The mustUnderstand element can have a value of either 1 or 0, with 1 indicating a positive condition requiring the application to understand the element. A nonexistent mustUnderstand attribute is the same has having it set to 0, or otherwise represents a false condition.

SOAP Body Elements

The Body element is the primary piece of a SOAP packet with which an end-point application is concerned. The Body element represents the SOAP packet's payload.

Child elements of the Body element are called *body entries*. Each body entry is encoded as an independent element within the SOAP body element. A body entry requires a namespace URI and local name. The encodingStyle attribute can be used within body entries to indicate their encoding style.

Error Message and SOAP Fault

The SOAP Fault element is used to communicate error conditions back to a calling application. The SOAP Fault may be used to communicate any type of failure relevant to your application.

Fault element

A Fault element may have the following four children elements:

faultcode

The faultcode element is required to appear within Fault elements, and provides a numeric code to applications for easier management of error messages. The SOAP specification defines a few fault codes automatically, covered in the "Fault codes" section.

faultstring

The faultstring element is required within Fault elements, and can be any type of description appropriate for the error.

faultactor

The faultactor element is used to pinpoint which actor caused the fault if the message followed along a message path. If present, this element indicates the origin of the fault. If an intermediary application causes a fault, the specification requires that the intermediary shows itself in the faultactor element. The value of a faultactor element is a URI.

`detail`

> The `detail` element allows for application-specific information associated with the XML payload in the `Body` element. For example, if a business logic error occurs in your distributed SOAP-powered application, the business error detail rides in the `detail` element. On the other hand, if an intermediary causes a problem during the routing process, the `detail` element is not used to communicate the information. Like the `Body` element, the `detail` element allows for *detail entries* to be present as immediate children of the detail element.

Fault codes

The fault codes defined by the SOAP specification list four different error conditions. If one of these conditions occurs, the following fault codes must be used. These fault codes are in the space defined by the URI prefix *http://schemas.xmlsoap. org/soap/envelope/*. The SOAP specification hopes the fault codes are extensible and will be used by developers. By default, the specification includes:

VersionMismatch

> Used when an invalid namespace is used for the SOAP `Envelope`.

MustUnderstand

> Used when an element is not understood or processed by an application, but its `mustUnderstand` attribute is set to 1.

Client

> Used when the message is not well formed, or did not contain required information for success.

Server

> Used when the message cannot be processed by the server for reasons other than physical makeup. That is, you may have formatted your `GetLocalTemperature` call correctly, however the server could be offline momentarily. When this error comes up, it is possible that the application may try again at a later time.

The Client and Server classes of errors are meant to be extensible, so that a programmer could define a fault such as *Client.AccessDenied* or *Server.Unavailable*. The complete URI for *Client.AccessDenied* is *http://schemas.xmlsoap.org/soap/envelope/Client.AccessDenied*.

For faults that are not described by the SOAP specification, it is legal to use URIs that begin with a different prefix.

SOAP Encoding Techniques

SOAP encoding defines a format for data types communicated in SOAP packets. If SOAP is to be used for Remote Procedure Calls (RPC) between applications, then application-specific data must be marshaled to and from the involved parties. These applications must be able to understand the types of data—to be able to distinguish, for example, arrays from strings and numbers from letters.

In the world of SOAP encoding, the SOAP specification sees two types of data. Simple scalar types (dog = "foo") and compound types (dog = {"foo" : "bar", "bar" : "foo"}). SOAP encoding uses the namespace URI *http://schemas.xmlsoap.org/soap/encoding/*.

SOAP does acknowledge that other types of encoding schemes may be used, but for applications to be interoperable, it's easiest if they use the same encoding.

SOAP Encoding Rules

There are nine golden rules for data serialization using SOAP. These rules establish guidelines for both simple and complex data types and data representation. These nine rules are explored and illustrated in practice following these simple guidelines.

1. All data values must be represented as element content. This means that data is inside elements, not inside attributes as in:

   ```
   <specialSymbol>DataValues</specialSymbol>
   ```
   and not:
   ```
   <specialSymbols symbol1="DataValue1" symbol2="DataValue2"/>
   ```

2. When an element contains a data value, the value must have one of the following features:
   - Have an xsi:type attribute
   - Be contained within an element with a SOAP-ENC:arrayType attribute
   - Have a type determinable from a schema

3. Simple values are represented as character data without any child elements. Simple values must have a type referenced in the XML Schemas Specification.

4. Compound values are represented as a sequence of elements. Access methods are represented by an element with a matching name. Qualified names must be used unless the access names are local to their containing types.

5. Multireference simple or compound values are represented as independent elements with a local attribute ID of type ID (the ID type listed in the XML Specification, which must be unique within any XML document instance). Any access to this simple or compound value must have an attribute named href that points to a URI fragment identifier referencing the element.

6. Strings and byte arrays should be multireference simple types, but rules exist for efficient representation in common cases. See the specification at *http://www.w3.org* for details.

7. Multiple references to a value can all be encoded separately, but only if the meaning of the XML instance is unaltered as a result.

8. Arrays are compound values. Arrays must have a type of SOAP-ENC:Array or a derived type. SOAP arrays may be multidimensional, with the rightmost index advancing first. SOAP arrays need a SOAP-ENC:arrayType attribute that indicates

the contained element's type and dimensions. In its simplest form, the attribute may appear as:

```
arrayTypeValue: array-type array-size
```

where *<array-type>* is an XML Schema–defined type, and *<array-size>* is an integer indicating the size of the array. Things get trickier when encoding a multidimensional array. In the case of multidimensionality, *<array-size>* is a comma-separated list of integers.

9. A null value doesn't require an accessor element. However, a null value may be present and represented with an accessor with an `xsi:null` attribute set to 1.

While these rules may seem quite complicated, learning more about types helps demystify them. When working with some SOAP APIs (and hopefully all SOAP APIs), such strict data typing is not manually required, and is taken care of by the API.

Simple Types

The SOAP specification declares that it adopts the types found in the *XML Schema Part 2: Datatypes* specification. In other words, the SOAP drafters are not reinventing the wheel, but utilizing the work done for the XML Schema effort.

Using established data typing makes data encoding far simpler to understand than the list of nine rules presented in the previous section. For example:

```
<element name="FirstName" type="xsd:string"/>
<element name="LastName" type="xsd:string"/>
<element name="Address1" type="xsd:string"/>
<element name="City" type="xsd:string"/>
<element name="State" type="xsd:string"/>
<element name="Zip" type="int"/>
<element name="BalanceDue" type="float"/>
```

Compound Types

The SOAP specification recognizes two primary types of compound data: *structs* and *arrays*. A struct is a compound type in which members are given names, and the names are used to access the values. An array, on the other hand, is an ordered list in which an integer index is used to access the values.

SOAP over HTTP

SOAP fits naturally over HTTP. SOAP's request/response RPC-style transactions are perfect for HTTP's request/response protocol. When sending SOAP over HTTP, the content-type must be `text/xml`.

The SOAPAction header

The `SOAPAction` HTTP request header field is used to indicate the "intent" of the SOAP request. A client is required to supply this header in a request. The value of the header is a URI, but the specification places no restrictions on what the URI represents.

SOAP HTTP responses

SOAP over HTTP uses a hybrid combination of traditional HTTP response codes coupled with their equivalent meanings for the fate of the SOAP packet. That is, even if the HTTP request itself is okay, if for some reason there is an error on the server side while processing the request, the server must send back an HTTP 500 Internal Server Error. This is a slightly different process than that of HTTP, which only gives such a response when a CGI or ASP page ungracefully bails out of its execution. With SOAP, the execution of the SOAP server may proceed just fine, but if the logical execution of the SOAP message fails, the HTTP 500 error is returned.

SOAP for RPC

Using SOAP for RPC-style development is really nothing different from using SOAP for any other purpose. The semantics of request/response are still present. A SOAP method invocation is just a SOAP envelope with a method name as payload, accompanied by any data parameters. The response is either the return value or the error status, also within a SOAP envelope.

When performing RPC with SOAP, the method calls and return values are stored in the SOAP body.

Python SOAP Options

Support for web services in Python is emerging, but is not complete. At the time of this writing, there is lively debate in the XML-SIG (Python XML Special Interest Group; see *http://www.python.org/sigs/xml-sig/*) concerning SOAP client and server implementations and their ability to interoperate.

SOAP and WSDL, and therefore web services, are being driven largely by companies such as IBM and Microsoft. Microsoft has robust client and server support for web services in their SOAP Toolkit, while IBM is making headway contributing to the Apache SOAP project. Both camps feature support for two common styles of web service access: RPC-like proxy access, and SOAP Serialization access.

You can implement Python web service clients easily today by using one of Python's bridge mechanisms into subsystems such as COM and Java. Python's COM support is excellent and is enabled by installing PythonCOM (part of the *win32all.exe* package from the ActiveState web site). Detailed instructions are provided in the section "Requirements for Using MSSOAP" later in this chapter.

Through the accepted APIs of web services today, you'll likely be able to quickly adapt your Python code to use native Python web service support when it matures, although it may be more desirable to write your logic in Python but utilize APIs from Python that are implemented in faster C++. Python makes a great glue language due to its robust object model, sophisticated text and file manipulation, and component access. Utilizing components that are resource intensive (such as Parsers or SOAP clients) may work better if the components are written in fast native code and are driven by your Python code.

With one cross-platform exception, the Python client examples in this chapter rely primarily on using COM to bridge Microsoft's mature SOAP Serializer and SOAP Connector. Therefore, the Python examples in this section primarily run on Windows platforms, due to their utilization of COM. However, the SOAPy API is covered as well. This is a native Python RPC-like SOAP client implementation. SOAPy should run anywhere Python runs.

Working with SOAPy

As of this writing, SOAPy provides support for RPC-like interaction with WSDL-published web services. SOAPy is currently available on SourceForge (*http://soapy.sourceforge.net*). SOAPy is inherently cross-platform because it is a native Python implementation.

Working with SOAPy is very simple, as it's designed to transparently present a remote web service as if it were a local Python object. If you download one of the source distributions of SOAPy, you get a few examples that allow SOAPy to strut its stuff. For instance, the get_temperature example that ships with SOAPy allows you to enter a zip code and query a remote weather service for the current temperature. So, to check the temperature in Woodinville, Washington:

```
C:\c9>python get_temperature.py 98072
Temperature for 98072 = 53.0 degrees F
```

While this application is impressive, it immediately inspires curiosity as to how SOAPy works. SOAPy performs this trick in three lines of code:

```
import soap
server = soap.get_proxy('http://www.xmethods.net/sd/TemperatureService.wsdl')

temperature = server.getTemp(zipcode=zip)
```

The secret is that SOAPy interprets the WSDL file, and creates a local stub object for you to work with that seemingly has all of the methods of the remote service.

Ideally, when working with SOAPy, the only method you call is get_proxy. Afterwards, you should be able to use the methods described in the WSDL file located at the remote service.

Working with MSSOAP

When working with MSSOAP, you have the option of using an RPC client or a Serialization client.

The RPC client works essentially the same way that SOAPy does; however, there are some subtle differences. For example, to initialize a connection with remote service description, use the `mssoapinit` method as opposed to SOAPy's `get_proxy`, but the net effect is the same as shown here:

```
import win32com.client

sc = win32com.client.Dispatch("MSSOAP.SoapClient")
sc.mssoapinit("http://WebServiceDomain/service.wsdl")

response = sc.methodName(param, param)

print(response)
```

Again, the net effect of web service RPC implementations is to allow you to work with a remote object as if it were local. The Serialization method works slightly differently, but gives you finer control over how an actual SOAP request is structured, and allows you to work with a service without necessarily relying upon a service description WSDL file.

MSSOAP Serialization Basics

Using serialization is more involved than using RPC, but it has its own advantages as well as drawbacks. Serialization gives you fine control over exactly how a SOAP XML request appears. Implementing serialization also allows you to interact with a web service without having to understand WSDL, something that may be of considerable value as SOAP implementations (both client and server) mature.

The main trade-off between RPC and Serialization is the WSDL file. The WSDL file provides an RPC implementation with the information it needs about the service end-point, such as the URIs and namespaces involved, or the parameters and their types. Without RPC and WSDL, you'd need to supply these extra details manually.

Adding URIs and namespaces

Creating a SOAP packet with MSSOAP requires a few objects, but start with the connector and the serializer. You must give the connector information that is normally held in a WSDL file. For example, you need to supply the end-point, the SOAP Action URI, and the namespace:

```
import win32com.client

SoapActionUri = "http://tempuri.org/action/Calc.Add"
ElementNamespace = "http://tempuri.org/message/"
EndPointUrl = \"http://centauri/MSSoapSamples/Calc/Service/SrSz/AspVbs/Calc.asp"

connector = win32com.client.Dispatch("MSSOAP.HttpConnector")
connector.SetProperty("EndPointURL", EndPointUrl)
connector.SetProperty("SoapAction", SoapActionUri)
connector.BeginMessage( )
```

The connector is now prepared to connect to the service. All that is left to do is to prepare the SOAP envelope and execute the call. The SOAP envelope is also prepared manually.

```
serializer = win32com.client.Dispatch("MSSOAP.SoapSerializer")
serializer.Init(connector.InputStream)
```

Once the serializer is created, it is *attached* to the connector for writing to the service.

Creating the SOAP envelope

You use the serializer's methods to actually construct the SOAP packet, including the method you are targeting, as well as to supply the parameters. The following lines prepare a SOAP packet for delivery to a calculator service expecting that parameters A and B are integer parameters to a method named Add:

```
# Create SOAP Envelope
serializer.startEnvelope( )
serializer.startBody( )
serializer.startElement("Add", ElementNamespace, '', "m")
serializer.startElement("A")
serializer.writeString("4")
serializer.endElement( )
serializer.startElement("B")
serializer.writeString("5")
serializer.endElement( )
serializer.endElement( )
serializer.endBody( )
serializer.endEnvelope( )

# Finish SOAP message
connector.EndMessage( )
```

As shown in the previous code, the connector is then instructed that the complete SOAP message has been prepared with a call to EndMessage.

Making the call

After you've completed constructing your serializer and connector, a final step is to instantiate a reader object to check for errors with the service and to retrieve the result of the call.

```
reader = win32com.client.Dispatch("MSSOAP.SoapReader")
reader.Load(connector.OutputStream)
```

Here, the reader is associated with the connector's output stream in order to retrieve the result of the call to the service. The Fault attribute of the reader indicates success or failure.

```
if reader.Fault:
  print("Error: ", reader.faultstring.Text)

print reader.RPCResult.Text
```

The response from the service is contained in the reader.RPCResult object. In this particular case, the response from the calculator service is "9," and the sum of the supplied parameters is 4 and 5.

Example SOAP Server and Client

As of this writing, server-side implementations of SOAP services are virtually non-existent. The few that do exist stray from the emerging standards and are likely to continue to morph as they discover what the users really want.

The most stable web service sample implementations come from Microsoft and IBM. In this section, we create a Python client that utilizes the calculator service that ships with Microsoft's free SOAP Toolkit 2.0, available from *http://msdn.microsoft.com*. As such, the service must run on either Windows NT Server 4.0 or Windows 2000 Server. The clients may run anywhere COM runs. The toolkit sets up very easily on these platforms, and is ready to go after the install script is finished.

The Python client created in this section uses COM to connect with the MSSOAP type library objects, and interacts with the service. The clients can run on virtually all flavors of Windows, provided they have access to the services and WSDL files residing on the server. Note that the clients can easily (and probably most conveniently) run on the same machine as the servers.

Requirements for Using MSSOAP

SOAP and web services are new, and as such require the installation of software for developers who wish to experiment the technology. The rest of this chapter relies on COM; therefore, if you are not familiar with the workings of COM and Python, this section helps to get things set up.

The following steps are required in order to run the Python client example in this section.

1. The Microsoft SOAP Toolkit 2.0 must be installed on a server.

2. The WSDL and service implementations that ship with the SOAP Toolkit must be visible via HTTP on your network, per the installation examples that ship with the toolkit. This is true even if you are running the client and server on the same machine.

3. Python clients must have *win32all.exe* (Python COM Support available from *http://aspn.activestate.com* and developed by Mark Hammond) installed, and the utility script *makepy.py* must be applied against the SOAP Type Library. Additionally, if running the clients on a different machine, the SOAP Toolkit, or at least the COM object *.dll* files, must be installed.

Getting Microsoft SOAP Toolkit 2.0

Microsoft has made available client DLLs and robust client and server example implementations in their SOAP Toolkit 2.0. This is a free download, fully supported as well as available from *http://msdn.microsoft.com/downloads/default.asp*.

When installing the toolkit, you automatically receive an updated MSXML 3.0 package, which fully supports XSLT. Appendix E covers working with Python and the MSXML parser.

Making the samples web-visible

When you install the samples, you need to follow the instructions for creating a virtual directory in IIS (Internet Information Server, the default HTTP implementation on Windows servers) that can point to the samples. The instructions call for putting an entry for MSSOAPSampleServer in your *hosts* file (*c:\winnt\system32\hosts*), but this step is optional, and is only required if you intend to run the Microsoft sample clients. For the purpose of this chapter, you are writing a Python client *from scratch*; therefore, your existing hostname is fine. You need to be able to see the samples directory via HTTP, as the instructions indicate.

If you plan on running the Python client from the same machine that hosts the samples, you won't need to install anything else (except perhaps Python COM support) to proceed.

Getting Python COM support

If you have not used COM from Python (and we haven't yet in this book), you need to download and install Python COM support. Start by retrieving the appropriate installer from the Web available at *http://aspn.activestate.com/ASPN/Downloads/ActivePython/Extensions/Win32all*.

There are links and instructions to download *win32all.exe* for your version of Python; read the information on this web page carefully to be sure you get the right version. This installer provides full support for COM from your Python programs, and allows you to implement COM servers from other languages to use.

Fixing MSSOAP with makepy.py

Even if you already have Python COM support (or just installed it), you need to tweak Python's access to the SOAP Type Library. Unfortunately, the authors of the SOAP Toolkit objects rely on Visual Basic's and Windows Scripting's ability to set object properties like this:

```
Object.Property("PropertyName") = NewPropertyValue
```

That's not even legal syntax in Python! Visual C++ uses a slightly different syntax, allowing an overloaded operator to provide syntax that matches Python's dictionary assignment syntax:

```
Object.Property["PropertyName"] = NewPropertyValue
```

Great! This syntax works just fine in Python if you are assigning a value to an element of a member dictionary. Unfortunately, the COM API does not automatically convert this COM construct to Python member dictionaries. For this specific object, Property is a method, and there is no way to assign a value in Python to an object method. Typically, components implement access methods, or at the minimum, implement SetProperty and GetProperty type constructs. Thankfully, the *makepy.py* script that ships with *win32all.exe* wraps another Python interface on top of the COM objects and uses a lower-level API to access them correctly, allowing you to overcome this aspect.

To run *makepy.py*, launch it from within the *win32com\client* directory of your Python installation (typically, *C:\Python20\win32com\client*):

```
C:\Python20\win32com\client>python makepy.py
```

A dialog GUI pops up that displays all of the different type libraries registered on your system. Find *Microsoft SOAP Type Library (1.0)* and click **Ok**. The script suddenly produces a flurry of activity (evidenced by frequent text output) and writes a *.py* file with a monstrously long name inside the folder *C:\Python20\win32com\gen_py*. You probably will not need to see that file again, as you can use a standard call to win32com.client.Dispatch to invoke the object and it will seek out the updated Python-friendly interface that *makepy.py* created. Figure 9-1 shows the dialog in action with *Microsoft SOAP Type Library (1.0)* highlighted.

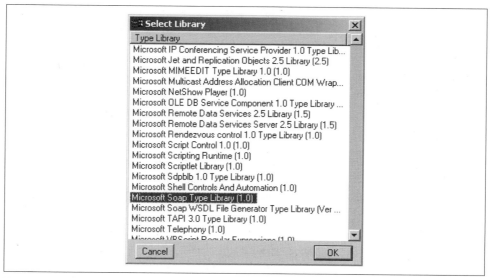

Figure 9-1. Selecting the SOAP Type Library with makepy.py

Once you've created the Python interface for the object by selecting **Ok**, you may go about instantiating the object normally, but now you can call constructs such as:

```
Object.SetProperty("PropertyName", "NewValue")
```

The *makepy.py* accomplishes more than just correcting property assignments for Python syntax, as it can also be used to smooth out parameter types and properties for all sorts of COM objects. See the makepy documentation for more information.

Server Setup

Before we get into developing the client, it's important to understand the server setup. SOAP and web services are inherently cross-platform. While you are running services implemented on Windows, clients can conceivably be written on any platform, provided they can either create the correct kind of SOAP packet to invoke the services, or interpret the published WSDL to wrap the services with a local stub object.

The Python client implemented here uses COM access to a SOAP connector and serializer; however any SOAP implementation should be able to connect to these services and utilize them.

The server setup that ships with the toolkit is merely a collection of WSDL files describing services, as well as service end-points that implement them. The end-points are in a variety of languages and techniques, ranging from Active Server Pages to ISAPI plug-ins. The interface to these services is purely SOAP.

A Python SOAP Client

The SOAP Toolkit ships with a Calculator service. This service offers four different operations that it performs on two supplied parameters, much like a basic calculator. This example is similar in functionality to the VBScript sample client that ships with the Toolkit. The most significant difference between the two is that your client is implemented entirely in Python from scratch, not in VBScript.

The calculator operations are add, subtract, multiply, and divide. If your SOAP Toolkit is freshly installed, it's a good idea to verify that the calculator service is running properly by testing it with one of the sample clients that ships with the toolkit—it certainly aids in the debugging phase of things (if you need to debug!) In other words, knowing that your web server and SOAP implementations are working helps to isolate any problems or errors that may occur when running your Python client.

Defining reusable basics

To properly build the SOAP packet, define a portion of the SOAP Action URI, allowing for the appending of different method names. You also want to reuse the namespace URI between method invocations. These two reused items, along with the service end-point, are defined up front as global variables:

```
import win32com.client

# SOAP Action URI
```

```
BaseSoapActionUri = "http://tempuri.org/action/Calc."

# Namespace
WrapperElementNamespace = "http://tempuri.org/message/"

# Service End Point
EndPointUrl = \
    "http://centauri/MSSoapSamples/Calc/Service/SrSz/AspVbs/Calc.asp"
```

You can take calculator functionality and embed it within a method, allowing the method to take a string representing the operation you wish to perform, along with the parameters. This method can then repeatedly be called to generate answers:

```
def Calculate(Op, Val1, Val2):
    """Return a result based on the operator 'Op' and two input values."""
    # Instantiate HttpConnector
    connector = win32com.client.Dispatch("MSSOAP.HttpConnector")
```

Immediately as the function begins, the HTTP SOAP connector is created as shown in the preceding code. The connector is then handed some critical information regarding the location of the service:

```
# Set properties (will fail if makepy.py wasn't run
#                 on SOAP type library)
connector.SetProperty("EndPointURL", EndPointUrl)
connector.SetProperty("SoapAction", BaseSoapActionUri + Op)

# Start SOAP message
connector.BeginMessage()
```

What's critical in this code snippet is the SetProperty call to change the value of SoapAction. If you note, the BaseSoapActionUri is concatenated with the desired operation Op. If using the add method, create a SoapAction string similar to:

http://tempuri.org/action/Calc.Add

Now the task turns to actually creating the SOAP envelope.

```
# Create a serialization object
serializer = win32com.client.Dispatch("MSSOAP.SoapSerializer")

# Attach it to the connector created earlier
serializer.Init(connector.InputStream)
```

The serializer is bound to the connector's input stream, so that the SOAP packet actually finds its way to the service end-point. Creating the rest of the packet follows the same pattern shown earlier, with methods representing the starting and ending of elements:

```
# Create SOAP Envelope
serializer.startEnvelope()
serializer.startBody()
serializer.startElement(Op, WrapperElementNamespace, '', "m")
serializer.startElement("A")
serializer.writeString(Val1)
```

```
serializer.endElement( )
serializer.startElement("B")
serializer.writeString(Val2)
serializer.endElement( )
serializer.endElement( )
serializer.endBody( )
serializer.endEnvelope( )

# Finish SOAP message
connector.EndMessage( )
```

The reader is brought in to read and interpret the result of the call to the service. As discussed earlier, in the section "The Emerging SOAP Standard," the reader is attached to the connector's output stream, and digests the information as it is returned:

```
# Create SOAP reader object
reader = win32com.client.Dispatch("MSSOAP.SoapReader")
reader.Load(connector.OutputStream)

# check for errors
if reader.Fault:
  print "Error: ", reader.faultstring.Text

# Return calculation value
return reader.RPCResult.Text
```

If there has been an error, it is reflected in the reader.Fault property. When a SOAP call fails, the SOAP server sends a fault entry back to the client. SOAP uses many of the same semantics as HTTP regarding propagating error conditions back to the caller. In fact, when using SOAP over HTTP, SOAP is bound to some of the same exact error conditions—SOAP must send back an HTTP 500 Internal Server Error, even if the web server behaves as expected but the code handling the SOAP request fails. (This is required to ensure that knowledge of the implementation details of the server is not needed by the client; it is not a failing of the SOAP or HTTP protocols.)

Example 9-1 shows the complete listing of *PyCalcSerial.py*.

Example 9-1. PyCalcSerial.py

```
"""
Python MSSOAP Serializer Example
"""
# import support for COM
import win32com.client

# SOAP Action URI
BaseSoapActionUri = "http://tempuri.org/action/Calc."

# Namespace
WrapperElementNamespace = "http://tempuri.org/message/"

# Service End Point
```

Example 9-1. PyCalcSerial.py (continued)

```python
EndPointUrl = \
  "http://centauri/MSSoapSamples/Calc/Service/SrSz/AspVbs/Calc.asp"

# Calculate(operation, value1, value2)
#   Takes an operator (as a word like "Add") along
#   with two values and returns the result
def Calculate(Op, Val1, Val2):
  # Instantiate HttpConnector
  connector = win32com.client.Dispatch("MSSOAP.HttpConnector")

  # Set properties (will fail if makepy.py wasn't run
  #                 on SOAP type library)
  connector.SetProperty("EndPointURL", EndPointUrl)
  connector.SetProperty("SoapAction", BaseSoapActionUri + Op)

  # Start SOAP message
  connector.BeginMessage()

  # Create a serialization object
  serializer = win32com.client.Dispatch("MSSOAP.SoapSerializer")

  # Attach it to the connector created earlier
  serializer.Init(connector.InputStream)

  # Create SOAP Envelope
  serializer.startEnvelope()
  serializer.startBody()
  serializer.startElement(Op, WrapperElementNamespace, '', "m")
  serializer.startElement("A")
  serializer.writeString(Val1)
  serializer.endElement()
  serializer.startElement("B")
  serializer.writeString(Val2)
  serializer.endElement()
  serializer.endElement()
  serializer.endBody()
  serializer.endEnvelope()

  # Finish SOAP message
  connector.EndMessage()

  # Create SOAP reader object
  reader = win32com.client.Dispatch("MSSOAP.SoapReader")
  reader.Load(connector.OutputStream)

  # check for errors
  if reader.Fault:
    print "Error: ", reader.faultstring.Text

  # Return calculation value
  return reader.RPCResult.Text
```

Example 9-1. PyCalcSerial.py (continued)

```
# Main line-- do some calculations
print "Using Service:", EndPointUrl
print "Calculate 3 * 4: \t",
print Calculate("Multiply", 3, 4)

print "Calculate 4 - 3: \t",
print Calculate("Subtract", 4, 3)

print "Calculate 345 + 1004: \t",
print Calculate("Add", 345, 1004)

print "Calculate 115 / 5: \t",
print Calculate("Divide", 115, 5)
```

To run the example, just launch it from your command line. You should then see output similar to the following:

```
C:\my-dir> python PyCalcSerial.py
Using Service: http://centauri/MSSoapSamples/Calc/Service/SrSz/AspVbs/Calc.asp
Calculate 3 * 4:        12
Calculate 4 - 3:        1
Calculate 345 + 1004:   1349
Calculate 115 / 5:      23
```

SOAP is the heart of web services, at least as they are being described by most of the big players. WSDL, if implemented correctly, is seldom even seen by developers as it can be automatically generated from object source files. When support for WSDL matures, most languages (most likely including Python) will have WSDL generators that generate WSDL directly from class code. Of course, these tools can also be provided by SOAP server implementations, or by Python object servers such as Zope.

What About XML-RPC?

Before the first version of the SOAP specification was completed, a simpler specification for a remote procedure call mechanism employing XML over HTTP was created by Dave Winer of UserLand Software; this specification is known as XML-RPC. This specification builds in less support for complex data types, but has the advantage of simplicity. Uptake among the developer community has been very rapid, in part because it filled a void before SOAP was available, and in part because the simpler specification allowed implementations to be easy to work with.

The simplicity of XML-RPC comes largely from the willingness of the authors of the specification to nail down many of the details required to implement the specification. Where SOAP allows the use of alternate transport protocols and data serialization rules, XML-RPC specifies HTTP POST requests and a single set of serialization rules. Though the flexibility offered by SOAP can be valuable for some projects, many developers suspect that this will be used to bloat middleware components and achieve vendor lock-in, which is something many XML users are trying to avoid.

Fredrik Lundh's `xmlrpclib` module, which will be part of the Python standard library as of Python Version 2.2, is available for older versions of Python at *http://www. pythonware.com/*. It presents a proxy interface very similar to that of SOAPy for clients to use, and provides support for basic server implementations as well.

For more information on XML-RPC, refer to *Programming Web Services with XML-RPC* by Simon St.Laurent, Joe Johnston, and Edd Dumbill (O'Reilly, 2001). This book includes information on using XML-RPC with Python.

## CHAPTER 10

Python and Distributed Systems Design

In this chapter, we pull all of the techniques and knowledge illustrated thus far into a distributed sample application. In addition to exercising what you've learned, this chapter blazes new ground with an analysis of XML network flow—a key to creating scalable, flexible XML applications. This chapter can be used as a design catalog and tutorial reference for interfacing XML with all sorts of distributed systems.

Thus far, you've learned about: XML DOM, and SAX manipulation; XSLT for transformation; XPath for searches and extraction, validation and dialects; Internet APIs; and finally SOAP and web services. In this chapter, we put many of these technologies to work.

One aspect of distributed XML development that you haven't touched on yet is the best way to move XML between distributed systems. As this chapter shows, a poor traffic design in your distributed systems can mean the difference between an eight-lane expressway and a bogged-down two-lane highway.

Sample Application and Flow Analysis

We will create a large sample application to illustrate many different concepts and show how they can be used together. An intelligent XML switch that knows how to move XML in the right direction holds the distributed application together. We also discuss how these switches can be daisy-chained together to form scalable networks of XML data. The components that are connected to the switch include a user input application, a customer profile SQL database, and an XML information store. Figure 10-1 shows a diagram of the application.

This application is meant to illustrate how several different applications that may have different purposes can utilize the same flow of XML traffic in the network by building intelligence between them, and not retrofitting them. The key to this application's success is in the way the XML is moved between the applications in a decoupled fashion. From a high-level, the application appears as a portal web site to end-users.

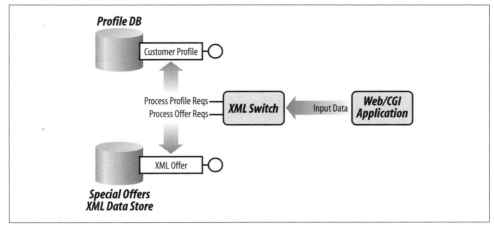

Figure 10-1. The sample distributed application

Backend systems of different types are integrated by exposing XML messaging APIs, allowing the portal to work. Other applications connect along the peripheral boundary of the main processing, to participate in the flow of XML information.

Decoupling Application Systems

Take for instance the Web/CGI application on the righthand side of Figure 10-1. Typically, it is connected directly to a database that contains the information it needs. However, in this scenario, the database is decoupled from the Web/CGI application by the XML switch. The Web/CGI application only submits an XML packet (a SOAP-like packet in this chapter) asking for relevant data. The switch interprets this packet and forwards it to the right location (in this particular case, a Python class that can perform the appropriate work). When the database responds, the information is "routed" back to the original caller. This allows for flexibility in the location or design of the database. In fact, it lets distributed systems commit to XML interfaces as they expose their functionality, instead of committing to the intricacies of table design or specific stored-procedure names.

Routing Adds Flexibility

This type of design is similar in architecture to message queuing designs, with some subtle and powerful differences. By decoupling different pieces of an enterprise, you're able to share their functionality more broadly, and enjoy the independence of not being tightly bound to any specific application that consumes the data. In addition, by placing an intermediary between data sources and data consumers, you allow for business logic to exist at a level above and between applications, and not programmed directly into them. For example, in Figure 10-1, you could conceivably swap out the Profiles database, and instead use a third-party service on the Internet that contains customer data. That is, if you find that a web service provides better personalization and consumer data than you, you can connect with the service, develop an XML interface that is familiar to your network, and swap out the old database for the new service partner. The local applications as consumers of the information would be none the wiser, as the XML switch is still accepting their XML requests and results are still being routed back to the applications.

Routing Adds Scalability

In addition to flexibility in system components, routing also adds another degree of scalability to a system. By routing XML requests for information around your network, you enable the ability to manage them as you would other types of network traffic. For example, you can replace individual systems with system farms consisting of multiple servers, and load balance the XML packets that are sent between them. In another case, XML switches could be daisy-chained together, much like routers and hubs are chained together for TCP/IP traffic. This concept enables you to do things such as broadcasting and duplication of read-only signals. It also allows you to create redundancy and multiple network paths to the same location.

Understanding the Scope

The sample application is the most ambitious example presented in this book yet. As such, it's a good idea to create a checklist and breakdown of what is involved and what dependencies exist.

This application can be created on one machine, but that machine needs to have all the different components installed. Ideally, two machines are a better fit. Regardless, the five pieces involved are as follows:

A simple relational database that hosts one simple table.   I used SQL Server, but MySQL or Postgres should work just fine.

Data Access Object.   This native Python class will encapsulate the data held within the SQL database behind an XML-friendly interface.

An XML data store.   This is a flat file that you create, coupled with an object to access the data using XML for both input and output.

The XML Switch.   The XML Switch itself is a Python-based interpretive XML-routing and object-brokering mechanism. If loaded with a routing table, it could analyze an incoming XML SOAP packet with XPath and determine which destination it should travel to. It could send a SOAP packet anywhere, including to web servers. In this example, the switch uses XML messages as RPC calls into the objects it hosts.

Web/CGI Application.   This a Python-based CGI script and accompanying web page similar to the CGI scripts created earlier in this book. It should run on any web server (IIS, Apache) that has been configured for CGI.

The code used in these examples is intended as a starting point for educational purposes. Understand that it does not have the necessary error handling or robustness to be used directly in applications. This chapter should be considered a design exercise showing a collection of different techniques for doing a whole scope of the things required in integrating distributed systems with XML.

Building the Database

Explaining the installation of a specific database is outside the scope of this book. However, if you are completely new to databases, we provide a quick overview of how this particular database was set up and used in this example. This overview broadly applies to any database systems, including SQL Server, Postgres, and MySQL. As a Python XML developer gluing together applications, understanding at least the fundamentals of working with databases will serve you well.

We used Microsoft SQL Server during the creation of this example as our relational database. However, only one simple table is created, and any database that supports SQL queries should be fine. A SQL table creation script is provided that should work on just about any SQL platform. However, the Python connectivity code presented here uses ODBC for access. If you choose to use a different database than SQL Server, you may need to download a Python API to access it. For example, the MySQLdb API is available at *http://sourceforge.net/projects/mysql-python/* to provide access from Python to MySQL databases. Regardless of your connectivity API, the SQL calls shown in this chapter should be identical.

Creating a Profiles Database

If you've installed your database of choice, your first task is to create a database inside of the system. If you are using SQL Server or your database offers an administrative GUI, this process may be as easy as typing a database name into a dialog box. For example, if using SQL Server, just browse to the databases folder using *SQL Enterprise Manager*. Once there, right-click and choose **New Database**. The name of the database should be Profiles. If you don't have a GUI, a SQL statement as simple as the following should suffice:

```
CREATE DATABASE Profiles
```

Once created, you may want to enable an account that has read and write privileges to this database, but to no others. Consult your database's documentation for details on creating specific user accounts. For the purposes of this example, in SQL Server the user webuser has been created, with a password of w3bus3r. The authentication information is required in the ODBC connectivity code.

Creating a Customer Table

Once you've created a database using either a GUI or SQL statements, create one simple table named Customer. This table represents some basic user information. It will be used by the different distributed applications as the one and only customer information record. While the fields in this table only cover the basics, you could easily expand them with other types of information related to the system.

The Customer table can be created with a GUI in SQL Enterprise Manager for SQL Server, or with the following SQL in any database:

```
CREATE TABLE Customer (
        firstname varchar (255) NULL,
        lastname varchar (255) NULL,
        address1 varchar (255) NULL,
        address2 varchar (255) NULL,
        city varchar (255) NULL,
        state varchar (2) NULL,
        zip varchar (10) NULL,
        customerId varchar (40) NULL)
```

The table is very simple. All of the data types are varchar and can easily be handled in Python as strings and integers. One thing to note about the Customer table is the varying length of the different fields. For example, most of the customer information may be zero to 256 characters in length. However, others in the table must conform to constraints such as two characters for a state abbreviation, and a 10-digit requirement on the zip code.

If you are using SQL Server, remember to expose your new database as an ODBC source on the machine you're running any database clients on—in this example application, only the XML Switch, which loads the CustomerProfile class, needs database connectivity. To enable connectivity to SQL Server, use the ODBC manager in the Windows' Control Panel to choose your database. Once this step is completed, the ODBC code presented here will work.

Populating the Database

You can populate the fields in your new table with an SQL statement similar to the following:

```
insert into Customer values('John',
  'Smith',
  '123 Evergreen Terrace',
  '',
  'Podunk',
  'WA',
  '98072',
  '234-E838839')
```

This statement creates a new row in the database table with the corresponding values contained in quotes. If you want to fill your database with several rows, you can resort to good, old-fashioned data entry with the *popdb.py* script shown in Example 10-1. This simple script just reads input from the command line and inserts it into the database. It's designed for use with the ODBC module and SQL Server, so if using another database, you need to adapt the connectivity code.

Example 10-1. popdb.py

```
"""
popdb.py - populate the Profiles/Customer DB with ODBC calls
"""
import dbi, odbc
conn = odbc.odbc("Profiles/webuser/w3bus3r")
cmd = conn.cursor( )

# loop to get input values.
while 1:
  firstname = raw_input("firstname:")
  lastname  = raw_input("lastname:")
  address1  = raw_input("address1:")
  address2  = raw_input("address2:")
  city      = raw_input("city:")
  state     = raw_input("state, 2 letter max:")
  zip       = raw_input("zip, 10 digit max:")
  customerId = raw_input("Customer ID, 40 character max length:")

  # execute SQL statement
  cmd.execute("insert into Customer values('"
              + firstname  + "', '"
              + lastname   + "', '"
              + address1   + "', '"
              + address2   + "', '"
              + city       + "', '"
              + state      + "', '"
              + zip        + "', '"
              + customerId + "')")

  # ask for additional entries
  finished = raw_input("another? [y/n]:")
  if (finished == "n"):
      break
```

There is no error checking in *popdb.py*, so if you violate one of the table constraints, you get an exception, and that particular row won't be inserted.

Building the Profiles Access Class

In addition to the `Profiles` database is the `CustomerProfile` Python class. This object performs XML input and output against the database, and exposes methods for use by the XML Switch. The basic profile actions allow you to retrieve, insert, update, and delete profiles. Arguments to these methods are XML versions of profile data. By making the customer profile packets in XML, it's easy for other applications to generate and consume the packets without any concern for the structure of the database, or even how to access it directly. In fact, a `CustomerProfile` can easily become the payload of a SOAP message. A profile packet appears as:

```
<CustomerProfile id="555-99JKK39">
  <firstname>John</firstname>
  <lastname>Doolittle</lastname>
  <address1>396 Evergreen Terrace</address1>
  <address2/>
  <city>Springfield</city>
  <state>WA</state>
  <zip>98072</zip>
</CustomerProfile>
```

Note that the `address2` element exists, even though it is empty. The DTD for such a document appears as:

```
<!ELEMENT firstname (#PCDATA)>
<!ELEMENT lastname (#PCDATA)>
<!ELEMENT address1 (#PCDATA)>
<!ELEMENT address2 (#PCDATA)>
<!ELEMENT city (#PCDATA)>
<!ELEMENT state (#PCDATA)>
<!ELEMENT zip (#PCDATA)>
<!ATTLIST CustomerProfile
    id CDATA #REQUIRED>
<!ELEMENT CustomerProfile
  (firstname, lastname,
   address1, address2,
   city, state, zip)>
```

An instance of the document using the DTD needs to have the declaration within the document as well:

```
<?xml version="1.0"?>
<!DOCTYPE CustomerProfile SYSTEM "CustomerProfile.dtd">
<CustomerProfile id="555-99JKK39">
  <firstname>John</firstname>
```

In order to keep things within the scope of this chapter, DTD enforcement is not a part of the `CustomerProfile` Python class, although the DTD rides along with the document and may be utilized at a later date. When embedding `CustomerProfile` elements within an XML message, the prolog is stripped out, and only the `CustomerProfile` element is inserted into the XML message.

The Interfaces

The `CustomerProfile` class supports four distinct operations. These operations allow for retrieval, insertion, updates, and deletes. This class is used by the XML switch to manage the insertion and retrieval of `CustomerProfile` information at runtime in the distributed system. All communication to and from this class takes the form of XML—this enables greater flexibility in how the data is stored on the backend. This also alleviates the burden of requiring distributed applications to connect directly to the database and understand the structure of its tables. In this scenario, distributed applications only need to understand structure of a `CustomerProfile` document.

getProfile(*id*)

> This method accepts a customer profile ID and returns the corresponding information in a well-formed, valid `CustomerProfile` document in the form of a string.

getProfileAsDom(*id*)

> This method is identical to `getProfile`, except that the return value is not a string of XML, but rather a DOM instance. The DOM can then be used for further manipulation.

insertProfile(*strXML*)

> The `insertProfile` method takes a valid, well-formed `CustomerProfile` document as a string and inserts it into the database.

updateProfile(*strXML*)

> Similar to `insertProfile`, this method takes a fresh XML `CustomerProfile` chunk and updates the existing record in the database based on the customer ID. Under the covers, it performs a delete and insert respectively.

deleteProfile(*id*)

> This method takes a customer ID as a parameter, and deletes the corresponding record from the database.

With the exception of the `getProfile` and `getProfileAsDom` methods, these methods return either 1 or 0 (`true` or `false`) to the caller, enabling them to be used as arguments to `if` statements.

Getting Profiles

The `CustomerProfile` class for retrieving profiles exposes two methods: `getProfile` and `getProfileAsDom`. Both methods take a `customerId` as an argument. In a simple test case, you could use the methods as follows:

```
from CustomerProfile import CustomerProfile
from xml.dom.ext import PrettyPrint

cp = CustomerProfile( )

print "String of XML:"
print cp.getProfile("234-E838839")

print "Or retrieve a DOM:"
dom = cp.getProfileAsDom("234-E838839")
PrettyPrint(dom)
```

This assumes that you have populated a record in the database with a `customerId` of 234-E838839. The result of running this code is the output of two identical XML representations:

```
G:\pythonxml\c9>python runcp.py
String of XML:
```

```
<?xml version='1.0' encoding='UTF-8'?>
<!DOCTYPE CustomerProfile SYSTEM "CustomerProfile.dtd">
<CustomerProfile id='234-E838839'>
  <firstname>John</firstname>
  <lastname>Smith</lastname>
  <address1>123 Evergreen Terrace</address1>
  <address2>
  </address2>
  <city>Podunk</city>
  <state>WA</state>
  <zip>98072</zip>
</CustomerProfile>

Or retrieve a DOM:
<?xml version='1.0' encoding='UTF-8'?>
<!DOCTYPE CustomerProfile SYSTEM "CustomerProfile.dtd">
<CustomerProfile id='234-E838839'>
  <firstname>John</firstname>
  <lastname>Smith</lastname>
  <address1>123 Evergreen Terrace</address1>
  <address2>
  </address2>
  <city>Podunk</city>
  <state>WA</state>
  <zip>98072</zip>
</CustomerProfile>
```

Whether you would like a raw XML string or a DOM really depends on what you want to do with the record after you obtain it. If passing it back to another application, it's wise to send the string, or make the string a piece of another document such as a SOAP packet (extracting the prolog declarations, of course). If you wish to manipulate the result, and perhaps insert it into the database once again, a DOM may be more convenient to work with.

Connecting with the database

The code for getProfile is straightforward. First, some simple validation is performed on the parameters, and then a database connection is prepared with a simple SQL statement:

```
def getProfile(self, strId, dom=0):
    """
    getProfile - returns an XML profile chunk based on
    the supplied id.  Returns None if not found.
    """
    if not strId:
      return None

    # generate connection
    conn = odbc.odbc(CONNECTION_STRING)
    cmd = conn.cursor()
    cmd.execute("select * from customer where " +
              "customerId = '" + strId + "'")
    conn.close()
```

In this code, that `strId` is inspected before anything else occurs, and the database command is of a simple `select *` variety. Of note is the third default parameter, `dom=0`, present in the method definition. This is flipped on by `getProfileAsDom` to require that `getProfile` return a DOM instance instead of a string.

Building the XML document

Next, the record is retrieved, and an XML document is prepared using the `DOMImplementation` class.

```
# get data record
prof_fields = cmd.fetchone()
if prof_fields is None:
  return None

# generate XML from fields
# generate CustomerProfile doctype
doctype = implementation.createDocumentType(
  "CustomerProfile", "", "CustomerProfile.dtd")

# generate new document with doctype
newdoc = implementation.createDocument(
  "", "CustomerProfile", doctype)
rootelem = newdoc.documentElement

# create root element id attribute
rootelem.setAttribute("id", prof_fields[CUSTOMER_ID])
```

In this code, the `DOMImplementation` class is used to build an XML document. In the beginning of the snippet, `prof_fields` is populated with the raw list of values from the database using the `fetchone` method, which returns one row. The indexes into `prof_fields` are given as named constants defined in the `CustomerProfile` module; the definitions are listed in the complete source listing for the module in Example 10-2, later in this chapter. Next, a document type object is created, citing the `CustomerProfile.dtd` file created earlier. This object is then used in the call to `implementation.createDocument` to generate an empty XML document element.

At this point, the simplicity of using the `DOMImplementation` to build your XML document (as opposed to manually constructing a string of XML, which is done later) is illustrated when we construct the elements in a simple loop:

```
# create list with field values
fields = ["firstname", prof_fields[FIRSTNAME],
          "lastname",  prof_fields[LASTNAME],
          "address1",  prof_fields[ADDRESS1],
          "address2",  prof_fields[ADDRESS2],
          "city",      prof_fields[CITY],
          "state",     prof_fields[STATE],
          "zip",       prof_fields[ZIP],
          ]
# loop through list adding elements and element text
```

```
for pos in range(0, len(fields), 2):
  # create the element
  thisElement = newdoc.createElement(fields[pos])

  # check for empty values and convert to soft nulls
  if fields[pos + 1] is None:
    fields[pos + 1] = ""
  thisElement.appendChild(newdoc.createTextNode(fields[pos+1]))
  rootelem.appendChild(thisElement)
```

What is interesting about this code is that you place all of the database values in a list, and then iterate the list creating and appending elements as you go. Use a list to hold the data values instead of a dictionary, because you need to create elements in the XML document in a specific order or it won't comply with the DTD. (Python dictionaries return their keys in an unpredictable order, and certainly do not maintain the order you in which you inserted them).

Using a list over a dictionary poses no big feat, as the Python range function is used to hop through the list in steps of two, allowing the code to use the current list member as the element name, and the next list member as the element's character data content.

With the XML in hand, a decision is made whether to return a string of XML or a DOM, based on how the method was called (remember, getProfileAsDom calls getProfile with additional parameters):

```
# return DOM or String based on how we were called...
if dom:
  return newdoc
else:
  # return string
  strXML = StringIO.StringIO()
  PrettyPrint(newdoc, strXML)
  return strXML.getvalue()
```

At this point, the caller's request has been satisfied. If a string is returned, the StringIO class is used in conjunction with the PrettyPrint method to write the XML into the string as if it were a file. Using a DOMImplementation to create your document, as opposed to manually constructing one with a string, offers several benefits. First, it removes tricky details such as preparing a DTD and encoding declarations from inside string assignment statements. It's far easier to maintain the code if you can programmatically alter the encoding or Document Type, without resorting to editing XML by hand inside string assignment statements. Second, greater flexibility is enabled if you need to change the structure of the document. It's easier in the long run to manipulate nodes and their position in the document with a DOM than to parse and manipulate a text string. However, there are many times when you may want to concatenate a string of XML together and create a fresh DOM (in this case, you still wind up with a programmatically accessible DOM representation of the XML).

Returning a DOM instead of a string

Using getProfileAsDom works the same as getProfile, but a DOM instance is returned to you instead of a string of XML.

```
def getProfileAsDom(self, strId):
    """
    This method calls getProfile with the
    dom option set on, which causes getProfile
    to return its created DOM object, and not
    an XML string
    """
    return self.getProfile(strId, 1)
```

This approach was taken because it's often easier to provide intuitive convenience functions as opposed to loading down a method with conditional parameters that a user must learn.

Inserting and Deleting Profiles

The insertProfile method is the other workhorse method of the CustomerProfile class. Whereas getProfile builds a DOM, insertProfile deconstructs a DOM to place its values in the database. Deleting profiles is relatively easy as just a single SQL statement is sent straight to the database with a supplied customer ID.

The insertProfile method is used to add new XML CustomerProfile documents to the database. This interface prevents client applications from having to connect to the database or understand the table structure. Arguably, sharing the structure of XML documents among distributed applications is easier than sharing database structure and potentially having to require support for proprietary data types.

Use insertProfile with a string of XML such as the following:

```
cp = CustomerProfile( )
cp.insertProfile("<string of XML>")
```

The method returns true on success, and false on failure. Additionally, exceptions may be propagated if they occur in handling code.

Inserting a profile

The code for insertProfile is simple as well, but touches on some intricate DOM manipulation. It starts off, as does getProfile, with some simple validation and the retrieval of a DOM instance (as opposed to a DOMImplementation in getProfile):

```
def insertProfile(self, strXML):
    """
    insertProfile takes an XML chunk as a string,
     parses down its fields, and inserts it into the
     profile database.  Raises an exception if XML is
     not well-formed, or customer Id is missing, or if
     SQL execution fails.  Returns 1 on success, 0 on failure.
```

```
"""
if not strXML:
    return 0

# Begin parsing XML
try:
    doc = FromXml(strXML)
except:
    print "Error parsing document."
    return 0

# Normalize white space and retrieve root element
doc.normalize()
elem = doc.documentElement
```

Probably the most important things in the preceding code are the calls to `FromXml` and the call to the `normalize` method of the instantiated document object. The `FromXml` method is part of the `Sax2` reader package, and allows for the construction of a DOM object from a raw string of XML data.

The call to the `doc.normalize` method is important as well. The structure of a `CustomerProfile` XML chunk is quite simple. The character data residing in the elements is short, and needs no peripheral whitespace. That is, if a web form or GUI has placed carriage returns inside the elements, they can be safely eliminated. This step is critical to how the elements are processed inside `insertProfile`. Without the normalization call, it's possible that the text contained in the element may be contained in multiple nodes, and the `firstChild` attribute provides only the first of these; the call to `normalize` ensures that all adjacent text nodes are collapsed into a single node.

Next, the values are extracted out of the fresh XML DOM and used to populate a SQL statement.

```
# Extract values from XML packet
customerId = elem.getAttributeNS(None, 'id')
firstname = self.extractNodeValue(elem, "firstname")
lastname  = self.extractNodeValue(elem, "lastname")
address1  = self.extractNodeValue(elem, "address1")
address2  = self.extractNodeValue(elem, "address2")
city      = self.extractNodeValue(elem, "city")
state     = self.extractNodeValue(elem, "state")
zip       = self.extractNodeValue(elem, "zip")

# prepare SQL statement
strSQL = ("insert into Customer values ("
          "'" + firstname  + "', "
          "'" + lastname   + "', "
          "'" + address1   + "', "
          "'" + address2   + "', "
          "'" + city       + "', "
          "'" + state      + "', "
          "'" + zip        + "', "
          "'" + customerId + "')")
```

Here, the `customerId` attribute is extracted from the root element, and then a series of calls to the `extractNodeValue` helper method are issued. This small method (shown next) takes the current element and attempts to extract a target's text value beneath itself. Since this step is repeated for every element you need, it's easier to relegate it to an internal function rather than duplicate the code in each method that uses it. The preparation of the SQL statement takes the results of the calls to `extractNodeValue` and assembles a SQL insert statement. The work of `extractNodeValue` is shown as follows:

```
def extractNodeValue(self, elem, elemName):
    """
    Internal method to parse UNIQUE elements for text value or
    substitute empty strings.
    """
    e = elem.getElementsByTagName(elemName)[0].firstChild
    if e is not None:
        return e.nodeValue
    else:
        return ""
```

This method attempts to extract a child element from the element it is given, and also tests for its character data content. If not available, an empty string is returned.

Now that the SQL statement is prepared, it can be sent to the database:

```
# generate connection
conn = odbc.odbc(CONNECTION_STRING)
cmd = conn.cursor()

# execute SQL statement
if not cmd.execute(strSQL):
    return 0

conn.close()
return 1
```

If communication with the database proceeds as expected, the method returns a positive 1 to the caller.

Deleting a profile

The code to delete a profile from the database is easy, and relies mainly on taking the supplied customer ID and using it as a parameter in a SQL delete statement:

```
def deleteProfile(self, strId):
    """
    deleteProfile accepts a customer profile ID
    and deletes the corresponding record in the database.
    Returns 1 on success, 0 on failure.
    """
    if not strId:
        return 0

    # generate database connection
```

```
conn = odbc.odbc(CONNECTION_STRING)
cmd = conn.cursor()
ok = cmd.execute("delete from customer where customerId = '"
                 + strId + "'"):
conn.close()
return ok and 1 or 0
```

The result of the SQL operation is indicated to the caller by either a 1 or 0 return value.

Updating Profiles

The process of updating a profile using the `CustomerProfile` class is simple. When calling `updateProfile`, you supply a new chunk of XML data. The `customerId` of this XML chunk must match an existing ID in the database. If so, the old record is deleted, and the new one is inserted.

As mentioned earlier, the `updateProfile` method uses `insertProfile` and `delete-Profile` internally, but is exposed to make the `CustomerProfile` class easier to use.

In order to extract the `customerId` from the supplied chunk of XML, a DOM object is briefly instantiated to parse the data:

```
def updateProfile(self, strXML):
    """

    This convenience function accepts a new customer
    profile XML packet.  It extracts the customer ID
    and then calls deleteProfile and insertProfile using
    the new XML.  The return value for the insert is propagated
    back to the caller, unless the delte fails, in which case
    it is propagated back and insert is never called.
    """
    # parse document for customer Id
    try:
        doc = FromXml(strXML)
        customerId = doc.documentElement.getAttributeNS(None,'id')
    except:
        print "Error parsing document."
        return 0
```

As the preceding code shows, `FromXml` is used once again to convert the string-based XML data into a DOM object. The `customerId` is then extracted using a call to `getAttributeNS`. Since the `reader.Sax2` package is used, you must use a namespace-oriented DOM method as opposed to the normal `getAttribute` method (this is a debated bug in the implementation that will *hopefully* be removed by the time of this printing, at which point `getAttribute` will work as well. To participate in the lively commentary, join the XML-SIG at *http://www.python.org*). With the `customerId` in hand, you can utilize the existing insert and delete methods:

```
# attempt to delete and insert based on customerId
if self.deleteProfile(customerId):
    return self.insertProfile(strXML)
```

```
    else:
        return 1
```

Here returns from these functions are propagated back to the caller as the return value of a call to this function.

The Complete CustomerProfile Class

The CustomerProfile class is quite a workhorse. It allows customer information to be stored on the network as XML. Any distributed application that can access the CustomerProfile class can utilize its functionality without knowing anything about the underlying database or storage medium. Additionally, it's possible to route XML to an application hosting the CustomerProfile class to perform an update. In this best-case scenario, the calling application need not even know of the CustomerProfile class, but instead just construct the appropriate SOAP or XML message format, and submit it to the network. We perform this operation later in this chapter after building the XML switch, in the sections "The XML Switch Client" and "The CGI Functionality."

The complete listing of the CustomerProfile class is shown in Example 10-2.

Example 10-2. CustomerProfile.py

```
"""
CustomerProfile.py
"""
import dbi
import odbc
import StringIO

from xml.dom                import implementation
from xml.dom.ext            import PrettyPrint
from xml.dom.ext.reader.Sax2 import FromXml

# define some global members for the class
CONNECTION_STRING = "Profiles/webuser/w3bus3r"
FIRSTNAME         = 0
LASTNAME          = 1
ADDRESS1          = 2
ADDRESS2          = 3
CITY              = 4
STATE             = 5
ZIP               = 6
CUSTOMER_ID       = 7

class CustomerProfile:
    """
    CustomerProfile - manages the storage and retrieval
    of XML customer profiles from a relational database.
    """
    def getProfileAsDom(self, strId):
```

Example 10-2. CustomerProfile.py (continued)

```
    """
    This method calls getProfile with the
    dom option set on, which causes getProfile
    to return its created DOM object, and not
    an XML string
    """
    return self.getProfile(strId, 1)

def getProfile(self, strId, dom=0):
    """
    getProfile - returns an XML profile chunk based on
    the supplied id.  Returns None if not found.
    """
    if not strId:
      return None

    # generate connection
    conn = odbc.odbc(CONNECTION_STRING)
    cmd = conn.cursor( )
    cmd.execute("select * from customer where " +
                "customerId = '" + strId + "'")
    conn.close( )

    # get data record
    prof_fields = cmd.fetchone( )
    if prof_fields is None:
      return None

    # generate XML from fields
    # generate CustomerProfile doctype
    doctype = implementation.createDocumentType(
      "CustomerProfile", "", "CustomerProfile.dtd")

    # generate new document with doctype
    newdoc = implementation.createDocument(
      "", "CustomerProfile", doctype)
    rootelem = newdoc.documentElement

    # create root element id attribute
    rootelem.setAttribute("id",prof_fields[CUSTOMER_ID] )

    # create list with field values
    fields = ["firstname", prof_fields[FIRSTNAME],
              "lastname",  prof_fields[LASTNAME],
              "address1",  prof_fields[ADDRESS1],
              "address2",  prof_fields[ADDRESS2],
              "city",      prof_fields[CITY],
              "state",     prof_fields[STATE],
              "zip",       prof_fields[ZIP],
              ]
    # loop through list adding elements and element text
    for pos in range(0, len(fields), 2):
      # create the element
```

Example 10-2. CustomerProfile.py (continued)

```
      thisElement = newdoc.createElement(fields[pos])

      # check for empty values and convert to soft nulls
      if fields[pos + 1] is None:
        fields[pos + 1] = ""
      thisElement.appendChild(newdoc.createTextNode(fields[pos+1]))
      rootelem.appendChild(thisElement)

    # return DOM or String based on how we were called...
    if dom:
      return newdoc
    else:
      # return string
      strXML = StringIO.StringIO()
      PrettyPrint(newdoc, strXML)
      return strXML.getvalue()

  def insertProfile(self, strXML):
    """
    insertProfile takes an XML chunk as a string,
    parses down its fields, and inserts it into the
    profile database.  Raises an exception if XML is
    not well-formed, or customer Id is missing, or if
    SQL execution fails.  Returns 1 on success, 0 on failure.
    """
    if not strXML:
      raise Exception("XML String not provided.")

    # Beign parsing XML
    try:
      doc = FromXml(strXML)
    except:
      print "Error parsing document."
      return 0

    # Normalize whitespace and retrive root element
    doc.normalize()
    elem = doc.documentElement

    # Extract values from XML packet
    customerId = elem.getAttributeNS(None, 'id')
    firstname = self.extractNodeValue(elem, "firstname")
    lastname  = self.extractNodeValue(elem, "lastname")
    address1  = self.extractNodeValue(elem, "address1")
    address2  = self.extractNodeValue(elem, "address2")
    city      = self.extractNodeValue(elem, "city")
    state     = self.extractNodeValue(elem, "state")
    zip       = self.extractNodeValue(elem, "zip")

    # prepare SQL statement
    strSQL = ("insert into Customer values ("
              "'" + firstname  + "', "
              "'" + lastname   + "', "
```

Example 10-2. CustomerProfile.py (continued)

```
              "'" + address1   + "', "
              "'" + address2   + "', "
              "'" + city       + "', "
              "'" + state      + "', "
              "'" + zip        + "', "
              "'" + customerId + "')")

  # create connection
  conn = odbc.odbc(CONNECTION_STRING)
  cmd = conn.cursor( )

  # execute SQL statement
  if not cmd.execute(strSQL):
    raise exception.Exceptions("SQL Exec failed.")

  conn.close( )
  return 1

def extractNodeValue(self, elem, elemName):
    """
    Internal method to parse UNIQUE elements for text value or
    substitute empty strings.
    """
    e = elem.getElementsByTagName(elemName)[0].firstChild
    if e is None:
      return ""
    else:
      return e.nodeValue

def updateProfile(self, strXML):
    """
  This convenience function accepts a new customer
  profile XML packet.  It extracts the customer ID
  and then calls deleteProfile and insertProfile using
  the new XML.  The return value for the insert is propagated
  back to the caller, unless the delte fails, in which case
  it is propagated back and insert is never called.
    """
  # parse document for customer Id
  try:
    doc = FromXml(strXML)
    customerId = doc.documentElement.getAttributeNS(None,'id')
  except:
    print "Error parsing document."
    return 0

  # attempt to delete and insert based on customerId
  if self.deleteProfile(customerId):
    return self.insertProfile(strXML)
  else:
    return 1
```

Example 10-2. CustomerProfile.py (continued)

```
def deleteProfile(self, strId):
    """

    deleteProfile accepts a customer profile ID
    and deletes the corresponding record in the database.
    Returns 1 on success, 0 on failure.
    """

    if not strId:
      return 0

    # generate database connection
    conn = odbc.odbc(CONNECTION_STRING)
    cmd = conn.cursor( )
    ok = cmd.execute("delete from customer where customerId = '"
                    + strId + "'"):
    conn.close( )
    return ok and 1 or 0
```

One thing of note in *CustomerProfile.py* is the use of constants defined at the top of the file as field markers in the database record set. By defining constants, it's far easier to work with the different fields in the record set array.

Creating an XML Data Store

The third component of the distributed application built in this chapter is an "Offers XML Data Store." This is a content-based repository of "special offers" that retailers commonly offer to their customers. In this imaginary application, the Offers Data Store holds various offers, which are retrievable from the network at runtime. Different distributed applications can access the offers for different reasons.

For example, a web-based application may want to access the offers dynamically to present offers to users based on their recent purchases or spending habits. The web application applies a stylesheet to the offer information prior to displaying on a web page. Or, it's possible that an Intranet application may access the offers as part of management functionality in order to change or edit offers.

To that end, in this section, we construct an XML Offers Data Store. In the following section, we construct another Python class similar to `CustomerProfile`, which allows us to access the XML data store on the network rather transparently.

A Large XML File

The Offers Data Store consists of a large XML document residing on disk. The aforementioned access component developed later will take care of traversing this file and returning the correct offers back to the caller. The basic structure of an offer as empty elements is:

```
<offer>
  <id/>
```

```
    <internal-name/>
    <heading/>
    <description/>
    <discount/>
    <discount-type/>
    <expires/>
    <disclaimer/>
  </offer>
```

A complete starting XML store is presented in Example 10-3, with just two offers. If
you feel the need to add your own, please do so.

Example 10-3. OfferXMLStore.xml

```
<?xml version="1.0" encoding="UTF-8"?>
<OfferXMLStore>
  <offer>
    <id>9908d093j4p3j33</id>
    <internal-name>DiscountOver1000</internal-name>
    <heading>20% Off All Orders Over $1000.00</heading>
    <description>
    As an incentive for you to purchase more,
    we're offering a 20% volume discount on all
    orders totaling $1000 or more!  This amazing
    discount is being brought to you because you
    are such an important customer to us.  We love
    you so much!
    </description>
    <discount>20</discount>
    <discount-type>percent</discount-type>
    <expires>2002-11-21</expires>
    <disclaimer>
    Discount subject to certain restrictions.  Merchandise
    must not be under any other discounts, and discount is
    taken from MSRP only.  Discount may not be applied in
    some cases if we think you are likely to buy the product
    without a discount.  We may revoke this discount whenever
    we want, including after you place your order.  Sorry.
    </disclaimer>
  </offer>
  <offer>
    <id>222833fgjQZ3j30</id>
    <internal-name>Clearance</internal-name>
    <heading>20% Off All Clearance Items</heading>
    <description>
    In an effort to reduce our inventory of the items
    that just don't seem to sell as well as our other
    merchandise, we're offering a 20% deduction on all
    items marked clearance!  This is because you are
    such an important customer to us.  We love you so
    much.
    </description>
    <discount>20</discount>
    <discount-type>percent</discount-type>
```

Example 10-3. OfferXMLStore.xml (continued)

```
    <expires>2002-11-21</expires>
    <disclaimer>
    Discount subject to certain restrictions.  Merchandise
    must be marked clearance.  In some cases, some items
    marked clearance may have the mark removed at time of
    purchase.  If this happens to you, the full price of the
    product will be charged to your card.  Sorry.
    </disclaimer>
  </offer>
</OfferXMLStore>
```

These two offers are enough to get started. The OfferXMLStore is just a large XML file on disk. The larger the file gets, the overhead of parsing and manipulating the file increases. At a certain point, it is better to migrate the OfferXMLStore into a database. While an XML representation of the data is critical, using an actual database for the physical storage to disk is far more efficient then processing a large text file. XML is at its strongest as a document format and glue language. In other words, you don't want a gigabyte XML document full of information, you want a gigabyte of XML documents inside your database. Given the flexibility of the XML access object created in the next section, it is simple to change the underlying storage mechanism of the XML offers without affecting the XML information passing in and out.

Creating an XML Access Object

In this section, we create another access component to access data from the XML data store. This type of object comes in handy when encapsulating a data source from a user of the data source. This was done with the CustomerProfile object earlier when it hid the ODBC data source from view behind a veil of XML. The XMLOffer class puts forth several methods for storing, retrieving, and modifying offers maintained in the XML data store.

The interfaces

The interfaces for the XMLOffer class are very similar to the ones for CustomerProfile, with the notable addition of a getAllOffers method. These methods are intended to allow network applications the ability to interact with the XML data store using only XML, without needing to know or be concerned with what type of underlying storage mechanism the store is using. In fact, by sticking to the interface but rewriting the implementation, you could change the XMLOffer class to speak with a database rather than an XML file. This change is completely transparent to the clients who would have no visibility of it whatsoever.

getOffer(*id*)

This method takes an ID as a string, and retrieves the corresponding XML offer within the Data Store as a single XML chunk contained in a string.

`getOfferAsDomElement(id)`

> As you might suspect, this method works identically to the analogous method in `CustomerProfile`, returning a DOM `Element` object instead of a string.

`getAllOffers( )`

> This method returns the entire `OfferXMLStore` as a string.

`insertOffer(strXML)`

> This method takes an XML offer chunk as an argument, and places it inside the XML data store.

`updateOffer(strXML)`

> Similar to `CustomerProfile.updateProfile`, this method takes an offer as XML, deletes the corresponding offer from the store, and adds this one.

`deleteOffer(id)`

> As you may realize, this method takes an ID as an argument and removes the corresponding offer from the XML data store.

The interfaces exposed are meant to make working with the XML offers as easy as possible for applications running on the network.

This class will be hosted, alongside `CustomerProfile`, within the XML Switch. Of course, they could easily be placed behind the web server or CORBA servers, but for brevity, in this chapter they are accessible as loadable classes to the XML Switch.

Using the XMLOffer class

Use of the `XMLOffer` class is simple. Provided you have *OfferXMLStore.xml* available on disk (as shown in Example 10-3), you can begin using the `XMLOffer` class:

```
from XMLOffer    import XMLOffer
xo = XMLOffer( )
print xo.getOffer('9908d093j4p3j33')
```

The result is retrieval of the offer element with a matching ID child. Likewise, if your web site posted an offer to you, or your GUI app returned a text area's XML content as a string, you could use the `insertOffer` method:

```
xo.insertOffer(strXMLOffer)
```

The interfaces are all straightforward.

Creating the XMLOffer class

The `XMLOffer` class is simple, but relies heavily on use of the DOM and XPath to support its functionality. As with `CustomerProfile`, the `XMLOffer` class typically returns a 1 or a 0 after each method call. The exceptions are, of course, the methods that return XML.

To understand how the `XMLOffer` class wraps the large `OfferXMLStore` with convenience functions, such as get, insert, update, or delete, is to understand many different ways to manipulate XML. Implementing the `XMLOffer` class illustrates DOM usage as well as XPath.

Retrieval methods. When obtaining an offer, the class accepts an ID string from the caller, and uses XPath to find the offer with the corresponding ID in the store:

```
offerdoc = FromXmlStream("OfferXMLStore.xml")
offer = Evaluate("offer[id='" + strId + "']",
                offerdoc.documentElement)
```

The XPath looks for the supplied ID string (strId) within offer elements inside the XML store. When it hits the target, it is returned as the offer element. If you requested an element node (offer), you could call getOfferAsDomElement; however, for a string, you call getOffer:

```
if dom:
  return offer[0]
else:
    strXML = StringIO.StringIO()
    PrettyPrint(offer[0], strXML)
    return strXML.getvalue()
```

Of course, getOfferAsDomElement works in the same fashion as getProfile in the CustomerProfile class. The method simply calls its shorter-named cousin with an optional parameter and indicates to return the node rather than a string.

The getAllOffers method uses a simple direct approach to delivering the XML store—it just writes the whole file back to you as a string.

```
# scoop up offers file
fd = open("OfferXMLStore.xml", "r")
doc = fd.read()
fd.close()

# return big string
return doc
```

Modification methods. Several methods exist for modifying and managing offers within the XML store. The insertOffer method allows you to put new offers in the store. The methods updateOffer and deleteOffer allow for additional maintenance.

The insertOffer method creates a DOM instance out of the submitted XML to verify well-formedness (and potentially validity, if you put in the effort). It's converted to a string and swapped out with the OfferXMLStore's end element tag. This is a quick and easy way to add the new element to the document. You can work with strings because the submitted XML was at first a DOM instance, and could be validated while in that state.

The updateOffer extracts the ID, and then performs a delete followed by an insert. The deleteOffer method extracts an ID, and then removes the node from a DOM instance:

```
try:
  targetNode = Evaluate("offer[id=\"" + strId + "\"]",
                  xmlstore.documentElement)
```

```
    except:
      print "Bad XPath Evaluation."
      return 0

    # use Node.removeChild(XPathResult)
    try:
      xmlstore.documentElement.removeChild(targetNode[0])
    except:
      # either it didn't exist, or
      # the XPath call turned up nothing...
      return 0
```

XPath is used to target the specific ID, and the Evaluate call returns the actual node. The node is then handed off to the documentElement node's removeChild( ) method. At this point, the rest of the code writes the file back to disk. Example 10-4 shows *XMLOffer.py*.

Example 10-4. XMLOffer.py

```
"""
XMLOffer.py
"""
import StringIO

from xml.dom.ext.reader.Sax2 import FromXmlStream
from xml.dom.ext.reader.Sax2 import FromXml
from xml.dom.ext              import PrettyPrint
from xml.xpath               import Evaluate

class XMLOffer:
  def getOffer(self, strId, dom=0):
    """
    getOffer takes an ID as a parameter and returns
    the corresponding offer from the XML Data Store
    as a string of XML, or as a DOM if the third param
    flag has been set.
    """
    # create document from data store
    offerdoc = FromXmlStream("OfferXMLStore.xml")

    # use XPath to target specific offer element
    # by child ID character data
    offer = Evaluate("offer[id='" + strId + "']",
                     offerdoc.documentElement)

    # decide which version to return, DOM or string
    if dom:
      # return offer element
      return offer[0]
    else:
      # convert to string
      strXML = StringIO.StringIO( )
      PrettyPrint(offer[0], strXML)
```

Example 10-4. XMLOffer.py (continued)

```
      return strXML.getvalue( )

  def getOfferAsDomElement(self, strId):
      """
      getOfferAsDomElement works the same as getOffer
      but returns a DOM element instance, as opposed to
      a string.  This method just calls getOffer with the
      dom flag (the third parameter) set to 1.
      """
      return self.getOffer(strId, 1)

  def getAllOffers(self):
      """
      getAllOffers returns the whole store
      as a string.
      """
      # scoop up offers file
      fd = open("OfferXMLStore.xml", "r")
      doc = fd.read( )
      fd.close( )

      # return big string
      return doc

  def insertOffer(self, strOfferXML):
      """
      insertOffer takes a string of XML and adds it to the
      XML store.
      """
      if not strOfferXML:
          return None

      # generate DOM from input data
      newoffer = FromXml(strOfferXML)

      #----
      # Optional: you could validate here using
      # your new dom object and offer.dtd; see
      # chapter 7 for details on using xmlproc for
      # validation...
      #----

      # Pour DOM into String
      newXmlOffer = StringIO.StringIO( )
      PrettyPrint(newoffer.documentElement, newXmlOffer)

      # grab contents into buffer
      rd = open("OfferXMLStore.xml", "r")
      bf = rd.readlines( )
      rd.close( )

      # search and replace in buffer
      wd = open("OfferXMLStore.xml", "w")
```

Example 10-4. XMLOffer.py (continued)

```python
    for lp in range(len(bf)):
      if (bf[lp].rfind("</OfferXMLStore>") > -1):
        # replace root element end tag with fresh offer
        # and root element end tag
        bf[lp] = bf[lp].replace("</OfferXMLStore>",
          newXmlOffer.getvalue( ) + "</OfferXMLStore>")

    # write new buffer to disk
    wd.writelines(bf)
    wd.close( )

    return 1

  def deleteOffer(self, strId):
    """
    deleteOffer takes an ID string and deletes that offer Node
    from the OfferXMLStore.xml document
    """
    # read store into DOM, close store
    try:
      xmlstore = FromXmlStream("OfferXMLStore.xml")
    except:
      print "Unable to open xmlstore."
      return 0

    # use XPath to return the id Node
    # offer/[id='<id>']
    try:
      targetNode = Evaluate("offer[id=\"" + strId + "\"]",
                            xmlstore.documentElement)
    except:
      print "Bad XPath Evaluation."
      return 0

    # use Node.removeChild(XPathResult)
    try:
      xmlstore.documentElement.removeChild(targetNode[0])
    except:
      # either it didn't exist, or
      # the XPath call turned up nothing...
      return 0

    # reopen store,w
    # PrettyPrint the DOM in
    # close the store
    fd = open("OfferXMLStore.xml", "w")
    PrettyPrint(xmlstore, fd)
    fd.close( )
    return 1

  def updateOffer(self, strOfferXML):
    if not strOfferXML:
```

Example 10-4. XMLOffer.py (continued)

```
      return 0
  else:
    try:
      offerId = Evaluate("id/text( )",
                         FromXml(strOfferXML).documentElement)
      if (not self.deleteOffer(offerId[0].nodeValue)
          or not self.insertOffer(strOfferXML)):
        print "could not delete or insert."
        return 0
    except:
      print "unable to update offer."
      return 0

  return 1
```

The XMLOffer class is easy to use. The next component of the distributed system is the XML Switch, which brokers the individual messages among the different applications.

The XML Switch

The XML Switch is the centerpiece of the distributed system. It's the grand intermediary between information consumers and information suppliers. Overall, the XML Switch is about two things:

1. It is meant to act as an intermediary between frontend application systems and backend information systems.
2. It has a fundamental XML messaging structure for greater flexibility between the message sender and the message receiver.

XML Architecture

The overall architecture of the XML Switch is about messaging and RPC. The switch is an intermediary between frontend system applications, such as web servers and desktop applications, to backend systems, such as databases and remote services. By using a messaging paradigm rather than wiring the systems directly to each other, you gain a traffic pattern that is decoupled from the applications, and one that is manageable independently.

If you were to patch a CGI script directly into a database, you must use a specialized object to attach to the database as well as understand its schema and data types. By moving to XML, on the other hand, your application and others need only become familiar with an XML data structure. This data structure is produced by the database when asked with the right XML message. The main difference here is that these types of messages can be interpreted by any type of system that may need to understand them either today or years into the future. This sort of flexibility pays off greatly in the design of distributed systems that must evolve over long periods.

The XML Switch presented here is a simple messaging prototype to facilitate the use of XML messages in distributed Python systems. Ideally, your message format should be SOAP, or some other format that is easily shared between emerging commercial systems. The confines of this book do not allow for the complete development of a SOAP messaging server and example client applications, so instead a simple XML message format has been chosen that supports the same type of RPC and messaging functionality.

Core XML Switch Classes

The XML Switch is composed of three main pieces. First, there is the XMLMessage. This class is the base unit of the system. This class and its associated XML message structure are used as the basis of communication between the XML Switch and its neighboring applications. Any client, on any platform, can conceivably create the right kind of XML message for the switch to understand. The message format is paramount in allowing the system to work.

Of equal importance in the trilogy of supporting players is the actual XMLSwitchHandler. This class implements the HTTP handler used to catch calls against the server. It is the XMLSwitchHandler's duty to ensure that RPC messages are properly parsed and executed, and that their return results are quickly sent back to the caller in XML.

All of this messaging between the Switch and the backend systems that it's connected to (via objects) is initiated by clients. Clients of the XML Switch use the xsc class to send XML messages to the switch. True to their black-box designs, the messages disappear into the switch and information comes back out in XML format!

XMLMessage
> This class is defined in *XMLMessage.py*, shown in Example 10-7. This class encapsulates developers from the standard message format of the application. An example message (*message.xml*) is shown in Example 10-5.

XMLSwitchHandler
> This class is defined in *XMLSwitchHandler.py*, shown in Example 10-12, later in this chapter. This class runs the XML switching server that accepts XML messages from the end- user applications and pairs them with backend resources. The results returned by these resources are delivered back to the originating application in another XML message.

xsc
> This class offers a one-method client API to send messages into the XML Switch. The sendMessage method expects a well-formed XML message string as an argument, and sends the XML to the switch. If everything goes well, the server invokes the method and parameters on one of the hosted objects, and returns the result back to you.

The XMLMessage Class

In this distributed system, messages are sent between systems in a simple XML envelope. This envelope is similar in structure to SOAP. But given the nascent SOAP support in Python and the limited space available in a book such as this, the distributed system in this chapter uses the following simple message structure (in empty form):

```
<message>
  <header></header>
  <body></body>
</message>
```

As long as the document is organized this way, the elements can contain anything you like, including SOAP fragments, web pages, data records, or whatever you can place XML tags around.

XMLMessage format

Example 10-5 shows a complete, well-formed XML message:

Example 10-5. An example message.xml file

```
<message>
  <header><rpc/></header>
  <body>
    <object class="CustomerProfile"
            method="getProfile">
      <param>234-E838839</param>
    </object>
  </body>
</message>
```

The message format is really a thin envelope consisting of a message, a header, and a body. The message in Example 10-5 is an RPC call. When the server receives Example 10-5, it first examines the header to see that it's an RPC call. Next, it extracts the payload and invokes the correct object, method, and parameters. It then changes the XML message and sends it back to the original caller through the XML Switch.

XMLMessage class

Using the XMLMessage class is simple. Messages can either be created from an XML string, an XML document object, or loaded from a file. Once created, access functions allow you to get at specific parts of the message document more quickly. The methods getHeader and getBody allow you to quickly extract header or body data. The method setHeader and setBody allow you to manipulate an XML message before sending it to another system for processing. The whole message can be swapped in and out as either a string or a DOM object using getXMLMessage and setXMLMessage, along with their DOM counterparts getXMLMessageDom and setXMLMessageDom. The methods typically used to load and inspect an XML message (like the *message.xml* shown in Example 10-5) are shown in the short script illustrated in Example 10-6.

Example 10-6. runxm.py—using the XMLMessage object

```
"""
runxm.py - run xml message object
"""
import XMLMessage
from xml.dom.ext import PrettyPrint
#from xml.dom.ext.reader.Sax2 import FromXml

xm = XMLMessage.XMLMessage()

xm.loadXMLMessage("message.xml")

from xml.dom.ext import PrettyPrint
PrettyPrint(xm.getXMLMessageDom())

print "Change the body to: <body>Hello!</body>"
if xm.setBody("<body>Hello!</body>"):
  print xm.getXMLMessage()
```

This code produces the following output:

```
G:\pythonxml\c10>python runxm.py
<?xml version='1.0' encoding='UTF-8'?>
<!DOCTYPE message>
<message>
  <header>
    <rpc/>
  </header>
  <body>
    <!-- cp.getProfile("234-E838839") -->
    <object method='getProfile' class='CustomerProfile'>
      <param>234-E838839</param>
    </object>
  </body>
</message>
Change the body to: <body>Hello!</body>
<?xml version='1.0' encoding='UTF-8'?>
<!DOCTYPE message>
<message>
  <header>
    <rpc/>
  </header>
  <body>Hello!</body>
</message>
```

This output shows the successful loading of the original XML message, and the successful modification of its body element. The methods of the XMLMessage class are simple, and most behave the same. Here is a quick reference of the methods implemented by the XMLMessage class:

---

setBody(*strXML*)

    setBody takes a string of XML representing a well-formed body element and replaces the existing message's body element with the new content.

getBody( )

    Returns the body element as a string of XML (held in self._body).

setHeader(*strXML*)

    Replaces the existing header element with the supplied XML string.

getHeader( )

    Returns the header element as a string (held in self._header).

setXMLMessage(*strXMLMessage*)

    Takes an XML message document as a string. The supplied parameter is then used as the entire XML message. The new content is returned in all other calls to getBody, getHeader, and getXMLMessage.

setXMLMessageDom(*xmldom*)

    Identical to setXMLMessage but takes an XML DOM object representing a well-formed message instead of a string of XML.

loadXMLMessage(*file*)

    Sets the contents of the current XML message with the contents of *file*, provided they are well-formed.

getXMLMessage( )

    Returns the entire message XML document as a string.

getXMLMessageDom( )

    Returns the entire message XML document as a DOM instance.

The implementation process in creating these methods utilized much of the DOM work done in this book thus far. However, there are a few notable new techniques, mentioned in the next section.

XML message code architecture

Most of the work of the XMLMessage class is done by the setXMLMessage method. This method takes a hidden DOM parameter that indicates whether the new message is a string of XML or a DOM instance.

The complete document is created, and then the member elements are populated by extracting their respective element names from the document. This enables the XMLMessage class to expose access methods for the message's two most common elements: the header and the body.

```
if dom:
  self._dom = strXMLMessage
  Holder = StringIO.StringIO( )
  PrettyPrint(self._dom, Holder)
  self._xml = Holder.getvalue( )
else:
```

```
        dom = FromXml(strXMLMessage)
        self._dom = dom
        self._xml = strXMLMessage

    # header as string
    Holder = StringIO.StringIO( )
    PrettyPrint(self._dom.getElementsByTagName("header")[0],
                Holder)
    self._header = Holder.getvalue( )

    # body as string
    Holder = StringIO.StringIO( )
    PrettyPrint(self._dom.getElementsByTagName("body")[0],
                Holder)
    self._body = Holder.getvalue( )
```

By populating the member elements at the initial time of parsing, the data they represent are stored as strings and are immediately accessible to any caller. It's worthy of noting however, that when you replace an element such as the body or header, it's *reconstituted*, so to speak, and the document is reprocessed as a string:

```
def setBody(self, strXML):
    """
      setBody(strXML) - The supplied XML
      is used for the body of the XML message.
    """
    xmlstr = FromXml(str("<message>" +
                     self._header + strXML + "</message>"))
    return self.setXMLMessageDom(xmlstr)
```

This shortcut requires reparsing the entire document. Another approach is to parse the document out into a collection of nodes, each made read-and-write capable by access functions. However, this DOM-friendly approach requires considerably more code than what is presented here.

XMLMessage code listing

Example 10-7 shows the complete listing of *XMLMessage.py*.

Example 10-7. XMLMessage.py

```
"""
 XMLMessage.py - a wrapper for message.xml
 documents
"""
import StringIO

from xml.dom.ext              import PrettyPrint
from xml.dom.ext.reader.Sax2 import FromXmlStream, FromXml

class XMLMessage:
    """
    XMLMessage encapsulates a message.xml document
```

Example 10-7. XMLMessage.py (continued)

```
    from class users.
    """
  def __init__(self):
    self._dom = ""
    self._xml = ""

  def setBody(self, strXML):
    """
    setBody(strXML) - The supplied XML
    is used for the body of the XML message.
    """
    xmlstr = FromXml(str("<message>" + \
                self._header + strXML + "</message>"))
    return self.setXMLMessageDom(xmlstr)

  def getBody(self):
    """ return body as string
    """
    return self._body

  def setHeader(self, strXML, dom=0):
    """
    setHeader(strXML) - The supplied XML
    is used for the header of the XML message.
    """
    xmlstr = FromXml(str("<message>" + strXML + self._body + "</message>"))
    return self.setXMLMessageDom(xmlstr)

  def getHeader(self):
    """ return header as string
    """
    return self._header

  def setXMLMessage(self, strXMLMessage, dom=0):
    """
    setXMLMessage - uses supplied XML as entire
    XML message
    """
    try:
      if dom:
        # assign dom directly with parameter
        self._dom = strXMLMessage

        # populate StringIO object for self._xml
        Holder = StringIO.StringIO()
        PrettyPrint(self._dom, Holder)

        # assign string value of dom to self._xml
        self._xml = Holder.getvalue()
      else:
        # create dom from supplied string XML
        dom = FromXml(strXMLMessage)
```

Example 10-7. XMLMessage.py (continued)

```
        # set member dom property
        self._dom = dom

        # set member string property
        self._xml = strXMLMessage

    # header as DOM
    self._headerdom = self._dom.getElementsByTagName("header")[0]

    # header as string
    Holder = StringIO.StringIO()
    PrettyPrint(self._dom.getElementsByTagName("header")[0],
                Holder)
    self._header = Holder.getvalue()

    # body as DOM
    self._bodydom = self._dom.getElementsByTagName("body")[0]

    # body as string
    Holder = StringIO.StringIO()
    PrettyPrint(self._dom.getElementsByTagName("body")[0],
                Holder)
    self._body = Holder.getvalue()

  except:
    print "Could not create dom from message!"
    return 0

  return 1

def setXMLMessageDom(self, xmldom):
  """ call setXMLMessage with dom flag
  """
  return self.setXMLMessage(xmldom, dom=1)

def loadXMLMessage(self, file):
  """
    loadXMLMessage - build an XML message from
    a file or URL
  """
  try:
    dom = FromXmlStream(file)
  except:
    print "Could not load XML Message."
    return 0

  return self.setXMLMessageDom(dom)

def getXMLMessage(self, dom=0):
  """
    getXMLMessage - returns the entire message
    as either string of XML or Dom
```

Example 10-7. XMLMessage.py (continued)

```
    """
    if(dom):
      return self._dom
    else:
      return self._xml


  def getXMLMessageDom(self):
    """ return XML message dom property
    """
    return self.getXMLMessage(dom=1)
```

The XMLMessage class encapsulates a simple XML message format from developers with access methods. This approach can be used to wrap messages more complex than these, such as SOAP. This allows you to build parts of your distributed system to speak SOAP, or to begin migrating your distributed integration project to SOAP and Python.

The XML Switch Service

The XML Switch is a server process and client API that allow objects to have their methods and properties exposed over the Web. XML messages similar to SOAP calls are used to invoke methods on the server objects. Since SOAP support for Python is thin, and this book has limited space, a simple XML message format (described in the last section) was designed for this application. These messages, if marked with an rpc element in their header, are used by the XML Switch to invoke methods on an object, and return the results in another XML message.

The XML Switch service is provided in large part by the XMLSwitchHandler class, developed later in Example 10-12. The client applications developed in later portions of this chapter create XML messages and forward them to the server. The server then inspects these XML messages to see if they are RPC calls—if so, the correct object is loaded, the method executed, and the return results framed in another XML message and sent back to the caller.

There is no reason why a lookup table could not be built, and have routing rules applied to the XML messages as they arrive. There is also no reason why an XML Switch can't route an XML message to another XML Switch—letting it hop its way to its final destination. This enables message delivery to be decoupled between the sender and receiver. By chaining XML Switch units together, you can create a scalable, routed XML network.

The XML Switch Client

There are two primary clients of the XML Switch. The first, *postMsg.html*, is simply a web page that posts to the correct server and URL. The switch responds with raw

XML that the browser (if Internet Explorer) displays in a tree-view, or with something like Netscape, uses the content handler specified or shows you the file as plain text.

The XML Switch client is a Python API that also can be used as a command-line tool. The API features a single method to submit XML messages to the server, and get back the responses. In this section, we look at the clients of the XML Switch; afterward, we build the server itself.

Using postMsg.html to send back XML

The *postMsg.html* file allows you to post to the server and invoke the echoReponse method to test your server's functionality. The *postMsg.html* source is shown in Example 10-8.

Example 10-8. The postMsg.html file

```
<html>
<body>
<form action="http://centauri:2112/" method="POST">
<p>Input here:</p>
<p><textarea name="n" rows=20 cols=80>
    <message>
  <header><non-rpc/></header>
  <body><!-- cp.getProfile("234-E838839") -->
    <object class="CustomerProfile"
          method="getProfile">
      <param>234-E838839</param>
    </object>
  </body>
</message>
    </textarea>
</p>
<p><input type="submit" value=" submit data ">
</p>
</form>
</body>
</html>
```

Using the echoResponse method is a good way to test the server's functionality. If you use the *postMsg.html* file created in Example 10-8, you can post a sample message and get a response from the XML Switch, as shown in Figure 10-2.

If you create a message with a header that says `<rpc/>` instead of `<non-rpc/>`, you actually get the XML response that the message generates when the RPC is invoked by the server.

For example, if you enter the following XML in *postMsg.html*:

```
<message>
  <header><rpc/></header>
  <body>
    <object class="CustomerProfile"
```

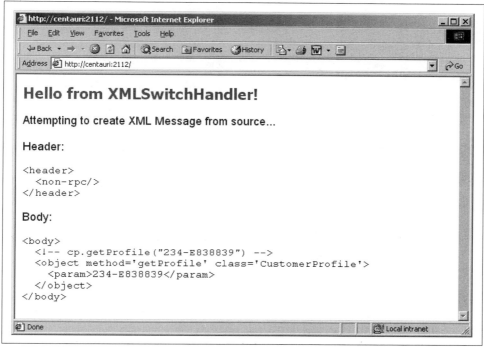

```
Hello from XMLSwitchHandler!

Attempting to create XML Message from source...

Header:

<header>
  <non-rpc/>
</header>

Body:

<body>
  <!-- cp.getProfile("234-E838839") -->
  <object method='getProfile' class='CustomerProfile'>
    <param>234-E838839</param>
  </object>
</body>
```

Figure 10-2. Using postMsg.html to connect to the server

```
          method="getProfile">
        <param>983-E2229J3</param>
      </object>
    </body>
  </message>
```

and hit submit data, you get back the raw XML packet from the server. With a browser like Internet Explorer, it is shown with the default stylesheet, as shown in Figure 10-3. This only works if you have a profile with the ID number 983-E2229J3 in your database. If not, just substitute the ID value with a value that exists in your database and things should work just fine.

In fact, *postMsg.html* should work for any valid XML message submitted to the server. To witness some real API work first hand, you need to run the xsc client from the command line or from Python code.

Using the XSC client

The xsc client *xsc.py*, shown in Example 10-11, allows you to make calls against the XML Switch and inspect the XML messages that are sent back in return. The XML messages must be kept in a local file if using xsc as a command-line tool.

The XML file is just a message document. Example 10-9 shows a sample message (*msgGetProfile.xml*) you can use with xsc.

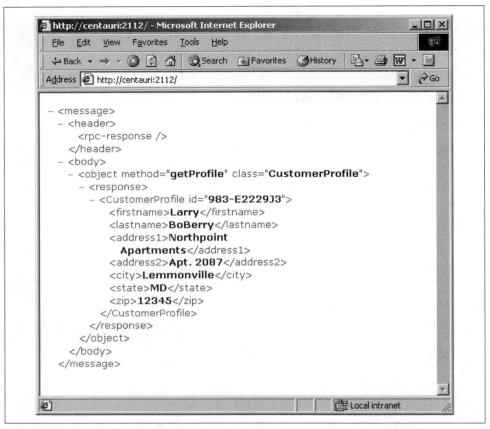

Figure 10-3. Posting an RPC call with postMsg.html

Example 10-9. msgGetProfile.xml

```xml
<message>
  <header><rpc/></header>
  <body>
    <object class="CustomerProfile"
            method="getProfile">
      <param>983-E2229J3</param>
    </object>
  </body>
</message>
```

Run the file with the message file as a parameter, as shown in Example 10-10.

Example 10-10. Running xcs.py from the command line

```
G:\pythonxml\c10> python xsc.py msgGetProfile.xml
XMLSwitch Server:  localhost:2112
[200 OK 522 bytes]
```

Example 10-10. Running xcs.py from the command line (continued)

Response:

```
<message>
  <header>
    <rpc-response/>
  </header>
  <body>
    <object method='getProfile' class='CustomerProfile'>
      <response>
        <CustomerProfile id='983-E2229J3'>
          <firstname>Larry</firstname>
          <lastname>BoBerry</lastname>
          <address1>Northpoint Apartments</address1>
          <address2>Apt. 2087</address2>
          <city>Lemmonville</city>
          <state>MD</state>
          <zip>12345</zip>
        </CustomerProfile>
      </response>
    </object>
  </body>
</message>
```

The xsc command-line operation prints out a status line indicating the server used, a line indicating the HTTP response code and message, as well as the size of the returned XML document. The returned XML is then dumped out to the command line.

Using the XSC API

You can also make calls to the XML Switch from your own programs. In fact, the client applications presented later in this chapter communicate with other systems via the xsc client and small XML rpc message invocations.

To use the xsc API, you must import xsc into your class.

```
import sys
import xsc

xc = xsc.xsc( )
```

Next you need to indicate the server and port combination where the XML Switch is running:

```
xc.server = "localhost:2112"
```

You also need some XML to send to the server. It never hurts to load the message from a file.

```
fd = open(sys.argv[1], "r")
xmlmsg = fd.read( )
fd.close( )
```

Finally, one method call is enough to send your XML message to the server and get the return result:

```
response = xc.sendMessage(xmlmsg)
print response
```

That is all it takes to invoke remote Python objects that peer into SQL databases and inspect XML stores for relevant information. The XML Switch acts as a broker, taking in your XML requests, and sending you back XML information.

The complete code to *xsc.py*, the file needed to do both command-line queries against the XML Switch as well as to use it programmatically, is shown in Example 10-11.

Example 10-11. xsc.py, the client to the XML Switch

```
"""
  xsc.py - XMLSwitch Client

  usage:
    python xsc.py myRequestFile.xml

"""
import sys
import httplib
from urllib import quote_plus

class xsc:
    """
    xsc - XMLSwitch Client
    This class is both the command line and module
    interface to the XMLSwitch.

    From the cmd line:
    $> python xsc.py msgFile.xml

    The third parameter is an XML file with a valid
    <message> within it.  The response <message> will
    be written back to the console.

    As an API:
    import xsc
    responseXML = xsc.sendMessage(strXMLMessage)

    The result is now in responseXML.
    """
    def __init__(self):
        """
        init - establish some public props
        """
        self.server = "localhost:2112" # host:port (80 is http)
        self.stats  = ""
```

Example 10-11. xsc.py, the client to the XML Switch (continued)

```python
    def sendMessage(self, strXMLMessage):
        """

        sendMessage(strXML) - this method sends the
        supplied XML message to the server in self.server.
        The XML response is returned to the caller.
        """
        # prepare XML message by url encoding...
        strXMLRequest = quote_plus(strXMLMessage)

        # connect with server...
        req = httplib.HTTP(self.server)

        # add HTTP headers, including content-length
        # as size of our XML message
        req.putrequest("POST", "/")
        req.putheader("Accept", "text/html")
        req.putheader("Accept", "text/xml")
        req.putheader("User-Agent", "xsc.py")
        req.putheader("Content-length", str(len("n=" + strXMLRequest)))
        req.endheaders( )

        # send XML as POST data
        req.send("n=" + strXMLRequest)

        # get HTTP response
        ec, em, h = req.getreply( )

        # content-length indicates number of
        # bytes in response XML message
        cl = h.get("content-length", "0")

        # stats us [http-code, http-msg, content-length]
        self.stats = ("[" + str(ec) + " " +
                    str(em) + " " +
                    str(cl) + " bytes]")

        # attempt to read XML resonse
        nfd = req.getfile( )
        try:
            textlines = nfd.read( )
            nfd.close( )
            # return XML data
            return textlines

        except:
            nfd.close( )
            return ""

# cmd line operation
if __name__ == "__main__":
    # instantiate server
    xc = xsc( )
```

Example 10-11. xsc.py, the client to the XML Switch (continued)

```
xc.server = "localhost:2112"

# read in the message file
fd = open(sys.argv[1], "r")
xmlmsg = fd.read( )
fd.close( )

# make call to server and print stats, and response
print "XMLSwitch Server: ", xc.server
response = xc.sendMessage(xmlmsg)
print xc.stats
print "Reponse: "
print response
```

The XMLSwitchHandler Server Class

The XMLSwitchHandler class is a BaseHTTPRequestHandler. The entire XMLSwitchHandler class is shown in Example 10-12. You can use the additional script *runxs.py* to actually run the server from the command line. The *runxs.py* script is shown in Example 10-13 (in the section "Running the XML Switch").

XMLSwitchHandler code architecture

The architecture behind the XMLSwitchHandler involves a great deal of XML. Probably the best method to highlight is processXMLMessagePost. This method is the real workhorse. The messages come in as URL-encoded data. To understand the message sent by the client, it's necessary to decode the data and try to get a DOM-friendly XMLMessage object from the results:

```
def processXMLMessagePost(self, strPostData):
    """

    processXMLMessagePost(strXMLMessage) - this
    method creates an XMLMessage from the supplied
    data and looks up a mapping from XMLMapping.xml
    to determine what object and method pair to
    invoke.
    """
    # create message by unquoting post data
    xmsg = XMLMessage( )
    xmsg.setXMLMessage(
        unquote_plus(strPostData).replace("n=", ""))
```

At this point, xmsg is a new XMLMessage object encapsulating the client's request. The header is inspected. If the header's text content is <rpc/>, then the server knows to process it as an rpc call. However, if it's anything else, it's considered non-rpc and is sent to the echoResponse method that uses HTML to send the request back to the client.

```
    # check header for <rpc/> element
    strHeader = xmsg.getHeader( )
    if strHeader.rfind("<rpc/>") < 0:
```

```
# send back an HTML echo resonse
self.echoResponse(strPostData)
return 0
```

If indeed the message is an RPC candidate, it's important to extract out the object name, the method name, and the parameters being supplied to the method invocation. This is not easy work, as the following code shows:

```
# eval out object.method(params)
msgDom      = xmsg.getXMLMessageDom( )
objElem     = msgDom.getElementsByTagName("object")[0]
object      = objElem.getAttributeNS('',"class")
method      = objElem.getAttributeNS('',"method")
params      = []
paramElems = msgDom.getElementsByTagName("param")

# Get parameters as strings
for thisparam in paramElems:
  strParam = StringIO.StringIO( )
  PrettyPrint(thisparam, strParam)
  parameter = strParam.getvalue().strip( )
  parameter = parameter.replace("<param>", "")
  parameter = parameter.replace("</param>", "")
  params.append(parameter)
```

After extracting the data necessary for the command, you can begin preparing the command string. The command string holds the name of the local object instance, along with the name of the method to invoke, as well as the parameters supplied. The command is prepared accordingly:

```
# instantiate correct object
if object == "CustomerProfile":
    from CustomerProfile import CustomerProfile
    inst = CustomerProfile( )

 if object == "XMLOffer":
    from XMLOffer import XMLOffer
    inst = XMLOffer( )

# '''''''''''''''''''''''''''''''''''''''''
# add additional object instantiations here
# '''''''''''''''''''''''''''''''''''''''''

# prepare cmd string
cmd = "inst." + method + "("

# add parameters to command if necessary, separated
# by """ and commas
if len(params) == 1:
   cmd += '"""' + params[0] + '""")'
elif len(params) > 1:
   for pmIndex in range(len(params) - 1):
     cmd += '"""' + params[pmIndex] + '""", '
   cmd += '"""' + params[len(params)-1] + '""")'
```

```
    # if no params, just close off parens: ()
    if not params:
        cmd += ")"
```

The preceding code shows the careful process of using the DOM to extract the necessary command values from the XML message. These different values are then combined to make a single cmd string. The highlighted lines of code show where the cmd value is being altered to fill out the command. The command for the previous *msgGetProfile.xml* calls would have to have been compiled by the XMLSwitchHandler to look like this:

```
    inst.getProfile("983-E2229J3")
```

The triple quotes are used to escape any single or double quotations that may be enclosed in the parameters. Of course, if triple quotes are used in the argument, then the process breaks down!

After preparing the methods, we can use the Python eval command to actually hit the objects and invoke the appropriate methods:

```
    result = eval(cmd)
```

After method invocation, the results are then used to build a response XML message. This is done by constructing a temporary DOM with the new values, and then writing a serialized form of that DOM to the socket connection to the client. Of course, once in DOM form it can be validated if you choose to, as well as be modified to remove a document prolog or other type of information that might not be appropriate for embedding inside another XML document.

XMLSwitchHandler listing

Example 10-12 shows the full listing of *XMLSwitchHandler.py*:

Example 10-12. XMLSwitchHandler.py

```
"""

 XMLSwitchHandler.py
"""
import sys
import BaseHTTPServer
import StringIO

from urllib                    import unquote_plus
from XMLMessage                import XMLMessage
from xml.dom.ext               import PrettyPrint
from xml.dom.ext.reader.Sax2 import FromXml

class XMLSwitchHandler(BaseHTTPServer.BaseHTTPRequestHandler):
    def do_GET(self):
        """

        do_GET processes HTTP GET requests on the
        server port.
```

Example 10-12. XMLSwitchHandler.py (continued)

```
    """
    # send generic HTML response
    self.send_response(200)
    self.send_header("Content-type", "text/html")
    self.end_headers()
    self.wfile.write("<html><body>")
    self.wfile.write("<font face=tahoma size=2>")
    self.wfile.write("<b>Hello from XMLSwitchHandler!</b>")
    self.wfile.write("</font></body></html>")

def do_POST(self):
    """
    do_POST processes HTTP POST requests and XML
    packets.
    """
    if self.headers.dict.has_key("content-length"):
        # convert content-length from string to int
        content_length = int(self.headers.dict["content-length"])

        # read in the correct number of bytes from the client
        # and process the data
        raw_post_data = self.rfile.read(content_length)
        self.processXMLMessagePost(raw_post_data)
        return 1

    else:
        # bad post
        self.send_reponse(500)
        return 0

def processXMLMessagePost(self, strPostData):
    """
    processXMLMessagePost(strXMLMessage) - this
    method creates an XMLMessage from the supplied
    data and looks up a mapping from XMLMapping.xml
    to determine what object and method pair to
    invoke.
    """
    # create message by unquoting post data
    xmsg = XMLMessage()
    xmsg.setXMLMessage(
        unquote_plus(strPostData).replace("n=", ""))

    # check header for <rpc/> element
    strHeader = xmsg.getHeader()
    if strHeader.rfind("<rpc/>") < 0:
        # send back an HTML echo resonse
        self.echoResponse(strPostData)
        return 0

    # eval out object.method(params)
    msgDom      = xmsg.getXMLMessageDom()
```

Example 10-12. XMLSwitchHandler.py (continued)

```
objElem    = msgDom.getElementsByTagName("object")[0]
object     = objElem.getAttributeNS('',"class")
method     = objElem.getAttributeNS('',"method")
params     = []
paramElems = msgDom.getElementsByTagName("param")

# Get parameters as strings
for thisparam in paramElems:
  strParam = StringIO.StringIO( )
  PrettyPrint(thisparam, strParam)
  parameter = strParam.getvalue().strip( )
  parameter = parameter.replace("<param>", "")
  parameter = parameter.replace("</param>", "")
  params.append(parameter)

# instantiate correct object
if object == "CustomerProfile":
  from CustomerProfile import CustomerProfile
  inst = CustomerProfile( )

if object == "XMLOffer":
  from XMLOffer import XMLOffer
  inst = XMLOffer( )

# '''''''''''''''''''''''''''''''''''''''''''
# add additional object instantiations here
# '''''''''''''''''''''''''''''''''''''''''''

# prepare cmd string
cmd = "inst." + method + "("

# add parameters to command if necessary, separated
# by """ and commas
if len(params) == 1:
  cmd += "\"\"\"" + params[0] + "\"\"\"" + ")"
elif(len(params) > 1):
  for pmIndex in range(0, (len(params) - 1)):
    cmd += "\"\"\"" + params[pmIndex] + "\"\"\"" + ", "
  cmd += "\"\"\"" + params[len(params)-1] + "\"\"\")"

# if no params, just close off parens: ()
if not params:
  cmd += ")"

# execute cmd and capture result
rezult = ""
rezult = eval(cmd)

# build response XML
returnDom = FromXml(
  "<message>\n\t<header>\n\t\t<rpc-response/>\n\t</header>\n" +
  "\t<body>\n\t\t<object class=\"" + str(object) + "\" method=\"" +
```

Example 10-12. XMLSwitchHandler.py (continued)

```
        str(method) + "\">\n\n\t\t\t<response>" + str(rezult) +
        "</response>\n\t\t</object>\n\t</body>\n</message>\n")

    # optional hook: validate against return dom or
    #               any other special logic

    # prepare string of document element
    # (cut out prolog for xml message)
    strReturnXml = StringIO.StringIO( )
    PrettyPrint(returnDom.documentElement, strReturnXml)
    xmlval = strReturnXml.getvalue( )

    # return XML over HTTP to caller
    self.send_response(200)
    self.send_header("Content-type", "text/xml")
    self.send_header("Content-length", str(len(xmlval)))
    self.end_headers( )
    self.wfile.write(str(xmlval))

    return 1

def echoResponse(self, strPostData):
    """
      echoResponse(postData) - returns the post data
      parsed into a header and body chunk.
    """
    # send response
    self.send_response(200)
    self.send_header("Content-type", "text/html")
    self.end_headers( )

    # send HTML text
    self.wfile.write("<html><body>"
                     "<font color=blue face=tahoma size=5>"
                     "<b>Hello from XMLSwitchHandler!</b></font><br><br>"
                     "<font face=arial,verdana,helvetica size=4>"
                     "Attempting to create XML Message "
                     "from source...<br><br>Header:<br><xmp>")

    msg = XMLMessage( )
    msg.setXMLMessage(unquote_plus(strPostData).replace("n=", ""))

    # parse message into header and body, display as
    # example on web page
    self.wfile.write(msg.getHeader( ))
    self.wfile.write("</xmp></font><font face="arial,verdana,helvetica"
                     " size="4">Body:<br><xmp>")

    self.wfile.write(msg.getBody( ))
    self.wfile.write("</xmp></font></font></body></html>")
```

Running the XML Switch

The file *runxs.py* is shown in Example 10-13, and actually is the primary script for the XML Switch service. The `XMLSwitchServer` object is an instance of the `BaseHTTPServer.HTTPServer`, so it is launched accordingly:

```
import XMLSwitchHandler
import BaseHTTPServer

XMLSwitchServer = BaseHTTPServer.HTTPServer(
    ('', 2112), XMLSwitchHandler.XMLSwitchHandler)

XMLSwitchServer.handle_request()
```

The `XMLSwitchHandler` is passed in at construction time along with the port number to listen to. Whenever a request comes in, the `HTTPServer` just launched invokes its `XMLSwitchHandler` to manage the request.

In this example, however, the `handle_request` method is used. Now the server runs only until it services one request. You can change this by calling `XMLSwitchServer.serve_forever`. Regardless, you can always use *runxs.py*, shown in Example 10-13, to start your server.

Example 10-13. The XML Switch launching script: runxs.py

```
"""
 runxs.py
"""
import XMLSwitchHandler
import BaseHTTPServer

# start up
print "XMLSwitch starting..."
XMLSwitchServer = BaseHTTPServer.HTTPServer(
    ('', 2112), XMLSwitchHandler.XMLSwitchHandler)

# run server
print "Running..."
for x in range(10):
  XMLSwitchServer.handle_request()
```

To launch the server, use a spare command or shell prompt:

```
G:\pythonxml\c10> python runxs.py
XMLSwitch starting...
Running...
```

The server outputs requests as they happen:

```
centauri - - [03/Jun/2001 15:12:02] "POST / HTTP/1.0" 200 -
centauri - - [03/Jun/2001 15:12:04] "POST / HTTP/1.0" 200 -
```

Beyond this, the only interaction you have with the server is by running *xcs.py* as shown in Example 10-10.

A Web Application

In this section, you develop a web site that is integrated with the XML Switch and the other systems running on your network (even if you're putting this all on one machine). In this web application, a user navigates through some HTML on the server, allowing them to login (in other words, retrieve their profile), edit their profile information, or view special offers. A CGI script runs next to the HTML, and is called by the HTML forms and other items to retrieve the information.

Typically, a web site or CGI script accesses a database directly to pull information out on behalf of a user. However, this application is different. In this web site example, the CGI script uses the xsc client created earlier to talk directly with the XML Switch. So instead of SQL queries, the web site submits XML messages to the switch. The switch then maps these to objects and invokes the correct method, resulting in the right information being either inserted or pulled back from the XML Switch. The returned information is then parsed and formatted into HTML, and displayed back to the user.

Connecting to a Web Service

This is how many web services may first be implemented. For example, with Microsoft's forthcoming web services (codenamed HailStorm), an independent business should be able to create a web site, as well as retrieve your user's HailStorm calendar by issuing SOAP calls from your web server (or the client) to Microsoft's services. The returned XML is then formatted by your web site (even "branded" with your logo) and returned to your user's browser. The application presented here follows the same type of bridged-services scenario, minus some considerable security and error handling.

Figure 10-4 shows a diagram focusing on the web site, and its relation to the XML Switch as well as the rest of the network.

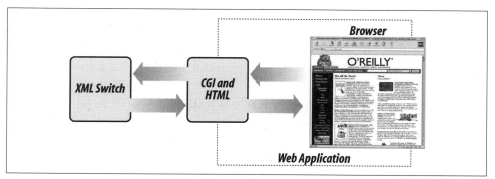

Figure 10-4. A detail of the web application

What Figure 10-4 doesn't show, and perhaps shouldn't, is that the XML Switch is in turn connected to other network resources, acting in effect as a black box to the CGI and HTML that just ask the Switch for data.

The Components

The Web/CGI application presented here is a standalone web application. It's fully integrated into the XML Switching–network built thus far. This web site uses an HTML page and a Python script on the server to generate dynamic data. The CGI script uses the XML Switch client to retrieve information from the switch and its backend resources. This web site has no idea that profiles are kept in SQL Server and that offers are kept in a big flat file. It only know that it formats an XML message a certain way, and that tossing the message to the XML Switch usually results in the right information being returned.

We deployed the HTML and CGI scripts to a five-line CGI server we wrote in Python. Having used Apache and IIS throughout this book, we sought some cross-platform simplicity in this chapter and used a very simple CGIHTTPServer in Python. The HTML page *intro.html*, and CGI script *sp.py*, should run under any CGI-capable web server.

In this section, we develop the following pieces:

intro.html
> This is a simple login page that accepts a user ID and posts you over to *sp.py*. The login box expects an ID that is valid within the database connected to the XML Switch. In other words, you need to put a valid ID here that corresponds to a record that you created in your database in the section "Building the Database," earlier this chapter.

sp.py
> This is a Python CGI script that retrieves information from the XML Switch and formats it for display. It is not named *.cgi*, although you should rename it that if your CGI server is only going to run *.cgi* files. This script is the main workhorse of the application, as it not only retrieves the data for you, it formats it into HTML and sends it back to the browser.

When putting these finished files in your web server area, remember to put *sp.py* in a *cgi-bin* directory beneath *intro.html*. The web form used in *intro.html* and *sp.py* expects *sp.py* to live at */cgi-bin/sp.py*.

Additionally, you should copy over *xsc.py* and *XMLMessage.py* (created in the section "The XML Switch," earlier this chapter) into the *cgi-bin* directory so that *sp.py* is able to load them as modules.

The Topology

As shown earlier in Figure 10-4, the CGI application is primarily a series of transactions between itself and a web browser. However, when the user requests dynamic information, the CGI script uses the XML Switch client to talk to the XML Switch on the network. This example has broad network implications: *intro.html* and *sp.py* are served up by your web server; the *sp.py* script uses the XML Switch client (xsc, created in Example 10-11) to connect back to wherever you are running the XML Switch server process. As long as the site's CGI script tells the Switch client where to find the Switch server, it gets the information it needs. Of course, an end user's browser needs only to point to the web site.

In the next few sections, we highlight some of the more XML-centric code used in building the site, and present full listings of the three primary files.

The Code Architecture

When creating any web site, the very first thing to do might be to code a start page. For the purposes of this chapter, the start page is *intro.html*. The *intro.html* file is a simple page that politely asks for an ID. Use the submit button to send your ID off to the server, and the information is returned and formatted by the CGI script, which presents you with additional, but dynamically created, HTML. Figure 10-5 shows *intro.html* loaded in a web browser.

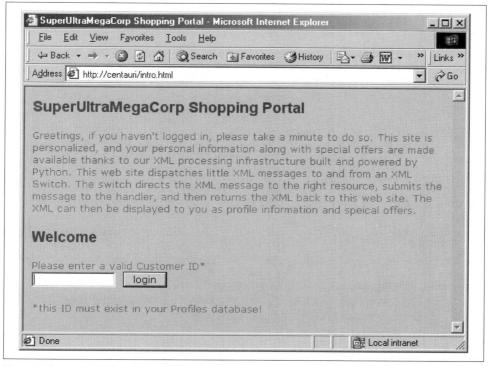

Figure 10-5. intro.html is the start page for the CGI example

As Figure 10-5 shows, *intro.html* is straightforward. Probably the most difficult part is tracking down a valid ID from your Profiles database. Example 10-14 shows the *intro.html.*

Example 10-14. intro.html

```
<HTML>
<HEAD>
<TITLE>SuperUltraMegaCorp Shopping Portal</TITLE>
</HEAD>
<BODY>
<P align="center"><h1>SuperUltraMegaCorp Shopping Portal</h1></P>

<P>Greetings, if you haven't logged in, please take a minute
   to do so.  This site is personalized, and your personal
   information along with special offers are made available
   thanks to our XML processing infrastructure built and
   powered by Python.  This web site dispatches little XML messages
   to and from an XML Switch.  The switch directs the XML message
   to the right resource, submits the message to the handler, and
   then returns the XML back to this web site.  The XML can then
   be displayed to you as profile information and speical offers.

<P>
  <h1>Welcome</h1>
  <form name=login action="/cgi-bin/sp.py"
        method="GET">
    Please enter a valid Customer ID* <br>
    <input type="text" size="15" name="id"> 
    <input type=submit value=" login ">
    <input type="hidden" name="mode" value="login">
    </form>
</P>
<p>*this ID must exist in your Profiles database!</p>
</BODY>
</HTML>
```

It's important to point out that in Example 10-14 the form features a hidden variable named mode, which is set to login. This is used as the primary indicator for the CGI script.

```
<input type="hidden" name="mode" value="login">
```

The CGI script encounters a mode of login, and executes the correct code accordingly.

The file *intro.html* and its stylesheet are of no value without somewhere to send them. The login box only takes an ID, but obviously doesn't do anything. The CGI script, on the other hand, takes the ID and runs with it.

The CGI Functionality

The CGI for this web application is *sp.py*, shown in Example 10-15, later in this chapter. The script has four primary purposes. The first is to take your customer ID and use it to extract your profile information from somewhere behind the XML Switch. The second purpose is to allow you to edit your profile information on the same page that it's presented on. The third purpose is to accept your update form and send the correct message back to the Switch. The fourth purpose is to display all offers currently in the OfferXMLStore. Of course, before any of this can begin, the script needs to import its dependencies. As mentioned earlier, the script needs access to both the XML Switch client (xsc) and the XMLMessage class. The script also imports some standard XML functionality:

```
import os
import cgi

from xsc                    import xsc
from XMLMessage             import XMLMessage
from xml.dom.ext.reader.Sax2 import FromXml
```

Before the server can do any of its four purposes, it must also do some common housecleaning, such as extracting the right data from the query string and figuring out which method it needs to call:

```
# ''''''''''''''''''''''''''''''''''''''''''''''''
# MAIN
#
qs   = cgi.parse_qs(os.environ["QUERY_STRING"])
mode = qs.get("mode", "")
id   = qs.get("id", "")

print "Content-type: text/html"
print ""
print "<html>"
print """<HEAD><TITLE>SuperUltraMegaCorp Shopping Portal (intro.html)
        </TITLE></HEAD><BODY>"""
print """<P align="center"><h1>SuperUltraMegaCorp Shopping Portal</h1></P>"""
print """<p><h3>click <a href='/intro.html'>here</a> to login</h3>"""
print """<h3>click <a href='/cgi-bin/sp.py?mode=getOffers'>here</a> to
        review offers</h3></p>"""

if mode[0] == "updateProf":
  doUpdateProfile()

elif mode[0] == "login":
  doLogin(id[0])

elif mode[0] == "getOffers":
  doGetOffers()

print "</body></html>"
```

As you can see, most of the work is done by three methods, doUpdateProf, doLogin, and doGetOffers. Let's examine each of these methods in greater detail, as that is where the XML action is.

Extracting profile information

When you hit the login button, the *intro.html* web form sends your user ID and mode to the server. As shown earlier, the script calls a doLogin method right off the bat when it encounters a login mode. The login method accepts an ID as a parameter and builds the appropriate getProfile XML message:

```
def doLogin(id):
    """

     doLogin(id) - this method grabs a user's profile
     and displays it as XML on the browser, and also
     provides a form that allows the user to edit their
     own data.
    """
    # Bring up XML Switch client
    xs = xsc( )
    xs.server = "centauri:2112"

    # prepare an XML message for the server
    xmlmsg = XMLMessage( )

    # format a getProfile message
    xmlmsg.setXMLMessage("""
        <message>
          <header><rpc/></header>
          <body>
            <object class="CustomerProfile"
              method="getProfile">
              <param>""" + id + """</param>
            </object>
          </body>
        </message>
                        """)
```

As the preceding code shows, the first thing that occurs is the instantiation of the XML Switch client, as well as assignment of the xsc.server property to centauri: 2112. This means we're running the XML Switch at a host named centauri, on port 2112. After instantiating the XML Switch client, a message is prepared as shown in the previous code. This message has the current user's ID placed within it, so the server presents the correct information.

What follows is the submission of your getProfile request, using the xsc class instantiated as xs:

```
# make the call to the XML Switch
xmlresp = xs.sendMessage(xmlmsg.getXMLMessage( ))

# display response
print "<P>Response received on your behalf:<br><xmp>"
print xmlresp
print "</xmp></p>"

# setup profile XML Message and retrieve response DOM
xmlmsg.setXMLMessage(xmlresp)
msgdom = xmlmsg.getXMLMessageDom( )
```

After the doLogin method has correctly formatted your message and sent it off to the server with a call to xs.sendMessage, it's time to parse the result.

```
CustProfElement = msgdom.getElementsByTagName("CustomerProfile")[0]
CustProfElement.normalize()

# pick out ID number
id = CustProfElement.getAttributeNS('', "id")
print "<tr>"
print " <td colspan=2><b>Greetings " + id + "</b></td>"
print "</tr>"

# iterate through children, creating pre-populated
# form as we go...
nodes = CustProfElement.childNodes
for node in nodes:
  if node.nodeType == node.ELEMENT_NODE:
    print "<tr><td>"
    print "<b>" + node.nodeName + "</b>"
    print "</td><td>"
    for ec in node.childNodes:
      print "<input type=text size=20 name='" + node.nodeName  + "' "
      print " value='" + ec.nodeValue + "'>"

    print "</td></tr>"
```

At this point, a new form is created allowing you to update and change fields within your profile. Figure 10-6 shows the prepopulated form sitting in the browser.

If you hit Submit, you would trigger a different event on the server *sp.py* script. Also, your mode changes to updateProf, and a different call is made to the XML Switch. Your ID and mode are ready and waiting for the next form submission via hidden fields in the form markup:

```
print "<input type='submit' value='update profile'>"
print "<input type='hidden' name='id' value='" + id + "'>"
print "<input type='hidden' name='mode' value='updateProf'>"
```

Although the hidden input fields don't show up in the browser, they are still submitted during a GET or POST operation.

Updating profile information

When you submit your profile-editing form, the same *sp.py* is called again, but this time your mode has been flipped to updateProf. As you saw earlier, depending on the mode, a corresponding function is called. In this case, it's the doUpdateProfile function.

To create the necessary XML message, the first thing the script does is attempt to extract the form values out of the query string and create valid XML message:

```
xmlmsg =  "<message><header><rpc/></header>\n"
xmlmsg += "<body><object class='CustomerProfile' method='updateProfile'>\n"
xmlmsg += "<param><CustomerProfile id="
xmlmsg += "'" + id[0] + "'>\n"
```

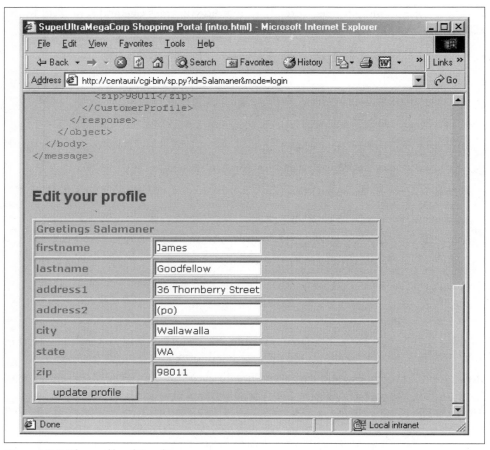

Figure 10-6. The profile-editing form

```
xmlmsg += "<firstname>" + qs.get("firstname","")[0].strip() + "</firstname>\n"
xmlmsg += "<lastname>"  + qs.get("lastname","")[0].strip()  + "</lastname>\n"
xmlmsg += "<address1>"  + qs.get("address1","")[0].strip()  + "</address1>\n"
xmlmsg += "<address2>"  + qs.get("address2","")[0].strip()  + "</address2>\n"
xmlmsg += "<city>"      + qs.get("city","")[0].strip()      + "</city>\n"
xmlmsg += "<state>"     + qs.get("state","")[0].strip()     +"</state>\n"
xmlmsg += "<zip>"       + qs.get("zip","")[0].strip()       +"</zip>\n"
xmlmsg += "</CustomerProfile></param></object></body></message>"
print xmlmsg
print "</xmp></p>"
```

In this code, each required field of an updateProfile XML request is populated with
something from the web form that was just submitted. With the XML message
freshly created, the doUpdateProfile method moves on to actually submit the message to the XML Switch:

```
xs = xsc()
xs.server = "centauri:2112"
```

```
resp = xs.sendMessage(xmlmsg)
print "<P>Response received:<br><xmp>"
print resp
print "</xmp></p>"

print "<h1>Log Back In?</h1>"
print "<form name=login action='/cgi-bin/sp.py' method='GET'>"
print "Use Current Customer ID:<br>"
print "<input type='text' size='15' name='id'"
print " value='" + id[0] + "'> "
print "<input type=submit value=' login '>"
print "<input type='hidden' name='mode' value='login'>"
print "</form>"
```

In addition to submitting the request and displaying the confirmation, the script also creates a new HTML form with your ID preloaded, allowing you to log back in and see your modified information.

Displaying all offers

The code to display offers is some hairy XML, but is not the most difficult if you've been following along thus far. At first, an XML message must be prepared that the CGI script will send off to the XML Switch:

```
xs = xsc()
xs.server = "centauri:2112"

xmlmsg =  str("""<message>
                    <header><rpc/></header>
                      <body>
                        <object class="XMLOffer"
                          method="getAllOffers">
                        </object>
                      </body>
                    </message>""")
resp = xs.sendMessage(xmlmsg)
```

As you can see, as soon as it is prepared it is immediately submitted. If everything went okay, the doGetOffers method attempts to display all valid offers:

```
offdom = FromXml(resp)
offers = offdom.getElementsByTagName("offer")

for offer in offers:
  offer.normalize()
  for node in offer.childNodes:
    if (node.nodeType == node.ELEMENT_NODE):
      if (node.nodeName == "heading"):
        print "<h3>" + node.firstChild.nodeValue + "</h3>"
      if (node.nodeName == "description"):
        print "<p>" + node.firstChild.nodeValue + "</p>"
```

Here you use some familiar methods and operations from the DOM. In this case, a node is traversed for its heading and description nodes. Once they are found, they are descended and their text extracted.

The Complete sp.py Listing

Example 10-15 shows the complete listing of *sp.py*.

Example 10-15. sp.py

```
"""
 sp.py - a series of web pages and forms that send messages
   to the XML Switch for data access.
"""
import os
import cgi

from xsc                  import xsc
from XMLMessage           import XMLMessage
from xml.dom.ext.reader.Sax2 import FromXml

def doLogin(id):
    """
    doLogin(id) - this method grabs a user's profile
    and displays it as XML on the browser, and also
    provides a form that allows the user to edit their
    own data.
    """
    # Bring up XML Switch client
    xs = xsc( )
    xs.server = "centauri:2112"

    # prepare an XML message for the server
    xmlmsg = XMLMessage( )

    # format a getProfile message
    xmlmsg.setXMLMessage("""
        <message>
          <header><rpc/></header>
          <body>
            <object class="CustomerProfile"
              method="getProfile">
              <param>""" + id + """</param>
            </object>
          </body>
        </message>
                        """)

    # Display how CGI is contacting XML switch
    print "<p>Message to be sent on your behalf:<br><xmp>"
    print xmlmsg.getXMLMessage( )
    print "</xmp></p>"
```

Example 10-15. sp.py (continued)

```
# make the call to the XML Switch
xmlresp = xs.sendMessage(xmlmsg.getXMLMessage( ))

# display response
print "<P>Response received on your behalf:<br><xmp>"
print xmlresp
print "</xmp></p>"

# setup profile XML Message and retrieve response DOM
xmlmsg.setXMLMessage(xmlresp)
msgdom = xmlmsg.getXMLMessageDom( )

# Create a form to edit this new profile data
print "<h1>Edit your profile</h1>"
print "<form action='sp.py' method='GET'>"
print "<table width=450 border=1>"

# parse result
try:
  CustProfElement = msgdom.getElementsByTagName("CustomerProfile")[0]
  CustProfElement.normalize( )

  # pick out ID number
  id = CustProfElement.getAttributeNS('', "id")
  print "<tr>"
  print " <td colspan=2><b>Greetings " + id + "</b></td>"
  print "</tr>"

  # iterate through children, creating pre-populated
  # form as we go...
  nodes = CustProfElement.childNodes
  for node in nodes:
    if (node.nodeType == node.ELEMENT_NODE):
      print "<tr><td>"
      print "<b>" + node.nodeName + "</b>"
      print "</td><td>"
      for ec in node.childNodes:
        print "<input type=text size=20 name='" + node.nodeName  + "' "
        print " value='" + ec.nodeValue + "'>"
      print "</td></tr>"
except:
    print "<tr><td>Exception</td><td>Encountered</td></tr>"

# finish up the form
print "<tr><td colspan=2>"
print "<input type=submit value='update profile'>"
print "<input type=hidden name='id' value='" + id + "'>"
print "<input type=hidden name='mode' value='updateProf'>"
print "</td></tr>"
print "</table>"
print "</form>"
```

Example 10-15. sp.py (continued)

```python
def doUpdateProfile():
    """

    doUpdateProfile() - this method is called to update a profile
    using the updateProfile XML message.
    """
    print "<p>Update message on your behalf:<br><xmp>"

    xmlmsg =  "<message><header><rpc/></header>\n"
    xmlmsg += "<body><object class='CustomerProfile' method='updateProfile'>\n"
    xmlmsg += "<param><CustomerProfile id="
    xmlmsg += "'" + id[0] + "'>\n"
    xmlmsg += "<firstname>" + qs.get("firstname","")[0].strip() + "</firstname>\n"
    xmlmsg += "<lastname>"  + qs.get("lastname","")[0].strip()  + "</lastname>\n"
    xmlmsg += "<address1>"  + qs.get("address1","")[0].strip()  + "</address1>\n"
    xmlmsg += "<address2>"  + qs.get("address2","")[0].strip()  + "</address2>\n"
    xmlmsg += "<city>"      + qs.get("city","")[0].strip()      + "</city>\n"
    xmlmsg += "<state>"     + qs.get("state","")[0].strip()     + "</state>\n"
    xmlmsg += "<zip>"       + qs.get("zip","")[0].strip()       + "</zip>\n"
    xmlmsg += "</CustomerProfile></param></object></body></message>"
    print xmlmsg
    print "</xmp></p>"

    print "Update in progress..."

    xs = xsc()
    xs.server = "centauri:2112"
    resp = xs.sendMessage(xmlmsg)
    print "<P>Response received:<br><xmp>"
    print resp
    print "</xmp></p>"

    print "<h1>Log Back In?</h1>"
    print "<form name=login action='/cgi-bin/sp.py' method='GET'>"
    print "Use Current Customer ID:<br>"
    print "<input type='text' size='15' name='id'"
    print " value='" + id[0] + "'> "
    print "<input type=submit value=' login '>"
    print "<input type='hidden' name='mode' value='login'>"
    print "</form>"

def doGetOffers():
    print "<p>Retrieving all offers...</p>"
    xs = xsc()
    xs.server = "centauri:2112"

    xmlmsg =  str("""<message>
                    <header><rpc/></header>
                      <body>
                        <object class="XMLOffer"
                         method="getAllOffers">
```

Example 10-15. sp.py (continued)

```
                        </object>
                        </body>
                    </message>""")
    resp = xs.sendMessage(xmlmsg)

    print "<p>Fromatting response from server..."
    print "<h1>Offers!</h1>"

    offdom = FromXml(resp)
    offers = offdom.getElementsByTagName("offer")

    for offer in offers:
        offer.normalize()
        for node in offer.childNodes:
            if (node.nodeType == node.ELEMENT_NODE):
                if (node.nodeName == "heading"):
                    print "<h3>" + node.firstChild.nodeValue + "</h3>"
                if (node.nodeName == "description"):
                    print "<p>" + node.firstChild.nodeValue + "</p>"

# ''''''''''''''''''''''''''''''''''''''''''
# MAIN
#
qs   = cgi.parse_qs(os.environ["QUERY_STRING"])
mode = qs.get("mode", "")
id   = qs.get("id", "")

print "Content-type: text/html"
print ""
print "<html>"
print """<HEAD><TITLE>SuperUltraMegaCorp Shopping Portal (intro.html)
        </TITLE></HEAD><BODY>"""
print """<P align="center"><h1>SuperUltraMegaCorp Shopping Portal</h1></P>"""
print """<p><h3>click <a href='/intro.html'>here</a> to login</h3>"""
print """    <h3>click <a href='/cgi-bin/sp.py?mode=getOffers'>here</a> to review offers
</h3></p>"""

if mode[0] == "updateProf":
    doUpdateProfile()

if mode[0] == "login":
    doLogin(id[0])

if mode[0] == "getOffers":
    doGetOffers()

print "</body></html>"
```

Running the Site as a User

Once you have completed all of the prerequisites for this mammoth web site and XML integration, you'll likely want to test it with a browser. There are eight steps to get things going:

1. Make sure your web server is running, and that *intro.html* and *sp.py* are functioning properly.

2. Make sure your XML Switch is running (*runxs.py*).

3. Make sure your web forms point to your web server and that your xsc calls point to your XML Switch server.

4. Browse to *intro.html* and place a valid ID from your database in the text box. Click **Login**.

5. You can review your profile, and edit it in the form at the bottom of the page.

6. If you've changed some items, click the **Submit** button on the new form to login again.

7. Verify that your data has changed, then click on the link to check your offers.

8. The offers should be presented as formatted HTML.

The Web/CGI application presented here is the tip of an iceberg of integration. The browser talks to the web site. The web site talks to the XML Switch. The XML Switch uses local objects to retrieve information from relational databases and flat files. By standardizing on XML messages between distributed systems and creating an intermediary routing capability between these applications, a much greater level of integration is afforded, with a greater capacity for scaling.

Installing Python and XML Tools

This appendix helps you get started with Python and the additional XML packages we use in this book. You will want to have an Internet connection in order to download the packages you'll be installing. Some packages may have additional installation notes online, which you'll want to look over as we'll generally be installing the latest versions. The online notes may well be more recent than this book, so please don't ignore them.

Installing Python

While this book is not an introductory text on Python, we review the installation process since you may be upgrading an older system to use Python 2; using one of the more recent versions of Python is strongly recommended if you'll be doing much work with XML. If you already have Python Version 2.0 or newer installed, you do not need to install a new version to use the examples in this book.

Python is available from *http://www.python.org/* for both Windows and Unix platforms. If you follow the download links on the Python web site, you are prompted to select a version. After selecting the most recent stable version, you are presented with selections for the Windows Installer, source code, and possibly installable packages for Linux or other platforms. (Version 2.1.1 is the most recent version available as this book goes to press, but Python 2.2 is expected to be available shortly thereafter and is expected to be fully compatible with everything in this book.)

Windows

If you are installing on Windows, download the Windows Installer and run it. The remainder of the installation process will seem very familiar to you as a standard Windows installation procedure. When the process is complete, the Python executable will be available to you in the *C:\Python21* directory unless you have elected a different location during the installation process. The trailing version number in the directory name may be different depending on the version of Python you install, but will never be more than two digits long.

You can run Python programs on Windows either by double-clicking the icon of the executable, or at the command line by typing:

```
C:\my-dir> c:\python21\python myProgram.py
```

If you want to run Python from the command line, you probably want to add Python's installation directory to your Path environment variable. If you're using Windows 2000, this needs to be done using the Control Panel. From **Start**, select **Settings → Control Panel** to open the **System** panel. Select the **Advanced** tab, and then choose **Environment Variables**. In the lower portion of the dialog, labeled **System Variables**, locate and select the Path variable, then choose **Edit**. In the **Variable Value** entry field, add the full name of the installation directory to the list of directories, separated from the others by a semi-colon (;). When you're done editing the Path value, click the **Ok** button for each of the three open dialogs. For other versions of Windows, you can edit the setting for the Path variable in your *autoexec.bat* file.

Linux and Unix

If you are installing on Linux or Unix (collectively referred to as Unix from now on), we suggest downloading the source code in *.tar.gz* format. You can unpack the package with something along the lines of:

```
$> gzip -dc Python-2.1.1.tgz | tar xf -
```

Either way, you wind up with a fresh new Python directory. Once created, use the *cd* command to go inside. On most Unix machines, all that is needed to build Python is:

```
$> ./configure
$> make
$> su
password:
$> make install
```

The *Python-2.1.1.tgz* archive installs Python in */usr/local/bin/python*. Depending on the security of your system, you'll likely need to be user root in order to install Python.

If you have an existing Python 1.*x* installation, after running make install, you may want to check that the new version of Python is in your execution path:

```
$> which python
/usr/local/bin/python
```

If you get back the following:

```
/usr/bin/python
```

you may want to consider adding */usr/local/bin* to your PATH environment variable before */usr/bin*. Some Linux installations require an older version of Python; until those installations are updated by the vendors, it may be better to install multiple versions than to replace an installation provided as part of the Linux distribution.

Other options include removing older versions before installing the latest and greatest, or deploying the new version into the same base path as the old. Unless your operating system requires the older version, their should be no conflicts aside from the executable loaded when you run *python* from the command line; older versions remain in place if installing from source. You can still run the older version by including the *major.minor* portion of the version number in the command line (for example, *python2.1*). In either case, if upgrading is an issue for you, the documentation included with the source distribution itself (the *README* file, *Misc/NEWS*, and other documents), as well as the release notes on *http://www.python.org/* should be consulted.

Installing PyXML

Once Python is installed, additional packages may be added with relative ease. PyXML takes advantage of the Python Distribution Utilities, or *distutils*. To get the PyXML package, visit the project's SourceForge project page and look at the available downloads for the most recent version (0.6.6 at the time of this writing). The web page is at *http://pyxml.sourceforge.net/*.

For Windows, there is a selection of installers; one for each supported Python version. For bug-fix releases of Python (such as 2.1.1), use the installer for the corresponding feature enhancement for Python (2.1 for this example), as binary compatibility is maintained. Download the installer and run it like any other Windows installer; it locates all the Python installations of the appropriate version as you select the installation to which you want to add PyXML. Once you've done so, installation proceeds and PyXML is available for that Python interpreter.

For Unix, retrieve the *.tar.gz* archive containing the version of PyXML you've selected and unpack it just as you did the Python source distribution. Change your working directory to be the top-level directory of the unpacked distribution. That directory contains a Python script named *setup.py*; run that with the Python interpreter for which you're installing PyXML and the command-line parameter build:

```
$> python setup.py build
```

This builds all the components of PyXML from their Python or C source code. Once this is complete, install the package so that Python can use it; this usually needs to be done by a privileged user:

```
$> su
Password:
%> python setup.py install
```

Be sure that the privileged user is using the same Python interpreter as the user who built the PyXML package.

Installing 4Suite

4Suite includes a variety of DOM implementations optimized for different types of applications, and includes support for XPath, XLink, XPointer, XSLT, and RDF. It is offered by Fourthought, Inc., and is available from a dedicated web site at *http://www.4suite.org/*. There are source and binary packages available for both Windows and Linux. For Windows, download the Windows installation binary of 4Suite and follow the on-screen instructions as they walk you through the process. If you add the new location to your path (visit *autoexec.bat* or your NT environment variables), use the *4xslt* script to perform XSLT transformations from the command line. You can download either a source or binary package for Linux systems. The *README* file contains the latest install instructions, but as with most new Python source packages, you can use the Distribution Utilities; see the description of the PyXML installation for details.

Once completed, the *4xslt* script will be available for you to perform transformations from the command line (provided you've added the directory it lives in to your PATH environment variable).

XML Definitions

This appendix details the definitions spelled out in the XML Specification. These terms are used frequently in connection with the DOM, and with XML technology in general. All of the terms are defined here for reference purposes. This appendix should serve as a companion to the previous specification walkthrough from Chapter 2. In order to extract the XML terms and definitions out of the specification, we thought it appropriate to write an XML-processing script that operates on the XML version of the W3C Recommendation. For a good example of how to reveal the utility of Python and XML, use the program in Example B-1 to parse terms out of the specification's XML.

Example B-1. gen-td.py—a script to print XML definitions

```
"""Generate HTML for terms and definitions
directly from XML specification.

XML source must come from standard input.
"""
import sys

from xml.sax import ContentHandler
from xml.sax import make_parser


class XMLSpecHandler(ContentHandler):
    """
    Class implements part of SAX API to pull term
    definitions out of the XML Specification source file.
    """
    inTermDef = 0

    def startElement(self, name, attrs):
        if name == "termdef":
            self.inTermDef = 1
            self.strTermDefContents = ""
            print "<p><b>" + attrs.get('term', "") + "</b><br>"
```

Example B-1. gen-td.py—a script to print XML definitions (continued)

```
    def characters(self, ch):
      if self.inTermDef:
        self.strTermDefContents += ch

    def endElement(self, name):
      if name == "termdef":
        self.inTermDef = 0
        self.strTermDefContents += "</p>"

        print self.strTermDefContents

# Main
if __name__ == "__main__":
  dh = XMLSpecHandler()
  parser = make_parser()
  parser.setContentHandler(dh)

  print "<html><head>"
  print "<style type='text/css'>"
  print "body { font-family: sans-serif; }"
  print "</style>"
  print "</head><body>"
  parser.parse(sys.stdin)
  print "</body></html>"
```

You can download the XML specification as an XML document from the W3C web site (*http://www.w3.org/TR/*). You can then run the script in Example B-1 against it to generate very simple HTML from the command line:

```
$[chris@spindle]> python gen-td.py < XMLSpec.py > termdef.html
```

If you load the *termdef.html* file in your web browser, you'll see all of the term definitions from the XML Specification neatly presented in simple HTML. Figure B-1 shows the *termdef.html* output running in a browser.

One note: the architects of the XML version of the specification didn't neatly keep the full text of each definition within the confines of the `termdef` tags. So, a little human intervention was necessary to truly present them accurately in this text. The definitions presented here are a subset of what appears in the specification, as definitions related only to the specification itself (and not to XML) have been removed, and the list has been alphabetized to be more human-friendly.

XML Definitions

Attribute

    The `Name-AttValue` pairs are referred to as the attribute specifications of the element.

Attribute Default

    If the declaration is neither `#REQUIRED` nor `#IMPLIED`, then the `AttValue` value contains the declared default value; the `#FIXED` keyword states that the attribute

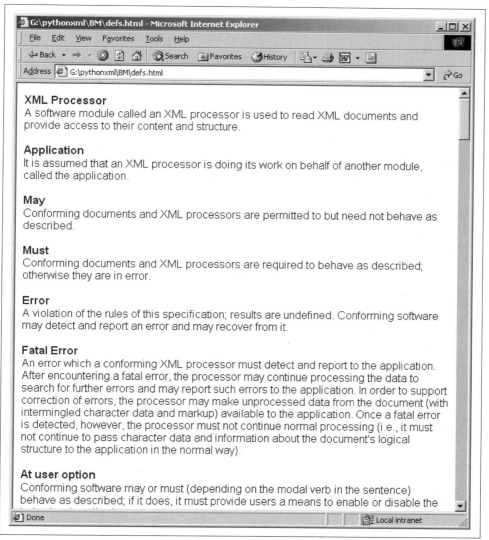

XML Processor
A software module called an XML processor is used to read XML documents and provide access to their content and structure.

Application
It is assumed that an XML processor is doing its work on behalf of another module, called the application.

May
Conforming documents and XML processors are permitted to but need not behave as described.

Must
Conforming documents and XML processors are required to behave as described; otherwise they are in error.

Error
A violation of the rules of this specification; results are undefined. Conforming software may detect and report an error and may recover from it.

Fatal Error
An error which a conforming XML processor must detect and report to the application. After encountering a fatal error, the processor may continue processing the data to search for further errors and may report such errors to the application. In order to support correction of errors, the processor may make unprocessed data from the document (with intermingled character data and markup) available to the application. Once a fatal error is detected, however, the processor must not continue normal processing (i.e., it must not continue to pass character data and information about the document's logical structure to the application in the normal way).

At user option
Conforming software may or must (depending on the modal verb in the sentence) behave as described; if it does, it must provide users a means to enable or disable the

Figure B-1. termdef.html loaded in a browser

must always have the default value. If a default value is declared, when an XML processor encounters an omitted attribute, it behaves as though the attribute is present with the declared default value.

Attribute-List Declaration

Attribute-list declarations specify the name, data type, and default value (if any) of each attribute associated with a given element type.

Attribute Name

The name in each pair is referred to as the attribute name.

Attribute Value

The content of the `AttValue` (the text between the ' or " delimiters).

CDATA Section

May occur anywhere character data may occur; used to escape blocks of text containing characters that would otherwise be recognized as markup.

Character

An atomic unit of text as specified by ISO/IEC 10646. Legal characters are tab, carriage return, line feed, and the legal graphic characters of Unicode and ISO/IEC 10646. The versions of these standards were current at the time of this writing. New characters may be added to these standards by amendments or new editions. Consequently, XML processors must accept any character in the range specified for Char. The use of compatibility characters is discouraged.

Character Data

All text that is not markup constitutes the character data of the document.

Character Reference

Refers to a specific character in the ISO/IEC 10646 character set—for example, one not directly accessible from available input devices.

Comment

Comments may appear anywhere in a document outside other markup; in addition, they may appear within the Document Type Declaration at places allowed by the grammar. They are not part of the document's character data; an XML processor may, but need not, make it possible for an application to retrieve the text of comments. For compatibility, the string must not occur within comments.

Conditional Section

Portions of the Document Type Declaration external subset, which are included in, or excluded from, the logical structure of the DTD, based on the keyword that governs them.

Content

The text between the start tag and end tag.

Content Model

In this case, the constraint includes a content model, a simple grammar governing the allowed types of the child elements and the order in which they may appear.

Document Entity

Serves as the root of the entity tree and as a starting point for an XML processor.

Document Type Declaration

The XML Document Type Declaration contains or points to markup declarations that provide a grammar for a class of documents. This grammar is known as a *Document Type Definition* (DTD). The Document Type Declaration can point to an external subset (a special kind of external entity) containing markup declarations, can contain the markup declarations directly in an internal subset, or can do both. The DTD for a document consists of both subsets taken together.

Element

Each XML document contains one or more elements, the boundaries of which are either delimited by start tags and end tags, or for empty elements, by an empty-element tag. Each element has a type, identified by name, which is sometimes called its generic identifier (GI), and may have a set of attribute specifications.

Element Content

An element type has element content when elements of that type must contain only child elements (no character data), optionally separated by whitespace (characters matching the nonterminal S).

Empty

An element with no content.

Empty-Element Tag

An empty-element tag takes a special form: `<tagName/>`.

End Tag

The end of every element that begins with a start tag must be marked by an end tag containing a name that echoes the element's type, as given in the start tag.

Entity

An XML document may consist of one or many storage units. These are called entities; all have content and all (except for the document entity and the external DTD subset) are identified by entity name.

Entity Reference

Refers to the content of a named entity.

Enumerated Attribute Values

Enumerated attributes can take one of a list of values provided in the declaration.

Error

A violation of the rules of the XML specification; results are undefined. Conforming software may detect and report an error and may recover from it.

Escape

Entity and character references can both be used to escape the left-angle bracket, ampersand, and other delimiters. A set of general entities (amp, lt, gt, apos, quot) is specified for this purpose. Numeric character references may also be used; they are expanded immediately when recognized and must be treated as character data, so the numeric character references #60; and & may be used to escape < and & when they occur in character data.

External Entity

If the entity is not internal, it is an external entity.

External Markup Declaration

Defined as a markup declaration occurring in the external subset or in a parameter entity (external or internal—the latter being included because nonvalidating processors are not required to read them).

Fatal Error

An error that a conforming XML processor must detect and report to the application. After encountering a fatal error, the processor may continue processing the data to search for further errors and may report such errors to the application. In order to support correction of errors, the processor may make unprocessed data from the document (with intermingled character data and markup) available to the application. Once a fatal error is detected, however, the processor must not continue normal processing (i.e., it must not continue to pass character data and information about the document's logical structure to the application in the normal way).

General Entity

Entities for use within the document content. In this specification, general entities are sometimes referred to with the unqualified term entity, if this leads to no ambiguity.

General Entity Reference

References to parsed general entities use ampersands (&) and semicolons (;) as delimiters.

Include

An entity is included when its replacement text is retrieved and processed in place of the reference itself, as though it is part of the document at the location the reference is recognized.

Internal Entity Replacement Text

If the entity definition is an EntityValue, the defined entity is called an internal entity. There is no separate physical storage object, and the content of the entity is given in the declaration.

Literal Entity Value

The quoted string actually present in the entity declaration, corresponding to the nonterminal Entity Value.

Markup

Markup takes the form of start tags, end tags, empty-element tags, entity references, character references, comments, CDATA section delimiters, Document Type Declarations, processing instructions, XML declarations, text declarations, and any whitespace that is at the top level of the document entity (that is, outside the document element and not inside any other markup).

Markup Declaration

An element type declaration, an attribute-list declaration, an entity declaration, or a notation declaration.

Mixed Content

An element type has mixed content when elements of that type may contain character data, optionally interspersed with child elements.

Name

A token beginning with a letter or one of a few punctuation characters, and continuing with letters, digits, hyphens, underscores, colons, or full stops. Together, these are known as name characters.

Notation

Identifies by name the format of unparsed entities, the format of elements that bear a notation attribute, or the application to which a processing instruction is addressed.

Notation Declaration

Provide a name for the notation, for use in entity and attribute-list declarations and in attribute specifications, and an external identifier for the notation, which may allow an XML processor or its client application to locate a helper application capable of processing data in the given notation.

Parameter Entity

Parsed entities for use within the DTD.

Parameter-Entity Reference

Parameter-entity references use percent-signs (%) and semicolons (;) as delimiters.

Parent/Child

For each nonroot element C in the document, there is one other element P in the document, such that C is in the content of P, but is not in the content of any other element that is in the content of P. P is referred to as the parent of C, and C as a child of P.

Process Declarations

While these are not required to check the document for validity, they are required to process all the declarations they read in the internal DTD subset and in any parameter entity that they read, up to the first reference to a parameter entity that they do not read. That is, they must use the information in those declarations to normalize attribute values, include the replacement text of internal entities, and supply default attribute values.

Processing Instruction

Processing instructions (PIs) allow documents to contain instructions for applications.

Public Identifier

In addition to a system identifier, an external identifier may include a public identifier.

Replacement Text

The content of the entity, after replacement of character references and parameter-entity references.

Root Element

There is exactly one element, called the root or document element, of which no part appears in the content of any other element.

Start Tag

Marks the beginning of every nonempty XML element.

System Identifier

The SystemLiteral is called the entity's system identifier. It is a URI reference (as defined in IETF RFC 2396 and updated by IETF RFC 2732), meant to be dereferenced to obtain input for the XML processor to construct the entity's replacement text.

Text

A parsed entity contains text (a sequence of characters), which may represent markup or character data.

Text Entity

A parsed entity's contents are referred to as its replacement text; this text is considered an integral part of the document.

Unparsed Entity

An unparsed entity is a resource whose contents may or may not be text, and if text, may be other than XML. Each unparsed entity has an associated notation, identified by name. Beyond the requirement that an XML processor make the identifiers for the entity and notation available to the application, XML places no constraints on the contents of unparsed entities.

Validity

An XML document is valid if it has an associated Document Type Declaration and if the document complies with the constraints expressed in it.

Validity Constraint

A rule that applies to all valid XML documents. Violations of validity constraints are errors; they must, at user option, be reported by validating XML processors.

Validating Processor

Must, at user option, report violations of the constraints expressed by the declarations in the DTD, and failures to fulfill the validity constraints given in this specification.

Well-Formed

A textual object is a well-formed XML document if:

1. Taken as whole, it matches the production labeled "document."

2. It meets all the well-formedness constraints given in the specification.

3. Each of the parsed entities referenced directly or indirectly within the document is well-formed.

Well-Formedness Constraint

A rule that applies to all well-formed XML documents. Violations of well-formedness constraints are fatal errors.

XML Declaration

XML documents should begin with an XML declaration that specifies the version of XML being used.

XML Document

A data object is an XML document if it is well-formed, as defined in this specification. In addition, a well-formed XML document may be valid if it meets certain further constraints.

XML Processor

A software module used to read XML documents and provide access to their content and structure.

Python SAX API

The Simple API for XML (SAX), is essentially a collection of interfaces. Python supports the second version of the SAX specification, often referred to as SAX 2. There are several interfaces defined by the SAX API, and the Python implementation includes convenient base classes that make it simple to define only the methods you are actually interested in providing. Also included in the Python version of the interface are some convenience functions that make working with SAX very easy for most basic applications.

The SAX interface is discussed in Chapter 3; several examples are given in that chapter. The official documentation for the Python version of SAX is part of the *Python Library Reference*, available online and in downloadable formats from the Python web site at *http://www.python.org/doc/current/lib/markup.html*.

Convenience Functions

Three important convenience functions make performing a SAX-based parse trivial. These are sufficient for most applications, especially if the only handler that's needed is the ContentHandler. These functions are provided in the xml.sax module and work with both the standard library and PyXML.

make_parser([*parser_list*])

> Returns a SAX XMLReader object. Most of the examples in Chapter 3 use this function to create a reader. See also the section "Advanced Parser Factory Usage," in that chapter, for more information on using the underlying parser factory objects.

parse(*source, content_handler[, error_handler]*)

> Creates a reader using make_parser, associates the provided content and error handlers, and parses an XML document. The document is identified by the *source* parameter, which may be a filename, URL, a file object open for reading, or an InputSource instance.

parseString(*text, content_handler[, error_handler]*)

> Similar to parse, but the input document is the text given by *text*.

XMLReader

This is the basic parser interface used in SAX 2. It provides methods to get and set the handler objects and a control variety of configurable options.

parse(*source*)

Starts the parser working on the document in the entity identified by *source*. The parameter may be a filename, a URL, or an InputSource object. The InputSource interface is described later in this Appendix.

getContentHandler( )

Returns the currently configured content handler, or None if there isn't one.

getDTDHandler( )

Returns the currently configured DTD handler, or None if there isn't one.

getEntityResolver( )

Returns the currently configured entity resolver, or None if there isn't one.

getErrorHandler( )

Returns the currently configured error handler, or None if there isn't one.

getFeature(*name*)

Get the current Boolean value for the feature identified by *name*. This method returns true if the feature is enabled, and false if it is disabled, or it raises the SAXNotRecognized or SAXNotSupported exception if name is not known or supported.

getProperty(*name*)

Returns the current value of the property identified by *name*. This method returns whatever Python object is appropriate for the specific property; the application must be written to follow the rules associated with that property. If the specific property for which the value is requested is not known or supported by the parser, the appropriate subclass of the SAXException is raised as an exception.

setContentHandler(*handler*)

Sets the content handler to *handler*, which must conform to the ContentHandler interface (described next). If *handler* is None, content events are not reported.

setDTDHandler(*handler*)

Sets the DTD handler to *handler*, which must conform to the DTDHandler interface described later in this reference. If *handler* is None, information about unparsed entities is not provided to the application.

setEntityResolver(*resolver*)

Sets the entity resolver to *handler*, which must conform to the EntityResolver interface. This interface is described in more detail later in this reference. If *handler* is None, the default behavior is to allow the parser to determine whether and how external entities are accessed. Many parsers have at least some ability to load external entities.

setErrorHandler(*handler*)

Sets the error handler to *handler*, which must conform to the ErrorHandler interface. This interface is described in more detail later in this reference. If *handler* is None, the default behavior is used.

setFeature(*name, value*)

Enables or disables the parser feature identified by *name*. The feature is enabled if *value* is true, or disabled if it is false. If the feature is not known, the exception

SAXNotRecognized is thrown; if the particular value is not supported, SAXNotSupported is raised. Some features must be set before the parse begins, and others may be set at any time.

setLocale(*locale*)

Sets the locale for the error messages from the parser. If the parser does not support the indicated locale, a SAX exception is raised. The application may choose to catch and ignore the exception, but the locale does not change. The application may change the locale at any time.

setProperty(*name, value*)

Sets the value of the property identified by *name* to *value*. The parser checks that *value* is of the right type for the specific property and may raise an exception if it is not. If the property *name* is not known or supported by the parser, the appropriate exception is raised. Some properties must be set before the parse begins, and others may be set at any time.

ContentHandler

The ContentHandler is the most used of the SAX handler objects. It is this handler that receives information about the elements being parsed, their attributes, and the content between start and end tags. The parse and parseString convenience functions described in the previous section require a ContentHandler implementation to be passed in.

setDocumentLocator(*locator*)

SAX parsers are encouraged to supply a *locator* for finding the origin of events within the document, so that you can determine the end position of any document-related event. The *locator* object conforms to the Locator interface, described later in this Appendix.

startDocument( )

When the parser begins a document, it calls this method first and only once, with the exception of setDocumentLocator, which is called first if implemented.

endDocument( )

This method is called only once as the very last method invoked by the parser.

startPrefixMapping(*prefix, uri*)

This method is called when a namespace declaration is encountered. The *prefix* parameter is the prefix string used in the document, and *uri* refers to the Universal Resource Indicator (URI) that the prefix represents.

endPrefixMapping(*prefix*)

This event occurs at the time the end element with the corresponding startPrefixMapping is called, indicating that the declaration for *prefix* has gone out of scope. It does *not* indicate that there is no mapping for *prefix*; an outer declaration may still be in scope.

startElement(*name, attrs*)

This event is called each time an element's opening tag is encountered. The name is the actual tag name of the element. The *attrs* parameter is a Python dictionary containing attribute names and values. This is called when Namespace processing is not being used.

`startElementNS(name, qname, attrs)`

In this method, *name* is a tuple containing the URI and localname. The *qname* parameter is the actual tag name used in the XML document. The *attrs* variable is once again the Python dictionary containing the attribute name and value pairs. This is called only when Namespaces are being used.

`endElement(name)`

This event is called when the end of an element is found, if the start of the element was reported by `startElement`.

`endElementNS(name, qname)`

This is the corresponding method and event for `startElementNS` event.

`characters(content)`

This method is called for each section of character data that is not part of an element or other markup. This method may be called multiple times in what might appear to be a contiguous section of character data. In other words, some parsers may call this method for each line of the document, or some may choose to aggregate lines and call the method between other sections of markup. Either way, all character data is passed through this method call. The *content* parameter contains the actual character data.

`ignorableWhitespace(whitespace)`

This method is called by validating parsers when reporting whitespace in element content. Similar to the `characters` method mentioned earlier, this might be called multiple times depending on the parser. Validating parsers must call this method. The *whitespace* parameter contains the actual whitespace encountered.

`processingInstruction(target, data)`

This method is called once for each processing instruction found by the parser. XML declarations and text declarations must not be reported in this fashion. Both the *target* and *data* parameters are string types containing the processing instruction's relevant information to the application.

`skippedEntity(name)`

The parser calls this method each time an entity reference is found and the content of the entity is not parsed. Nonvalidating parsers may skip external entities and any entities for which they have not seen a declaration.

DTDHandler

This handler allows the application to receive some information that may be useful when using unparsed external entities. This handler is not used often.

`notationDecl(name, publicId, systemId)`

This method is invoked when a notation declaration is encountered. At least one of the ID parameters must be populated, and if the *systemId* is present and is a URL, the parser must resolve it fully before passing it to the application through this event.

`unparsedEntityDecl(name, publicId, systemId, ndata)`

The notation name corresponds to a notation reported by the aforementioned `notationDecl` event. Again, if the *systemId* is a URL, then the parser must fully resolve it prior to passing it to the application.

EntityResolver

This handler interface is used to allow the application to control how external entities are loaded. This can be used to support the use of an application-level cache or use one or more of the techniques for mapping public identifiers to system identifiers.

resolveEntity(*publicId, systemId*)

The parser calls this method to convert the identifiers for an external entity into a system identifier to load. The *systemId* parameter is the URL provided in an entity declaration, and *publicId* is the public identifier, or None if there isn't one. This method should return a string giving a new system identifier as a string or an object that supports the InputSource interface.

InputSource

The application can use instances of the InputSource class, provided in the xml.sax. xmlreader module, as return values from the resolveEntity method of the EntityResolver interface, or as parameters to the parse convenience function or XMLReader method. There should not normally be a reason to use an alternate implementation of this class, but it is allowed. When the application prepares an InputSource to provide to the parser, it should use the various set methods to configure the object with as much information as it has about the input source.

When the parser receives the InputSource instance, it first attempts to use the character stream if it is available; otherwise it uses the byte stream. If neither of those is available, it uses the system identifier and attempts to open a byte stream itself.

getByteStream( )

Returns the byte stream associated with this input source. This is a stream that returns raw bytes from the input source rather than decoded Unicode characters.

getCharacterStream( )

Returns the character stream associated with this input source. A character stream provides the parser with decoded Unicode characters rather than raw bytes.

getEncoding( )

Returns the encoding of the byte stream if known. If it is not known, return None. If the encoding is not known, the parser applies the rules for auto-detection of the encoding based on the leading bytes of the input stream.

getPublicId( )

Returns the public identifier of the input source, or None if there isn't one or if it isn't known.

getSystemId( )

Returns the system identifier of the input source, or None if there isn't one or if it isn't known. The only time this should ever return None for a fully initialized input source is if the source is being used to provide the document entity and the input source is provided by the user instead of a URL or filename.

setByteStream(*stream*)

Sets the byte stream of the input source. This should be used if the bytes of the entity can be referenced more efficiently than the parser would be able to do based on the system identifier. This is appropriate when loading the document from a cache rather than loading it across the network.

setCharacterStream(*stream*)

Sets the character stream for the input source. This should be used if the source can provide Unicode characters directly.

setEncoding(*encoding*)

Sets the encoding of the byte stream to *encoding*. This may be known if the resource is being loaded using a protocol that provides this information directly. HTTP, for instance, can include information about the character encoding as the charset parameter to the Content-Type header in the response.

setPublicId(*id*)

Sets the public identifier to *id*.

setSystemId(*id*)

Sets the system identifier to *id*.

ErrorHandler

The way SAX deals with error conditions is described in the section "SAX Handler Objects" in Chapter 3. For the methods of the ErrorHandler interface, each is called with a parameter giving an SAXException instance as a parameter. The specific exception classes are described in the section "SAX Exceptions," later in this Appendix.

error(*exception*)

This method allows the application to respond to a recoverable error.

fatalError(*exception*)

Similar to error, this method indicates that the parser has encountered an error that is not recoverable. Applications are to assume that the document is unusable at this point.

warning(*exception*)

This method is called to communicate conditions that are not fatal, and not necessarily errors.

DeclHandler

The DeclHandler is used to receive information about the allowed structure of a document based on the DTD. It is supported only using PyXML; the standard library does not support it. A simple base class for this handler is available as the DeclHandler class in the xml.sax.saxlib module. The DeclHandler can be set using the setProperty method on the parser object, using the property constant property_declaration_handler from the xml.sax. handler module.

attributeDecl(*element, attribute, type, constraint, default*)

The parser calls this method for each attribute declared. The call represents the declaration of the attribute named *attribute* for the element type *element*. The data type of the attribute, given as *type*, is provided as a string with a value of CDATA, ENTITY, ENTITIES, ID, IDREF, IDREFS, NMTOKEN, NMTOKENS, or NOTATION, or as a list of strings for enumerated types. The *constraint* is given as a string or None, with the possible string values #FIXED, #IMPLIED, and #REQUIRED. If the attribute has a default value, it is provided as *default*; if no default is defined, *default* is None.

elementDecl(*name, contentModel*)

This method is called by the parser when it encounters an element declaration. *name* is the name of the element type, and *contentModel* is its content model. The content module is the string EMPTY, the string ANY, or a tuple containing the model separator character, the list of element type names, and the quantity modifier.

externalEntityDecl(*name, publicId, systemId*)

When the parsers see the definition of an external parsed entity, it calls this method to inform the application. The *name* is the name assigned to the entity, *publicId* is the public identifier or None, and *systemId* is the system identifier.

internalEntityDecl(*name, value*)

The parser calls this method when an internal general entity is defined. The *name* is the name assigned to the entity and *value* is a string giving the replacement text for the entity.

LexicalHandler

The LexicalHandler is used to receive information about syntactical events such as CDATA section boundaries and comments in a document. It is only supported using PyXML; the standard library does not provide this. A simple base class for this handler is available as the LexicalHandler class in the xml.sax.saxlib module. The LexicalHandler can be set using the setProperty method on the parser object, using the property constant property_lexical_handler from the xml.sax.handler module.

comment(*text*)

This method is called when the parser finds a comment in the document. The body of the comment, between the two occurrences of --, is passed as the *text* parameter.

startDTD( )

This method is called before the parser starts reading any DTD information, regardless of whether that information is in the internal or external subset. This method is called at most once.

endDTD( )

The parser calls this method after all DTD information is read; it is called at most once.

startEntity(*name*)

This method is called when the parser begins parsing the entity associated with the name *name* in the DTD. The only way to know about the names defined in the DTD is to provide a DeclHandler and implement the externalEntityDecl and internalEntityDecl methods.

endEntity(*name*)

The parser calls this method when it is finished parsing the entity identified by *name*. See startEntity for information about using entity names.

startCDATA( )

This method is called at the start of a CDATA section.

endCDATA( )

The parser calls this method at the end of a CDATA section.

Locator

Objects called *locators* are used to provide access to information about where events occur in the document. The application receives a locator by implementing the setDocumentLocator method on the content handler. Locator objects provide methods that allow the application to determine which entity was being parsed when the event occurred, and where in the entity the parse had reached. The SAXParseException exception class also conforms to the Locator interface.

The information provided by these methods can be extremely valuable in reporting problems with your documents in an application. For example, if a purchase order document has a price that is out of range, or a part number that does not exist in your database, you could aid in debugging by providing specific details about the location in the XML document where the problem occurred. This could be used to direct an editor widget to position the cursor where the problem is found so that the user can correct the document.

getColumnNumber( )
> Returns the character offset within the line on which the parse event occurred. The column is not adjusted for tab characters.

getLineNumber( )
> Returns the number of the line on which the parse event occurred. The first line is numbered 1 rather than 0.

getPublicId( )
> Returns the public identifier of the entity being parsed, if one is known. If there isn't one, None is returned.

getSystemId( )
> Returns the system identifier of the entity being parsed when the event occurred, if known. This may not be known, for instance, if the input data is being fed directly to the parser for the document entity. If the system identifier is not known, this returns None.

SAX Exceptions

SAX presents all errors, including exceptions raised by handler methods, to the application as instances of the SAXException exception class or its subclasses. Instances of this class have these methods:

getException( )
> Returns an exception caught by the SAX parser, if there was one, or None if there wasn't one.

getMessage( )
> Returns an explanation of the problem encountered by the parser as a string for human consumption. The message string may have been localized if the XMLReader's setLocale method is called.

The following subclasses of SAXException are defined by SAX.

SAXParseException

This exception is raised when there is a problem parsing the document. Instances of this exception also conform to the Locator interface.

SAXNotRecognizedException

When an application attempts to set or query a feature or property that is not recognized by the parser, this exception is raised. Parsers are required to recognize all features and properties defined as part of the SAX 2 specification, even if they don't support them.

SAXNotSupportedException

A parser raises this exception when the application attempts to set or query a feature or property that is recognized but not supported, or when the application attempts to set a feature or property to a value that is not supported.

Python DOM API

The DOM is essentially a collection of interfaces. All of the core interfaces are implemented in Python including DOMException, DOMImplementation, DocumentFragment, Document, Node, NodeList, NamedNodeMap, CharacterData, Attr, Element, Text, Comment, CDATASection, DocumentType, Notation, Entity, EntityReference, and ProcessingInstruction. These interfaces and their specific implementation in Python are detailed for reference in this appendix.

DOMException

DOM operations may occasionally encounter a problem and raise an exception. The abstract interface defined by the W3C DOM specification defines one exception and several constants. In this interface, specific exceptions are detected by catching the general exception and checking the code attribute of the exception object. Python extends this to behave more like other Python exceptions: there is the DOMException base class for the exceptions, and a derived class for each specific exception. The code attribute still takes one of the defined constants as a value. Code that is expecting to deal with only one particular exception should only name the specific derived exception in an except clause but code that expects to handle any DOM exception in a general way should name the DOMException base class. All of the exception classes and constants are defined in the xml.dom module.

In this list, the first name is the name of the exception class, and the second name is the name of the constant for the code attribute.

IndexSizeErr (INDEX_SIZE_ERR)
> Raised if an index of size is negative or greater than the allowed value.

DOMStringSizeErr (DOMSTRING_SIZE_ERR)
> Raised if the specified range of text does not fit into a DOMString.

HierarchyRequestErr (HIERARCHY_REQUEST_ERR)
> Used if any node is inserted somewhere it doesn't belong.

WrongDocumentErr (WRONG_DOCUMENT_ERR)
> Used if a node is used in a different document than the one that created it (which doesn't support it).

InvalidCharacterErr (INVALID_CHARACTER_ERR)
> Used if an invalid or illegal character is specified, such as in a name. Illegal characters are indicated in the XML specification.

NoDataAllowedErr (NO_DATA_ALLOWED_ERR)
> Used if data is specified for a node that does not support data.

NoModificationAllowedErr (NO_MODIFICATION_ALLOWED_ERR)
> Used if an attempt is made to modify an object where modifications are not allowed.

NotFoundErr (NOT_FOUND_ERR)
> Used if an attempt is made to reference a node in a context in which it does not exist.

NotSupportedErr (NOT_SUPPORTED_ERR)
> Used if the implementation does not support the requested type of object or operation.

InuseAttributeErr (INUSE_ATTRIBUTE_ERR)
> Used if an attempt is made to add an attribute that is already in use elsewhere.

InvalidStateErr (INVALID_STATE_ERR)
> Used if an attempt is made to use an object that is not, or is no longer, usable.

SyntaxErr (SYNTAX_ERR)
> Used if an invalid or illegal string is specified.

InvalidModificationErr (INVALID_MODIFICATION_ERR)
> Used if an attempt is made to modify the type of the underlying object.

NamespaceErr (NAMESPACE_ERR)
> Used if an attempt is made to create or change an object in a way that is incorrect with regard to namespaces.

InvalidAccessErr(INVALID_ACCESS_ERR)
> Used if a parameter or an operation is not supported by the underlying object.

DOMImplementation

The DOMImplementation interface provides a number of methods for performing operations that are independent of any particular instance of the Document Object Model.

hasFeature(*feature, version*)
> Tests if the DOM implementation has a specific feature. The return is a Boolean value.

createDocumentType(*qualifiedName, publicId, systemId*)
> Creates and returns an empty DocumentType node. Entity declarations and notations are not made available. It is expected that a future version of the DOM will provide a way for populating a DocumentType.

createDocument(*namespaceURI, qualifiedName, doctype*)
> Creates an XML Document object of the specified type and document element. The return value should be a Document object. *namespaceURI* and *doctype* may be None if they do not apply for the new document.

DocumentFragment   Inherits Node

DocumentFragment is a minimal document object. It is meant to be a storage container that applications can use when they want to isolate and deal separately with a portion of another document, or to hold temporary fragments during complex cut and paste operations. Document fragments can contain any type of nodes, and have some special behavior when inserted into the document tree. Most interestingly (and usefully), when a DocumentFragment is appended or inserted, the *children* of the fragment are inserted into the appropriate location, rather than the fragment itself.

The DocumentFragment is an interface that inherits from Node, buts adds no additional methods or attributes.

Document

The Document interface is the object representation of an entire XML document. It contains all of the root elements, as well as the document type. The contained child objects of the Document have their ownerDocument attribute associated with this parent.

doctype
> Contains the Document Type Declaration associated with the document. The value is read-only, and cannot be modified in DOM Level 2.

documentElement
> Represents the root element of the document. As you work with the DOM, dealing with elements is a natural thing, and being able to quickly extract the root element of any document object is desirable.

implementation
> The DOMImplementation object that handles this document.

createAttribute(*name*)
> Creates an Attr object with the *name* supplied. Support for namespaces is provided with the createAttributeNS method.

createAttributeNS(*namespaceURI, qualifiedName*)
> Does essentially the same task as createAttribute(*name*), however it creates the attribute with the given *namespaceURI*.

createCDATASection(*data*)
> Creates and returns a *CDATA* node section with the supplied data.

createComment(*data*)
> Creates and returns a comment node.

createDocumentFragment( )
> Creates and returns an empty DocumentFragment object.

createElement(*tagname*)
> Creates an element with the given element *tagname*. Returns an Element object.

createElementNS(*namespaceURI, qualifiedName*)
> Same as createElement; however the *namespaceURI* is associated with the element.

createEntityReference(*name*)
> Creates and returns an EntityReference object; may raise an invalid character exception if illegal characters are used.

createProcessingInstruction(*target, data*)
> Creates and returns a ProcessingInstruction node with the supplied *target* and *data*.

createTextNode(*data*)

    Creates and returns a text node that contains the text given by *data*.

getElementById(*elementId*)

    Returns an Element object with the corresponding ID. Returns None if there is no such element. Remember that ID attributes must be specified in the DTD. Simply creating a tag such as <account id="234"/> will not cause it to be returned by this method unless the DTD included assigns the attribute to be of the tokenized type ID. Additionally, the DOMImplementation object must be aware of which attributes have been given the type ID. Attributes of type ID must be unique within any given XML document.

getElementsByTagName(*tagName*)

    Returns a NodeList containing all of the elements matching *tagName*. They are returned in the order they were found when the original document is parsed.

getElementsByTagNameNS(*namespaceURI, localName*)

    Returns a NodeList of the elements that match both the *localName* and *namespaceURI*.

importNode(*importedNode, deep*)

    This method imports a node from another document into the current one. The Node has no parent. All attributes and the namespace of the imported Node are the same. Given the broad variety of nodes that can be imported, certain rules or side effects are applied.

- Imported nodes that are Attributes (Attr) have no owner element, and all children are imported as well.

- DocumentFragment nodes have their children imported as well if the *deep* parameter is set to true.

- Document nodes are not imported since a Document cannot contain another Document.

- Element nodes are imported as expected, complete with attributes. If the *deep* parameter is true, children of the element are imported as well.

- EntityReference nodes have only themselves copied, regardless of the *deep* parameter. If the entity has a value definition, it is imported as well.

- Notation nodes can be imported, but the DOM currently does not allow modification of the DocumentType.

- ProcessingInstruction nodes are imported as expected, in their entirety. Character-Data (including CDATASection and Comment nodes) are copied as expected with their data attribute.

Node

The granddaddy of much of the DOM, the Node class carries quite a lot of information.

Node Constants

Node defines several constants that can be used by application writers to determine the node's nodeType.

ELEMENT_NODE

    An Element node

ATTRIBUTE_NODE

    An Attr node

TEXT_NODE
  A Text node
CDATA_SECTION_NODE
  A CDATASection node
ENTITY_REFERENCE_NODE
  An EntityReference node
ENTITY_NODE
  An Entity node
PROCESSING_INSTRUCTION_NODE
  A ProcessingInstruction node
COMMENT_NODE
  A Comment node
DOCUMENT_NODE
  A Document node
DOCUMENT_TYPE_NODE
  A DocumentType node
DOCUMENT_FRAGMENT_NODE
  A DocumentFragment node
NOTATION_NODE
  A Notation node

Node Properties and Methods

attributes
  This contains a NamedNodeMap that contain the attributes of this node, or the value is None.

childNodes
  This contains a NodeList containing all children of this node. If no children exist then the list is empty.

firstChild
  The first child of the node. A convenient attribute if you know the structure of the document. If the node has no children, this is None.

lastChild
  Similar to its counterpart firstChild, but returns the last child node. If the node has no children, this is None.

localName
  Returns the local part of the qualified name of the node.

namespaceURI
  The namespace URI of the node or None if none exists.

nextSibling
  The node immediately following this node or None if none exists.

nodeName
  The name of the node, depending on its type. nodes of type Text and CharacterData do not have their own names, but rather just a string indicating that they are that specific type. For Element nodes, it's the tag name. For other named types, it returns their respective names.

nodeType

An integer representing the type of the node. This is directly correlated to the defined constants of the Node class.

nodeValue

The value of this node depending on its type. For attributes, it is the assigned value. For CDATASection, Comment, Text, and ProcessingInstruction nodes, it is their contents respectively. However, for Element nodes, this value is not the character data beneath the element, but None.

ownerDocument

The Document object to which this node belongs.

parentNode

The immediate parent of the node. This may be None if the node has just been created and has not been inserted as a child of another node. This is always None for attribute nodes.

prefix

This is the namespace prefix, or None if the node does not have a namespace prefix.

previousSibling

Similar to nextSibling, this attribute is associated with the node immediately preceding this one, or None.

appendChild(newChild)

This method adds the newChild node the end of the NodeList contained within this node. If the node already exists, it is removed and then added back.

cloneNode(deep)

This method returns a duplicate of the node. The duplicate node is not attached, and does not have a parent. The deep parameter, if true, indicates that the entire tree beneath this node should be included in the copy operation.

hasChildNodes()

Boolean method returns true or false depending on whether the node has children.

insertBefore(newChild, refChild)

Inserts the new node immediately prior to the refChild within the node's NodeList. If the newChild already exists within the list, it is deleted first and added again.

supports(feature, level)

This method returns true or false depending on whether the DOM implementation supports a specific feature for this particular node.

normalize()

This method descends to the full depth beneath this node, and ensures that only markup structure such as elements, comments, and processing instructions separate Text nodes. This eliminates empty (or whitespace) nodes existing in between chunks of text in your markup.

removeChild(childNode)

Returns and removes the childNode from the node's NodeList.

replaceChild(newChild, oldChild)

Replaces oldChild with newChild and returns oldChild to the caller. If newChild is already a child of some element, it is removed.

NodeList

The NodeList interface is a generic list containing the child nodes of the node, regardless of their specific subtype. In other words, Text nodes are in the list alongside Element and ProcessingInstruction nodes. This interface is not defined in terms of the Node interface.

length

> This read-only attribute indicates the number of nodes in the list. If the length is 10, then the actual indexes are 0 through 9.

item(*index*)

> This method returns the node with the corresponding index in the NodeList. If the index is out of range, None is returned.

NamedNodeMap

This interface is similar to a NodeList, but its designed to allow the accessing of nodes from the list by name. Nodes are not guaranteed to be in any particular order within the map. This interface is not defined in terms of the Node interface.

length

> The number of nodes in the map. As with the NodeList, if length is 10 then actual indexes are 0 through 9.

getNamedItem(*name*)

> This method retrieves the node specified by the parameter *name*. The node is returned if found, or None is returned if not.

getNamedItemNS(*namespaceURI, localName*)

> This method returns a node matching both the localName and namespaceURI supplied as parameters.

item(*index*)

> Returns the node at position *index*, or None if *index* is out of range.

removeNamedItem(*name*)

> Removes the node specified by *name*. If the node is an Attr (XML attribute) and has a default value (as specified in the DTD), the default value is then substituted and keeps the same namespace URI, local name, and prefix. The removed node is returned.

removeNamedItemNS(*namespaceURI, localName*)

> Identical to removeNamedItem, with one exception: the search criteria includes the *namespaceURI* as well as the *localName* to match a node from the map. The removed node is returned.

setNamedItem(*arg*)

> The first parameter, *arg*, is expected to be a node object. If a node with the same name already exists, it is replaced with the new one, and the old one is returned. A value of None is returned if nodes are added, but not replaced.

setNamedItemNS(*arg*)

> This method is essentially the same as setNamedItem, with the addition of a qualifying namespace URI as well as the local name (both taken from the *arg* of type Node).

CharacterData

The CharacterData interface is a subtype of Node that provides additional methods for working with text data. This interface does not correspond to concrete node types, but is used as a basis for defining the Text and Comment interfaces.

data
> This string represents the character data held within the node.

length
> The number of characters available through the data attribute and substringData method. If the object is empty, the value may be 0.

appendData(*arg*)
> This method appends the string *arg* to the end of the character data.

deleteData(*offset, count*)
> Removes a given number of characters from the character data beginning at *offset* and continuing through *offset* + *count*. If the supplied range exceeds the length of the string, the contents from *offset* through the end of the string are deleted.

insertData(*offest, arg*)
> This method allows you to insert character data into the node beginning at the position noted by *offset*.

replaceData(*offset, count, arg*)
> This method replaces the data beginning at offset, with the supplied data of *arg*, continuing through *offset* + *count*. If the length of the data is exceeded, then the additional replacement text is appended to the data.

substringData(*offset, count*)
> Extracts a portion of the data from the CharacterData node. If *offset* + *count* exceed the length, then all characters through the end of the node are returned.

Attr
Inherits Node

The Attr interface is the Node interface for attributes of an element. The DOM does not consider an Attr part of the tree, and therefore the attributes parentNode, previousSibling, and nextSibling are all None for Attr objects. Attributes should be considered properties of elements. Attr nodes cannot be immediate children of a DocumentFragment, but can be contained within an element of a document fragment.

The value for a node is its assigned value within the actual markup. Failing that, if a default value is specified in the DTD, it is used. Child nodes of an Attr may be Text nodes or of the type EntityReference.

name
> The name of the attribute.

ownerElement
> This property represents the Element node to which the attribute is attached.

specified
> This Boolean property lets you know if the value was explicitly stated in the markup (true), or if it is the default value as assigned by the DTD. The value also returns true if the value has been manipulated or is explicitly assigned, but still holds the default

value. If the `ownerElement` attribute is `None` (if this node is not currently associated with an element), then `specified` is also `true`.

value

>   This is the actual value of the key/value pair that makes up the `Attr` within any given `Element`.

Element 　

Inherits Node

The Element interface represents a markup element. In addition to its `Node`-like methods, it supports access methods to get at contained attributes.

tagName

>   The name of the element type. In `<stag drums="dale">`, a string with the value `stag` is returned.

getAttribute(*name*)

>   This method returns an attribute's value. This method bypasses retrieving the `Attr` object directly and using its accessor methods. In some cases, using the `Attr` node directly may be more appropriate, but the convenience methods on the element node usually suffice.

getAttributeNS(*namespaceURI, localName*)

>   Similar to `getAttribute`, but selects the return attribute based on namespace as well as name.

getAttributeNode(*name*)

>   This method returns the actual `Attr` object instead of its character value, as is the case with `getAttribute`. Returns `None` if no such attribute is found.

getAttributeNodeNS(*namespaceURI, localName*)

>   Returns an `Attr` node that matches both the name and namespace URI specified. Returns `None` if no such attribute is found.

getElementsByTagName(*tagName*)

>   This method returns a `NodeList` of descendant `Element` nodes that share the same element type name. The special value * matches all tags.

getElementsByTagNameNS(*namespaceURI, localName*)

>   Returns a `NodeList` of all descendant elements who match both the name and namespace URI supplied. The value * in either field matches all namespaces URIs or all local names; using * for both fields matches all elements in the tree rooted at this node.

hasAttribute(*name*)

>   This Boolean method returns `true` when an attribute with a given *name* is in the element or has a default value in the DTD.

hasAttributeNS(*namespaceURI, localName*)

>   This Boolean method returns `true` when an attribute of a specific name and namespace exists within the element or has a default value stated in the DTD.

removeAttribute(*name*)

>   Removes an attribute by the name indicated in the *name* parameter. If the removed attribute has a default value in the DTD, that value is immediately substituted upon its removal.

removeAttributeNS(*namespaceURI, localName*)

> Removes an attribute that matches both the local name and namespace supplied. If the attribute had a default value specified in the DTD, that value is immediately substituted upon removal.

removeAttributeNode(*node*)

> This method removes the specified attribute *node*. This method takes a complete Attr object as a parameter as opposed to a string name, as is the case with the removeAttribute methods. Return value is the removed node.

setAttribute(*name, value*)

> This method adds a new attribute to the Element with the supplied *name/value* pair. It replaces any elements that already exist with the same name. The text supplied as value is placed as a literal string, so any EntityReference or other more complex Attr structures are not created (see setAttributeNode instead).

setAttributeNS(*namesapceURI, qualifiedName, value*)

> This method works essentially the same as setAttribute, except a namespace URI and prefix are associated with the attribute.

setAttributeNode(*node*)

> This method adds a new attribute to the Element. If the supplied *node* parameter (of type Attr) contains any Text node or EntityReference children, they are added as well. If an attribute with a matching nodeName already exists within the element, it is replaced. Returns None unless an attribute is replaced, in which case the old attribute is returned to the caller.

setAttributeNodeNS(*node*)

> This method works essentially the same as setAttributeNode. If a node already exists with the same namespace URI and local name, it is replaced and returned to the caller. Otherwise, the new attribute is added and None is returned.

Text
Inherits CharacterData

The Text method represents textual data within an Element or Attribute. Text nodes are created for all chunks of text outside of regular markup within an XML document. The normalize method merges adjacent Text nodes into a single node for each chunk of Text. The methods of the CharacterData interface can be used on this object to gain access and manipulation of the text data.

splitText(*offset*)

> This method splits the node into two nodes at the point *offset*. All of the data in the node prior to the *offset* remain as a node. The data after the offset becomes part of a new, adjacent Text node, which is returned to the caller.

Comment
Inherits CharacterData

The Comment node holds the textual data of a Comment structure: <!-- Behold, a comment -->. The methods of CharacterData are available for manipulation of the Comment's data.

CDATASection

This interface allows you to manipulate CDATASection nodes. Unlike Text nodes, the normalize method does not merge adjacent CDATASection nodes. CDATASection nodes are used to hold special characters that may be mistaken as XML by a parser.

DocumentType

This interface represents the DTD of your XML document, or it is None if one does not exist. Its attributes are read-only, per the DOM specification, because the W3C is uncertain about how the different XML schema efforts will impact DTD usage.

entities
> This attribute returns a NamedNodeMap containing both external and internal entities declared within the DTD. Parameter entities aren't included and entities declared more than once are represented only by the first declaration. The members of the NamedNodeMap implement the Entity interface. If the information is not provided by the underlying parser, or if no entities are defined, this may be None.

internalSubset
> This attribute gives access to the internal DTD subset as a string, or None if no internal subset is given. The value of this string does not include the brackets that surround the internal subset.

name
> The name of the root element as given in the DTD.

notations
> This property represents a NamedNodeMap of the notations within the DTD. Each member of the map implements the Notation interface. Notations declared more than once are represented only by the first declaration. If the information is not provided by the underlying parser, or if no notations are defined, this may be None.

publicId
> This is the public identifier of the external subset. If there is no public identifier, this is None.

systemId
> This is the system identifier of the external subset. If there is no public identifier, this is None.

Notation

This interface represents a Notation declared in the DTD. The nodeName attribute inherited from Node is used as the declared name of the notation.

publicId
> The public identifier of the notation, or None if not present.

systemId
> The system identifier of this notation, or None if not present.

Entity

Inherits Node

This interface represents both parsed and unparsed entities. A parser may choose to expand entities before the structure model is passed to the DOM; in this case, there are no EntityReference nodes in the document tree.

External entity values in nonvalidating parsers may not be available, since nonvalidating parsers are not required to process external entities.

Entity nodes cannot be edited—they are read-only.

notationName
> This value is None for parsed entities, and is the name of the notation for unparsed entities.

puclicId
> The public identifier of the entity, or None if not present.

systemId
> The system identifier of the entity, or None if not present.

EntityReference

Inherits Node

This empty interface represents entity references in an XML document, or when you want to insert an entity reference. Character references, as well as references to predefined entities, may be expanded by the parser in creation of the DOM tree. In this case, EntityReference objects may not be created by the parser.

ProcessingInstruction

Inherits Node

This method represents a processing instruction. This straightforward interface has two string data properties representing the data and target of the ProcessingInstruction.

data
> The content of the processing instruction.

target
> The target of the processing instruction.

4DOM Extensions

The 4DOM package that accompanies PyXML contains some proprietary extensions that may eventually make their way into W3C offerings. These classes include methods for reading streams of XML, "pretty printing," and convenient splitting functions, among other things. These are documented in the *PyXML/doc/4DOM/extensions.html* file that ships with PyXML, and are not available using other DOM implementations.

Working with MSXML3.0

This appendix focuses on techniques for using the Microsoft MSXML3.0 XML parser from within Python. If you are working with the Windows platform and XML, chances are you've worked with MSXML.

Setting Up MSXML3.0

Fortunately, when using Python for your XML development, you don't have to give up MSXML3.0. The Microsoft parser is fully accessible from Python using Python's COM support.

If you haven't already, you'll need to visit *http://www.python.org/* and install *win32all.exe* as a supplement to your Python installation. This Windows-specific package provides support for Microsoft's Component Object Model (COM) framework. The *win32all.exe* package must be installed prior to using COM objects. More details of working with Python and COM can be found in Chapter 9, in which COM is used to access the MSSOAP collection of objects.

Version 3.0 is the latest incarnation of Microsoft's parser. It provides full support for XSLT, among other things. However, Version 3.0 might not be the version used in other applications, such as Internet Explorer. This may or may not be of concern to you. If you are somehow running Python inside an application, or using automation from Python to talk to another application, you need to be aware that a foreign application's parser may be an older version. Knowing the particular version of the user's copy of MSXML is primarily of concern for those writing client-side script inside Internet Explorer where the parser may be chosen for them (as in an XSLT stylesheet linked in an XML file). Standalone applications, on the other hand, can pick their own parser (as we do in this appendix).

If you are writing programs in Python, you typically use a program ID (ProgID) to instantiate a COM object. When using the ProgID, you can explicitly state that you wish to use 3.0 and not an earlier version. However, if you want to embed a stylesheet within your XML document and want Internet Explorer to use MSXML 3.0, you need to consult the documentation that ships with Microsoft's XML SDK for installing MSXML3.0 in "replace mode." For the purposes of the Python examples in this appendix, using the ProgID work just fine!

Basic DOM Operations

This section goes over different techniques for working with DOM, and highlights some of the features that MSXML supports but PyXML does not. In addition to these convenience functions added by Microsoft, working with MSXML means also working with COM, so examples are shown here to work with the various types returned by MSXML that may stray from your standard Python list types and tuples.

The Microsoft DOM supports the same operations as the PyXML DOM, but there are differences in using them. For starters, MSXML is only accessible via COM, so your Python needs to work as a COM client. Second, and related to the first, is MSXML is not a native Python implementation and therefore doesn't use Python types like the lists and tuples you'd find in PyXML. This section shows you the basics of working with this foreign parser from within Python.

To illustrate some node and document manipulation, you need some source XML to manipulate. You'll want structured data like *books.xml* shown in Example E-1, and try out your MSXML skills.

Example E-1. books.xml

```
<book name="Python and XML">
  <section name="Appendix E" type="Appendix">
    <chapterTitle>Appendix E</chapterTitle>
    <bodytext>This appendix focuses on techniques for using...
    </bodytext>
  </section>
</book>
```

Using MSXML, it's easy to take this document apart. But before you can work with MSXML, you have to import the correct library to access COM objects (win32com. client). Additionally, for the call to Dispatch, you need the ProgID of the Microsoft XML parser. If you've installed the latest Microsoft XML SDK, you have Version 3.0 of the MSXML parser. You may also have it if you're running Visual Studio.NET or Internet Explorer 6. However, if you aren't sure, you can download the XML SDK from Microsoft and install the newest version of the parser.

After importing the client package and calling Dispatch with the correct ProgID, use MSXML's load method to actually load a document:

```
>>> import win32com.client
>>> msxml = win32com.client.Dispatch("MSXML2.DOMDocument.3.0")
>>> msxml.load("books.xml")
1
```

The returned 1 indicates success in Python terms, and allows for the syntax:

```
if (msxml.load("books.xml")):
    # success
else:
    # failure
```

Now that the msxml instance is ready to go, you can begin plucking out nodes and experimenting with them.

MSXML Nodes

The MSXML objects will feel familiar to you if you've been working with the PyXML objects throughout this book. Retrieving a documentElement or getting a node's nodeName works as you might suspect:

```
>>> docelem = msxml.documentElement
>>> print docelem.nodeName
book
>>> print docelem.getAttribute("name")
Python & XML
```

MSXML throws in the occasional convenience like the text attribute of its Node class. This method returns all text content (or character data) beneath the current node:

```
>>> print docelem.text
Appendix E This appendix focuses on techniques for using...
```

This can come in handy when working with text-heavy documents. Related to the text attribute is the xml attribute. The xml attribute returns a string of XML representing the current node and its children:

```
>>> print docelem.xml
<book name="Python and XML">
        <section name="Appendix E" type="Appendix">
                <chapterTitle>Appendix E</chapterTitle>
                <bodytext>This appendix focuses on techniques for using...
    </bodytext>
        </section>
</book>
```

This is a definite shortcut (for your typing at least) over using the PrettyPrint method in the PyXML DOM extensions package. Of course, just like PyXML, some MSXML methods return collections of nodes rather than single nodes. In these cases, use the MSXML NodeList interface for dealing with the collections.

Using a NodeList

MSXML3.0 has great support for node lists, and provides a NodeList object for use in their manipulation. This is slightly different then the native and robust list type provided by Python and PyXML. The NodeList object has a built-in *iterator* that you can take advantage of by calling the nextNode method; note that this is different from the concept of iterators as they have been implemented in Python 2.2 and newer versions.

```
node = NodeList.nextNode()
while node:
  # do something here...
  node = NodeList.nextNode()
```

A while loop can be used until the nextNode method fails to return a node. Example E-2, *people.xml*, shows some sample XML describing workers and their job titles.

Example E-2. people.xml

```
<employees>
  <person title="Project Manager">Cal Ender</person>
  <person title="Development Lead">A. Buddy Codit</person>
  <person title="Customer Service Rep">Will Icare</person>
  <person title="Documentation Writer">E. Manual</person>
  <person title="Catering Specialist">Willy Eadit</person>
</employees>
```

In a structure such as this, a NodeList can be a convenient way to process all nodes of a certain type. A NodeList can be returned with a call to getElementsByTagName, or by using a string expression in one of the selectNodes and selectSingleNode methods of MSXML3.0. Example E-3 shows the NodeList in use in *nodelists.py*:

Example E-3. nodelists.py

```
"""
 nodelists.py - using the NodeList object
  from MSXML3.0
"""
import win32com.client

# source XML
strSourceDoc = "people.xml"

# instantiate parser
objXML = win32com.client.Dispatch("MSXML2.DOMDocument.3.0")

# check for successful loading
if (not objXML.load(strSourceDoc)):
  print "Error loading", strSourceDoc

# grab all person elements
peopleNodes = objXML.getElementsByTagName("person")

# begin iteration of NodeList with nextNode()
node = peopleNodes.nextNode()
while node:
  # print value of text descendants
  print "Name: ", node.text,
```

Example E-3. nodelists.py (continued)

```
    # print value of title attribute
    print "\tPosition: ", node.getAttribute("title")

    # continue iteration
node = peopleNodes.nextNode( )
```

When you run *nodelists.py* from the command prompt, you'll get a textual version of its contents:

```
C:\appD>c:\python21\python nodelists.py
Name:   Cal Ender       Position:   Project Manager
Name:   A. Buddy Codit  Position:   Development Lead
Name:   Will Icare      Position:   Customer Service Rep
Name:   E. Manual       Position:   Documentation Writer
Name:   Willy Eadit     Position:   Catering Specialist
```

MSXML3.0 Support for XSLT

MSXML3.0 provides support for XSL transformations without any additional software. The parser features a transformNode method that usually accepts a stylesheet as a parameter (in DOM form) and returns the result of processing the current document with the supplied stylesheet. For example:

```
objXML = win32com.client.Dispatch("MSXML2.DOMDocument.3.0")
objXSL = win32com.client.Dispatch("MSXML2.DOMDocument.3.0")
strTransformedXML = objXML.transformNode(objXSL)
```

In the simplest case, as shown in the preceding code, two DOM instances are created. One DOM instance is needed to hold the source document, the other contains the stylesheet. To get the result of the transformation, call transformNode on the source DOM, providing the stylesheet DOM as a parameter.

Source XML

Example E-4 shows *1999temps.xml*, a document containing monthly average temperatures for Woodinville, Washington. This is a simple XML document with a flat structure.

Example E-4. 1999 temps.xml

```
<CalendarYear value="1999" data="Average Monthly Highs">
  <Month name="January">45.0</Month>
  <Month name="February">49.5</Month>
  <Month name="March">52.7</Month>
  <Month name="April">57.2</Month>
  <Month name="May">63.9</Month>
  <Month name="June">69.9</Month>
  <Month name="July">75.2</Month>
  <Month name="August">75.2</Month>
```

```
    <Month name="September">69.3</Month>
    <Month name="October">59.7</Month>
    <Month name="November">50.5</Month>
    <Month name="December">45.1</Month>
</CalendarYear>
```

There are attributes indicating the year on record, and the type of data displayed. The Month elements have a name attribute, while the actual temperature is character data.

XSL Stylesheet

With your stylesheet, attempt to find the average yearly temperature, based on the average monthly temperatures. Using a combination of XPath's sum function and div operator yields the results needed. Example E-5 shows the stylesheet *temps.xsl*.

Example E-5. temps.xsl

```
<?xml version="1.0"?>
<xsl:stylesheet
 xmlns:xsl="http://www.w3.org/1999/XSL/Transform"
 version="1.0">

<xsl:variable name="average"
       select="sum(//CalendarYear/Month/text()) div 12"/>
<xsl:template match="/">
<html>
<body>
  <p>
  <font face="tahoma,arial,helvetica" size="2">
    <xsl:value-of select="/CalendarYear/@data"/> for
    <xsl:value-of select="/CalendarYear/@value"/>:
  </font>
  </p>
  <table border="1"
         bordercolor="#000000"
         cellpadding="5"
         cellspacing="0"
         width="350">
    <xsl:apply-templates/>
    <tr>
      <td colspan="2" bgcolor="#88BBEE" width="350"
         align="right">
        <p>
          <font face="tahoma,arial,helvetica" size="2">
            <b>Average:
              <xsl:value-of select="format-number($average, '0.00')"/>
            </b>
          </font>
        </p>
```

```
        </td>
      </tr>
    </table>
  </body>
</html>
</xsl:template>

<xsl:template match="Month">
  <tr>
    <td bgcolor="#CCCCCC" width="325" align="left">
      <p>
        <font face="tahoma,arial,helvetica" size="2">
          Month: <b><xsl:value-of select="@name"/></b>
        </font>
      </p>
    </td>
    <td bgcolor="#CCCCCC" width="25" align="left">
      <p>
        <font face="tahoma,arial,helvetica" size="2">
          <b><xsl:value-of select="./text()"/></b>
        </font>
      </p>
    </td>
  </tr>
</xsl:template>

</xsl:stylesheet>
```

The stylesheet performs its computational work in two parts. First, a variable is created that holds the average of the temperatures by using the sum function to add them together, then using the div operator to divide between the total number of months in a year:

```
<xsl:variable name="average"
    select="sum(//CalendarYear/Month/text()) div 12"/>
```

Finally, some formatting is performed within a template by calling format-number, using $average as a parameter:

```
<xsl:value-of select="format-number($average, '0.00')"/>
```

This ensures that the temperature figure contains at least two floating-point digits.

Running an MSXML Transformation

To apply the transformation from Python, create two instances of MSXML3.0, and supply one with the source XML and one with the stylesheet. Then use transformNode to complete the transformation process. Example E-6 shows *transform.py*, which completes the task.

Example E-6. transform.py

```
"""
transform.py - using MSXML3.0
XSLT support from Python
"""
import win32com.client

strSourceDoc = "1999temps.xml"
strStyleDoc  = "temps.xsl"

objXML = win32com.client.Dispatch("MSXML2.DOMDocument.3.0")
objXSL = win32com.client.Dispatch("MSXML2.DOMDocument.3.0")

if (not objXML.load(strSourceDoc)):
  print "Error loading", strSourceDoc

if (not objXSL.load(strStyleDoc)):
  print "Error loading", strStyleDoc

strTransformedXML = objXML.transformNode(objXSL)
print strTransformedXML
```

You can run the process from a command prompt, and write the output to an HTML file if you want to view the results in a browser.

```
>c:\python21\python transform.py > temps.html
```

Figure E-1 shows the transformed XML residing in a browser.

Handling Parsing Errors

The parseError object contains the most recent errors encountered by the parser. For example, consider loading a document that does not exist:

```
>>> msxml.load("NotReally.xml")
0
```

The return result of 0 is enough to indicate that something has gone wrong. At this point, you can retrieve the parseError object to inspect for damage:

```
>>> pe = msxml.parseError
```

The parseError interface is detailed at the end of this appendix's reference section. The object essentially encapsulates seven attributes of an XML parsing error and makes them available via the ParseError object:

```
>>> print pe.errorCode
-2146697211
>>> print pe.reason
The system cannot locate the resource specified.
```

The error conditions hint that it may be wise to also check the URL that the parser was using to load the document:

```
>>> print pe.url
NotReally.xml
```

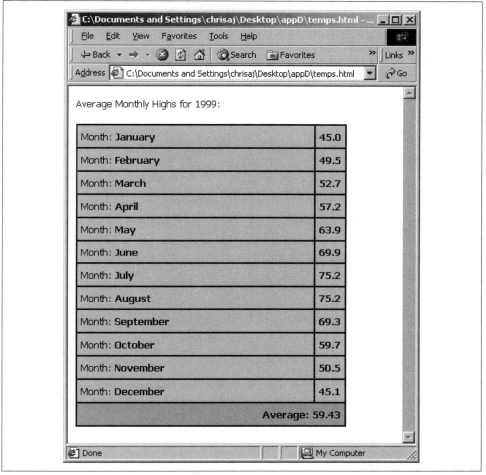

Figure E-1. The result of the transformation

As you can see, the problem is that the parser is after a file that does not exist. In addition to a reason and an errorCode, the parser also contains information concerning location within the file of a parsing error (filepos, line, and linepos).

MSXML3.0 Reference

This section provides a reference for the method exposed by MSXML3.0 that is available for use within Python. Based on the DOM, MSXML3.0 supports five main types of objects. A Node object contains the DOM interface for a node, and some Microsoft-built convenience functions as well. The Document supports the DOM interface for a Document, plus additional Microsoft extensions. Furthermore, MSXML supports a NamedNodeMap, a NodeList, and a ParseError object. This section lists the details of each object and its methods.

MSXML3.0 Document Object

The Document object supports the same functionality as the W3C DOM Document interface, but also features some Microsoft convenience extensions. For example, with MSXML3.0, you can use the validate method to validate your document against its DTD:

```
myDomDocument.validate( )
```

In addition to validation, support for XSLT transformations is built into the MSXML3.0 as well as with the transformNode method:

```
myDomDocument.transformNode(myXSLTDomDocument)
```

The transformNode method takes another DOM instance as a parameter that contains an XSLT stylesheet. The transformation is applied against the current document, and the result is returned to the caller. The following section is a reference for the different methods and properties of the Document object.

MSXML3.0 Document Object Methods

abort( )
> Aborts an asynchronous download operation, if in progress.

createAttribute(*name*)
> Creates an attribute using the *name* supplied as a parameter.

createCDATASection(*data*)
> Creates the character string *data* as a CDATA node and returns.

createComment(*data*)
> Creates and returns a new comment using the supplied *data* as the contents.

createDocumentFragment( )
> Creates and returns a new and empty document fragment.

createElement(*elementName*)
> Creates and returns a new element with the supplied name.

createEntityReference(*name*)
> Creates and returns a new entity reference object.

createNode(*type, name, namespaceURI*)
> Creates and returns a node of the given *type*, using the supplied *name*, within the given namespace context.

createProcessingInstruction(*target, data*)
> Creates and returns a new processing instruction with the given *target* and *data*.

createTextNode(*data*)
> Creates and returns a text node with the provided *data* as its characters.

getElementsByTagName(*elementName*)
> Returns a NodeList of elements matching the given name.

getProperty( )
> Returns the SelectionLanguage, ServerHTTPRequest, or SelectionNamespace properties.

load(*url*)
> Loads the URL supplied as a parameter. If it is a filename, the parser attempts to load the file; if it is a remote HTTP address, the parser attempts to connect and load the document. The existing contents of the document are discarded.

loadXML(*strXML*)

> Creates a document object from a well-formed string of XML. Only UTF-16 and UCS-2 text are accepted. Any existing contents of the document are discarded.

nodeFromID(*id*)

> Returns the node from the document using the supplied unique ID value.

save(*objTarget*)

> Attempts to save the XML document to the specified location.

setProperty( )

> Allows you to specify the value of the SelectionLanguage, ServerHTTPRequest, or SelectionNamespace property.

validate( )

> Performs validation against the document based on the declared DTD.

MSXML3.0 Document Object Properties

async

> This read/write property determines whether synchronous or asynchronous document retrieval is used when downloading.

doctype

> This read-only property contains the doctype associated with the XML document.

documentElement

> This read/write property contains the XML document's root element.

implementation

> This read-only property contains the DOMImplementation object for the document instance.

namespaces

> This read-only property contains a collection of all of the namespaces used in the document.

ondataavailable

> This read/write property represents the event handler that is called when data becomes available.

onreadystatechange

> This read/write property represents the event handler that is called when the readyState property changes.

ontransformnode

> This read/write property is set to the event handler called when the transformnode event is fired.

parseError

> This read-only property contains the document's ParseError object.

preserveWhiteSpace

> This read/write property determines whether whitespace is preserved during document parsing.

readyState

> This read-only property indicates the current state of the document instance.

resolvedExternals

> This read/write property determines whether external definitions are resolved during parsing.

url

> This read-only property represents the canonical URL for the most recently loaded XML document.

validateOnParse

> This read/write Boolean property indicates whether the parser should validate during its parsing pass.

MSXML3.0 Node Object

The Node object is the fundamental object of the DOM and of MSXML3.0. This interface supports the common methods used throughout this book when working with the DOM.

MSXML3.0 Node Object Methods

appendChild(*newChildElement*)

> Appends the supplied node to child NodeList for this element.

cloneNode( )

> Creates a new node that is a complete copy of this particular node.

hasChildNodes( )

> Returns true if the node has children.

insertBefore(*newChild, referenceChild*)

> Takes the node supplied as *newChild* and inserts it in this node's NodeList immediately prior to the supplied *referenceChild* node, which must be an existing child.

removeChild(*oldChild*)

> Removes the supplied node from this element's NodeList.

replaceChild(*newChild, oldChild*)

> Places *newChild* in the same location where *oldChild* was residing.

selectNodes(*pattern*)

> Returns a list of nodes matching the given pattern.

selectSingleNode(*pattern*)

> Returns the first node matching the given pattern.

transformNode(*stylesheet*)

> Takes a *stylesheet* that has been loaded into a DOM instance, and applies its rules against this node. The resulting transformation is returned to the caller of the method.

transformNodeToObject(*stylesheet, outputObject*)

> Works as *transformNode* does, but sends the output to the specified object.

MSXML3.0 Node Object Properties

attribute

> This read-only property contains the list of attributes attached to this node.

baseName

> This read-only property contains the base name for the name qualified within the namespace.

childNodes
This read-only property represents a `NodeList` of descendent children.
dataType
This read/write property indicates the data type for this node.
definition
This read-only property contains the definition of the node in the DTD.
firstChild
This read-only property represents the first immediate descendent element of the current node.
lastChild
This read-only property is similar to `firstChild`, but is the last node in the `NodeList`.
namespaceURI
This read-only property contains the URI for the namespace.
nextSibling
This read-only property returns the adjacent node in the list (in relation to this node and its parent).
nodeName
The element name of the node.
nodeType
The type of the node as defined in the DOM recommendation.
nodeTypedValue
A read/write property specifying the node's value as a defined data type.
nodeTypeString
This value is the node type in string format.
nodeValue
The data value of the node—for example, the text of a text node.
ownerDocument
This read-only property indicates which document owns this node.
parentNode
The node that is the parent of this one.
parsed
This Boolean value indicates whether the node and its descendants have been successfully parsed.
prefix
This read/write property is the namespace prefix of the node.
previousSibling
This read-only property returns the node immediately preceding this node in its parent's list of children.
specified
This read-only property represents whether an attribute node is explicitly specified, or if it is derived from a default value in the DTD or schema.
text
This read/write property contains the text of the node and its descendants.
xml
This read-only property contains the node in XML format (including its children).

MSXML3.0 NamedNodeMap Object

The NamedNodeMap object is MSXML3.0's support for namespaces and attribute nodes.

getNamedItem(*name*)

   This method retrieves the attribute with the given name.

getQualifiedItem(*baseName, namespaceURI*)

   This method retrieves the attribute but within the given namespace context.

item(*index*)

   This method returns the item at the given *index*. If there is no such item, None is returned.

nextNode( )

   This method returns the next node in the collection.

removeNamedItem(*name*)

   This method removes the given item from the node collection.

removeQualifiedItem(*name, namespaceURI*)

   This method removes the item from the node collection that also is within the supplied namespace.

reset( )

   This method resets the iteration count back to zero.

setNamedItem(*newItem*)

   This method adds the supplied node into the collection.

length

   The length attribute contains an integer representing the number of items in the collection.

MSXML3.0 NodeList Object

The NodeList is commonly returned by DOM methods that return a collection or list of Nodes. The NodeList features some special methods and properties to make working the list easier.

item(*index*)

   This method returns an item from the list at the given *index* (zero-based, as Python sequence indexes). If there is no node at *index*, returns None.

nextNode( )

   This method returns the next node in the list, based on the internal iterator.

reset( )

   This method resets the internal iterator to zero.

length

   This property indicates the number of items within the list.

MSXML3.0 ParseError Object

The ParserError object is a collection attributes populated when there is an error. The parser populates this object at the time of runtime errors.

errorCode
:   The number representing the error.

filepos
:   This byte-oriented position within the file.

line
:   The line number of the error.

linepos
:   The character position within the line that the error occurred on.

reason
:   This property contains the reason for the error, if known.

srcText
:   This property contains the full text of the line containing the error in the document.

url
:   This property represents the URL of the document.

APPENDIX F

Additional Python XML Tools

This appendix details some other options for working with Python and XML that didn't receive much coverage in the book. *Python and XML* has tried to cover the popular API standards, because they are most likely what is leveraged across multiple programming environments, languages, and even jobs. If you are going to work with XML, you must understand the DOM. Python happens to be a language where all of the standard APIs are available. For all of these reasons, this book focuses on the DOM, XPath, XSLT, SOAP, and others.

In this section, explore some of the alternatives for working with XML from Python. Some of these tools provide equivalent functionality to the tools used elsewhere in the book, but using an implementation that may be more appropriate in another context.

Pyxie

The Pyxie package, developed by Sean McGrath, is available from *http://pyxie. sourceforge.net/* and is based around a line-oriented notation known as PYX. PYX and Pyxie are an alternative to the SAX and DOM, and is, according to its author, geared for pipeline processing, in which one application's output is fed as input to the next application. This idiom is common among Unix tools, but is also used on Windows, though it is not common there for end-user tools.

Pyxie can parse an XML document into a line-oriented format known as PYX, which give signals as to the content of the document. It's similar to SAX in that it is event-driven; however, instead of implementing callback interfaces, the events are dumped to standard output as PYX notation. The PYX output can then be processed by other text manipulation tools such as *grep*, *sed*, and *awk*, or fed into other text-aware scripts you might write with Python and Perl.

PYX output appears as individual lines representing different types of markup. Consider the following XML:

```
<Book>
  <Name>Python and XML</Name>
  <Publisher>O'Reilly &amp; Associates</Publisher>
</Book>
```

The above XML would be converted to the following PYX using Pyxie or other PYX aware processors:

```
(Book
-\n
(Name
-Python and XML
)Name
-\n
(Publisher
-O'Reilly & Associates
)Publisher
-\n
)Book
```

One thing to note about the PYX output is that each document construct that is being dealt with is given its own line. This makes it very accommodating to Unix-style command-line processing tools. Additionally, the PYX markup starts each line with a symbol giving an indication of the node type encountered:

(The left parenthesis is used to denote start elements.

)   The right parenthesis is used to denote the ends of elements

A   A capital A is used to mark attributes.

-     A dash (or minus) is used to mark character data.

?   A question mark is used to denote a processing instruction.

These symbols don't cover every type of construct in XML. For example, there is no support for CDATA sections, DTDs, or comments.

Having experience with Unix system administration, we can honestly state that the line-oriented markup of the PYX syntax would be of incredible value for those familiar with sed, awk, and grep, and need to parse an XML document, but don't want to take the time to code with a parser against the document.

Another powerful feature of PYX is the ability to quickly examine the contents of a document—leading to searchable grep-like features. The line-oriented contents can easily be searched for with a utility such as grep allowing for some complex operations on the document. For example, using grep and PYX, you could invoke grep's options on the output of PYX data. For instance:

```
$> <PYX-generating-command> | grep -v "Celsius"
```

If your PYX output is full of temperature reports with text such as "38 degrees Celsius" the previous grep command ensures that Celsius temperatures are not included in the output. Such filtering is far more complex with XPath and the DOM. Likewise, we don't think PYX will help very much if your task is to convert SQL record sets to XML while at the same time adding DTDs and Namespaces. In a complex case like that, working with the DOM is necessary.

Python XML Tools

The Python XML Tools collection is built on top of PyXML and features two GTK widgets: XmlTree and XmlEditor. The Python XML Tools are available from *http://www.logilab.org/xmltools/*. These packages are used to display XML files (XmlTree), as well as edit them (XmlEditor).

XmlTree displays XML files in a tree-like form, familiar to those who've used file browsers on Windows, KDE, or GNOME. This structure takes the form of a GTK widget—it's derived from the GtkCTree Widget.

The API features several methods for setting the XML document for display, setting XPath filters for the tree, and a class for generating metadata about the tree.

In addition to API methods, the tree features configurable key bindings. For example, pressing an asterisk (*) recursively expands the selected node, while the / key closes them.

The XmlEditor is also a GTK widget, but XmlEditor allows for the editing of XML documents. It uses the aforementioned XmlTree for display. The structure available for editing is currently centered around a DTD, but may change to use schema at a later date.

In addition to a simple API for driving the editor, the XmlEditor also features an add_change_listener method that allows you to supply a callback function. The callback function is then executed whenever the **Apply** or **Ok** buttons are pressed on the editor.

XML Schema Validator

The XML Schema validator is available from *http://www.ltg.ed.ac.uk/~ht/xsv-status.html*. While still cutting-edge (like XML Schema itself), the software is frequently updated and appears to be making progress. XSV seeks to be one of the first open source Schema-aware XML processors. This provides a nice complement to the TREX validator in PyXML and the Schematron validator in 4Suite.

Sab-pyth

Sab-pyth is a module that interfaces with the Sablotron XSLT processor written in C++. Sab-pyth allows your Python programs to call the Sablotron APIs. The API is small and effective, but has its own quirks and special constants. Sablotron also allows for the addition of custom-written handlers. By adding handlers, you can intercept messages generated by the processor.

The Sab-pyth documentation is available online at: *http://www.ubka.uni-karlsruhe. de/~guenter/Sab-pyth/doc/html/sabpyth/*.

Redfoot

James Tauber and Daniel Krech developed this toolkit for working with Resource Description Framework (RDF) data. The tools include an RDF parser and serializer, RDF database, an API for queries, a convenient user interface, and a web server that provides an interface for viewing and editing RDF in the database. A number of sample applications built on top of Redfoot are available as well.

More information is available at *http://redfoot.sourceforge.net/*, as well as the implementation and complete documentation.

XML Components for Zope

Zope is an open source application server written in Python and C, developed by Zope Corporation (*http://www.zope.com/*); the implementation and more information on Zope itself can be found at the Zope users' web site at *http://www.zope.org/*. While not specifically an XML project itself, there are a number of interesting components available that can be used in building web sites that use XML.

Parsed XML

Parsed XML is an optional Zope component that can be used to store a persistent DOM in Zope's object database. The project, started by Karl Anderson, is now led by Martijn Pieters. The underlying DOM implementation is primarily the work of one of the authors of this book, Fred L. Drake, Jr.. More information, including the plan for future development, is available at *http://dev.zope.org/Projects/ParsedXML/*. The package includes an extensive test suite for DOM implementations.

Page Templates

Page Templates are another optional Zope component. This one is designed to apply presentation to results of the operations of a web site that implement the business logic that forms the site's underpinnings. The template language is defined so that the templates may continue to be edited using the graphical tools that site designers love without breaking the linkages to the business logic implemented by the site's programmers. The templates themselves may be written in HTML, XML, or XHTML. The leadership for the project comes from Evan Simpson, who also provided much of the expertise on creating Zope components. Fred L. Drake, Jr. (the co-author of this book) and Guido van Rossum provided much of the non-Zope–specific portions of the package.

Online Resources

The Python/XML community is centered around the Python XML Special Interest Group, or XML-SIG. The group has a web page at *http://www.python.org/sigs/xml-sig/*.

As with most Python SIGs, everything really happens on a mailing list. Information on the mailing list, including both links to the list archives and a subscription form, is available at the XML-SIG web page.

The XML-SIG is not only responsible for maintaining the PyXML package used extensively in this book, but also the *Python/XML Topic Guide,* containing overviews of what's available for working with XML in Python and links to additional online and published resources. The Topic Guide is available at *http://pyxml.sourceforge.net/topics/*.

Index

We'd like to hear your suggestions for improving our indexes. Send email to *index@oreilly.com*.

InvalidModificationErr exception, 312
InvalidStateErr exception, 312
ISO (International Organization for
        Standardization), language support
        and, 6
ISO-8859-1 character set, 25
iteration
    NodeList object, 325
    stylesheet elements, 138

J

Java XML APIs, 1

L

language identification, markup, 30
language support, 5
large XML files, 245
lastChild attribute, nodes and, 88
Latin-1 character set, 25
levels, DOM, 81
LexicalHandler, SAX, 51, 308
libraries, Python standard library, 12
line-feed characters, 29
linked resources, entities, 24
Linux, Python installation, 290
literal entity values, XML, 298
literal special characters, markup, 26
literals, 32
loading documents
    4DOM, 86
    minidom, 87
    MSXML, 324
location paths, XPath, 112
    abbreviated location paths, 112
Locator objects, SAX, 309

M

mailing lists, 342
make_parser function (SAX), 302
makepy.py file, 218
markup, 4
    character data and, 26
    characters used, 26
    end-of-line handling, 29
    external declaration, 297
    language identification, 30
    literal special characters, 26
    XML, 298
markup languages versus meta-languages, 7

match attribute
    template element, 134
    xsl:template element, 131
Message Path, SOAP, 206
messages, SOAP
    encoding, 207
    exchanging, 206
    Message Path, 206
    serialization, 208
meta-languages, 7
method
    urlencode, 182
method attribute, stylesheet elements, 134
method definitions, genxml.py, 72
method tag, web form, 158
method template, pyxml.xml
        conversion, 141
methods
    appendChild( ), 93
    appendStylesheetUri( ), 146
    attributeDecl( ), 307
    characters( ), 305
    comment( ), 308
    crateProcessingInstruction( ), 313
    createAttribute( ), 313
    createAttributeNS( ), 313
    createCDATASection( ), 313
    createComment( ), 313
    createDocument( ), 312
    createDocumentFragment( ), 313
    createDocumentType( ), 163
    createElement( ), 164, 313
    createElementNS( ), 313
    createEntityReference( ), 313
    createTextNode( ), 314
    deleteProfile( ), 239
    Document object (MSXML), 332
    elementDecl( ), 308
    endCDATA( ), 308
    endDocument( ), 304
    endDTD( ), 308
    endElement( ), 305
    endElementNS( ), 305
    endEntity( ), 308
    endPrefixMapping( ), 304
    error( ), 307
    externalEntityDecl( ), 308
    fatalError( ), 307
    fromXML( ), 99
    getAttribute( ), 92
    getAttributeNode( ), 92

W

warning( ) method, 307
web application sample, 275
 CGI, 278
 code architecture, 277
 components, 276
 connecting to web service, 275
 profile updating, 281
 start page, 277
 testing as user, 288
 topology, 276
 see also sample application
web applications
 Article class, 98–102
 ArticleManager class, 104–107
 control, 107–110
 script execution, 97
 server preparation, 97
 site logic, 103–110
 Storage class, 102
 structure, 98–103
 write permissions, 97
web forms, 150
 Bill Summary and, 158
web services, 204
 connecting to, 275
 content syndication, 204
 support, 205
web sites, 342
 connecting, 180
 XML specifications, 9
Web/CGI application
 components, 276
 sample application, 228
well-formed, 22
well-formed documents, XML, 300
well-formedness constraint, XML
 documents, 300
What, 164
whitespace, character data, 28–29
Windows
 Python installation, 289
 PyXML installation, 291
 thumbnails, 66
Word, revision tracking, 3
workflow, 177
 primary objective, 177
write permissions, web applications, 97
writing handlers, SAX, 53
WrongDocumentErr exception, 311
WSDL (Web Services Description
 Language), 205

X

XHTML (Extensible Hypertext Markup
 Language), 44
XLink, 44
XML
 advantages of, 2
 international language support, 5
 platform neutrality, 5
 attribute-list declarations, 295
 attributes, 18, 294
 defaults, 294
 names, 295
 values, 296
 values, enumerated, 297
 Canonical XML, 41–42
 CDATA sections, 296
 characters, 24–26, 296
 child, 299
 comments, 32
 conformance, 22
 conversion
 flat file, 170
 validation, 171
 converting
 to HTML, 69–76
 to PYX, 339
 declarations, 18
 definitions, 293–301
 displaying, CGI, 172
 document structure, 18
 document types, 19
 documents
 characters in, 24–26
 data types and, 19
 parsing, Pyxie, 338
 prolog, 30
 well-formed, 300
 well-formed constraint, 300
 XLink, 44
 XPath expressions and, 111
 DOM, 82
 DTDs, 20
 elements, 18, 31
 empty, 18
 empty elements, 31
 files, XSLT and, 125
 as foundation, 8
 intelligence, 54
 Java XML APIs, 1
 large XML files, 245
 namespaces, 8, 43
 parsing, 3

About the Authors

Christopher A. Jones has an extensive background in Internet systems programming and XML. He is the co-founder of Planet 7 Technologies, a Seattle-based commercial software company specializing in XML transport software. He is also the author of *Open Source Linux Web Programming* (IDG, 1999) and *Unix Shell Objects* (IDG, 1998).

Fred L. Drake, Jr. is a member of the Python Labs team and has been contributing to Python since 1995. He took over maintenance of Python's documentation in 1998, changing the face of both the printed and online forms. He has been active in the PyXML project since it started. He also helps maintain the Expat XML parser, which is used in many major applications that utilize XML, including PyXML, Apache, and Mozilla. He holds a Bachelor of Architecture degree, as well as a Master of Science in computer science.

Colophon

Our look is the result of reader comments, our own experimentation, and feedback from distribution channels. Distinctive covers complement our distinctive approach to technical topics, breathing personality and life into potentially dry subjects.

The animals on the cover of *Python and XML* are elephant shrews. Different types of elephant shrews are found throughout Africa, most residing along the coast. The elephant shrew's long nose, which resembles an elephant's trunk, is the source of its name. The shrew pokes this trunk under leaves and, with its even longer tongue, flicks food into its mouth. It feeds mostly on termites and ants, but also eats shoots, berries, and roots.

Elephant shrews have long, soft fur that is sandy brown on the surface, fading to pale orange or gray. Their bodies range from 3.7 to 4 inches in length, and their tails, 3.7 to 5 inches. They weigh between 1 and 1.7 ounces. Elephant shrews grow to full size in about 46 days, and leave their shelters anywhere from 18 to 36 days after birth. Because they mature and leave their nests so quickly, predators rarely invade the nests.

Most elephant shrews do not burrow, as their feet are not well adapted for digging, but instead find depressions in the ground in which to nest. As they settle into these depressions, they pull leaves and debris over their heads for cover. The elephant shrew is very territorial, as it is mainly a solitary animal. When others approach, the shrew will break into a sudden flurry of kicking, screaming, sparring, and snapping until it is alone once more.

Mary Brady was the production editor and copyeditor for *Python and XML*. David Futato was the proofreader. Matt Hutchinson and Claire Cloutier provided quality control. Edith Shapiro and Camilla Ammirati provided production support. Johnna VanHoose Dinse wrote the index.

Emma Colby designed the cover of this book, based on a series design by Edie Freedman. The cover image is an original illustration from *Mammalia*. Emma Colby produced the cover layout with QuarkXPress 4.1, using Adobe's ITC Garamond font.

David Futato designed the interior layout. Mihaela Maier converted the files from Microsoft Word to FrameMaker 5.5.6, using tools created by Mike Sierra. The text font is Linotype Birka; the heading font is Adobe Myriad Condensed; and the code font is LucasFont's TheSans Mono Condensed. The illustrations that appear in the book were produced by Robert Romano and Jessamyn Read using Macromedia Free-Hand 9 and Adobe Photoshop 6. The tip and warning icons were drawn by Christopher Bing. This colophon was written by Linley Dolby.

Whenever possible, our books use a durable and flexible lay-flat binding.

 # More Titles from O'Reilly

XML

XML in a Nutshell

By Elliotte Rusty Harold & W. Scott Means
1st Edition December 2000
400 pages, ISBN 0-596-00058-8

XML in a Nutshell is just what serious XML developers need in order to take full advantage of XML's incredible potential: a comprehensive, easy-to-access desktop reference to the fundamental rules that all XML documents and authors must adhere to. This book details the grammar that specifies where tags may be placed, what they must look like, which element names are legal, how attributes attach to elements, and much more.

Java and XSLT

By Eric M. Burke
1st Edition September 2001
528 pages, ISBN 0-596-00143-6

Learn how to use XSL transformations in Java programs ranging from stand-alone applications to servlets. *Java and XSLT* introduces XSLT and then shows you how to apply transformations in real-world situations, such as developing a discussion forum, transforming documents from one form to another, and generating content for wireless devices.

Learning XML

By Erik T. Ray with Christopher R.Maden
1st Edition January 2001
368 pages, ISBN 0-596-00046-4

XML (Extensible Markup Language) is a flexible way to create "self-describing data"—and to share both the format and the data on the World Wide Web, intranets, and elsewhere. In *Learning XML*, the authors explain XML and its capabilities succinctly and professionally, with references to real-life projects and other cogent examples. *Learning XML* shows the purpose of XML markup itself, the CSS and XSL styling languages, and the XLink and XPointer specifications for creating rich link structures.

XSLT

By Doug Tidwell
1st Edition August 2001
473 pages, ISBN 0-596-00053-7

XSLT (Extensible Stylesheet Language Transformations) is a critical bridge between XML processing and more familiar HTML, and dominates the market for conversions between XML vocabularies. Useful as XSLT is, its complexities can be daunting. Doug Tidwell, a developer with years of XSLT experience, eases the pain by building from the basics to the more complex and powerful possibilities of XSLT, so you can jump in at your own level of expertise.

Java & XML, 2nd Edition

By Brett McLaughlin
2nd Edition September 2001
528 pages, ISBN 0-596-00197-5

New chapters on Advanced SAX, Advanced DOM, SOAP, and data binding, as well as new examples throughout, bring the second edition of *Java & XML* thoroughly up to date. Except for a concise introduction to XML basics, the book focuses entirely on using XML from Java applications. It's a worthy companion for Java developers working with XML or involved in messaging, web services, or the new peer-to-peer movement.

XML Pocket Reference, 2nd Edition

By Robert Eckstein with Michel Casabianca
2nd Edition April 2001
102 pages, ISBN 0-596-00133-9

The *XML Pocket Reference* is both a handy introduction to XML terminology and syntax, and a quick reference to XML instructions, attributes, entities, and datatypes. Although XML itself is complex, its basic concepts are simple. This small book combines a perfect tutorial for learning the basics of XML with a reference to the XML and XSL specifications. The new edition introduces information on XSLT (Extensible Stylesheet Language Transformations) and Xpath.

Scripting Languages

Programming Python, 2nd Edition

By Mark Lutz
2nd Edition March 2001
1256 pages, Includes CD-ROM
ISBN 0-596-00085-5

Programming Python, 2nd Edition, focuses on advanced applications of Python, an increasingly popular object-oriented scripting language. Endorsed by Python creator Guido van Rossum, it demonstrates advanced Python programming techniques, and addresses software design issues such as reusability and object-oriented programming. The enclosed platform-neutral CD-ROM has book examples and various Python-related packages, including the full Python Version 2.0 source code distribution.

Learning Python

By Mark Lutz & David Ascher
1st Edition April 1999
384 pages, ISBN 1-56592-464-9

Learning Python is an introduction to the increasingly popular Python programming language—an interpreted, interactive, object-oriented, and portable scripting language. This book thoroughly introduces the elements of Python: types, operators, statements, classes, functions, modules, and exceptions. It also demonstrates how to perform common programming tasks and write real applications.

Python Programming on Win32

By Mark Hammond & Andy Robinson
1st Edition January 2000
674 pages, ISBN 1-56592-621-8

Despite Python's increasing popularity on Windows, *Python Programming on Win32* is the first book to demonstrate how to use it as a serious Windows development and administration tool. This book addresses all the basic technologies for common integration tasks on Windows, explaining both the Windows issues and the Python code you need to glue things together.

Tcl/Tk Tools

By Mark Harrison
1st Edition September 1997
678 pages, Includes CD-ROM
ISBN 1-56592-218-2

One of the greatest strengths of Tcl/Tk is the range of extensions written for it. This book clearly documents the most popular and robust extensions—by the people who created them—and contains information on configuration, debugging, and other important tasks. The CD-ROM includes Tcl/Tk, the extensions, and other tools documented in the text both in source form and as binaries for Solaris and Linux.

Exploring Expect

By Don Libes
1st Edition December 1994
602 pages, ISBN 1-56592-090-2

Written by the author of Expect, this is the first book to explain how this part of the Unix toolbox can be used to automate Telnet, FTP, passwd, rlogin, and hundreds of other interactive applications. Based on Tcl (Tool Command Language), Expect lets you automate interactive applications that have previously been extremely difficult to handle with any scripting language.

Tcl/Tk in a Nutshell

By Paul Raines & Jeff Tranter
1st Edition March 1999
456 pages, ISBN 1-56592-433-9

The Tcl language and Tk graphical toolkit are powerful building blocks for custom applications. This quick reference briefly describes every command and option in the core Tcl/Tk distribution, as well as the most popular extensions. Keep it on your desk as you write scripts, and you'll be able to quickly find the particular option you need.

Scripting Languages

Ruby in a Nutshell

By Yukihiro Matsumoto
With translated text by David L. Reynolds Jr.
1st Edition November 2001 (est.)
200 pages (est.), ISBN 0-59600-214-9

Written by Yukihiro Matsumoto ("Matz"), creator of the language, *Ruby in a Nutshell* is a practical reference guide covering everything from Ruby syntax to the specifications of its standard class libraries. The book is based on Ruby 1.6, and is applicable to development versions 1.7 and the next planned stable version 1.8. As part of the successful "in a Nutshell" series *Ruby in a Nutshell* is for readers who want a single desktop reference for all their needs.

Python Pocket Reference, 2nd Edition

By Mark Lutz
2nd Edition December 2001 (est.)
128 pages (est.), ISBN 0-596-00189-4

This book is a companion volume to two O'Reilly animal guides: *Programming Python* and *Learning Python*. It summarizes Python statements and types, built-in functions, commonly used library modules, and other prominent Python language features.

Tcl/Tk Pocket Reference

By Paul Raines
1st Edition October 1998
94 pages, ISBN 1-56592-498-3

A companion volume to *Tcl/Tk in a Nutshell*, the *Tcl/Tk Pocket Reference* is a handy reference guide to the basic Tcl language elements, Tcl and Tk commands, and Tk widgets. It provides easy access to just what you need and includes easy-to-understand summaries of Tcl/Tk language elements. Covers Tcl Version 8 and Tk Version 8.

Python & XML

By Christopher A. Jones & Fred Drake
1st Edition December 2001 (est.)
400 pages (est.), ISBN 0-596-00128-2

This book has two objectives: to provide a comprehensive reference on using XML with Python and to illustrate the practical applications of these technologies (often coupled with cross-platform tools) in an enterprise environment. Loaded with practical examples, it also shows how to use Python to create scalable XML connections between popular distributed applications such as databases and web servers. Covers XML flow analysis and details ways to transport XML through a network.

Python Standard Library

By Fredrik Lundh
1st Edition May 2001
300 pages, ISBN 0-596-00096-0

Python Standard Library, an essential guide for serious Python programmers, delivers accurate, author-tested documentation of all the modules in the Python Standard Library, along with over 300 annotated example scripts using the modules. This version of the book covers all the new modules and related information for Python 2.0, the first major release of Python in four years.

PHP Pocket Reference

By Rasmus Lerdorf
1st Edition January 2000
120 pages, ISBN 1-56592-769-9

The *PHP Pocket Reference* is a handy quick reference for PHP, an open-source, HTML-embedded scripting language that can be used to develop web applications. This small book acts both as a perfect tutorial for learning the basics of PHP syntax and as a reference to the vast array of functions provided by PHP.

How to stay in touch with O'Reilly

1. Visit Our Award-Winning Web Site

http://www.oreilly.com/

★ "Top 100 Sites on the Web" —PC Magazine
★ "Top 5% Web sites" —Point Communications
★ "3-Star site" —The McKinley Group

Our web site contains a library of comprehensive product information (including book excerpts and tables of contents), downloadable software, background articles, interviews with technology leaders, links to relevant sites, book cover art, and more. File us in your Bookmarks or Hotlist!

2. Join Our Email Mailing Lists

New Product Releases

To receive automatic email with brief descriptions of all new O'Reilly products as they are released, send email to:
ora-news-subscribe@lists.oreilly.com
Put the following information in the first line of your message (not in the Subject field):
subscribe ora-news

O'Reilly Events

If you'd also like us to send information about trade show events, special promotions, and other O'Reilly events, send email to:
ora-news-subscribe@lists.oreilly.com
Put the following information in the first line of your message (not in the Subject field):
subscribe ora-events

3. Get Examples from Our Books via FTP

There are two ways to access an archive of example files from our books:

Regular FTP

• ftp to:
ftp.oreilly.com
(login: anonymous
password: your email address)
• Point your web browser to:
ftp://ftp.oreilly.com/

FTPMAIL

• Send an email message to:
ftpmail@online.oreilly.com
(Write "help" in the message body)

4. Contact Us via Email

order@oreilly.com
To place a book or software order online. Good for North American and international customers.

subscriptions@oreilly.com
To place an order for any of our newsletters or periodicals.

books@oreilly.com
General questions about any of our books.

cs@oreilly.com
For answers to problems regarding your order or our products.

booktech@oreilly.com
For book content technical questions or corrections.

proposals@oreilly.com
To submit new book or software proposals to our editors and product managers.

international@oreilly.com
For information about our international distributors or translation queries. For a list of our distributors outside of North America check out:
http://www.oreilly.com/distributors.html

5. Work with Us

Check out our website for current employment opportunites:
http://jobs.oreilly.com/

O'Reilly & Associates, Inc.
1005 Gravenstein Hwy North
Sebastopol, CA 95472 USA
TEL   707-829-0515 or 800-998-9938
      (6am to 5pm PST)
FAX   707-829-0104

O'REILLY®

Titles from O'Reilly

PROGRAMMING

C++: The Core Language
Practical C++ Programming
Practical C Programming, 3rd Ed.
High Performance Computing,
  2nd Ed.
Programming Embedded Systems in
  C and C++
Mastering Algorithms in C
Advanced C++ Techniques
POSIX 4: Programming for
  the Real World
POSIX Programmer's Guide
Power Programming with RPC
UNIX Systems Programming
  for SVR4
Pthreads Programming
CVS Pocket Reference
Advanced Oracle PL/SQL
Oracle PL/SQL Guide to Oracle8i
  Features
Oracle PL/SQL Programming,
  2nd Ed.
Oracle Built-in Packages
Oracle PL/SQL Developer's
  Workbook
Oracle Web Applications
Oracle PL/SQL Language
  Pocket Reference
Oracle PL/SQL Built-ins
  Pocket Reference
Oracle SQL*Plus:
  The Definitive Guide
Oracle SQL*Plus Pocket Reference
Oracle Essentials
Oracle Database Administration
Oracle Internal Services
Oracle SAP
Guide to Writing DCE Applications
Understanding DCE
Visual Basic Shell Programming
VB/VBA in a Nutshell: The Language
Access Database Design
  & Programming, 2nd Ed.
Writing Word Macros
Applying RCS and SCCS
Checking C Programs with Lint
VB Controls in a Nutshell
Developing Asp Components,
  2nd Ed.
Learning WML & WMLScript
Writing Excel Macros
Windows 32 API Programming with
  Visual Basic
ADO: The Definitive Guide

USING THE INTERNET

Internet in a Nutshell
Smileys
Managing Mailing Lists

WEB

Apache: The Definitive Guide,
  2nd Ed.
Apache Pocket Reference
ASP in a Nutshell, 2nd Ed.
Cascading Style Sheets
Designing Web Audio
Designing with JavaScript, 2nd Ed.
DocBook: The Definitive Guide
Dynamic HTML:
  The Definitive Reference
HTML Pocket Reference
Information Architecture
  for the WWW
JavaScript: The Definitive Guide,
  3rd Ed.
Java & XML, 2nd Ed.
JavaScript Application Cookbook
JavaScript Pocket Reference
Practical Internet Groupware
PHP Pocket Reference
Programming Coldfusion
Photoshop for the Web, 2nd Ed.
Web Design in a Nutshell, 2nd Ed.
Webmaster in a Nutshell, 2nd Ed.
Web Navigation: Designing the
  User Experience
Web Performance Tuning
Web Security & Commerce
Writing Apache Modules
  with Perl and C

UNIX

SCO UNIX in a Nutshell
Tcl/Tk in a Nutshell
The Unix CD Bookshelf, 2nd Ed.
UNIX in a Nutshell,
  System V Edition, 3rd Ed.
Learning the Unix Operating System,
  4th Ed.
Learning vi, 6th Ed.
Learning the Korn Shell
Learning GNU Emacs, 2nd Ed.
Using csh & tcsh
Learning the bash Shell, 2nd Ed.
GNU Emacs Pocket Reference
Exploring Expect
Tcl/Tk Tools
Tcl/Tk in a Nutshell
Python Pocket Reference

USING WINDOWS

Windows Me: The Missing Manual
PC Hardware in a Nutshell
Optimizing Windows for Games,
  Graphics, and Multimedia
Outlook 2000 in a Nutshell
Word 2000 in a Nutshell
Excel 2000 in a Nutshell
Windows 2000 Pro:
  The Missing Manual

JAVA SERIES

Developing Java Beans
Creating Effective JavaHelp
Enterprise JavaBeans, 3rd Ed.
Java Cryptography
Java Distributed Computing
Java Enterprise in a Nutshell
Java Examples in a Nutshell, 2nd Ed.
Java Foundation Classes
  in a Nutshell
Java in a Nutshell, 3rd Ed.
Java Internationalization
Java I/O
Java Native Methods
Java Network Programming, 2nd Ed.
Java Performance Tuning
Java Security
Java Servlet Programming
Java ServerPages
Java Threads, 2nd Ed.
Jini in a Nutshell
Learning Java

GRAPHICS & MULTIMEDIA

MP3: The Definitive Guide
Director in a Nutshell
Lingo in a Nutshell

X WINDOW

Vol. 1: Xlib Programming Manual
Vol. 2: Xlib Reference Manual
Vol. 4M: X Toolkit Intrinsics
  Programming Manual, Motif Ed.
Vol. 5: X Toolkit Intrinsics Reference
  Manual
Vol. 6A: Motif Programming Manual
Vol. 6B: Motif Reference Manual,
  2nd Ed.

PERL

Advanced Perl Programming
CGI Programming with Perl, 2nd Ed.
Learning Perl, 2nd Ed.
Learning Perl for Win32 Systems
Learning Perl/Tk
Mastering Algorithms with Perl
Mastering Regular Expressions
Perl Cookbook
Perl in a Nutshell
Programming Perl, 3rd Ed.
Perl CD Bookshelf
Perl Resource Kit – Win32 Ed.
Perl/Tk Pocket Reference
Perl 5 Pocket Reference, 3rd Ed.

MAC

AppleScript in a Nutshell
AppleWorks 6: The Missing Manual
Crossing Platforms
iMovie: The Missing Manual
Mac OS in a Nutshell
Mac OS 9: The Missing Manual
REALbasic: The Definitive Guide

LINUX

Learning Red Hat Linux
Linux Device Drivers, 2nd Ed.
Linux Network Administrator's
  Guide, 2nd Ed.
Running Linux, 3rd Ed.
Linux in a Nutshell, 3rd Ed.
Linux Multimedia Guide

SYSTEM ADMINISTRATION

Practical UNIX & Internet Security,
  2nd Ed.
Building Internet Firewalls, 2nd Ed.
PGP: Pretty Good Privacy
SSH, The Secure Shell:
  The Definitive Guide
DNS and BIND, 3rd Ed.
The Networking CD Bookshelf
Virtual Private Networks, 2nd Ed.
TCP/IP Network Administration,
  2nd Ed.
sendmail Desktop Reference
Managing Usenet
Using & Managing PPP
Managing IP Networks
  with Cisco Routers
Networking Personal Computers
  with TCP/IP
Unix Backup & Recovery
Essential System Administration,
  2nd Ed.
Perl for System Administration
Managing NFS and NIS
Vol. 8: X Window System
  Administrator's Guide
Using Samba
UNIX Power Tools, 2nd Ed.
DNS on Windows NT
Windows NT TCP/IP Network
  Administration
DHCP for Windows 2000
Essential Windows NT System
  Administration
Managing Windows NT Logons
Managing the Windows 2000
  Registry

OTHER TITLES

PalmPilot: The Ultimate Guide,
  2nd Ed.
Palm Programming:
  The Developer's Guide

O'REILLY®

TO ORDER: **800-998-9938** • order@oreilly.com • www.oreilly.com
ONLINE EDITIONS OF MOST O'REILLY TITLES ARE AVAILABLE BY SUBSCRIPTION AT safari.oreilly.com
ALSO AVAILABLE AT MOST RETAIL AND ONLINE BOOKSTORES

International Distributors

http://international.oreilly.com/distributors.html • international@oreilly.com

UK, Europe, Middle East, and Africa (except France, Germany, Austria, Switzerland, Luxembourg, and Liechtenstein)

INQUIRIES
O'Reilly UK Limited
4 Castle Street
Farnham
Surrey, GU9 7HS
United Kingdom
Telephone: 44-1252-711776
Fax: 44-1252-734211
Email: information@oreilly.co.uk

ORDERS
Wiley Distribution Services Ltd.
1 Oldlands Way
Bognor Regis
West Sussex PO22 9SA
United Kingdom
Telephone: 44-1243-843294
UK Freephone: 0800-243207
Fax: 44-1243-843302 (Europe/EU orders)
or 44-1243-843274 (Middle East/Africa)
Email: cs-books@wiley.co.uk

France

INQUIRIES & ORDERS
Éditions O'Reilly
18 rue Séguier
75006 Paris, France
Tel: 33-1-40-51-71-89
Fax: 33-1-40-51-72-26
Email: france@oreilly.fr

Germany, Switzerland, Austria, Luxembourg, and Liechtenstein

INQUIRIES & ORDERS
O'Reilly Verlag
Balthasarstr. 81
D-50670 Köln, Germany
Telephone: 49-221-973160-91
Fax: 49-221-973160-8
Email: anfragen@oreilly.de (inquiries)
Email: order@oreilly.de (orders)

Canada

(French language books)
Les Éditions Flammarion ltée
375, Avenue Laurier Ouest
Montréal (Québec) H2V 2K3
Tel: 1-514-277-8807
Fax: 1-514-278-2085
Email: info@flammarion.qc.ca

Hong Kong

City Discount Subscription Service, Ltd.
Unit A, 6th Floor, Yan's Tower
27 Wong Chuk Hang Road
Aberdeen, Hong Kong
Tel: 852-2580-3539
Fax: 852-2580-6463
Email: citydis@ppn.com.hk

Korea

Hanbit Media, Inc.
Chungmu Bldg. 210
Yonnam-dong 568-33
Mapo-gu
Seoul, Korea
Tel: 822-325-0397
Fax: 822-325-9697
Email: hant93@chollian.dacom.co.kr

Philippines

Global Publishing
G/F Benavides Garden
1186 Benavides Street
Manila, Philippines
Tel: 632-254-8949/632-252-2582
Fax: 632-734-5060/632-252-2733
Email: globalp@pacific.net.ph

Taiwan

O'Reilly Taiwan
1st Floor, No. 21, Lane 295
Section 1, Fu-Shing South Road
Taipei, 106 Taiwan
Tel: 886-2-27099669
Fax: 886-2-27038802
Email: mori@oreilly.com

India

Shroff Publishers & Distributors Pvt. Ltd.
12, "Roseland", 2nd Floor
180, Waterfield Road, Bandra (West)
Mumbai 400 050
Tel: 91-22-641-1800/643-9910
Fax: 91-22-643-2422
Email: spd@vsnl.com

China

O'Reilly Beijing
SIGMA Building, Suite B809
No. 49 Zhichun Road
Haidian District
Beijing, China PR 100080
Tel: 86-10-8809-7475
Fax: 86-10-8809-7463
Email: beijing@oreilly.com

Japan

O'Reilly Japan, Inc.
Yotsuya Y's Building
7 Banch 6, Honshio-cho
Shinjuku-ku
Tokyo 160-0003 Japan
Tel: 81-3-3356-5227
Fax: 81-3-3356-5261
Email: japan@oreilly.com

Singapore, Indonesia, Malaysia, and Thailand

TransQuest Publishers Pte Ltd
30 Old Toh Tuck Road #05-02
Sembawang Kimtrans Logistics Centre
Singapore 597654
Tel: 65-4623112
Fax: 65-4625761
Email: wendiw@transquest.com.sg

Australia

Woodslane Pty., Ltd.
7/5 Vuko Place
Warriewood NSW 2102
Australia
Tel: 61-2-9970-5111
Fax: 61-2-9970-5002
Email: info@woodslane.com.au

New Zealand

Woodslane New Zealand, Ltd.
21 Cooks Street (P.O. Box 575)
Waganui, New Zealand
Tel: 64-6-347-6543
Fax: 64-6-345-4840
Email: info@woodslane.com.au

Argentina

Distribuidora Cuspide
Suipacha 764
1008 Buenos Aires
Argentina
Phone: 54-11-4322-8868
Fax: 54-11-4322-3456
Email: libros@cuspide.com

All Other Countries

O'Reilly & Associates, Inc.
1005 Gravenstein Hwy North
Sebastopol, CA 95472 USA
Tel: 707-829-0515
Fax: 707-829-0104
Email: order@oreilly.com

O'REILLY®

TO ORDER: **800-998-9938** • **order@oreilly.com** • **www.oreilly.com**
ONLINE EDITIONS OF MOST O'REILLY TITLES ARE AVAILABLE BY SUBSCRIPTION AT **safari.oreilly.com**
ALSO AVAILABLE AT MOST RETAIL AND ONLINE BOOKSTORES